ISBN 978-0-331-34118-8
PIBN 11090137

NORTH CAROLINA GEOLOGICAL AND ECONOMIC SURVEY

JOSEPH HYDE PRATT, State Geologist

ECONOMIC PAPER No. 35

GOOD ROADS DAYS

NOVEMBER 5 AND 6, 1913

Compiled by
JOSEPH HYDE PRATT, State Geologist and Miss H. M. BERRY, Secretary

RALEIGH

GEOLOGICAL BOARD

LETTER OF TRANSMITTAL.

CHAPEL HILL, N. C., May 1, 1914.

To His Excellency, HON. LOCKE CRAIG,
Governor of North Carolina.

SIR:—I herewith submit for publication, as Economic Paper No. 35, a Report on the results of the work done on "Good Roads Days, November 5th and 6th, 1913." This report gives in detail the proclamation, the work of organization, and the results of this coöperative road building, as obtained through correspondence and through the press. It is believed that the publication of the results of this undertaking will be of considerable interest to all those interested in the promotion of the good roads cause.

Yours respectfully,
JOSEPH HYDE PRATT,
State Geologist.

TABLE OF CONTENTS

LIST OF ILLUSTRATIONS

GOVERNOR LOCKE CRAIG ON THE BEAVERDAM ROAD, BUNCOMBE COUNTY, WHERE THE ROAD WAS STRAIGHTENED, A NEW PIECE BEING BUILT THROUGH THE LANDS OF WALTER HAYNES, AN ASHEVILLE ATTORNEY, A DISTANCE OF ABOUT 300 YARDS.

GOOD ROADS DAYS, NOVEMBER 5 AND 6, 1913

Compiled by
JOSEPH HYDE PRATT, State Geologist, and Miss H. M. BERRY, Secretary

---

INTRODUCTION.

At a special meeting of the North Carolina Good Roads Association on September 24, 1913, a resolution was unanimously adopted, calling on Governor Craig to set apart two days in November following to be devoted to the building and improvement of the highways by the people of the State. In accordance with this, on the 27th day of September, 1913, Governor Locke Craig conceived the plan of setting aside certain days to be known as "Good Roads Days" and calling upon all able-bodied citizens in the State in every walk of life to get together and work on the public roads. In connection with this project, he called upon the North Carolina Geological and Economic Survey to take charge of the organization of the State, so as to get the most benefit possible from the two days' labor which, it was expected, would be given by every citizen in his own respective county, township, or town,

The Governor also called on Dr. J. Y. Joyner, Superintendent of Public Instruction, to interest the schools, so that they should contribute their share to the success of this coöperative movement. Dr. Joyner, in turn, called upon the Geological Survey to prepare a pamphlet giving data and instructions as to road work and road building, which could be put in the hands of the school children with profit, and to combine with this an Arbor Day feature. Such a pamphlet was prepared and issued, and has been distributed among all the schools of the State.

The University, the State Normal, and a number of the preparatory schools of the State took a very active part in this movement, and in a letter from Acting-President Graham, he says:

"The value of these days will come not so much in the actual road constructed, though that will be great; but in driving home the fundamental idea, so difficult to hold steadily in mind, that our Government is primarily a coöperative enterprise in constructive achievement. Every blow struck on our highways makes emphatic and personal this great idea.

"The Road is not merely an avenue of trade and community intercourse; it is a symbol of community strength, and a test of our grasp of the meaning of Democracy."

EXECUTIVE DEPARTMENT

STATE OF NORTH CAROLINA

GOOD ROADS PROCLAMATION BY THE GOVERNOR.

Whereas the modern highway is essential to material prosperity, and to the advancement of the social life of every community; every people that aspires to join the forward procession and that hopes for the opportunities of our time is beginning to realize the necessity of improved roads; all sections and all progressive citizens are demanding them and determined to have them; the whole country has awakened to their importance; everywhere there is a generous rivalry to have the best, and everywhere enthusiasm for them is apparent, and increasing; and

Whereas, the people of North Carolina are losing, according to reliable estimate, twelve million dollars annually on account of bad roads—this vast sum paid as a tribute to mud:

Now, therefore, recognizing the universal sentiment for road improvement, and realizing the benefits which must result therefrom to all the people, I, Locke Craig, Governor of North Carolina, do set apart Wednesday, the fifth day of November, and Thursday, the sixth of November, one thousand nine hundred and thirteen, as Good Roads Days, and do appoint these days as holidays and days of festival throughout the State, to celebrate the beginning of an era wherein improved highways shall be built in every neighborhood, that all the people of farm and city may enjoy the opportunities which they bring.

I call upon all patriotic people throughout the State to work upon the public roads and refrain from all other occupations on these appointed days; and I call upon every able-bodied man to shoulder his shovel and march out and strike a blow for progress. Let the farmer, the merchant, the lawyer, the doctor, the minister of the Gospel, the rich and the poor, and the men of all the walks of life enlist as volunteers in this mighty army for grand accomplishment.

Let no man be above this work, nor forget his duty to himself and to his neighbors. It will be an honor to every man on these days to labor with his fellow-man to banish from the country the curse of bad roads and the evils that accompany them.

Let all the people of every station, high or low, be moved by the same patriotic impulse to work for the common weal. To all the benefit will come. Let all participate.

I do appoint and set apart these days, the fifth and sixth of November, that the people may have an opportunity to give substantial expression to the universal desire and determination of the State, in action inspired by hope, and rejoicing that will resound in one unbroken chorus from the mountains to the sea.

I call upon all the women to participate. In every hour of danger they have inspired the men of North Carolina with faith and courage; in this day of realization, they with their children will come to lend to this noble cause the charm and the encouragement of their presence. They can provide good things to eat, and decorate every worker with a badge of honor.

Let every citizen do his duty, and these days will be long remembered for the impetus they gave to the cause of good roads and a finer civic spirit.

I call upon the county commissioners of every county in the State to issue a proclamation urging the people to go out on the fifth and sixth days of November and labor for the welfare of their respective counties and communities, as well as for the whole State of which they constitute a part.

I call upon the president of the Farmers' Union to issue his proclamation to the farmers of North Carolina, and to their various local organizations, that this great body of our citizenship, constituting as it does the bone and sinew of the State, may join with energy and enthusiasm in this movement. More than any other class of our people, they are dependent upon the country road. More attractive homes, better farming, and a finer rural life will result from the building of modern highways.

Let the work be completely organized so that it will reach to every neighborhood, "and be conducted in a systematic and business way, to the end that at sunset of the second day there will be no community in all the State where the hand of progress and toil has not left its mark in permanent road improvement, and the progressive spirit its impression in the hearts and minds of the people."

I call upon the ministers of the Gospel, the educators, and the press of the State to use their mighty influence for this work, which means not only material development, but moral and intellectual development.

I call upon all road overseers, good roads associations, boards of trade, chambers of commerce, and all associations and organizations for the public welfare and civic betterment to give to this movement the energy of their influence.

I call upon the mayor of every town and city of North Carolina to issue his proclamation that his people may enlist in this organization, and in the building of roads upon which the prosperity of town and city depends.

Let every North Carolinian show by his work that he is for the improvement of his State. "Let us labor that we may enjoy the fruits today, and our children a fuller fruition tomorrow."

Done at our city of Raleigh, this the twenty-seventh day of September, in the year of our Lord, one thousand nine hundred and thirteen, and in the one hundred and thirty-eighth year of our American Independence.

LOCKE CRAIG,
Governor.

By the Governor:
JNO. P. KERR,
Private Secretary.

GOVERNOR CRAIG ON HAW CREEK ROAD, BUNCOMBE COUNTY, HANDLING SCRAPER. THE ROAD AT THIS POINT WAS CHANGED FOR SEVENTY-FIVE YARDS, ELIMINATING A VERY STEEP HILL.

ORGANIZATION.

It was realized at the start that if any effective work was to be accomplished on the days set apart by the Governor's Proclamation, it would be necessary for the work to be systematized, and that a plan for organization of the various forces to take part in the work should be made. Plans were made to bring to the attention of all the people of the State the Governor's Proclamation. This was done by letters, circulars, newspaper notices, etc. Letters were written by the Governor to the editors of State papers, to the chairmen of the boards of county commissioners, to the mayors of the cities and towns, to the presidents of the chambers of commerce, boards of trade, women's clubs, and civic leagues, to assist in this organization. Copies of these are given below:

To the Editors of the Newspapers of the State:

STATE OF NORTH CAROLINA, EXECUTIVE DEPARTMENT, RALEIGH.

October 1, 1913.

MY DEAR SIR:—Enclosed you will find a copy of my proclamation designating Wednesday, November 5th, and Thursday, November 6th, as Good Roads Days in North Carolina for this year. The article sets forth the objects and purposes which prompted the issuance of the proclamation, and I am writing to ask if you will accord it a place in the columns of your paper. You can readily comprehend the benefits to the State that are contemplated in this call for service, in a cause which means so much to the people of North Carolina. I am asking this in the hope of enlisting your earnest and active coöperation in presenting a plan for quick and effective road building to the people of the territory covered by your splendid publication.

I am persuaded to believe that when the plan proposed has been unfolded to the people, they will cheerfully respond to the call. Hence, I am relying upon the newspapers of the State to acquaint their readers with the plan for action promulgated herewith, and offer it for their consideration. It is needless to suggest that a better system for constructing and maintaining her public highways is one of the greatest needs of the State today, and I venture to hope that the event contemplated will mark the dawn of a new day for road building in North Carolina. May I hope that you will keep this matter constantly before your readers until the day for actual service arrives, and also give the proposition your endorsement.

With personal regards, I am

Yours sincerely,

(Signed) LOCKE CRAIG,

Governor.

To the Chairmen of the Boards of County Commissioners:

October 1, 1913.

My dear Sir:—Enclosed you will find copy of my proclamation designating Wednesday, November 5th, and Thursday, November 6th, as Good Roads Days in North Carolina for this year. The article sets forth the objects and purposes that prompted the issuance of the proclamation, and I am writing to ask that you will assist in every way possible to make these days a success in your county, by helping to organize the whole county, giving it wide publicity, and having the work laid out, so that whatever is done can be done to the best advantage of the road work in the County. You can readily comprehend the benefits to the State that are contemplated in this call for service in a cause which means so much to the people of North Carolina. I am asking this in the hope of enlisting your earnest coöperation in presenting a plan for quick and effective road building to the people of your county.

I am inclined to believe that when the plan proposed has been unfolded to the people of your county, they will cheerfully respond to the call. I have asked the newspapers of your county to do whatever they can to give wide publicity to the scheme; but a great deal of work will have to be done by you along the line of organizing the different townships and neighborhoods. It is needless to suggest that a better system for constructing and maintaining her public highways is one of the greatest needs of the State today. And I venture to hope that the event contemplated will mark the dawn of a new day for road building in North Carolina. May I hope you will give this your earnest support, and that you will get your county to make this a splendid day of achievement and arouse the sense of civic duty, which only lies dormant in the hearts of our citizens?

With personal regards and best wishes, I am

Yours sincerely,

(Signed) Locke Craig,

Governor.

To the Mayors of the Towns and Cities:

October 8, 1913.

My dear Sir:—Enclosed is copy of my proclamation designating November 5th and 6th as Good Roads Days in North Carolina for this year. The article sets forth the objects and purposes which prompted the issuance of the Proclamation, and I am writing to ask you to assist us in the organization of this movement by issuing a similar proclamation calling the citizens of your city together and arousing enthusiasm for the success of the project. The city should be divided up into portions, appointing an organizer to take charge of each portion to get the names of those who are willing to "strike a blow for progress," organize these men into squads and plan out their work for them to undertake on these days. It would also be well to have organizers for the portions of the township outside of the city, also to get the ladies of any civic league you may have in the city or clubs to get together and prepare lunches for the men who work on the roads during these two days. We are told that Missouri sent out "250,000 men, consisting of bankers, clerks, farmers, governors and convicts, who served without pay in a pick-and-shovel army pledged to pull Missouri out of the mud." I believe the people of North Carolina have an equal amount of patriotism and civic pride.

I have asked Dr. Joseph Hyde Pratt, State Geologist, to prepare a pamphlet giving directions as to what had best be done to the various kinds of country roads at this time of the year, and you can announce to those having this work in charge in your town or township that they can communicate with him at Chapel Hill as to the practical working out of the plan.

Aside from the work which may be accomplished on these days for the betterment of the public roads, it is expected that the net results of these days of civic enlistment will be to bring to each participant a clearer and fuller realization of what true citizenship means—the giving on the part of the individual of his time and thought and money and effort for the common good.

With personal regards and best wishes, I am

Yours sincerely,
(Signed) LOCKE CRAIG,
Governor.

To the Presidents of the Chambers of Commerce and Boards of Trade:

October 8, 1913.

MY DEAR SIR:—Enclosed is copy of my proclamation designating November 5th and 6th as Good Roads Days in North Carolina for this year. The article sets forth the objects and purposes which prompted the issuance of the proclamation, and I am writing to ask that your organization coöperate with us and with the Mayor of your city in every way possible to advertise and make a success of these two days. It will be well to have organizers for your town, township, and the other townships in the county, so that the men can be divided up into squads and thoroughly organized and instructed by the leader or captain of the squad, to the end that all the work done may be done systematically and be of real value to the county. You should get the ladies of each neighborhood organized, and let them know as nearly as possible how much dinner to prepare and where to take it. I would suggest that men who are especially interested in road work be instructed in regard to the kind of work to be done and appointed to take charge of from 15 to 20 men, and be able to tell them where to work and what to do.

I have asked Dr. Joseph Hyde Pratt, State Geologist, to prepare a pamphlet giving directions as to what had best be done to the various kinds of country roads at this time of the year and you can announce to those having this work in charge in your town or township that they can communicate with him at Chapel Hill as to the practical working out of the plan.

Aside from the work which may be accomplished on these days for the betterment of the public roads, it is expected that the net results of these days of civic enlistment will be to bring to each participant a clearer and fuller realization of what true citizenship means—the giving on the part of the individual of his time and thought and money and effort for the common good.

With personal regards and best wishes, I am

Yours sincerely,
(Signed) LOCKE CRAIG,
Governor.

October 16, 1913.

To the Women's Clubs, Civic Leagues, etc.:

MY DEAR MADAM:—I am enclosing herewith a copy of my proclamation, which will tell you what we are undertaking to do in connection with our Good Roads Days. We would like very much indeed to have the coöperation of the women of the State in making these Good Roads Days a success, and I will appreciate it if you will get in touch with the mayor of your town, board of trade or chamber of commerce, or whoever is in charge of the organization of the volunteers from your town and county, and plan to prepare dinners or lunches for the men who are working the roads on these days. It might be a good plan for you to get in touch with the women of the county, and arouse in them an interest in this civic undertaking.

Trusting that you will do whatever you can to make this occasion a success, I am, with best wishes,

Yours sincerely,
(Signed) LOCKE CRAIG,
Governor.

The State Geologist* prepared a pamphlet giving suggestions for organization of work on these Good Roads Days:

*Letters were written by the State's Geologist to the Chairmen of Boards of County Commissioners and to Road Officials, enclosing this pamphlet.

SUGGESTIONS FOR ORGANIZATION AND WORK ON GOOD ROADS DAYS

November 5 and 6, 1913

By JOSEPH HYDE PRATT, State Geologist

FOREWORD

The proclamation recently issued by Governor Locke Craig, setting apart Wednesday and Thursday, November 5th and 6th, as Good Roads Days throughout the State of North Carolina for this year, will undoubtedly have more far-reaching results than any other the Governor may issue. In this proclamation he calls upon all the people of the State to unite on these two days and work on the public roads.

In addition to the improvement of a certain number of miles of road on these days, the result of such a movement will be to bring a large number of our citizens to a fuller realization of what a system of good roads will mean in the industrial development of the State and will cause them to give more thought to such legislation as will insure the proper location and construction of the public roads, to the necessity for a system of maintenance of all the roads, and to the need of a more businesslike expenditure of our road funds.

To accomplish the best results on these days, it will be necessary for the citizens of each county and township to thoroughly organize in advance. I have been asked by Governor Craig to map out, as far as possible, a general plan of organization for the counties and make suggestions regarding work that can be done to advantage on the public roads.

Better results will be obtained if work is concentrated on certain roads instead of each group of men trying to do work entirely within their community or each man trying to do work on the road in front of or near his own place. If the labor is concentrated on particular sections of road, it will be found that a road can be pretty well constructed for a long distance across a township or county and, in some instances, will be the beginning of a good road connecting outlying sections with town and will become one of the main highways of the county.

ORGANIZATION.

The Governor has called upon all people throughout the State to assist in this work. Therefore, meetings should be called and well advertised in each city, town, and township, by the mayor, secretary chamber of commerce or board of trade, township or county good roads associations, or individuals who are interested in the road work of their township. A call should be made upon all civil and road engineers, road superintendents and foremen who have or have had charge of road work to volunteer their services in planning out the work and taking charge of and organizing the groups mentioned below.

Arrangements should also be made for each ten squads of men to be under a road engineer, superintendent or foreman, who will plan out the work to be done and instruct the captains as to the work their squads should do and the tools that each squad will require. The captains in turn should instruct each man as to his work and what tool or tools to bring.

Captains should also determine how many teams can be secured and report same to engineer or superintendent in order that these teams can be used to the best advantage.

Where there are no engineers, superintendents, or foremen to plan out the work for the several squads, the captains should follow as closely as possible the suggestions given below regarding road work.

Picnic dinners to be furnished by the women of the communities to the different groups would help to give cheer to the occasion. Captains should notify the women just about how many they should prepare lunch or dinner for.

EQUIPMENT.

The equipment required will be wheelbarrows, picks, axes, mattocks, shovels, crowbars, plows, and teams. As far as possible, new or nearly new tools should be used; picks and axes sharpened, wheelbarrows oiled, and all equipment put in as good condition as possible.

ROAD WORK THAT CAN BE PROFITABLY DONE.

Perhaps the most profitable road work that can be done on such an occasion as this is as follows:

Cutting and clearing right-of-way on new road locations.

Grading the new road.

Surfacing road already graded.

In cutting a right-of-way, the material should be piled and burned as completely as possible.

In grading, the road should be constructed with a width of 24 feet and with no grade over four and one-half per cent.

As far as practicable, curves on a highway should have at least a 40-foot radius.

Where a road has already been graded to the right width, work can be done to advantage in surfacing this with gravel, topsoil or making a sand-clay road.

Gravel or topsoil should be put on the road to a thickness of at least 9 inches, so that when it is compacted there will be a gravel or topsoil surface of at least 6 inches.

In making a sand-clay road, the directions are briefly as follows:

CLAY BASE.

1. Have the top of the clay grade smooth and about 4 or 5 inches lower than it will be when finished.

2. Plow and harrow the top 3 to $3\frac{1}{2}$ inches for the width the sand is to be put on, leaving loose but smooth, with no big lumps.
3. Spread an even layer of sand about 4 inches deep over the top and plow and harrow.
4. Spread 4 more inches of sand over the top and harrow and drag thoroughly.
5. Use clean coarse sand, even if it has to be hauled some distance.
6. When possible, harrow just after a rain.

SAND BASE.

1. Smooth the sand road, leaving it perfectly flat.
2. Spread the clay the desired width and from 4 to 6 inches thick.
3. If the sand base is clean sand, drag it up on the clay for a thickness of 4 inches and plow, harrow, and drag thoroughly, preferably after a rain.
4. If the sand base contains loam, haul clean sand from a pit.
5. Use natural sand-clay mixture in preference to pure clay.

IMPROVEMENT OF PRESENT ROADS.

There are many roads that have been constructed with the right grade, but are too narrow and have many sharp curves. Effective work can be done on such roads by widening them and constructing the curve with a longer radius.

If the center of such a road is surfaced, care should be taken that in widening none of the dirt is thrown on the surfaced portions. If it is a dirt road which is being widened, no new dirt should be thrown on the compact centers of the road except what may be necessary to fill up holes and bad ruts.

Many surfaced roads and many dirt roads on grade can be improved by putting in culverts to carry the water *under* the road, whereas now it is being carried across the surface of the road. These culverts can be made of rock or terra cotta or metal. Any captain who is planning to use his squad of men for putting in culverts should make arrangements for the materials for the culverts to be on hand the morning of the first day.

IMPROVEMENT OF DIRT ROADS.

There are many old dirt roads which can be very much improved during these two days' work by removing stumps and rocks from the road and filling up the holes thus made and other holes with dirt of the same character or texture as the balance of the road.

Ditches and drains should be cleaned out, but the material from these ditches *should not be thrown on the roads,* but onto the adjacent land.

Holes or ruts in a road should never be filled with brush and rock, but should be cleaned out and filled with dirt of the same character as the balance of the road.

Don't leave the center of the road the lowest point, but make it the highest point and slope the surface of the road about 1 in 20 to the side ditch.

If sufficient teams can be obtained, road machines, drags, and scrapes can be used to splendid advantage. Men can be found in nearly every community who are familiar with operating these machines.

In eastern North Carolina many main roads through the swamps can be very materially improved by deep ditching. The ditches should be at least 30 feet apart. In many of these swamps good surfacing material can be obtained in close proximity to where the roadway is being ditched.

A road that is in very good condition for most of its distance may contain a steep grade for a short distance which very materially reduces the value of the road. The reduction of this grade to one not over 4½ per cent, and in some cases even less, will enable the users of the road to get full value out of it.

Letter written by the State Geologist to the Chairmen of the Boards of County Commissioners:

NORTH CAROLINA GEOLOGICAL AND ECONOMIC SURVEY.

October 1, 1913.

DEAR SIR:—Enclosed is copy of proclamation made by Governor Craig in regard to Good Roads Days for North Carolina. I have been requested by the Governor to assist the County Road Commissioners in every way possible to make these Good Roads Days successful and of real value to the counties of the State.

As suggested in his letter, I sincerely hope you will pass a resolution at your October meeting calling the attention of the people of your county to the Governor's proclamation, declaring these days County Road Days, at which time you will assist with the county road forces to superintend and direct the work that will be done on these two days. Please authorize the Chairman of the Board of County Commissioners to coöperate with all available forces of the county and State to make the work done in the county of value to the road work of the county; and to carry out to the fullest extent possible the request Governor Craig has made in his message.

In determining where to do the work on these Road Days, it should be borne in mind that in many parts of the State it will not be a good plan to throw up loose materials on our roads at this time of the year. Splendid work, however, can be done in clearing rights-of-way for new locations and grading these. Also many of our dirt roads can be very much improved by eliminating stumps, rocks, filling up holes, and cleaning out ditches and drains. Care should be taken to instruct all the workers that all materials taken out of the ditches should be thrown *away* from the road, and not on the road. The split-log drag can probably be used to good advantage in many places on these days. I am

A. GOVERNOR CRAIG AND SQUAD FACING A MOVING PICTURE MACHINE AT A PLACE ON WEAVERVILLE-GOLD VIEW ROAD, BUNCOMBE COUNTY.

B. THREE CHEERS AND A TIGER FOR GOVERNOR CRAIG ON THE SUMMIT OF GOLD VIEW ON THE 6TH, AFTER THE BARBECUE DINNER.

preparing a bulletin, giving suggestions as to how we can use to advantage the workers who offer their services on these days.

I think it would be a good plan for you to appoint one man to take general charge of different townships and neighborhoods, thus organizing the whole county, so that we can reach them all. Write me the name and address of the man who will have entire charge, so that I can communicate with him as to how much literature he will need in order to effectively organize the county.

We can make this a success all over the State, if every county will do its part toward thoroughly organizing the county and getting the people out.

With best wishes, I am

Yours very truly,
(Signed) JOSEPH HYDE PRATT,
State Geologist.

Letter written by the State Geologist to Road Officials:

October 15, 1913.

MY DEAR SIR:—Enclosed I am sending you copy of a proclamation of Governor Craig, setting apart Wednesday and Thursday, November 5th and 6th, as Good Roads Days. He has asked me to assist in making these two days of value to the road work in North Carolina. I am, in turn, calling upon all the road engineers, road supervisors, road superintendents, road commissions, etc., to assist in making a success of this State-wide campaign for *good roads*. In order for it to be a success, all of the counties and townships must be thoroughly organized and the work laid out in advance of the time.

I am enclosing a circular with suggestions regarding the organization of your county or township, and suggestions regarding the road work to be done; and I will appreciate it if you will join with the others who are working to make this occasion a success, and assist in laying out the work, instructing the captains who are appointed to take charge of different squads of men as to what work should be done, tools to be used, etc. I will be very glad to coöperate with you in any way I can, and want you to feel free to write me for any assistance that I can render you.

The Governor has written the mayors of the cities and towns, the chambers of commerce, the boards of trade, the chairmen of the boards of county commissioners, etc., to assist in the organization of the counties; and, if you can get in touch with these people, I feel that much can be accomplished.

Trusting that you will do what you can to make this occasion a success, and with best wishes, I am

Yours sincerely,
(Signed) JOSEPH HYDE PRATT,
State Geologist.

Letter written by the State Geologist to the Postmasters:

October 14, 1913.

MY DEAR SIR:—Enclosed I am sending you copy of Governor Craig's Good Road Proclamation, and I will appreciate it very much if you can have same put up in conspicuous place in your post office. If we will all get together and do our part in carrying out this proclamation of Governor Craig, we can make November 5th and 6th memorable days in the history of the road work in North Carolina.

Thanking you for your coöperation in this matter, I am

Yours very truly,
(Signed) JOSEPH HYDE PRATT,
State Geologist.

Letter written by Joseph Hyde Pratt, Secretary of the North Carolina Good Roads Association, to members of this Association:

NORTH CAROLINA GOOD ROADS ASSOCIATION, NORTH CAROLINA DIVISION, NATIONAL HIGHWAYS ASSOCIATION.

CHAPEL HILL, October 15, 1913.

DEAR SIR:—Enclosed I am sending you copy of the recent proclamation of Governor Craig, setting apart Wednesday and Thursday, November 5th and 6th, as Good Roads Days. He has asked me to assist in making these two days of value to the road work in North Carolina. I am, in turn, calling upon the members of the North Carolina Good Roads Association to join in this work and help to make this occasion a success in the various counties and townships represented in our Association. It is necessary that the counties and townships be thoroughly organized, if good results are to be obtained.

I am enclosing a circular giving suggestions regarding the road work which can be done, and I will appreciate it very much if you will join with others in seeing that your county is thoroughly organized and ready for work on November 5th and 6th. I will be very glad indeed to coöperate with you in any way I can, and want you to feel free to write me for any assistance that I can render you.

The Governor has written the mayors of the cities and towns, chambers of commerce, boards of trade, chairmen of boards of county commissioners, etc., to assist in the organization of the counties; and I believe the members of our Association who are particularly alive to the need of *good roads,* and have been working for this cause, will help to make this a memorable occasion in the history of our State.

With best wishes, I am

Yours sincerely,
(Signed) JOSEPH HYDE PRATT,
Secretary.

Letter written by Joseph Hyde Pratt, Secretary of the North Carolina Good Roads Association, to the members of the County Good Roads Associations:

October 14, 1913.

Dear Sir:—Enclosed I am sending you copy of the recent proclamation of Governor Craig, setting apart Wednesday and Thursday, November 5th and 6th, as Good Roads Days. He has asked me to assist in making these two days of value to the road work in North Carolina. I am, in turn, calling upon all the affiliated associations of the North Carolina Good Roads Association to join in this work. It is necessary that the counties and townships be thoroughly organized, if good results are to be obtained.

I am enclosing a circular with suggestions regarding the organization of county or township, and suggestions regarding road work, and I will appreciate it very much if you will join with others in seeing that your county is thoroughly organized and ready for work November 5th and 6th. I will be glad indeed to coöperate with you in any way I can, and want you to feel free to write me for any assistance that I can render you.

The Governor has written the mayors of cities and towns, the chambers of commerce and boards of trade, the chairmen of the boards of county commissioners, to assist in the organization of the counties, but I have felt that the County Good Roads Associations, which are alive to the need of good roads, and are working for good roads, would be willing to make a special effort to see that their county is well organized.

With best wishes, I am Yours sincerely,

(Signed) Joseph Hyde Pratt,
Secretary.

In all of the letters sent out, there was included a copy or copies of the Governor's proclamation; and, to the road officials and county commissioners were sent, in addition, the pamphlet containing plans for organization. There was also mailed to all the preachers of the State a copy of the Governor's proclamation.

There was prepared for distribution amongst the county superintendents, boards of education, and teachers, a special bulletin on "Civic Days" (Good Roads Day—Arbor Day), which gave material and suggestions for a program that would be suitable for celebrating Good Roads Days. This bulletin was prepared by the North Carolina Geological and Economic Survey, and was published and distributed as a bulletin of the Department of Education. An edition of 20,000 was sent out.

CIVIC DAYS.*

GOOD ROADS DAY—ARBOR DAY.

Letter of Superintendent of Public Instruction:

RALEIGH, October 15, 1913.

To County Superintendents, Boards of Education and Teachers:

The Governor of North Carolina, by proclamation, has set apart the 5th and 6th of November as Good Roads Days, to be celebrated as holidays by all the people throughout the State. The schools should contribute their share to the success of this commendable coöperative movement for better roads in North Carolina. The children should have the opportunity to participate in this celebration and thereby learn a valuable, practical lesson in community service for civic betterment. I deem it wise and proper, therefore, to request and direct all county superintendents to notify and instruct all teachers of their counties to set apart and celebrate the last of these days—Thursday, November 6th —as "Good Roads Day" in the public schools.

A part of this day should be devoted to reading and discussing with the children in school, the valuable information contained in the bulletin on Good Roads and Arbor Day, kindly prepared by Miss Berry and Mr. Holmes of the North Carolina Geological and Economic Survey. The remainder of the day should be spent in actual work by the children, under the direction of the teachers, in improving and beautifying the school grounds, the school building, and the outhouses, and in laying off and grading walks through the school yards and roads leading thereto. Valuable suggestions for such work will be found in this bulletin.

I suggest that the road workers be requested and urged to spend Thursday, or at least a part of that day, in working the roads leading to the schoolhouses, and that they be invited by the women of the neighborhood to meet at the schoolhouse on that day for dinner, and to join with the children in their work on the school grounds. The women of the neighborhood might be invited to come to the schoolhouse, Thursday morning, and participate with the children and teachers in the celebration and in the improvement work of the morning.

The gathering of all the best citizens of the school district about the school on this day, spending a social hour together at dinner, joining with the children and teachers in an afternoon's work, side by side, for the improvement of their school, will afford a fine opportunity to become acquainted with the conditions and needs of their school—to meet and to know teachers and children, and will result, I doubt not, in awakening interest and stimulating pride in the school and incalculable benefit in many ways to the school and community.

*Bulletin XXII of the office of the Superintendent of Public Instruction, compiled by Miss H. M. Berry, Secretary, and J. S. Holmes, Forester of the North Carolina Geological and Economic Survey.

To become permanent, all great movements for civic and industrial improvement must begin with the teaching of the children in the schools. The rising generation should be taught the necessity and importance of good roads in North Carolina; should be brought to see the relation of these to the future comfort, progress and prosperity of the State along all lines. Nothing is more essential than good roads for increasing the efficiency of our country schools. Consolidation and transportation, so necessary for larger schools, larger taxing areas, better houses and equipment, more and better teachers, with better organized, more advanced and more practical courses of study, for better preparation for life and its daily occupations, are practically impossible without good roads. Good attendance and good health during the winter months are almost impossible in the country schools without good roads. This one day, therefore, will be most profitably spent in our public schools in impressing upon the children, by precept and by example, the value and necessity of good roads and the civic duty of helping to secure them for their communities and their State.

County Superintendents are earnestly requested and officially directed to distribute these bulletins to the teachers of their county without delay, and to urge them, by written or personal communication, to begin at once preparation for the successful celebration of this day. Teachers are urged to spare no effort to enlist the children and the citizens of the community in making the day pleasant and profitable.

This bulletin should be filed in the library and preserved for future reference and instruction.

J. Y. Joyner,
Superintendent Public Instruction.

COMMENTS OF THE PRESS AND INDIVIDUALS ON THE UNDERTAKING.

The *News and Observer* of November 2nd, 1913, wrote as follows:

Wednesday and Thursday are to be made notable days in North Carolina.

They are to be "Good Roads Days," having thus been designated by Governor Craig, who in a proclamation has called upon all able-bodied citizens of North Carolina to do actual work on those days.

President H. Q. Alexander, of the North Carolina Farmers' Union, has issued a notice to the farmers of the State, asking that they observe the day and do road work which will be of value to the whole State.

President Henry B. Varner, of the North Carolina Good Roads Association, has issued a call to all good roads advocates to get busy on "Good Roads Days" and aid in the work of making better highways.

At the State University and at various colleges in the State, Wednesday and Thursday, November 5th and 6th, are to be observed by actual road work and by discussions as to the making of highways. And the same is true of a great number of the schools of the State.

In many of the cities, towns and counties notices have been issued by mayors, county commissioners and road officials calling upon all citizens to get to work on the roads on "Good Roads Days," and it is expected there will be a response all along the line.

Governor Locke Craig is to set the example by doing actual road work for the two days, and last night the news came from Washington that Governor Elliott, Governor Major, of Missouri, and Governor Hodges, of Kansas, who worked the roads in their states, expect to spend the two days in North Carolina, assisting Governor Craig in working the roads. Governor Hodges went over into Missouri and helped Governor Major work the roads of that State.

It is to be two days of big work for North Carolina in the making of good roads. Every man who can handle a road working tool of any kind should get on the job.

The *Charlotte Observer* of September 28th, remarks editorially as follows:

The *Observer* prints a proclamation by Governor Craig appointing November 5th and 6th as "Good Roads Days" in North Carolina. The plans of the Governor will be understood by a reading of the paper. He believes that when the people once grasp the idea, they will respond to the call and make the two days of some account. The State is in need of a better system of constructing and maintaining public roads and the plan of the Governor is calculated to have an inspirational effect. This call to service means much to the people of North Carolina, for good roads building really is just now getting an impetus. The *Observer* will give its endorsement to any movement calculated to make a county that does not spider-web itself with good roads feel ashamed of its backward condition.

The *Durham Sun* of October 1st wrote as follows:

Wednesday and Thursday, November 5th and 6th, are "good roads days" in North Carolina. Don't forget that under any circumstances.

Two days have been observed in other states in such a way for this purpose as to bring about great transformations in improved highways. Why not in North Carolina? The proclamation of Governor Locke Craig will be found in another column and it should be read by all so that they will appreciate the fullness and hopefulness of this rally of all to picks and shovels. The proclamation for holidays and other purposes are seldom very novel or instructive, but this public document is both. It will repay every one that reads it, as it is progressive and inspiring in welfare, coöperative work and public spirit.

The observances of road days in other states have been accompanied by much amusement when all get together for outings on the roads. In Missouri, where the movement was inaugurated, the benefit to the roads was wonderful, and at the same time the people had more fun than on any other two days in the history of that state. Everybody should arrange now to work the roads two days the first week in November. We have no elections for excitement this year, and we can all get out on the roads and "holler" as we go shoveling along, "Hurrah for 'Good Roads'!"

The *Western North Carolina Times,* published at Hendersonville, on October 3rd, commented as follows:

Declaring that the people of North Carolina lose $12,000,000 annually because of the poor condition of the State's highways, Governor Craig issued a proclamation designating November 5th and 6th as "Good Roads Days" and calling on all patriotic people throughout the State to work upon the public roads of the State on those days.

The Governor pointed out that the modern highway is essential to the material prosperity and social advancement of every community, and declared the country has awakened to the importance of improved roads.

Characterizing the vast sum lost annually to North Carolina through lack of good roads as a "tribute paid to mud," Governor Craig's proclamation calls upon every able-bodied man "to shoulder his shovel, march out and strike a blow for progress."

Summoning the people of every station to answer the call of patriotism, the proclamation calls on the "farmer, the merchant, the lawyer, the doctor, the minister of the gospel, the rich and the poor, to enlist as volunteers in this mighty army for grand accomplishment."

The work will be organized and conducted in a systematic manner, so that at the end of the second day every community in the State will show permanent road improvement. All road overseers, good roads associations and organizations for public welfare and civic improvement are urged to aid the movement. County commissioners are called on to issue proclamations urging the people to participate in the work.

Declaring that the farmers, more than any other class, are dependent upon the country road, Governor Craig's proclamation says: "I call upon the president of the Farmers' Union to issue his proclamation to the farmers of North Carolina, that this great body of our citizenship, constituting as it does the bone and sinew of the State, may join with energy and enthusiasm in the movement."

The women are summoned to lend their presence.

In conclusion the Governor says: "Let every North Carolinian show by his work that he is for the improvement of the State."

The *Enterprise,* of Williamston, Martin County, had this to say:

North Carolina's Governor, Hon. Locke Craig, is wearing the title of Good Roads Governor deservedly. He has recently issued a Good Roads Proclamation in which he declares that "the modern highway is essential to material prosperity, and to the advancement of the social life of every community; all sections and all progressive citizens are demanding them and determining to have them." He further states that the people of North Carolina are annually losing twelve millions of dollars on account of bad roads, which is a vast sum to contribute to mud.

He sets apart the 5th and 6th of November, 1913, as Good Roads Days, and appoints these days as holidays throughout the State. On these days he calls upon every citizen in every walk of life to shoulder his shovel and march out, and strike the blow for progress. The women are asked to have a part in the work by providing good things to eat and by inspiring the men with faith and courage.

The Commissioners of every county are asked to set apart these days and to urge the people to labor for the welfare of their respective counties. "Let the work be conducted in a systematic way, to the end that at sunset of the second day there will be no community in all the State where the hand of progress and toil has not left its mark in permanent road improvement, and the progressive spirit its impression in the hearts and minds of the people."

The setting apart of these days is a wise stroke on the part of Governor Craig. Everywhere, signs of progress are appearing, and better highways make for an advanced civilization, and help the material wealth of any community. The citizens of Martin County should appreciate this opportunity to further the work on their township roads. We urge official notice of the plan by the Board of County Commissioners and the Mayors of every town.

The *Greensboro Daily News* of October 1st, wrote as follows:

The proclamation of Governor Craig bids you, if you are an able-bodied man, help to build some roadway in North Carolina during the period designated as Good Roads Days, November 5th and 6th.

This request may be regarded as personal to you from the chief magistrate of your state. He himself will probably be found with overalls on and pick in hand setting this example of citizenship. If every man who likes to call himself a good and patriotic citizen heeds the mandate of this proclamation, and the work is systematized beforehand, so that most of what is done will be of a really constructive and permanent nature, there will be accomplished something grandly worth while.

To the average man living in a town or city, perhaps, this work will be found an educational novelty. You have been reading and talking of good roads, perhaps writing of them; and you certainly have a practical and painful knowledge of the subject of bad roads. If you do your duty on the good roads days you will hereafter know considerably more of your subject when you discuss good roads.

The village dwellers and farmers have nearly all done some road building, of a sort, and to them the occasion has no glamour of novelty. They knew that a great deal of hard work can be done on a road, without adding anything much to its permanent improvement. "Working the roads" is an institution in North Carolina; a patchwork process upon which the law has compelled men to waste a great deal of time without accomplishing very much. The people see that they are not doing anything, not getting anywhere, and so "working the road" in many communities of the state has come to mean a neighborhood loafing. It may be a little difficult to arouse these citizens, sophisticated in "working the road" to any degree of enthusiasm, but it will be necessary to arouse them if this enterprise is to accomplish anything. A few years ago, Dr. Pratt was of a notion to have the folks along the line turn in and build the central highway from mountains to sea at one fell swoop; and the central highway is not built yet. However, most of it is. That is to say, most of it is good road in summer and passable in winter.

It is earnestly to be hoped that citizens everywhere, irrespective of condition—laborers, business men, farmers, professional men, teachers—will fall in with the Governor's plan. We must create in North Carolina an enthusiasm, a spirit, a determination to anticipate future development, to pledge the great resources of the state to build GOOD highways for all the people in all parts of the state; and these good roads days will be at once a means of deepening that enthusiasm and of testing it. It will be magnificently educational, it can be made a means of proclaiming to the world that we are determined to throw off our bondage to the mud tax. We, in North Carolina, are struggling mightily with the railroads to grant partial relief from freight overcharges of five million dollars; it is in our own power to abate a bad roads overcharge of twelve million dollars a year.

Of course the able-bodied men of the state are not going to build a system of highways in two days, nor could they do it in a week or month. But here is the opportunity for a magnificent new beginning; and if the people will unite, if all will get together in the communities and build some roads and devote two days concentrated thought and discussion to it, it will mean that North Carolina will be a good roads state in a few years.

The *Wilmington Star* of October 7th very enthusiastically wrote:

Every man in North Carolina owes his good old State a service. Instead of being put on the roads we've got a chance to go to the roads voluntarily and do a little road work either on the 5th or 6th of November. According to Governor Craig's proclamation those dates have been appointed Good Roads Days and he calls upon all able-bodied men to turn out and do some sort of work on the roads. He is going to take a hand himself, and all those "high" State officials will no doubt take great pleasure in becoming constructionists like the Good Roads Govcruor. By the way, the judges and the lawyers should keep an eye on those dates, November 5th and 6th, and avail themselves of the opportunity to take a little exercise "on the roads." They will set a good example and learn how it feels to be "sent to the roads."

The *Star* wants to emphasize the fact that Governor Craig's good roads proclamation is a capital idea and that his call upon all citizens alike was a ten strike. It challenges the attention of every individual North Carolinian to the importance and value of good roads, and it emphasizes their necessity in the development of the State. That proclamation is well calculated to arouse interest on the part of all men to the utility and economy of modern highways. If it will make every man a good roads man it will be worth untold millions in bringing about the availability of the great agricultural resources of the State. Good roads will do that in the same proportion that modern methods of agriculture will. Improved cultural methods and good roads go hand in hand, for the one depends on the other. In fact, we are pretty safe in saying that good roads bring about the highest type of agricultural development. We never saw a good road that did not accomplish that result. The farmer who wants to do modern farming invariably locates on a good road or gets a good road located in his community. A modern highway is the basic economy in rural development and the wideawake man knows it. Every man ought to know it, if he don't and so we can say that nothing will so accentuate the good roads cause as Governor Craig's timely proclamation. If it interests every man in improved roads and makes a good roads advocate of all classes of people, North Carolina will take a stride that will astonish the natives. Mark well our words—the South Atlantic State which first networks itself with good roads will take the loan of all of them and it won't be long in doing it either.

Some man who heeds the Governor's proclamation and turns out to work the roads may do the grunting while others will do the work, but that's all right. It will show his interest in a great cause and enlist him as an advocate and supporter of better highways for the better development of his State. If a half million men and boys turn out on Good Roads Days, it will mean a militant army faced about in the direction of Progress. It will set the pace. It will make North Carolina sit up and look straight ahead. We will get a visualization of North Carolina's future, with all the immeasurable possibilities that the matchless versatility of the State foreshadows from its ocean strand to its mountain vales.

If a half million North Carolinians should turn out on Good Roads Days it would be a good sign. The State would get the benefit of the new inspiration that would come to them, while if the State got the equivalent of $1,000,000 in work done on the highways of the state it would mark the beginning of a State-wide good roads movement. It would arouse a constructive sentiment and inspire a progressive spirit from the mountains to the sea.

No man, the millionaire or the workingman, could do two days of greater work for the State than to respond to the constructive impulse of the State's Governor. If, on the 5th and 6th of November, we give thought to the cause, the magnitude of the result cannot be conceived. If we but view our roads and become susceptible to a sense of shame at their neglect, we can form a new resolve that will cut the ground from beneath the feet of the last remnant of mossbackism that hampers the progress of a State with more diversified resources than can be found elsewhere on the American continent.

Governor Craig has given us all a chance to hit a lick for North Carolina.

The *Asheville Citizen* of September 29, 1913, wrote as follows:

In his praiseworthy proclamation setting aside November 5th and 6th as good roads days in North Carolina, Governor Craig has justly earned the title of "Good Roads Governor," by which he will always be known to posterity. It is not necessary to go into details of the plans which are set forth in the proclamation published in the *Citizen* yesterday; the general scheme looks to the enlistment of all able-bodied men in the active support of the good roads movement and on the days mentioned it is hoped to have hundreds of men with shovels, citizens of high and low degree, out on the county roads. No man need consider it "infra dig" to take up his shovel and work, since the governor himself will set the example by actually turning dirt on the public roads. While the people of North Carolina have been imbued with a large part of the good roads spirit there is room for much more enthusiasm than has heretofore been shown; so many of us have lain back while others did the work. Now, it is proposed to fan the smoldering embers of good roads enthusiasm into brightly burning flames by giving every man the opportunity to contribute to the cause in a practical manner. It is not given to all men to give of their funds for the good roads cause, but none is too poor to wield a shovel. The *Citizen* believes that the respouse to Governor Craig's appeal for the observance of good roads days will be a most generous one.

Governor Craig, in his proclamation, called attention to the fact that North Carolina loses $12,000,000 every year because of the poor conditions of the state's highways, a condition which he very aptly describes as paying tribute to mud. Surely our people are not content to calmly brook without protest a loss so enormous; a loss which might be averted by the application of energy to a problem which will be with us as long as men remain indifferent. Indeed, the solution of this problem seems so simple, so easily within arm's length, that the only cause for wonder is that determined efforts at solution have not been made before.

The *Biblical Recorder* of October 8th, 1913, commended the project as follows:

Recalling the fact that the people of North Carolina are losing twelve million dollars annually on account of bad roads, believing that the modern highway is essential to material prosperity, and recognizing the universal sentiment for road improvement, Governor Craig has set apart Wednesday and Thursday, November 5th and 6th, as Good Roads Days, appointing them as holidays and days of festival throughout the State in order to especially mark the beginning of an era wherein improved highways shall be built in every neighborhood of the Commonwealth.

His Excellency is to be warmly commended for directing public attention to this vital matter. It is hoped that every man who can possibly do so will himself "shoulder his shovel and march out and strike a blow for progress." The Governor continues "Let the farmer, the merchant, the lawyer, the doctor, the minister of the Gospel, the rich and the poor, and the men of all walks of life, enlist as volunteers in this mighty army for grand accomplishment."

Good roads will not only promote general prosperity, but we should also have improved highways for the onward march of the Gospel. How many good people are hindered from church attendance by bad roads! We dare say there is not a minister in our entire brotherhood who does not believe in the gospel of good roads. Nor is there one who will withhold his influence and coöperation from the Governor and the Commonwealth in this noble undertaking.

The *State Journal* of October 24th wrote as follows:

Some sections of the State are beginning to make great preparations for working their roads on November 5th and 6th, the special days set apart by Governor Craig. The Governor has announced that he, following his proclamation for every man to go, not send, will don his overalls, shoulder his shovel and work two days along with the other folks. The Governor is to be congratulated upon his willingness to practice what he preaches. Dr. Alexander, President of the Farmers' Union, has issued a proclamation to local unions throughout the State to assemble on Friday, the 31st, and arrange for work in their localities on the days set apart. The County Commissioners of Rowan County will give one thousand dollars in three prizes to the townships of that county which makes the best showing on the two days. Buie's Creek Academy, in Harnett County, has announced that it will turn 250 students loose on the roads for two days, and no doubt other schools will follow.

The *Asheville Gazette-News* of September 29th comments as follows:

In setting aside two good roads days in North Carolina, by proclamation, when the people are asked to gather together and work on the roads, Governor Craig is following a scheme which was carried out with signal success by the Governor of Missouri. The idea of coöperative labor, however, is by no means new; it is as old in this country as the country; but in late years the practice has only survived in the quiltings and "corn shuckings" of a few vicinities. It would be well if the neighborhood "workings" could be brought into popularity again, at least so far as the roads are concerned; for they have ever been an effective plan of labor. To be sure, the working out of roads by popular labor survives, and in reality it is a gathering together of the people to work for the general good; but there is all the difference in the world in having to work and being invited to work—the difference between doing all you can and doing as little as you can. It is little wonder that method of road working was never effective. It is in the form of a tax; and possibly there is in the makeup of all of us just a little rebellion against tax paying. But if the objection to paying taxes came to us from our ancestors, by the same token the greater percentage of the population ought to respond to the call of Governor Craig.

While Missouri is used as an example of the state-wide movement of this kind, we do not have to go out of western North Carolina to learn of its effectiveness.

The *Union Republican* (Winston-Salem) of October 24th wrote as follows:

A good many counties in the State are making preparations to actively and practically observe Governor Craig's Good Roads Days, November 5th and 6th, and citizens in their respective townships will pull off their coats during the specified time. The proclamation of His Excellency will serve good purposes. It shows a willingness to carry out a proclamation by our Chief Executive, will result in considerable work being done on the roads and stimulate an interest generally in the good roads work by a united effort instead of depending entirely on bond issues and ceaseless interest payments to build them. Much money is appropriated every year to road building. Forsyth county alone collects in taxes, something like $80,000. Much of it is wasted in experiments, shoddy work, and the employment of men who are not conversant with this kind of business. Realizing our needs it is well to profit by past experiences and in future make every dollar count or find out the reason why.

The *Asheboro Courier* of October 17th wrote:

If all the able-bodied male population of North Carolina will turn out and work the public roads on the 5th and 6th of November, much can be accomplished towards improving the earth roads of the State. It is to be hoped that all the plows will stop on these days, and all the factories, the engines, and machinery stop and that the shops and offices will be closed and that everybody will turn out and work the roads. This movement is a fine beginning. It means an increased interest in road building. It is an idea that is borrowed from an Eastern State but it is a good one. The principal road question for North Carolina is how to keep the earth roads in repair, but the ordinary man knows so little about building and repairing any kind of road, earth or otherwise, that something like this is necessary to increase the interest to such an extent as to cause the average man to learn how to build and keep in repair earth roads.

The *News and Observer,* under date of November 2nd, wrote editorially as follows:

There is to be opportunity at hand this week for the people of North Carolina to show that they are imbued with the spirit of good roads. Not alone that they want good roads, but their hearts are in the cause for the making of better highways in North Carolina.

By proclamation Governor Craig has set aside Wednesday and Thursday of this week as "Good Roads Days" in North Carolina, two days on which all people in North Carolina, can devote themselves to actual work on the roads. In person he will set the example, and will "serve" two days in road work in Buncombe county.

If there is a general response to the call to work the roads on November 5th and 6th, there can be much effective work done in repairing old roads and in putting in shape new roads. This will make the two days of practical value because of the work which will be done, but the days can be made of far more lasting and valuable service than the road building which is done.

This greater service is for good roads advocates to make of "Good Roads" an example of their value to the State, and of their interest in the making of highways of which the State can be proud. The time when it was necessary to argue the value of good roads has passed. This is a thing recognized. What is now needed is to get into the minds of the people everywhere the desire to have them, to have good roads everywhere in North Carolina. Unfortunately there are sections of North Carolina where the spirit of good roads does not exist, and it is to bring such a spirit as this to all the State that Wednesday and Thursday of this week should be used.

The opportunity is here for a work which will redound in good to all the State. Let no man who wants good roads in North Carolina fail to take advantage of it.

The *Kinston Free Press* of October 11th endorsed the movement as follows:

Every community in the State ought to observe good roads days, November 5th and 6th. The Governor has called upon the public to make these days two distinctively good roads days, and citizens would do well to heed his advice. Not only will doing so largely increase the good roads mileage in the State, but such action would bear much larger fruit in the enhanced good roads sentiment that it would foster. Remember the days, November 5th and 6th!

The *Weekly News Letter* of the Brett Engineering and Contracting Company of November 6th, 1913, wrote as follows:

"UP AND AT THEM."

It is a heavy tax which North Carolina pays for having bad roads, and they are relieving themselves of burdens when they "get the habit" of having good roads. To get these always means a fight, but "up and at them" should be the battle cry when there is an assault on bad roads and the resultant evil.

To-day and to-morrow, November 5th and November 6th, North Carolina is to have two "Good Roads Days" in which, by proclamation, the people are called upon in every part of North Carolina to do actual work on good roads. It is not meant that these days be made play time events, but that real work on the roads be done.

Throughout the State the people are reported as having seized upon the idea presented, and the indications are that there will be much work in making better highways. In cities and towns and country, able-bodied men are to shovel dirt to-day in an effort to help North Carolina to become bigger and better North Carolina. That is the spirit behind the work of to-day and to-morrow.

And what is done on these two days is going to have an influence on the future of good roads in the State, for interest shown to-day by good roads advocates will be of avail in bringing forth a great spirit of interest in a cause which means for a greater North Carolina in many ways.

The call, then, is for every man to do his full duty to-day in the cause of good roads. Shovel dirt with the purpose to make this a factor in building up the spirit for good roads. "Up and at them," up and at the bad roads so that North Carolina may get out of the mud and travel on a broad and smooth highway which leads on to progress and prosperity.

Many letters in regard to the observance or non-observance of the Good Roads Days were received, the following being representative:

WINSTON-SALEM, N. C., October 13, 1913.

HON. LOCKE CRAIG,
Governor of North Carolina, Raleigh, N. C.

MY DEAR SIR:—Your esteemed favor of the 9th inst. with reference to coöperation of this organization in the objects and purposes of the proclamation made by your Excellency, naming the 5th and 6th of November as good roads days, was received and has been given careful attention. Referring thereto I beg to advise as follows:

About the time your proclamation was issued, the writer canvassed the matter with a number of our citizens and it appeared to be the view that this county, having some years back passed through the good roads rally spirit and having taken up the matter of road building very much as a routine proposition with about $80,000 per annum available for road building, that we would not be able to count much on getting the citizens to turn out with their picks and shovels to do actual work on the roads. However, we did not desire to repose in this view of the matter, but have been on the lookout for the indications of a sentiment, at least in some parts of the county, that, with proper encouragement and coöperation, could be crystallized into some active work along the line of your proclamation on the days named therein.

One such instance came to light on Saturday last just after the receipt of your letter and we have taken it up actively with the parties promoting the movement, and with the Chairman of the County Highway Commission, we shall follow it up vigorously and hope it may lead to some real active work in road improvement on the days set apart in your proclamation.

We think now that such a sentiment may also develop in other neighborhood centers, and beg to assure you that we stand ready to coöperate in every way possible and do everything that we can do to aid you in making good roads days a great success in the way of practical accomplishment for road improvements.

We are not only interested in the roads improvement involved in the proclamation, but are in hearty sympathy with the sentiment contained in the closing paragraph of your letter in regard to the opportunity which it affords for developing, as you state, a clearer and fuller realization of the obligations and duties of citizenship in promoting the common good.

Very respectfully yours,

(Signed) J. L. LUDLOW,
President.

The Clerk of the Board of County Commissioners of Mitchell County wrote as follows:

BAKERSVILLE, N. C., October 11, 1913.

HON. LOCKE CRAIG,
Governor, Raleigh, N. C.

DEAR SIR:—This is to notify you that the County Commissioners of this County called a meeting of the citizens of this County on the 6th inst. and heartily endorsed your Proclamation on the two days' free labor movement. After considerable discussion and display of enthusiasm, the people present unanimously recommended Dr. R. E. Stack to organize and carry out this good roads movement. You will please address all communications to Dr. R. E. Stack.

Yours very truly,
(Signed) J. H. MCKINNEY,
Clerk to the Board of County Commissioners.

From Register of Deeds of Edgecombe County:

TARBORO, N. C., November 5, 1913.

JOSEPH HYDE PRATT,
Chapel Hill, N. C.

DEAR SIR:—The Board of Commissioners of Edgecombe County, at their regular meeting last Monday, requested me to acknowledge receipt of the Governor's Proclamation and say, while this Board and the people of this County are most heartily in sympathy with the good roads movement, unfortunately the people of this County have in Tarboro, the County seat, an agricultural fair in which there is much general interest taken. Owing to this there can be no good roads work in this county this week.

Yours truly,
(Signed) H. S. BUNN,
Clerk to Board.

The Chairman of the Highway Commissioners of Morehead Township, Carteret County, wrote as follows:

MOREHEAD CITY, N. C., October 15, 1913.

DR. JOSEPH HYDE PRATT,
Chapel Hill, N. C.

DEAR SIR:—I beg to acknowledge receipt of your favor in reference to the Governor's proclamation. We are making arrangements to work the roads these two days, and certainly appreciate your suggestions in regard to organization.

Yours very truly,
(Signed) G. D. CANFIELD,
Chairman.

Hon. John H. Small, Congressman from the First District, wrote:

WASHINGTON, D. C., October 11, 1913.

DR. JOSEPH HYDE PRATT,
Chapel Hill, N. C.

DEAR SIR:—I am simply writing to say that it is my purpose to be at my home on November 5th and 6th, the two good roads days, and put in two days work for the roads. Have you been able yet to organize Beaufort County for this work? Yours sincerely,

(Signed) JOHN H. SMALL.

The Chairman of the Board of County Commissioners of Columbus County wrote as follows:

TABOR, N. C., October 16, 1913.

DR. JOSEPH HYDE PRATT,
Chapel Hill, N. C.

DEAR SIR:—After due consideration by the Board of Commissioners of Columbus County, the Board decided that the most effective way of organizing for the road work ordered by the Governor the fifth and sixth of November was to organize by school districts, making the chairman of each school committee in Columbus County a leader in the procession of road working. The Board of Commissioners ordered the clerk of the Board to furnish you with the name of each chairman of the school committee, expecting at the same time for you to furnish each one with some road literature. We decided that this would be the best plan to fall upon, as all the school districts are connected by roads. We are obliged in this way to reach nearly every road in the county. We further requested the Superintendent of Education to call off his school those two days. Our salvation for road building lies in the young men.

If the clerk of our Board has not furnished you with the names of the chairmen of each district, you will oblige me by letting me know at once. We want you to have their names so you can furnish them with the road literature, as this is part of our plan. Any suggestion of yours to help us on in organizing will be highly appreciated, as we want to make this a success.

I remain, Yours very truly,

(Signed) C. C. PRIDGEN,
Chairman Board of Commissioners.

The Chairman of the Board of County Commissioners of Carteret County had the following to say:

MOREHEAD CITY, N. C., October 8, 1913.

HON. LOCKE CRAIG,
Raleigh, N. C.

DEAR SIR:—Yours of October 1st is to hand and contents noted. The Board of County Commissioners of Carteret County acting under your suggestion to make November 5th and 6th good roads days have taken up the matter and will endeavor to get our people to act accordingly.

I thank you very much for the interest you have taken in this matter and hope that it will be the means of awakening our people along the line of good roads building.

Yours very respectfully,
(Signed) J. B. MORTON,
Chairman.

The Carolina Metal Products Company of Wilmington:

WILMINGTON, N. C., October 15, 1913.

MR. JOHN P. KERR, *Private Secretary,*
Raleigh, N. C.

DEAR SIR:—The Good Roads Proclamation issued by the Honorable Locke Craig, Governor, should be given as much publicity as possible, and should be read by each citizen of North Carolina.

To assist the Governor and State to arouse enthusiasm, and to bring men and women from their daily tasks to the Roads, we had in mind the sending out to all names on our mailing list, in North Carolina, a copy of the Governor's Good Roads Proclamation; consequently, we would appreciate your sending us two thousand (2,000) copies.

If there is any expense incurred in complying with our request we are only too glad to pay for these proclamations, as we deem it our duty to assist in this worthy cause. Yours very truly,

THE CAROLINA METAL PRODUCTS COMPANY.
(Signed) GEORGE P. GALVIN,
General Manager.

The offer of the Carolina Metal Products Company was accepted and 2,000 of the Governor's Proclamation were forwarded to them for distribution.

PROCLAMATION BY DR. H. Q. ALEXANDER, PRESIDENT FARMERS' UNION OF NORTH CAROLINA.

Whereas, his Excellency, Locke Craig, Governor of North Carolina, has issued his proclamation setting apart the fifth and sixth days of November, 1913, as Good Roads Days, and appointing these days as holidays and days of festival throughout the State, to celebrate the dawn of a new day in North Carolina—a day in which the march of progress toward a higher and better civilization is made easier by Good Roads, with modern schools as signboards guiding the people onward and upward; and

Whereas, his Excellency has called upon the president of the Farmers' Union to issue his proclamation to the organized farmers of North Carolina to enlist in this great movement for the betterment of all the people and the development of both country and town;

Therefore, as president of the Farmers' Union, I hereby call upon all the local unions in the State to assemble at their regular meeting places on Friday afternoon or night, October 31st, and there organize and arrange to work every able-bodied man in the community on the community roads on Wednesday and Thursday, November 5th and 6th.

Let all farmers unite with all other classes of our citizenship, and, shovel in hand, realize that it is one of the very few instances in life where brawn will hold its own with brain.

And in this union of effort in a "common cause," may all men come to realize that every movement for the development of North Carolina and the upbuilding of her citizenship is a "Common Cause" that should enlist the united coöperation of all classes.

And as we are thus for two days brought personally under the divine edict "by the sweat of thy face shalt thou eat bread" may all men be brought into a closer and larger sympathy with that large class of our people that spend all their days in labor and toil.

And as we tire under the burden of the day may we be stimulated to greater guidance by the thought that we are thus lessening the burden of North Carolina's twelve million dollar Bad Road Tax—that we are thus helping to bring country and town nearer together, reducing the cost of marketing to the one and lowering the high cost of living to the other, that we are thus making possible an increased attendance on church and school, thereby elevating the people spiritually, morally and intellectually.

And may these Good Roads Days arouse a universal demand for good road building that will soon extend these arteries of trade to the humblest home in North Carolina.

And may this meeting and mingling and laboring together bring all men of all classes to recognize the rights of others and the part that each class must take in the development of a greater civilization; and may we never be content with a prosperity that does not extend to every class and every section of our State.

All State and county papers please publish.

Fraternally,

H. Q. ALEXANDER,

President Farmers' Union of North Carolina.

4. ACTUAL ROAD WORK.

Volunteers from the University community will be available in large numbers to work any given piece of road, if the Survey find practical a plan for using them on the afternoons of November 5th and 6th.

We will appreciate any suggestions you may make supplementary to this program.

Sincerely yours,

(Signed) EDWARD K. GRAHAM,

Acting President.

Mr. J. F. Webb, of the Granville Commercial Club, wrote as follows:

OXFORD, NORTH CAROLINA, September 30, 1913.

DR. JOSEPH HYDE PRATT,

Chapel Hill, N. C.

DEAR SIR:—We want to do something in this county during the "Good Roads Days." We should like to have you come to Oxford some day before that time, as early as you can, and help us make some definite plans. You will find the business people here interested. We just need a little assistance in rounding up the energy of our people and directing it into practical channels.

Very truly,

(Signed) J. F. WEBB.

Mr. T. F. Hickerson, Highway Engineer of the Survey, was detailed by the Geological Survey to assist in this work.

Elaborate plans for the carrying out of the so-called "Good Roads Bee Campaign" were formulated by the Salibury Industrial Club, Mr. J. H. Warburton, the Secretary, being untiring in his efforts to make these days a success in Rowan County.

The following letters are given to indicate the widespread interest that was aroused for Good Roads Days, and are from people from all sections of North Carolina, and illustrate the type of letters received:

The following letter to Governor Craig from Greensboro shows the interest of an individual there:

GREENSBORO, N. C., October 10, 1913.

His Excellency, HON. LOCKE CRAIG,

Raleigh, N. C.

DEAR SIR:—As you have designated November 5th and 6th as Good Roads Days in North Carolina I would like to offer my services to you in any way that I could assist you in this good cause. If there is anything that I can do for you in Greensboro I would be pleased if you will call upon me.

Wishing you very great success in this good work, I beg to remain

Very truly yours,

(Signed) MAX T. PAYNE.

The following letter from Mr. W. C. Boren, Chairman of the Board of County Commissioners, under date of October 10th, states as follows:

"As per your request of October 1st, we have appointed a Committee in each township in Guilford County to assist in organizing for work on Good Roads Days, and wish you would mail a copy of your bulletin giving suggestions as to this work to the enclosed list."

The following letter from Weaverville will be of great interest as coming from a man well along in age and of wide experience, which contains some sound advice to road builders:

WEAVERVILLE, N. C., October 18, 1913.

HON. JOSEPH HYDE PRATT,
Chapel Hill, N. C.

DEAR SIR:—I am just in receipt of your letter enclosing therewith the Governor's Proclamation, which I have posted as requested. Although I am 65 years old, I shall be on the roads D. V. on the 5th and 6th prox. But I must say that, notwithstanding I have always been a firm believer in good roads, and as commissioner in Buncombe County in 1897 succeeded in having put down the first one-half mile of macadam in this country; still I must say that I can't feel as hearty in my effort for good roads as I should be if we had a law to induce, impel, or compel the use of *wide tires* on our roads. You don't have to be told that our roads could be kept in good condition with one-half or less money with the use of wide tires. Then why is it that there is no agitation of that feature of the road question?

I am informed that France not only requires the use of wide tires but that the axles be of different length, so that the wheels will not "track."

Yours truly,
(Signed) T. H. WEAVER,
Postmaster.

The letter given below is from Mr. George I. J. Elliott, Postmaster at Jackson Hill, North Carolina:

JACKSON HILL, N. C., October 22, 1913.

DEAR MR. PRATT:—The proclamation received and same posted. I am real glad to have the opportunity to do something for better roads. If you have any literature of any kind for distribution would be glad to have a supply to hand out, or anything that I can distribute to get the people to thinking and doing. I am anxious to do what I can for Better Roads.

If you have anything that I can mail out from this office to parties that I may suggest, I will take pleasure in doing so.

Yours very truly,
(Signed) GEORGE I. J. ELLIOTT,
Postmaster.

The following letter is from Mr. R. H. Bradshaw of Herrell, Mitchell County:

HERRELL, N. C., October 17, 1913.

DR. JOSEPH HYDE PRATT,
Chapel Hill, N. C.

DEAR MR. PRATT:—I have your letter in regard to roads. We had a public meeting at Bakersville, N. C., on the first Monday and laid some plans. Dr. R. E. Stack of Bakersville was appointed to look after the county work. You may send any plans to him that you may suggest. Our board is doing all we can to help the thing along. The clerk to our board was to send you our proceedings, but guess he has failed to do so. I am doing all I can and will continue to do so.

Hope we will have a great rally on the 5th and 6th of next month.

Yours very truly,
(Signed) R. H. BRADSHAW.

Mr. John C. Drewry, President of the Raleigh Chamber of Commerce, wrote as follows in regard to organization:

RALEIGH, N. C., October 20, 1913.

DR. JOSEPH HYDE PRATT,
Chapel Hill, N. C.

MY DEAR DOCTOR:—Your favor of the 18th inst. is received.

I note with pleasure that you have sent literature and copies of the Governor's Proclamation to the list of names that I recently sent you.

I believe that I am going to get all the people in my township interested in going out on the roads and working on November 5th and 6th.

I note with pleasure that you have also written our Commissioners, Supervisors, and Superintendents of Roads in this county. I will keep right behind them and write them other letters, and see if we can't get them interested.

We ought to organize this county in every township, and if the County Commissioners and Road Supervisors and Superintendents will take an interest in this movement, and will thoroughly organize this county, they can obtain good results on our roads. I sincerely trust that they will realize the importance of this work, and will get busy and organize as they should.

With best wishes,

Yours truly,
(Signed) JOHN C. DREWRY,
President.

Mr. S. P. Cross, Secretary of the Gates County Good Roads Association, wrote as follows:

GATESVILLE, N. C., October 17, 1913.

DR. JOSEPH HYDE PRATT,
Chapel Hill, N. C.

MY DEAR DOCTOR:—In reply to your communication dated a few days ago, beg to thank you for the offer so kindly made us and we are taking advantage of it.

I am handing you herewith a list of citizens living at various parts of the county. While the list shows a great many having the same post-office, they are on R. F. D.'s. This list contains the names of magistrates, road overseers, township organizers, appointed by county commissioners for the 5th and 6th of November, and other men of influence who will take part in the work. In order to get them and all their neighbors thoroughly worked up, we want you to mail each a copy of the Governor's proclamation and a copy of your excellent "Suggestions for Organization."

I am anxious to increase the sentiment for good roads that has been created during the last two years in our county, and your help has been of an incalculable benefit to us. We desire to thank you in advance for this kindness to the Gates County Good Roads Association and the cause, in general.

With best wishes, I ask to remain

Yours very truly,
(Signed) S. P. CROSS,
Secretary.

Mr. W. R. Lynch, Manager of the Department of Welfare and Health at Spray, North Carolina, wrote as follows:

SPRAY, N. C., October 7, 1913.

MR. JOSEPH HYDE PRATT,
Chapel Hill, N. C.

DEAR SIR:—We note the Governor has set aside two days in November as good roads days, and we are very much interested and would like to take advantage of these days in our county and township, if possible. Would you kindly advise us what other communities are going to do and if anything is to be done by the Textile communities that you know of?

Will appreciate very much a line from you in this connection and any suggestion that you may have to offer.

Yours very truly,
DEPARTMENT OF WELFARE AND HEALTH,
W. R. LYNCH, *Manager.*

Mr. J. R. Griffin, of Edenton, Chowan County, wrote the following letter:

EDENTON, N. C., October 6, 1913.

HON. LOCKE CRAIG,
Raleigh, N. C.

MY DEAR GOVERNOR:—I am very much interested in your proclamation issued in reference to working the public highways, and am writing to ask you to send me some copies, if you have them available for that purpose. I am a rural letter carrier and am allowed the privilege of advocating any sentiment that may make for the betterment of our public highways. Therefore, if you can send me some copies of your proclamation I think I can use them to good advantage. I can use 1,000 or more.

Hoping to hear from you with a favorable reply, I beg to remain,

Yours truly,

(Signed) J. R. Griffin.

Mr. J. M. Britt, Mayor of Benson, Johnston County, wrote as follows:

Dr. Joseph Hyde Pratt, Benson, N. C., October 17, 1913.
Chapel Hill, N. C.

Dear Sir:—I am in receipt of a letter from Governor Craig with reference to the good roads days. He states that he has asked you to prepare a pamphlet on this work. If you have them ready, will you please mail me a few copies of the same?

I am hopeful that this move will mean something for the betterment of roads of our country. Yours very truly,

(Signed) J. M. Britt.

Mr. Cicero Ritchie, Mayor of Richfield, wrote as follows:

Dr. Joseph Hyde Pratt, Richfield, N. C., October 15, 1913.
Chapel Hill, N. C.

Dear Sir:—Will you please send me 50 or more "Suggestions for Organization and Work on Good Roads Days," and any other literature that you may have that will help to work up the good roads spirit for November 5th and 6th.

If such literature and the postage on same is not paid by the State, I will remit you the price upon receipt of your bill.

Very truly,

(Signed) Cicero Ritchie,
Mayor.

Mr. Z. T. Watson, Chairman of the Board of County Commissioners of Watauga County, wrote the following letter:

Hon. Joseph Hyde Pratt, Brookside, N. C., October 13, 1913.
Chapel Hill, N. C.

Dear Sir:—Your letter of recent date to hand, asking that I give you the name of some men to take charge of the different townships and neighborhoods of Watauga County, so as to more effectively organize the people to the importance of the "Good Roads Movement." I accordingly recommend that you communicate with Mr. L. N. Perkins, Boone, N. C., who is very much interested in good roads. I will do all I can to help bring about the desired road movement in Watauga County.

I am, Yours very truly,

(Signed) Z. T. Watson,
Chairman Board of County Commissioners.

RESULTS ACCOMPLISHED.

It has been impossible to obtain full statistics regarding the results accomplished on the Good Roads Days, but every means has been taken to get full returns from the counties. Information has been sought from county and road commissioners, and various individuals in the different counties. In other cases information has been taken directly from newspaper notices. These results are given below by counties:

Anson County.

The *Wadesboro Courier* of November 26th gives in detail the work done in Lilesville Township on the Good Roads Days as follows:

The 5th and 6th of November were great days in Lilesville Township. We are still boasting that to the per capita we did more work and better work than any other individual township in North Carolina. There were three squads of hands working on three different roads leading into Lilesville and two squads working on roads leading into Pee Dee. The following who responded gives some evidence of what the citizenship of Lilesville Township stands for in good roads spirit:

On the Lilesville to Morven road there were 52 white men who worked, and 46 colored.

On the Diggs and Wall Ferry road between W. C. Henry's and Lilesville, 41 white men and 38 colored men worked.

Between Pee Dee and Diggs Ferry road, 12 white men and 23 colored men worked.

On the road between Wall Ferry and Pee Dee, 3 white men and 20 colored men worked.

On the mountain road near B. J. Webb's, 19 white men and 12 colored men worked.

The list shows that 259 hands worked on the roads of Lilesville Township during the two days—123 white and 136 colored. This is a great compliment to the colored people, that they outnumbered the whites by thirteen. Of course some of them got pay for their work, but I don't believe over thirteen on the whole list in Lilesville Township accepted pay for their work. I certainly want to thank them for this spirit of patriotism. We made almost a half-mile of permanent road in the two days. We think the Governor's action was timely, and Lilesville Township has moved several spans toward the goal of "good roads" in every community.

(Signed) J. E. KERR.

The *Messenger and Intelligencer* of Wadesboro wrote as follows on November 6th in regard to the work done in that township:

Quite a number of Wadesboroites turned out yesterday, and they did considerable work on the Morven road in the worst places. Still more are expected to shoulder shovels or picks and go out to-day. The road is said to be considerably improved, and one of the enthusiastic workers yesterday said he did more work in two hours than a road hand would do in a year.

Reports from the various other townships of the county say that some work was done in all of them, and in some sections the people turned out en masse, and gave most of the day to work. It is being continued to-day.

The same paper also says in regard to the work at Polkton:

A number of our people observed "good roads" days by doing some road work with pick and shovel. It is rather a busy time to expect farmers and laboring men to take a "couple of days off." A number of us will put in full time later.

Beaufort County.

The following letter gives the results of the work done in Beaufort County:

WASHINGTON, N. C., Dec. 12, 1913.

DR. JOSEPH HYDE PRATT,
Chapel Hill, N. C.

DEAR SIR:—I am in receipt of your letter of the 8th inst., asking for information as to the work done on Good Roads Days in this County, etc. In some sections the call of the Governor met with very hearty response. In Pantego Township, which includes Belhaven and Pantego towns, there was a great deal of good work done. All of the stores and factories closed on those days and the work entered into with enthusiasm. While I have no record as to the matter, I am informed that in that township there were as many as five hundred men working on the two days. In the other townships, where we have a special road tax, the people did not respond to any great extent, although from Washington and several other places quite a number went out and did some very good work. I suppose that there were possibly seven hundred men in the entire County who worked on those days. It gave quite an impetus to the good roads spirit and I think good was accomplished in more ways than the actual work done.

Yours very truly,
(Signed) HARRY McMULLAN.

Bertie County.

A great deal of interest was shown by the public-spirited citizens of Aulander, Bertie County, in good roads days. The citizens of this town went out en masse, and as a result of their efforts, three excellent pieces of road were built, estimated to be worth from $300 to $350.

Mr. C. H. Jenkins was elected general director of the work, and Messrs. J. H. Mitchell, J. L. Harrington, Herbert Jenkins, and Cherry Minton were elected overseers of the groups to assist. The town schools were closed, and the Superintendent put in charge of the school forces. Mr. W. S. Dunning was put in charge of the bridge building forces, and rendered excellent service in repairing over thirty bridges in two days. The Messrs. Rawls furnished six large mules and a road machine. Others sent wagons and carts, plows, drags and scoops.

Bladen County.

The Wilmington *Morning Star* of November 6th writes as follows in regard to the Bladen County work:

In compliance with the proclamation of Governor Craig, road working was the order here to-day. In groups ranging from the ministers of the Gospel to the humblest of the colored race, the people were seen in places, all bending their efforts towards repairing the bad roads around the place. Your correspondent had the pleasure of working part of the day in a gang under the supervision of Sheriff J. M. Clark and composed of two ministers, the register of deeds, a doctor of medicine, a clerk in a store, a telegraph operator, and several plain ordinary citizens, both white and colored. All were throwing dirt with one aim and purpose. Much good has been accomplished in the two days on the roads in the county by this means and—could all the people have turned out there would have been many miles of good roads built.

Buncombe County.

Very elaborate preparations were made by Buncombe County for the carrying on of the work on these good roads days, and the following taken from the *Asheville Citizen* of October 18th will give you an idea as to their method of organization:

For the purpose of arousing interest in the observance of "good roads days" in this county next month, the Board of Trade is sending out letters to the residents of the various townships of this county, asking their coöperation in making the movement a successful one. It is felt that in view of the fact that this is Governor Locke Craig's county, Buncombe cannot afford not to make an excellent showing, and the members of the Central Committee are putting forth their very best efforts to arouse intense interest in the celebration. Four thousand letters are being mailed, signed by the following: J. E. Rankin, mayor; N. A. Reynolds, chairman of the Board of County Commissioners; Frank M. Weaver, president of the Board of Trade; J. D. Murphy, chairman of the County Board of Education; E. C. Chambers, president of the Good Roads Association of Asheville and Buncombe County; Dr. A. W. Calloway, president of the Asheville Motor Club; J. W. Neely, president of the Asheville Merchants' Association; George S. Powell, Judge J. C. Pritchard, E. D. Weaver, J. J. Britt, W. W. Rollins, W. H. Hipps, superintendent of County schools; Marcus Erwin, clerk of the Superior Court.

The letters read as follows:

"We appeal to the people of Asheville and Buncombe County to organize themselves, as hereafter suggested, and make this the banner county for carrying out the wishes of Governor Craig as set forth in his proclamation designating November 5th and 6th as holidays and good roads days for North Carolina. To this end we suggest that meetings be held in the townships at the places hereafter named, on Saturday, October 25th, at two o'clock, and that organizations be formed at these meetings and officers elected to take charge of squads of about twenty-five men, who will pledge themselves to devote at least part of the two days designated to unselfish work for the public good, and that the women be asked to form organizations for the purpose of furnishing good things to eat. We also suggest that the persons pledging themselves to work on these days state what kind of implements they will furnish, also the number of teams, wagons, plows, etc., so that the captains of squads will know exactly how to plan for the work.

"It is not the purpose of the Governor in his proclamation to make these days of drudgery for any one, but for the people to come together in a spirit of coöperation and spend these two days together doing such work as will not be burdensome, and bring about a better feeling of fellowship among the people of the State. It is peculiarly appropriate that the people of Buncombe County make this a great success. The business men of the city and county will be asked to close their places of business and participate in this celebration; the public schools will also be asked to close so that the children may participate; and we suggest that in order that they may take part, plans be made by which the children can beautify some of the roads in the county by planting honeysuckle, wild roses and other plants along the roadside, thereby adding to the pleasure, as well as the comfort, of those who pass over these roads. We also suggest that in some cases it may be best to build paths for the use of the school children in places where they are forced to wade through muddy roads.

"Representatives from the Board of County Commissioners, the Good Roads Association, the Board of Trade, and other organizations will be at the places of meeting on the 25th of the month for the purpose of aiding the organization and forming plans for the good roads days. The Central Committee, composed of the chairman of the Board of County Commissioners, president of the Good Roads Association, president of the Board of Trade, the mayor, president of the Motor Club, and others will be glad to coöperate with any of the townships in selecting suitable roads on which to work. In this connection it is thought that the best results can be had by either building new sections of roads, building paths to public schools and repairing dirt roads.

"The following places are suggested for the meetings to be held on the 25th:

"Avery's Creek, at school house near Ingram's.

"Lower Hominy, at Sand Hill.

"Upper Hominy, at Candler.

"Leicester, at Leicester.

"Sandy Mush, at Brick Church school house.
"Limestone, at Skyland.
"Fairview, at Fairview.
"Swannanoa, at Swannanoa.
"Reem's Creek, at Weaverville.
"Flat Creek, at Georgetown.
"Ivy, at Barnardsville.
"Black Mountain, at Black Mountain.
"French Broad, at Alexander.

"The meetings for Asheville township are called for Friday evening, October 24th, at eight o'clock, at the following places: County Court House, Biltmore and West Asheville."

The *Asheville Gazette-News* of November 1st gives additional facts in regard to the organization for Good Roads Days:

H. A. Coggins, who has been selected as captain for the squad that is to work the roads of his section on Governor Craig's "good roads days," November 5 and 6, has issued a challenge to all other townships of Buncombe, and to all other counties of the State, to beat him and his cohorts in the amount of actual work done on these days. He says he does not believe it can be done, but he is willing for any that want to try to see what showing they can make.

In addition to this general challenge, he extends a special challenge to the following: J. J. White, captain for Swannanoa; Victor Sorrels, captain for Azalea, and Marion Roberts, captain for the Riceville people. All these challenges are put down in black and white in a letter to Mr. N. Buckner, and Mr. Coggins proposes to make good on them. He says that the people of Bee Tree are really enthusiastic over road improvement and the means that Governor Craig has selected for arousing a greater sentiment for road building.

Further interest among the people of Biltmore will be aroused in a mass meeting to be held in the schoolhouse at that place to-night. There was a mass meeting there last Friday night when committees were appointed to make arrangements for the work to be done, and the chairmen of these committees will be asked to make reports to-night. A large gathering is expected, and an announcement is predicted to the effect that all shops and mills in and around Biltmore, employing men, will be closed during "good roads days."

The *Asheville Citizen* of November 7th described the work in Buncombe County on Good Roads days as follows:

"If ever the real location of the Garden of Eden is discovered, I am convinced it will be found right here in the French Broad Valley."

Standing in an automobile on the highest point of Goldview, with a majestic view of the mountains, and a panorama of gold, green and red, combined with an azure sky forming a background, Governor Locke Craig yesterday paid this beautiful tribute to his native county and announced once again his intention of returning to Asheville when his term of office is ended, to spend the balance of his days among "his people."

SPLENDID ADDRESS.

It was one of the best speeches made by the "Little Giant of the West," the occasion being the big barbecue held at Goldview yesterday for the good roads workers who had turned out in response to the call issued by Governor Craig. All morning long, the crowd present with a few exceptions, had toiled on the roads, and they were more than ready for the feast of good things that J. Baylis Rector, of the Langren, with two cooks from the hotel, had been busily preparing since the night before.

Following the cue, General Theodore F. Davidson arose in an automobile for what he termed a "most extraordinary idea; the introduction of Governor Locke Craig to a Buncombe County gathering."

"He needs no introduction to the mountain people," declared General Davidson, "for he has shown by his actions on more than one occasion, and on none better than the present, his fondness for the mountain people. All portions of the State wanted the Governor on these two days, but he preferred to return to his 'own people.' "

Governor Craig began his address with an appreciation of the opportunity to eat with the mountain people again, and said that, while he did not have his overalls for the second day, he understood that he was to eat and did not see the use of overalls in eating anyway.

GOOD WORK DONE.

"Good work has been done all over the State yesterday and to-day," declared Governor Craig. "I have had many reports and they were all to the effect that much interest was being manifested in the good roads days. But most important of all is the spirit for good roads that is being engendered by the work of these two days, attracting the attention of people all over the State to the value of good roads. The time is coming when there will be no bad roads, and the people are rapidly awakening to the necessity for the early arrival of that time. A bad road is more expensive than a good road, as it absorbs money all the time, whereas a good road pays more than one hundred per cent dividends each year."

Governor Craig then told of the different janitors that had climbed to the fourth floor of the building at Chapel Hill every hour daily for years to sound the bell announcing classes. He said that they continued to climb until Dr. Winston thought to bore a hole down through the ceilings to the ground and drop the rope down.

"People today are just as stupid in some districts," declared the Governor. "They will plow through muddy roads to their homes rather than start a movement for betterment of those roads. This is a great era of thought, and men are beginning to realize the importance of good roads, and to get away from the idea of following the trails made by the bears, followed by the cows and finally by man. A good road is a big factor in the problem of transportation, and transportation is the great educational force of the present time, bringing us, as it does, into communication with each other, so that we can obtain each other's ideas."

Governor Craig also referred to the defeat of the proposed $300,000 bond issue for roads in Buncombe County, defeated by the vote of the country people, and expressed himself as confident that such a move would now have their endorsement.

GOOD ROADS A NECESSITY.

"Good roads are not only desirable, but they are a necessity if we wish to keep pace with the march of progress," declared the Governor. "A man cut off from the rest of his race by a sluice of mud, which ought to be a road, is necessarily deprived of the ideas of his neighbors and fails to make any progress."

Governor Craig also referred to the Appalachian Park Association, and told of his hope that the government would consider favorably the proposition of the association to transform the great forest reserves recently purchased into a national park. He said he had talked to representatives and senators from North Carolina, and others and had high hopes of the ultimate transformation of the reserves into a great park, which will attract people from all over the world. Good roads leading to these reserves, he declared, would be necessary to make them attractive.

The Governor also spoke of the aristocracy of labor and said that only the man who accomplishes something, however small, is entitled to the hall mark of the aristocrat. He said that the election of Woodrow Wilson was brought about by the fact that he stood for the great principle of "equal opportunity for all."

"After all, this is a world of individual lives," concluded the Governor. "This is our land, our heritage, and we must improve it or the Great World Builder will send another race to accomplish what we fail to do. When my term of office is ended, I hope to be spared many years to return and live out my allotted span in these beautiful mountains, veritably God's footstool, for, I believe, that if the Garden of Eden is ever discovered, it will be found right here in the French Broad Valley."

GIVEN AN OVATION.

Governor Craig was given an ovation at the conclusion of his address and was frequently compelled to pause on account of the applause greeting his remarks.

At the conclusion of the Governor's speech, Judge Phil C. Cooke announced the presence of a visitor at the barbecue from McDowell County, and introduced Hon. Will Pless, of that county. Mr. Pless expressed his appreciation at being able to be present with the Buncombe County workers and said that McDowell County was doing its part on the good roads days.

George S. Powell then called on Rev. C. B. Waller, who made a short talk, assuring the crowd that his heart was in the work.

Al Bartlett, representing the Pathe Freres Company, was present with a moving picture machine, and took "movies" of the barbecue and Governor Craig. Mr. Bartlett went to the barbecue with Harry Bickford, of the Classis theatre, and Paul E. Wilkes, of Grove Park Inn, in Mr. Wilkes' machine.

J. G. Robinson, accompanied by Secretary Buckner, of the Board of Trade, and a representative of the *Citizen,* also formed a party which went to Goldview in Mr. Robinson's machine, and Mr. Robinson succeeded in getting some excellent pictures of the meeting.

The meeting was probably the best held in the State yesterday, and was largely due to the presence of Governor Craig.

With ideal weather, the workmen got an early start in the various townships of Buncombe County yesterday morning, and the second of the "good roads days" was even more successful than the first. Many of those who failed to work on the first of the holidays couldn't resist the temptation to join their neighbors and friends on the roads while the workers who had experienced a day swinging picks, shovels and axes, didn't feel disposed to give up the task until it was completed. Hundreds of men did a hard day's work and more women turned out to inspire the laborers than on the previous day.

GOLDVIEW ROAD.

A large force of workmen reported on the Goldview road, where Governor Locke Craig served the last day of his term. Many workers from the city of Asheville visited the highway, carrying their road working implements, and they were joined by residents of the county from a radius of several miles of the highway. The work began at sunrise and lasted until a late hour, the barbecue being the feature of the celebration of the day.

BILTMORE WORKERS.

A squad of fifty able-bodied men spent the day working at Biltmore. As a result of the activities of the residents of the town, the Biltmore school building has been "pulled from the mud," the workmen spending the day on roads leading to the school. Two walks were constructed to the structure, one of sand and rock and the other of cinders. Dinner was served on the school grounds at noon by the women of the town.

WEST ASHEVILLE.

The residents of West Asheville continued their activities yesterday and as a result of the observance of good roads days, the streets of the recently incorporated town have been greatly improved. Holes in the roads have been filled, good grades have been established on the streets and ditches have been cleaned out.

BARNARDSVILLE WORKERS.

Practically all of the residents of Barnardsville turned out on the roads yesterday and the streets of the town show the results of the activities of the laborers. An improved highway, a mile in length, leads to the schoolhouse and the students can go to their classes now without wading through the mud. Good sidewalks have been built through the town and many fills have been eliminated. The Barnardsville women took an active part in the celebration of the two days, providing dinners for the men, and many of them did active road work with their husbands, sons and brothers. Robert Buckner was the captain of the forces.

SASSAFRAS GAP ROAD.

The Sassafras Gap road was worked by eighteen men, who had two teams and a road scraper. The road was widened from twelve to twenty feet and a new link of road through the land of Walter Haynes was constructed with a good grade. This is one of the country's most attractive scenic highways, the view of Asheville and surrounding points being very attractive. It is the intention of the workers to continue the highway several miles through upper Beaverdam. Yesterday the work was done under the general supervision of T. M. Creasman, while John Drake was the captain of the squad. Mrs. Creasman served dinner at noon and the meal was thoroughly enjoyed. One of the workmen declared that he would spend the remainder of his life on the roads if he could secure a promise of such dinners as have been served during the "good roads days."

Reports from all sections of the State indicate that the observance of the holidays will mean much to the improvement of the system of highways of North Carolina. Various counties report that their citizens have been very active during the past two days and as a result of the Governor's proclamation, many miles of roads have been built and improved during the days set aside for road work.

The *Asheville Gazette-News* of November 6th, wrote as follows with regard to the work of the Farm School:

The students of the Farm School are taking an active part in the construction of roads in Buncombe County during Governor Craig's "good roads days." There are over 100 boys attending the school, and the principal announced some time ago that these boys would give 100 days' work for the cause at this time. There has been a scarcity of tools for all of them, however, and during the two days there will probably be about 40 or 50 days' work done. The remainder, it is announced, will be made up tomorrow and Saturday.

The work is being done under the direction of Allan Coggins, who was appointed for this purpose by Chairman N. A. Reynolds of the board of county commissioners. The section of road from the Pickens Schoolhouse, on the sand-clay road, to the macadam road at Bee Tree is being worked, and it will probably be in good condition before the work is completed.

Burke County.

The *News-Herald* of Morganton on November 13th, wrote as follows:

Although there was no thorough organization, considerable work was put on the roads in different sections of the county last Wednesday and Thursday—Good Roads Days. Now, let the spirit grow until there are frequent county and township good roads days and good roads in every section.

Cabarrus County.

The *Concord Times* of October 27th, reports that cards and ribbons had been sent out all over the county with pledges in regard to working the roads on November 5th and 6th. This card was as follows:

GOOD ROADS DAYS, NOVEMBER 5TH AND 6TH.

I hereby promise to work the roads on the days mentioned above.

Township No............

....

For the purpose of perfecting an organization of the good road forces in the county and making plans for the good roads days a meeting of citizens was held at the court house Saturday afternoon. While the meeting was not largely attended every citizen there manifested great interest in the undertaking. All the townships were represented except one. Prof. C. E. Boger was made chairman of the meeting and John M. Oglesby and W. J. Weddington, secretaries.

Upon request of the chairman, who opened the meeting by stating that it was called for the purpose of arousing interest in good roads and executing plans for working the roads as set forth in the Governor's proclamation, Superintendent J. M. Burrage suggested to the meeting his idea of the work that might be accomplished on the two days.

Mr. Burrage suggested that each township select a committee and that the work in the townships be left in the hands of the committee. He thought a good idea would be for the committee to select the roads leading into the main roads the first day and on the second day work on the main roads until noon. At that hour dinner could be served and the afternoon spent in general picnic fashion. He said that it should be understood on the 6th where the meeting place for dinner would be located and that those working, plan to reach that point about the noon hour. In speaking of the town's part in the work, Mr. Burrage said that he thought it would be a good idea for the people in town who did not volunteer to work the roads to go out in the afternoon of the sixth and carry refreshments to the workers.

VOLUNTEERS ON NATIONAL HIGHWAY, CABARRUS COUNTY.

Upon motion the committees named below were selected from the various townships. These committees are to meet and decide on how they will conduct the work. Every township's work will be left in the hands of the committee and they will have charge of the work which will be done as they deem best. The secretaries were instructed to notify the members of the committee by letter as to the place they will meet to perfect the plans.

Capt. Q. E. Smith, who has volunteered to place his services in the hands of the organization, distributed the cards and ribbons as previously mentioned, and requested that every citizen who signs a card (and they are all expected to sign) mail it to the chairman, Mr. C. E. Boger, Concord, and the names of the signers will be published daily.

A great many signatures were received to these cards, and also contributions of money were made. As far as could be learned about $100 in money was subscribed; and other citizens contributed scoops, plows, wagons, and many tools in addition to the county tools.

Committeemen were elected from each School District to take charge of working the roads on November 5th and 6th.

So far as could be ascertained, the work undertaken was as follows:

No. 6 Township will grade the big hill between M. W. Harkey's and Berry Beaver's. They will also open up the new road recently graded by the county commissioners.

In No. 11 Township a representative reports that grit will be hauled and the road worked from the red hill to Nelson Carrigan's.

In No. 10 Township it was decided for the citizens of each neighborhood to work the section of road which would be of most benefit to their community.

A letter was received from Mr. Q. E. Smith, Road Engineer of Cabarrus County, in part as follows:

CONCORD, N. C., April 25, 1914.

DR. JOSEPH HYDE PRATT,

Chapel Hill, N. C.

SIR:—Your inquiry of late date in reference to the road work done in Cabarrus County on November 5 and 6, 1913, received, and in reply will state that we raised two hundred and fifty dollars, by subscription to repair the National Highway from Kannapolis to Concord, that part of which has the surface treatment. The Texaco people furnished the asphalt without the cost. The work has not been done, owing to the fact that the asphalt did not arrive until the weather was too cold. The citizens of Kannapolis furnished labor, teams, and cash enough to put the remaining part of the National Highway from the macadam to the Rowan County line (four miles) in good shape.

Mr. Smith also states that the Winecoff High School and Jackson Training Schools did considerable work on these days. This will be brought in under schools.

Carteret County.

The following letter from the Chairman of the Highway Commissioners of Morehead Township, Carteret County, tells of the work in this County:

DR. JOSEPH HYDE PRATT, MOREHEAD CITY, Dec. 15, 1913.
Chapel Hill, N. C.

DEAR SIR:—Your favor of the 8th in reference to work done on Good Roads Days received. There was considerable interest manifested all over the County, but it is impossible to give the exact number of men and teams. There were not less than 300 men and 30 teams working on the roads these two days. There has been a great improvement in the public roads in Carteret County, especially in the western end. Newport township has shown more interest in good roads than any section in Eastern North Carolina that I know of, and are working on the roads every Thursday, from 40 to 50 men and from 10 to 15 teams taking part. There were about two miles of new road built in the County on November 5th and 6th, and at least 25 miles improved.

Yours very truly,
(Signed) G. D. CANFIELD,
Chairman.

The *News and Observer* of November 18th stated:

A great deal of enthusiasm was shown in the Good Roads work in this county. It is said that at least 175 men with about 40 teams were on the central highway west of here and in the western section of Carteret County to-day. A great deal of valuable work on the roads and great impetus to good roads were the result.

Caswell County.

DR. JOSEPH HYDE PRATT, YANCEYVILLE N. C., Dec. 20, 1913.
Chapel Hill, N. C.

MY DEAR SIR:—Little attention was given to "Good Roads Days" in Caswell. In two or three townships some little effort was made to observe the days, and through the influence of the County Board of Education, many of the school children worked on the schoolhouse grounds.
(Signed) T. J. HENDERSON.

Catawba County.

The following letter was received from Mr. A. K. Joy, of Hickory, N. C., in regard to the work in Catawba County on November 5th and 6th:

DR. JOSEPH HYDE PRATT, HICKORY, N. C., December 11, 1913.
Chapel Hill, N. C.

DEAR SIR:—Dr. W. H. Nicholson handed us your letter of the 8th inst., requesting us to give you the information desired with reference to the work done on public highways on November 5th and 6th.

Upon solicitation of our Chamber of Commerce, the Mayor of Hickory issued a proclamation requesting the closing of all places of business on those days, and calling upon all citizens to work on the city streets. In the meantime, the City Engineer had one mile of street graded, and pins placed for topsoiling, as well as having the topsoil plowed up at nearby points ready for hauling. As a result of this movement, we had about 40 two-horse teams and about 200 hands working November 5th and 6th, and completed permanent improvement of one mile of city streets on the two days. Luncheon was served by the ladies of Hickory, with music by the Hickory Band.

In our opinion, the development of the community spirit was of infinitely greater value than the actual work done, although that itself was of considerable importance. Many men who had contributed money to employ substitutes could not resist the inspiration of the occasion, and used their shovels all day. As one lady remarked, "There are men working to-day that I did not think could do manual labor."

In the country districts, about three miles of roads were graded. It is estimated that about 75 teams and 200 men were at work on those two days. In addition to this, the Road Commissioners of Hickory Township furnished their entire road equipment, including 40 mules and dump-carts to help along the work in the country.

Another point worth mentioning in this connection is that the good work is still going on. We heard this morning of a group in a community who were not prepared to do their work on November 5th and 6th, but were ready now to do their part.

With kindest personal regards, we remain,

Very respectfully yours,

(Signed) A. K. Joy,
Secretary.

The *Catawba County News* of November 7th read as follows:

Wednesday was a great day in Catawba County. In Hickory it is reported that more than one thousand men worked.

On the public road leading to Mr. A. L. Sigmon's by the George Moose place, there was a great day's work done.

The convicts, more than forty in number, were there. Forty-six white volunteers and three colored ones were on duty. Eleven volunteer teams to haul dirt, plow, etc., were there.

The dinner was great as well as the work. The good women had prepared for the inner man. They know how to do this very thing in Catawba County. If you have any doubt about this dinner as to amount and as to quality, ask Mr. L. C. Bickett. "They do say" that what he did for that dinner was "a plenty," but he moved dirt too.

The convicts were furnished dinner by the good women—just as good as all the rest had—and they did enjoy it immensely. Mr. A. L. Sigmon furnished a treat of apples. It was a glad day in the life of the convicts.

Hon. W. B. Gaither made a speech at the dinner hour that was enjoyed by all. He also did his duty with the shovel.

A special to the *Charlotte Observer* relating to the work in Conover section states as follows:

At a mass-meeting of the citizens of Conover, it was decided to postpone the working of the roads until November 20th, at which time the same call will be put to the men of that section as was put to the entire State last week. This action was taken in view of the fact that many were too busy now with their Fall work to put in two days at this time. A committee was appointed to make all plans and the ladies requested to furnish dinner.

The work done in Conover section is given in the *Newton Enterprise* of November 27th as follows:

The two road working days at Conover were a great success. Mr. B. A. Huitt tells us that there were over 100 hands and 25 teams and wagons at work on each day and the ladies served two of the biggest dinners he ever saw. About a half mile of as good sand-clay road as there is in the county was made in place of one of the worst that came into Conover.

Chowan County.

The following letter from Mr. Frank Wood, of Edenton, North Carolina, states:

Dr. Joseph Hyde Pratt, Edenton, N. C., Dec. 10, 1913.
Chapel Hill, N. C.

Dear Dr. Pratt:—Your letter of the 9th inquiring about the road work on November 5th and 6th is received.

I cannot fully answer your inquiries and have to say that in only a few localities in this county was road work done by the public on those days, and I do not know the extent.

The farmers in this country have been too short of labor and too far behind in housing their crops to give their time to road work in that busy period.

Yours very truly,
(Signed) Frank Wood.

Columbus County.

The following letter was received from Dr. W. Ross Davis, of Whiteville:

Whiteville, N. C., Dec. 23, 1913.
Dr. Joseph Hyde Pratt,
Chapel Hill, N. C.

Dear Sir:—Your inquiry of the 8th of December to Mr. K. Clyde Council, Wananish, N. C., has just reached me for answer. Without taking further time to make diligent inquiry, I will have to estimate that 150 men and 30 teams did service on Columbus County roads on

November 5th and 6th re-shaping and patching eight or ten miles of road. Want of system and definiteness as to where and what to do prevented more and better work.

Yours very truly,
(Signed) W. Ross Davis,
Chairman Board of Commissioners.

Craven County.

Not a great deal of work was done in this County on the Good Roads Days. Some citizens turned out for work on the Central Highway in and near the Newport Pocosin. Since the Good Roads Days, the people in two sections have contributed in labor 24 days and $34.

Cumberland County.

About 100 white and colored citizens of Fayetteville responded to Mayor Underwood's call for work Thursday at the market house, where they were supplied with shovels and other road working implements. It was later reported that Mayor Underwood had a force of fifty on North Street extending to Myrtle Hill, and that good work was done. The balance of the force was turned over to Mr. Tillinghast, who did fine work on Robinson Hill. Another force put a section of the Murchison road in good fix.

Mayor Underwood estimated that at least $1,000 worth of road work was done in Cross Creek Township; while in the county the work done was worth over $2,000.

Currituck County.

The following letter tells of the work in Currituck County:

Moyock, N. C., November 7, 1913.

Dr. Joseph Hyde Pratt,
Chapel Hill, N. C.

My dear Sir:—I am pleased to advise you that the Governor's request in setting apart November 5th and 6th as Good Roads Days was duly observed in and around Moyock.

Our people, old and young, of both colors, responded to the call to a greater degree than was expected. Through our Farmers' Organization the work was placed and arrangements made beforehand. The results show three miles of newly graded road and repair work on three miles previously graded. Very truly yours,

(Signed) R. O. Bagley.

Davidson County.

The *Twin City Daily Sentinel* of November 6th states as follows:

Good Roads Day has been well observed in Lexington and through Davidson County. Practically every community that has been heard from is busy building and repairing roads. Squads of men with plows, teams, wagons and road scrapers have been on the various roads doing good work.

Gates County.

The following letter was received from the Secretary of the Gates County Good Roads Association:

GATESVILLE, N. C., November 7, 1913.

DR. J. H. PRATT,
Chapel Hill, N. C.

DEAR SIR:—We beg to submit the following facts concerning the observance of Good Roads Days, November 5th and 6th:

The Governor's Proclamation was generally complied with throughout the County. Men from 94 years down to boys 8 years old did hard work. Ministers, lawyers, bankers, doctors, County officials, and merchants worked. Principals of schools led their boys in a body to the roads. Branning Manufacturing Company placed its train and crew at our sole disposal. Dr. Pratt's plans and suggestions adhered to in construction; various sections vied with each other in regard to model stretches of road; barbecues and picnics reported from several localities. Peace and harmony, sand and clay, and standard work filled the days. True sentiment and increased enthusiasm are certainly with us. Mintonsville Township led in work, which amounted to 500 days; Reynoldson comes next with more than 364 days to its credit; Gatesville has so far reported about 350 days to her credit. Holly Grove is hard at work every day—bonds, machines, better roads. Conservative estimate gives total number of days throughout the County as more than 1,500. The same estimate places the value of all work at $3,000. Five or six sections have asked for another chance.

Yours very truly,
(Signed) S. P. CROSS,
Secretary.

Granville County.

About 300 men went out in squads of about 50 each with picks, hoes, and shovels.

The Superintendent of the Orphan Asylum took his boys to make some much needed improvement in the roads near the Asylum grounds. It is reported that Judge Graham donned overalls and worked with the vigor of a young man, and encouraged the work with the earnestness which characterizes all his undertakings.

Guilford County.

Quite a number of the citizens of Greensboro volunteered for work on the streets of the city during the Good Roads Days. Men and women, white and black, occupied full time allotted in the day. Citizens, whose vocations find them behind desks and counters; students, who otherwise would have been engaged in classes, were there. From 50 to 75 men of the city worked the streets in the northern and southern sections. The ladies and the women's clubs served hot lunches from a big automobile truck with hot coffee.

Guilford College, the State Normal and Industrial College, and A. & M. College for the Colored Race took part in the work, which will be given in detail later on.

Mr. W. C. Boren, Chairman of the Board of County Commissioners, sent out a circular letter calling attention to the Governor's Proclamation, and asking the people of the county to coöperate.

Halifax County.

Very little work was done in this county for the betterment of the roads on November 5th and 6th. It is reported that there was a smattering of soil work, shoveling work, etc., near Brinkley and Heathsville.

Harnett County.

The chief work done in Harnett County was by the students of Buie's Creek Academy, and will be given under the head of Schools and Colleges.

Haywood County.

The principal work done in Haywood County on the Good Roads Days was in Beaverdam Township. At least three miles of the road leading out of Canton was re-graded and coated with a good layer of cinders, given for the purpose by the Champion Fibre Company. The Southern Railway also aided the cause by moving their cars free of cost. The working gangs in the town were well organized, and worked systematically. All classes of citizens were well represented, and everything donned overalls. The Champion Fibre Co. made it so that a great many of their hands could engage in this work.

It is not reported as to whether or not any work was done in other portions of Haywood County.

Henderson County.

The following from the *Asheville Citizen* of October 31st shows what Henderson County was expecting to do on good roads days:

While there has been little noise about it, there is every likelihood that the people of Henderson County will do their full duty on "good roads days" in pursuance to the Governor's Proclamation. It is expected that the work of road building and repairing will be systematized so that all of the roads most in need of work will receive most attention. Some of Henderson County's sons who have moved to other places and some who have become exalted in affairs of state, have written that they will be here on the days designated by Governor Craig to help in good work. A letter received by P. F. Patton, road supervisor, from Hon. M. L. Shipman, Commissioner of Labor and Printing, shows that gentleman's patriotism and is as follows:

Mr. P. F. Patton,
Hendersonville, N. C.

My Dear Sir:—This is to offer my services on the public roads of Henderson County for November 5th and 6th, the days designated by

Governor Craig as "Good Roads Days" and requesting all citizens to join in the movement towards better conditions throughout the State. I am yours for service, but prefer an assignment on the section of road leading from Little Willow creek, above Bowman's Bluff, to the Transylvania County line, where I used to work when I first attained "road age." Sentiment prompts this request, as I want to touch elbows with old associates and demonstrate to them my ability still to handle the shovel and other implements of war against mud.

Hoping you have arranged for a systematic observance of these days in every section of Henderson County and that thousands of citizens may respond to the call, I am, Sincerely yours,

(Signed) M. L. SHIPMAN.

It was stated in the *Asheville Citizen* of November 18th that during the two days, the people of Hickory Nut Gap turned out in large numbers, and helped sand-clay the road between Bat Cave and Rutherford County line, which has been graded by the State convicts. The schools at Bat Cave and Bearwallow closed, and the children helped work.

Iredell County.

"Good Roads Days" were not observed in this county because the county had built its roads with a $400,000 bond issue, getting 225 miles of graded, surfaced road, and repairing dirt roads with a gasoline traction engine at the rate of ten to fifteen miles per day.

Jackson County.

The *Sylva* (Jackson County) *Journal* of November 7th read as follows:

The work that has been done on the roads of Jackson County this week will be a source of pride for years to come. "By their work we shall know them" and the majority of folks certainly did work and they accomplished something. It is estimated that $10,000 worth of work was done and aside from the material results the patriotism and public spirited interest in the welfare of the county thus expressed can not be measured in dollars and cents but will tell in the future of the county. We are a united people working to a common good, placing Jackson County in her proper place among the leaders of the State. Much credit is due the men who answered the call of the Governor and we must not forget to extend the appreciation of the men to the ladies for their moral support and for the excellent dinners they served. The women of North Carolina have never failed at any crisis and have again been weighed in the balance and not found wanting.

The Cashiers Valley folks went out in large numbers and put in their time on the automobile highway to Walhalla; Webster did a fine lot of work on its roads and Cullowhee did the same.

At Sylva the folks went out in large numbers to Cal Love's field and when they got there, they sure did work on the grading of the

Sylva-up-the-river road, under the direction of W. J. Fisher. They put the road in fine condition for its early completion.

At about 12 o'clock of both days, we were all certainly glad to see the ladies and the dinner.

Although the work was satisfactory and everybody feels good over that thousand dollars' worth of work done in Sylva, Wednesday and Thursday.

Lee County.

From every section of the county, it is reported that the "Good Roads" days were observed. We have been unable to find out, however, just how many men worked, and how much work was done.

McDowell County.

The following letter from the Chairman of the Old Fort Township Highway Commission will give some idea of the work accomplished in that township on "Good Roads" days:

OLD FORT, N. C., December 6, 1913.

DR. JOSEPH HYDE PRATT,
Chapel Hill, N. C.

DEAR SIR:—Replying to yours of recent date, addressed to Mr. W. T. Morgan and referred to me, I would say, at Old Fort the "Good Roads" days were enthusiastically observed on November 5th and 6th. Ours is a small town, but regardless of occupation, vocation or avocation, merchants, farmers, bankers, doctors, ministers, trainmen, manufacturers and others were represented until on the first day fully one hundred and six or eight teams with picks, axes, shovels, wagons and scrapers were on the scene to work.

The women, the constant inspiration and well wishers of men, encouraged the good work by frequent visits and words of cheer. As evidence that the enthusiasm was genuine and not ephemeral, it was resolved at the end of the second day that an additional day be observed on the following week, when the ladies would serve dinner "on the grounds." So a third day we worked—and have to show for it about one mile of new road (on the Central Highway) where a great deal of blasting and building of walls were required.

Like the men who have voluntarily contributed to any cause, we are now more interested in good roads than ever: "For where your treasure is, there will your heart be also."

Yours very truly,
(Signed) P. H. MASHBURN,
Chairman Old Fort Township Highway Commission.

Macon County.

The following letter from Mr. G. L. Jones, of Franklin, gives an idea of the work accomplished in this county:

FRANKLIN, N. C., Dec. 24, 1913.

DR. JOSEPH HYDE PRATT,
Chapel Hill, N. C.

MY DEAR DR. PRATT:—I am just home after several days absence and find your letter of the 8th relative to the work done in the county on "Good Roads" days. I am sorry to say that our township let the days pass without observing the Governor's request. There were two townships, however, that did very good work. Cartoopchage Township took the worst piece of road they had and made about 100 yards of sand-clay road. They report that there were twenty-four men who worked the first day and eighteen the second, with eight teams the first day and four the second.

In Highland Township, four separate pieces of road were worked on, with, as well as I can ascertain, almost all the men in the township working. They had teams, scrapes, wagons, etc., but I am unable to learn just the number. They report that they made four pieces of good roads.

No money was raised in either place.

With personal regards, I am, Very truly yours,
(Signed) G. L. JONES.

The following excerpt from a letter of Mr. R. J. Phillips, of Shortoff, Macon County, dated Feb. 6, 1914, relates to the work done in Highland Township:

We did about 225 days' work on "Good Roads" Days and had twenty-five teams out both days. We estimated that there was $500 worth of work done in the township on the 5th and 6th.

Madison County.

Practically all the merchants in Marshall and many others in the rural sections of the county closed their stores, in order that the employees might join them on the public highways, and it is stated over a 1,000 men worked on the roads during the two days.

The women furnished dinners, and the workmen put in their very best efforts.

In No. 1 Township (Marshall) 280 men and 12 teams worked the bigger part of two days and graded three quarters of a mile of a link of the Central Highway near Marshall. The road was eighteen to twenty feet wide with no grade over 4½ per cent.

At Walnut, also in No. 1 Township, 30 men and 8 teams built 800 feet of new grade, consisting largely of a fill near Walnut, on the Central Highway.

On the edge of No. 1 Township and No. 3 (Mars Hill) Township, 40 men and 6 teams graded approximately one-half mile of new road on the Mars Hill Highway.

In No. 7 (Pine Creek) Township, there were about forty men at work grading a new road.

Mecklenburg County.

Mayor Bland of Charlotte, issued a call for the volunteers to work on November 5th and 6th; but, so far as has been ascertained, but very little interest was taken in this work in Mecklenburg County.

Moore County.

The following letters from Moore County will give some idea of the work accomplished:

PINEHURST, N. C., December 12, 1913.

DR. JOSEPH HYDE PRATT,
Chapel Hill, N. C.

MY DEAR DR. PRATT:—Your letter of the 8th in regard to the observance of Good Roads Days in this county has just been received, and in reply would say that there was no concerted action in the matter over all the county. However, in about half the county the different communities gathered in crews and spent the day at work on the roads improving them very much in some places. The work was generally intelligently done, and was usually done where not much interest had been manifested in the improvement of the road before.

As far as I have been able to learn, there was about seven miles of new road built besides a number of miles had the worse placed repaired. I am very sorry that I am not able to send you photographs of the work, as there were none taken, so far as I know.

Very truly yours,
(Signed) J. R. McQUEEN.

CARTHAGE, N. C., January 6, 1914.

DR. JOSEPH HYDE PRATT,
Chapel Hill, N. C.

DEAR DR. PRATT:—It is difficult to give the full amount of good that was done in Moore County on November 5th and 6th.

In one township there were four squads of men who built and shaped up about seven and one-half miles. Part of this road (about one-half mile) was graveled and clayed; the rest was grubbed and cleared out. In our township, which is Carthage Township, all stores closed, and everybody went out and worked. One crowd built and graveled three-quarters of one mile. At least 65 men worked together with eight teams, and two other crowds remodeled and repaired from two to three miles of road. Another township built a new road, one-fourth of a mile long, and many small forces of about 45 men built short pieces of road. In another township three miles were clayed, working 6 to 10 teams and 50 men or more; besides several small pieces of road all over the county were worked.

The work and spirit in our county will run up into the thousands of dollars. The road work is being continued in some sections on account of the money raised; and we are more than pleased over the results. It has done a lot of good. (Signed) D. A. McDonald.

A special to the *News and Observer* of November 11th, reads as follows in regard to the work done in Moore County:

People turned out in force to do their duty towards the betterment of the roads in this section. From Carthage, the county-seat, over two hundred men, representing all grades and professions, donned their overalls and with pick, rake and shovel worked steadily for ten hours of each of the days. Every available team was volunteered and the automobiles, which every owner offered, were in continuous operation transporting workers, and acting as commissary trains in distributing to the crews the excellent meals that were prepared by the women for them.

One gang, of one hundred hands and fifty teams, under the direction of C. F. Leavitt, had among its personnel such men as the mayor, the county commissioners, the clerk of the Superior Court, the register of deeds, the county superintendent of schools, two preachers, the prominent attorney, Mr. Curtiss Muse, and many other men prominent in various walks of life, who, by this show of public spirit, set a worthy example. This efficient crew accomplished very notable work, for as a result of their labors, the approaches to the famous sand-clay roads of the southern half of the county have been brought up to the standard of the highways to which they lead. Carthage, in consequence, has a system of broad, level and smooth highways leading into Pinehurst, Southern Pines, and Jackson Springs, which are as fine roads as any the State affords.

The negroes of this region too, showed remarkable public spirit, and colored gangs, under supervision of their own men, contributed in the fullest measure to the betterment of the roads in the county.

Nash County.

While considerable work may have been done in Nash County, yet the only record we have received is that of the Bailey High School at Bailey, which will be taken up under Schools and Colleges.

New Hanover County.

The following letter from Mr. M. S. Willard, of New Hanover County, gives the amount of road work done in this county during the Good Roads Days:

Wilmington, N. C., December 27, 1913.

Dr. Joseph Hyde Pratt,

Chapel Hill, N. C.

Dear Sir:—Replying to your letter of December 8th in regard to the work done in New Hanover County on Good Roads Days, November

5th and 6th, I will say that there were two points in the county in which good work was done.

In Masonboro Township the school children, together with some grown persons to direct them, built a very good road from our main macadamized road to Masonboro Church. The road was ditched and graded and the county furnished some road material to make a hard surface. This road is about one quarter of a mile in length.

In Cape Fear Township the colony of truckers (chiefly Hollanders) did considerable work in improving their neighborhood roads. The county furnished them a road machine which they used for grading, and there were also a number of teams worked on those days. Several miles of road were worked over and improved but no new roads were built.

Of course our regular work by the county was continued as usual on those days. I have been hoping to secure several photographs of the work done, and if I can get them within the next few days will forward them to you.

Yours very truly,
(Signed) M. S. Willard,
Chairman.

Orange County.

The principal work done in this county was in Chapel Hill and Carrboro, and was done by the students of the State University. This will be taken up under the head of school work.

The work of Chapel Hill was planned out in detail as follows:

Battle Dormitory:—In front of Battle Dormitory, cut back turf to bring ditch in alignment with ditch in front of campus. Put culvert across entrance to campus. 12″ culvert, 24 feet long. Mr. Woolen to have charge of removal of turf, and returfing after ditch made. The road is to be crowned, surfaced with gravel, and sloped evenly to ditches.

Tankersley's Store:—Slope of road should be graded so as to take care of drainage.

MacNider's Corner:—Drainage is bad at this corner, and road needs to be sloped in order to take care of water.

Patterson's Store:—Road needs to be crowned and raised with even slope to ditch. Ditch line should be opened nearer curbing.

University Inn:—Bad place just at University Inn where water accumulates. This should be raised, and the road sloped from the crown over this place, so that the water will drain into ditch.

In front of the Inn where water now flows toward the center of the road should be sloped, so that it will flow each side into the ditch from the crossing.

Pickard's Hotel: Pull back all turf and black soil to side of road at least 10 feet from center. Pile up grass and leaves and mulch not needed in filling places for turfing and have hauled away. Everything should be raked from the road toward the ditch, so that all the good dirt can be used in bringing an even slope from the center of the road to the ditches. The road will need crowning.

A. T. O. Hall: Same as Pickard's Hotel.

MacRae's House: Same as Pickard's Hotel.

Corner of Raleigh Road: Road needs crowning badly, and drainage prepared for taking care of water that comes from the Venable lot. It should be turned into side ditches, and not allowed to cross the road.

Venable House: Same as Pickard's Hotel.

Kluttz House: Ditch needs filling for nearly a foot, in order to give grade for taking care of water to pass through culvert at Raleigh road, and also to give right slope from crown of road to ditch.

If hill is cut down in front of Howell's house, sufficient material should be obtained to fill ditch.

Corner of Battle Road: Needs crowning and shoulders and slopes made to turn water into ditches and keep it out of center of road.

Mangum Driveway: A fill is needed in order to turn water into ditch. This fill should be made so as to slope gently from the crown of the road to the ditch.

Holmes & Herty: Several holes in front of these houses should be filled with gravel.

Herty's Driveway: Stone should be taken out of middle of road.

Lawson's East Driveway: Take out rock in middle of road, build up road crown, and slope so as to turn water into ditches.

Williams' House: On side of road in front of Lawson's driveway, cut down shoulders, so that the water can flow into ditches instead of being turned into middle of road.

SURFACING.

The road from in front of Battle's Dormitory until near top of hill in front of Howell's House to be surfaced evenly with gravel, 9 feet wide and 8 inches in center, sloping to 4½″ at the edges.

CULVERTS.

One 24 foot 12″ culvert at entrance of campus, east end of Battle Dormitory.

The results of the work done in Chapel Hill Township are given below:

On November 5th and 6th splendid work was done on the public roads in many sections of North Carolina, but in no section of the State was there greater enthusiasm and better work done than in Chapel Hill Township, Orange County, especially in the towns of Chapel Hill and Carrboro.

Not only the citizens of these towns responded willingly and enthusiastically to the Governor's Proclamation, but students of the State University responded with splendid enthusiasm and vigorous work.

The work to be done on these two days had been previously planned out and was concentrated on two roads, the main street of Chapel Hill and the new road through Carrboro connecting the two with the new location of the county road to Saxapahaw, a link of the Central Highway.

As teams were needed for carrying out the plans for the road work. subscriptions to a road fund for Chapel Hill was made by the stores, banks, and individuals, who thought they would not be able to work the roads. A sufficient fund was collected to enable the Special Committee for this occasion to hire teams for hauling the gravel with which to surface the road.

The Chapel Hill road work was under the supervision of Joseph Hyde Pratt, State Geologist, and Professor T. F. Hickerson, of the University.

Beginning in front of Battle Dormitory, the street was graded, ditched and crowned for a distance of 1,800 feet; and surfaced with gravel for a width of twelve feet. The working force was composed largely of students from the University with a goodly sprinkling of the citizens of the town and members of the Faculty. Professor Graham, Acting President of the University, was one of the first to put in appearance on Wednesday morning and begin work on the road.

In addition to the students working on the road, there were other squads under the direction of the Rev. W. T. D. Moss and Rev. Homer Starr, clearing up the streets and paths of Battle Park; and they did most efficient work.

These two days were also set apart as "Clean-up Days" by the Community Club with the most gratifying results. The negroes did their part, and cleaned up Potter's Field as it was never done before.

At Carrboro, Mayor Parker assembled his forces which were augmented on the first day by the Second-Year Medical Class of the University; and on the second day by the First-Year Medical Class under the leadership of Dr. Charles S. Mangum. The class turned out en masse. The result of the work at Carrboro was the opening of the new road connecting with the new county road to Saxapahaw. Right-of-way was cleared; stumps grubbed; rocks dug up; road graded, ditched, and made ready for surfacing materal. The people of Carrboro appreciated this very much and highly praised the work of the "Meds." On Wednesday noon they served lunch to the students, and on Thursday they treated them to a barbecue, which the students pronounced the "best ever."

The work at Carrboro was supervised by H. W. Collins, one of the Senior engineers in the course of Highway Engineering in the University.

Other members of this Engineering Class assisted in supervising the work on the Chapel Hill street. Another senior engineer, Bascom Field, went to Buie's Creek to assist the boys of this Academy in working the roads.

Altogether, over 400 of the students assisted in the road work, and the united efforts of these young men, together with the citizens of the towns of Chapel Hill and Carrboro, resulted in the construction of some excellent sections of good road, of which they are all justly proud. This demonstrated that good roads can be built in Chapel Hill.

On Tuesday morning at Chapel exercises, Professor Stacy made a talk on road work in Orange County, and Wednesday morning during Chapel exercises, Dr. Joseph Hyde Pratt, State Geologist, made a talk on the road situation in North Carolina. On Wednesday evening, Mr. L. H. Boykin of the U. S. Office of Public Roads gave an illustrated lecture on roads.

As a net result of the work done and enthusiasm aroused, it is believed that the students of the University have realized actual road conditions now facing the State; and that they will be in a better position, when they return to their homes, to help solve those difficult problems for their respective counties and townships. The splendid enthusiasm with which they entered upon this call from the Governor of the State shows that the University students have an active sense of civic duty, which can be easily kindled into splendid enthusiasm and accomplishment.

Polk County.

It is reported that in Tryon Township along the Howard Gap Road much work was done. Several culverts were put in, and sand and clay hauled from the river banks and filled into the soft spots along the road. This work was done by a dozen men and teams. A substantial dinner was served at the home of Captain Howard by the ladies of the neighborhood.

The day was observed by the Columbus High School, and some good work done.

Randolph County.

The following is an interesting description of the work done in Randolph County:

Asheboro, N. C., December 13, 1913.

Dr. Joseph Hyde Pratt,
Chapel Hill, N. C.

Dear Dr. Pratt:—On November 5th and 6th there was much work done on the roads of this county. The work throughout the county was general. There was no money subscribed but there were probably one hundred and fifty teams and wagons at work, and there were probably two thousand men and boys who gave two days' work each to the cause of good roads. This estimate may not be correct, but it is given from information which I have received in talking to people from nearly all over the county.

There were some eight miles or more of road graded and something like one and a half miles of road graveled.

Yours truly,
(Signed) W. C. Hammer.

The following from the *Concord Times* of November 6th tells about the enthusiasm in Randolph County:

Practically everybody closed up shop and put in full day on the roads today. They met at the courthouse this morning at 7:30 and divided into squads. The large squad worked on the road to Randleman. Mr. Jansen, the United States road expert was in charge, assisted by H. H. Kennedy, E. Whatley, Seth W. Laughlin. There were about 300 men and 30 teams. Judge B. F. Long adjourned Superior Court for the occasion. He was on the road early and used a pick with great skill. Solicitor W. C. Hammer plowed with four big mules.

The *Asheboro Courier* of November 13th says:

There was a notable response to the call of the Governor to work the roads November 5th and 6th, and in many counties the colored people turned out as well as the whites. There was work throughout this county pretty generally. Most of the work done in Asheboro Township was done on the old plank road in the direction of Randleman, and what is known as the Cox road south. There was much grading done on the old plank road, and about the same amount of work done on the Cox road. An effort will be made to gravel these two roads to the township line between now and Christmas. The business men of the town, ministers, clerks, bookkeepers, lawyers and officials turned out and worked faithfully and well all day. The merchants with two or three exceptions did not turn out to work. It is claimed that there are 24 hands assigned to the old plank road between the corporate limits of Asheboro and the Back Creek Township line, and none of them worked.

Robeson County.

The *Robesonian* of November 6th, states that very little work was done in Robeson County during the two days.

Rockingham County.

The following letter from the Superintendent of Roads of Rockingham County will tell of the interesting work done in that county:

SPRAY, N. C., December 31, 1913.

DR. JOSEPH HYDE PRATT,
Chapel Hill, N. C.

DEAR SIR:—Yours asking about "Good Roads Days" in Rockingham County received. I divided the roads of the county in about two and one-half mile sections, and appointed a foreman for each section. The town people, especially those of Reidsville and Leaksville-Spray entered into the work with enthusiasm, and did fine work. As a rule, the country people did not do so well, however, there were many notable exceptions.

As a whole the Good Roads Days were a success. I should say that as many as 500 men worked two days each in the entire county.

Respectfully yours,
(Signed) JAMES V. PRICE,
Superintendent of Roads.

Much enthusiasm was shown on the part of the citizens of Reidsville and Spray, and it it stated in these towns the stores and banks and other places of business were closed, so that all could observe Good Roads Days.

The *Webster Weekly* of Reidsville, of November 7th gives an interesting description of the work done on these days. This says:

Early Wednesday morning working squads went out on all the roads leading into the city and put in faithful service in repairing bad places, stopping breaks, opening drains, etc., and at the close of the day work had been done approximating $1,500 in value. The banks, warehouses, and nearly all the stores closed for the day, and the streets had a deserted appearance.

The workers embraced merchants, tobacconists, lawyers, doctors, ministers, and those accustomed to manual labor, and there was no make-believe about it. They dug dirt, used the shovel, drove teams, guided the plow, and did other things that made the sweat come. The work done on all the roads will be appreciated when the bad weather comes, if not before. Some of the worst places on the roads of this section were put in good fix. Pipe was laid, sand hauled, and some real pieces of good road constructed. Perhaps the best work of all was done on the Greensboro road near Mr. J. T. Amos'; on the Thompsonville road, near Mr. William Clark's; on the Lawsonville road, near Mr. J. T. McKinney's; and on the Leaksville road near Mrs. Tom Burton's. Real construction work was done on these bad places.

As a rule, very few of the farmers turned out, it being a very busy time with them, and besides a great many who could have spared the time had a notion that the town folks did not mean business. Had all hands joined in, the roads of the whole county would have been put in good shape for winter traffic. Some excellent work was done, however, in some sections of the county by the handful of workers who responded to the Governor's call.

This scribe's experience at road working was gained on the first stretch of the Ruffin road from the corporate limits to Palmer's crossing. The supervisor, Mr. J. W. Bennett, was at home, sick, and it looked like nothing would be done, but as the sun climbed up the force increased to seven. Mr. J. H. Laster acted as leader of the squad, and besides repairing a bridge in the corporate limits the holes in the road were repaired, the ditches opened, and the road put in what Judge Humphreys, on the squad, pronounced "apple-pie order." The judge used the shovel like a veteran as did also Mr. Laster and his two sons, Will and Jim. Three colored men, Andy Hooper, who was sent by Major Allan, and Ott Lawson and John Scales, also did faithful and efficient work. The little squad could have done better service had they been provided with a team to haul sand.

Mr. J. A. Lovelace of Sadler, 73 years old, was out bright and early Wednesday and put in the entire day mending the bad places between

A. MAYOR WOODSON OF SALISBURY, ROWAN COUNTY, AND OTHER CITIZENS DOING STREET WORK. SEVERAL BLOCKS OF DIRT STREETS WERE PUT INTO GOOD SHAPE.

B. CITIZENS OF ROWAN COUNTY WORKING ROADS ON NOVEMBER FIFTH AND SIXTH.

his house and Palmer's crossing. The jolly old gentleman worked by himself, no one going to his aid, it is said.

We would like to mention by name every person, white or black, who worked the roads in this section of the county.

Rowan County.

The following letter from the Secretary of the Salisbury Industrial Club gives the results of the road work in Rowan County:

SALISBURY, N. C., December 14, 1913.

DR. JOSEPH HYDE PRATT,
Chapel Hill, N. C.

DEAR DR. PRATT:—The reports turned in show that about 550 days of work for one man were done in the county. About two miles of good sand-clay road were built in one place, and about ten miles of scraping and grading done in other parts of the county. This is according to reports turned into the courthouse after the campaign. There was other work which has never been reported. Four or five blocks of Salisbury street were put in good condition, and there were a good many farmers over the county who worked here and there without any organization.

The county commissioners were interested in the campaign, and they gave a $1,000 in prize money for the work done. The prizes were given to the townships that did the most and best work. Unity township won the $500 prize, and will use this money for repair work on the township roads. Cleveland Township won the $300 prize, and this money will be used on the Cleveland Township roads where most needed. Franklin Township won the third prize of $200.

Franklin Township built a mile and a half or more of good sand-clay road, and Mr. Will Hall has agreed to keep it in good repair. Mr. Hall won the gold watch given as a prize by Leonard's Jewelry Store through the Rowan County Good Roads Association. He reported ninety-two men working in his squad.

The work of Mayor Woodson, Col. H. B. Smith, and Chairman of the County Commissioners, H. C. Trott, should receive notice. Mr. R. B. Bailey, leader of the work in Unity Township, should receive credit for good work and much accomplished. The negro college boys and instructors also did some good work.

I am,

Yours very truly,
(Signed) J. H. WARBURTON,
Secretary.

Rutherford County.

The following letter of Mr. L. D. Miller relates to the good roads work done in Rutherford County on these days:

RUTHERFORDTON, N. C., December 10, 1913.

HON. JOSEPH HYDE PRATT,
Chapel Hill, N. C.

DEAR SIR:—Regarding the two days' work on November 5th and 6th, will say that owing to the fact that we have voted bonds to build roads in this county and that the work is now being done by the Road Commision, there was not a general turning out by the people.

However, the people here and in other localities, did considerable work in repairing the roads. Possibly 500 people in the county worked the two davs. Something over 200 turned out in Rutherfordton Township and did fine work on the roads and the streets and sidewalks in this town. A splendid road was built from the Seaboard to the Southern depot, something over a mile, and also a road from the Rutherford Hospital to the Hickory Nut Gap road, on the western part of the town, a distance of about a mile; also a graded road from Rutherfordton to the Southern depot, about a mile.

All classes of people—professional men and laborers, worked side by side, entering into the spirit of better roads, and upholding the Governor's hands in a splendid manner. Yours very truly,

(Signed) L. D. Miller.

Stanly County.

The following from the *Albemarle Enterprise* of November 13th tells of the road work done in Stanly County:

It is a pity that the Governor's proclamation for Good Roads, November 5th and 6th, was not taken more seriously by the citizens of the State.

The majority of Albemarle citizens were evidently too busy to work the roads. A goodly number, however, worked with enthusiasm on both days. Stepping stones were laid at important points, dirt was thrown to advantage, and the scraper used in uneven places.

The lesson of the days seems to be that the Good Roads Days should be made an annual affair. There is every reason to believe that he who shovels dirt for good roads will deal less in hot air and take a more vital interest in the cause.

Surry County.

The following special to the *Greensboro Daily News* of November 7th gives some idea of the work done on Good Roads Days:

Yesterday and to-day were great days for Surry County and its citizenship responded nobly to Governor Craig's appeal for better roads, for hundreds of them worked faithfully and together for the splendid cause. Reports from every township in the county indicates that not only a large percentage of the people worked hard under the direction of competent overseers, but the work executed was of superior quality.

While all the townships worked faithfully, it is said that scarcely a man in Westfield or Long Hill remained at home, and there were several instances where whole families worked the entire two days. In Westfield Township William Needham and his five sons worked the entire time, while Esquire Frank Snoddy had charge of a road machine, several horses and 17 men. In Stewart's Creek Township the ladies prepared and served dinner at the roadside where the men were at work.

Taken as a whole the movement was a great success and will no doubt mean much to this particular section, where only one township, Mt. Airy, has done anything in the way of road improvement.

Transylvania County.

It is reported that there were numerous good roads workers active in Transylvania County. The stores at Brevard, were closed during one day and the workmen got an early start on the roads. Men of all walks of life picked and shoveled dirt together, and the captains experienced no trouble in keeping the men under their supervision busy. In fact, the task of performing the duties of captain was such an easy one that in many instances the foreman forgot to "boss" the job and got down in the trenches with the other laborers.

Tyrrell County.

The following is a rather discouraging report from Tyrell County:

COLUMBIA, N. C., December 11, 1913.

DR. JOSEPH HYDE PRATT,
Chapel Hill, N. C.

DEAR SIR:—I regret to say that nothing whatever was done on Good Roads Days in this county. Our people so far have not manifested any enthusiasm on this subject. A year or two ago I was elected President of the Good Roads Association, but I never could get anyone to attend meetings so I gave up in disgust and, I might say, despair.

I hope at some future time sentiment may change.

Yours truly,
(Signed) J. R. PINNER.

Union County.

MONROE, N. C., December 8, 1913.

DR. JOSEPH HYDE PRATT,
Chapel Hill, N. C.

DEAR SIR:—I am in receipt of your letter of December 2d, and have delayed reply in order to get a little information, and from all the information I have been able to get, there was no work done by the public on the public roads of Union County on November 5th and 6th. I am very sorry to make this report, nevertheless it is true. I am an enthusiast on the good roads question, and anything that I can do to help this movement, I am always ready to do.

Please command me if I can be of service to you in any way whatever.

Yours truly,
(Signed) M. K. LEE.

Wake County.

The following letter from the President of the Chamber of Commerce at Raleigh tells of the good work done in portions of Wake County on the Good Roads Days:

RALEIGH, N. C., December 12, 1913.

DR. JOSEPH HYDE PRATT,
Chapel Hill, N. C.

MY DEAR DR. PRATT:—Replying to your favor of recent date, in regard to work done in Wake County on November 5th and 6th, Good Roads Days, I beg to state as follows:

In Raleigh Township two miles of new road were built. The people of this township were materially aided by the International Harvester Company. This Company had a number of their road machines here that had been exhibited at the State Fair, and their men joined forces in this township and some splendid work was done. Hon. J. Bryan Grimes, Secretary of State, and Dr. A. W. Knox of this city were in charge of this work.

In House Creek Township we had about fifty men that turned out. Six mules were furnished by the citizens of this township, and the company furnished one of its best road machines, with one of its men in charge of the machine. In this township about three miles of roads were built. The ladies of the township furnished a barbecue dinner to the men who worked on the roads, and splendid results were accomplished.

Good work was also done in Barton's Creek Township, St. Matthews' Township, and Middle Creek Township. About a half-mile of road was built in each of these townships.

In St. Matthew's Township, the ladies turned out and some of them worked on the roads, picking up loose rock and pulling brush out of the roads as they were building a new road in this township. Mr. John C. Drewry had charge of the work in House's Creek Township.

Altogether splendid work was done in this county, and I believe a good sentiment was created.

With best wishes,

Yours truly,
(Signed) JOHN C. DREWRY,
President.

Warren County.

WARRENTON, N. C., December 3, 1913.

DR. JOSEPH HYDE PRATT,
Chapel Hill, N. C.

DEAR SIR:—It is with great regret that I am forced to inform you that no interest was taken in Good Roads Days in this county. A small crowd of us, the enthusiastic good road men, attempted to get the citizenship out on the 5th and 6th of November—but without any success whatever.

We had just a short time before the Good Roads Days been through an election for bonds for the county; this election engendered quite a little feeling and the opponents of the Bond Issue, who were in the majority, threw all their strength against working on the 5th and 6th of November.

But to their surprise we were victorious in our election for bonds for this township—Warrenton. We carried the election by a majority of 218 out of a total vote of 268.

I now believe the county as a whole is awakening to the fact that good roads are a necessity. Each day I hear some citizen from a small, far-off, and thinly populated township express himself as being in favor of good roads. Yours very truly.

(Signed) B. B. WILLIAMS.

Watauga County.

BOONE, N. C., December 23, 1913.

DR. JOSEPH HYDE PRATT,
Chapel Hill, N. C.

DEAR SIR:—I have been away from home for several days helping to survey and locate new roads, or would have answered sooner.

I am sorry to say that there was very little work done on the roads in this county on the days mentioned. I have no accurate figures but from the best information obtainable there were about one dozen teams and perhaps fifty men who did volunteer work. Several of the overseers of public roads ordered out their hands and worked. The people are to some extent awakened to the necessity of good roads, and several new roads are being constructed in the county on good grades; but many more are yet needed. We have two turnpikes kept up by toll in this County, is perhaps one reason why there was not more interest in good roads days. Yours very truly,

(Signed) L. N. PERKINS.

Wayne County.

GOLDSBORO, N. C., December 20, 1913.

DR. JOSEPH HYDE PRATT,
Chapel Hill, N. C.

MY DEAR DR. PRATT:—I have your letter of December 8th, relative to work done in our county on November 5th and 6th. I regret to say that there was not very much work done. I suppose, all told, there were 250 people who worked in different parts of the County. No money was subscribed and no new roads graded or laid off. It came just after an election in two or three townships for bond issues, and there seemed to be a feeling among our people that forces of hands would be put upon the roads under said issue, and therefore did not take the interest they would have otherwise. Yours truly,

(Signed) GEORGE C. ROYALL.

Wilkes County.

The Farmers' Union of Wilkes County issued a call to its members, urging them to work the roads on the Good Roads Days. The county commissioners issued the following call:

Whereas, we the County Commissioners of Wilkes County, deeming it one of the greatest needs of our county to-day to better the conditions

very few places where it is more than 4 per cent. For scenery it is unsurpassed, and it will open up a country richer than anything in the eastern part of the State. I guess you know of Ashe and Watauga counties' resources.

With personal regards and the compliments of the season, I am

Yours truly,

(Signed) H. W. HORTON.

Wilson County.

So far as has been learned little or no road work was done in this county at this time, although the Good Roads Days were observed by the school children of Wilson.

Yadkin County.

The county commissioners passed a resolution in which the overseers of every road in the county were asked to summon their hands for the two days' work. The Board of Education passed the following resolution:

Resolved, that the teachers of the county be requested to suspend their respective schools on November 5th and 6th, and the teachers and pupils render such assistance as they can in making a success of working the public roads on the two days as requested by the Governor.

The following were the ones who worked the roads on Good Roads Days:

John W. Doub, 2 days.
S. L. Doub, 2 days and a team one and a half days.
John Henry Doub, one and one-half days.
W. S. North, one-half day.
E. H. Wooten, one day.
Henry Churchill, two days.
C. H. Binkley, one day.
Anderson Phillips, one day.
Wiilliam Pilcher, 2 days, and a horse and plow a half day.
Elmer Pilcher, one day.
Cicero Binkley, two days.
Gray Binkley, two days.
Arl Binkley, two days.
Garfield Lakey, two days.
Dalt Carter, 2 days and a horse and plow one and a half days.

Yancey County.

The following letter from Yancey County will give the work done in this County:

WINGATE, N. C., December 12, 1913.

DR. JOSEPH HYDE PRATT,
Chapel Hill, N. C.

MY DEAR DR. PRATT:—Your letter of the 8th inst., has reached me and the same would have received my attention earlier but for my absence.

Permit me to say that I am not able to give you a full report of the work done in Yancey County on November 5th and 6th on account of the failure of the different townships reporting, and on account of my leaving there about that time.

In Burnsville Township 1,000 feet were turnpiked and drained with 400 feet surfaced with iron slag, furnished by the Black Mountain Railroad. There were on an average of 60 men and 12 wagons and teams working.

In Micaville Township they sanded about 250 feet of road and this is about all the work done in that township.

Yours very truly,

(Signed) IRA B. MULLIS.

A. SOME VIEWS OF STATE NORMAL AND INDUSTRIAL COLLEGE GIRLS CLEANING CAMPUS, ON NOVEMBER FIFTH AND SIXTH.

B. ANOTHER VIEW OF NORMAL GIRLS.

WORK DONE BY COLLEGES AND SCHOOLS.

UNIVERSITY OF NORTH CAROLINA.

As indicated in the program outlined in Acting President Graham's letter on page 43, very elaborate preparations were made by the University for carrying out the work on November 5th and 6th, in accordance with the Governor's proclamation. Pages 73-76, under Orange County, give in detail the program which was actually carried out.

About 400 students responded, and the number was limited only by the number of tools that could be secured for them to work with. The members of the Faculty also assisted in the work, those in the Engineering Department taking charge of squads of men. A squad of medical students worked at Carrboro opening up a new road, clearing out stumps, grading, ditching, and shaping the road.

In the town of Chapel Hill, one quarter of a mile on Franklin Street was shaped up, ditches cleared out, and a 6-foot layer of gravel, 9 feet wide, tapering to 12 feet, was the result of the work done. A number of culverts were put in. Plate VII shows views of the students at work on Franklin Street.

STATE NORMAL AND INDUSTRIAL COLLEGE.

The students of this college responded splendidly to the call for civic improvement, and the following letter from President Foust gives some idea of the work done by them:

GREENSBORO, N. C., December 12, 1913.

DR. JOSEPH HYDE PRATT,
Chapel Hill, N. C.

MY DEAR DR. PRATT:—I have received your letter of the 8th inst., and have sent you under separate cover several photographs of the students at work on our campus. It was impossible for our students to render service by working the roads on Good Roads Days. I, therefore, determined to make it a civic improvement day for the college and requested the students to thoroughly clean the campus in the forenoon and to spend the afternoon in putting the dormitories in first-class condition. Without any urging on my part I never saw a crowd of people enter into anything more enthusiastically than did the students. They thoroughly cleaned every nook and corner of the campus and the teachers who live in the dormitories tell me that the work in the dormitories was even better than it was on the campus. I feel that the occasion meant a great deal to them and will mean much to the State. As you know the young women of this College nearly all teach and they got a very good lesson about what could be accomplished by coöperation.

Thanking you for your letter, I am

Very truly yours,
(Signed) JULIUS I. FOUST,
President.

Plates VIII and IX show the girls at work in clearing up their campus.

AGRICULTURAL AND MECHANICAL COLLEGE AT RALEIGH.

Some of the students of this college did some special work on the road leading from A. & M. College to the Methodist Orphanage. Professor W. C. Riddick led the college corps. It contained engineers, students, children, and women. Another force worked at Pamlico Junction.

GUILFORD COLLEGE.

Plans were made by Guilford College to do road work on the Good Roads Days, but the details of what was accomplished have not been obtained.

BUIE'S CREEK ACADEMY.

Principal J. A. Campbell offered to give one day, November 5th, as a holiday to enable the boys of his academy to work on the roads. Application was made to the Geological Survey for an engineer to superintend the work, and Mr. Bascom Field, one of the students in Road Engineering, was detailed for this work. He went down a day ahead of time so as to have everything in readiness for work, when the day came. It is reported that more than 300 boys turned out for the work. The picture in Plate X represents the boys after they had returned from their work.

The *Benson Spokesman* of November 28th, says:

"These workers represented the new idea of coöperation between schools and community life, and the zeal of this age for the good roads movement."

CULLOWHEE NORMAL SCHOOL.

The students of this college observed both good roads days, and wrought a wonderful transformation in the old muddy roads and walks of their community.

LENOIR COLLEGE.

The students of this college did some excellent work on Good Roads Days on the roads of Catawba County, the students and faculty marching in a body to the scene of action.

JACKSON TRAINING SCHOOL, CABARRUS COUNTY.

This school repaired macadam and scraped the National Highway for a distance of a mile on each side of the school.

WINECOFF HIGH SCHOOL, CABARRUS COUNTY.

This school furnished the labor and the citizens the teams (18) to gravel one mile of the Statesville road, and scraped and filled up mud holes for a distance of two miles.

COLUMBUS HIGH SCHOOL, POLK COUNTY.

In this school the Principal talked to his pupils about road building, its history, and value to the County, State, and Nation. The pupils worked on the school grounds, and it is believed that the students

STUDENTS OF BUIE'S CREEK ACADEMY AT WORK ON NOVEMBER FIFTH AND SIXTH.

gained a better idea of true citizenship, because of the lessons inculcated during those days.

HILLSBORO HIGH SCHOOL, ORANGE COUNTY.

The Hillsboro High School gave an object lesson to the whole county in civic pride. Exercises were held on Thursday, November 6th, and the teachers joined hands with the student body to clear up the school grounds.

BAILEY HIGH SCHOOL, NASH COUNTY.

This school celebrated the Good Roads Days with much patriotic zeal and enthusiasm. At 8:30 the students and patrons met in the auditorium and carried out the following program:

Song: "America," by school.

Song: "Ho for Carolina!" by school.

Reading of the Governor's Proclamation, setting apart the Good Roads Day by Superintendent and Principal, J. E. Redfern.

Good Roads song, by school.

Essay: "How to Improve School Grounds," by Zetta Bissett.

Essay: "How to Improve School Rooms," by Frost Lewis.

Five minute talks by the following high school students on Good Roads: Smith Lewis, Lemon Johnson, Robert Underwood.

After the above program, the students hauled gravel and macadamized the school walks, set out shade trees, and cleaned up all the school rooms and beautified them. The students and patrons ate dinner in picnic fashion on the school grounds. It was a great day for the Bailey High School.

CHAPEL HILL SCHOOL, ORANGE COUNTY.

This school had Civic Day Exercises, consisting of talks from the Principal and from the State Forester in regard to tree planting. A tree was planted by the School with appropriate exercises, songs sung, etc., and the girls cleaned up the schoolhouse and the boys the school grounds.

It is believed that the schools pretty generally all over the State observed one of these Civic Days, in accordance with the suggestions and information outlined in the pamphlet called "Civic Days," prepared by the North Carolina Geological and Economic Survey and distributed by the State Board of Education.

AGRICULTURAL AND MECHANICAL COLLEGE FOR THE COLORED RACE AT GREENSBORO.

The students and teachers of this College put in two days of work for better roads, better sanitation, better living environments, and a more beautiful city. City Commissioner Foushee sent the steam roller and road scraper near the college at an early hour. This was met by many picks and shovels in the hands of the students, and long before

PRESS COMMENTS ON GENERAL WORK ACCOMPLISHED.

The *Morganton News Herald* quotes from the *Baltimore Sun* as follows:

North Carolina has followed Missouri's example in establishing "Good Roads Days," and Governor Craig, in overalls, led the embattled farmers with picks and spades on Wednesday in improving a stretch of highway near Asheville. Returns from various points estimate the value of the road work done by volunteers in North Carolina, Wednesday, at $25,000, and possibly as much more was accomplished on Thursday, the second day. These are paper figures, and perhaps an engineering survey might not sustain them. But if the volunteer army does not build up permanent roads, it at least helps to build up permanent good roads sentiment. And that, after all, is the real thing. For where there's a will, there's sure to be a highway).

The *Charlotte Chronicle* of November 10th says:

It is not what the 100,000 men who worked the roads last week actually did that is worth while, but what they will encourage 200,000 to do in the future that gives us cause for encouragement.

The *News and Observer* of October 26th reads:

The importance to good road development in North Carolina of the "Good Roads Days" of November 5th and 6th cannot be overestimated. It means more to the State than simply the amount of work on the roads which will be done on that day, and its purpose is to accomplish more than two days' improvement of roads in the State.

It is the spirit of road development which can be shown in a large degree which will prove of benefit to North Carolina. That spirit in some counties and in some sections of the State is largely developed, and the result is that without hesitation and with great majorities the people have voted to tax themselves to build up the roads, to make real good roads. But there are counties and sections in which good roads are needed in which this spirit is needed.

The advocates of good roads for all North Carolina can do a service of benefit on November 5th and 6th. If in all parts of the State they take part in the work of the day, if they follow the lead of Governor Craig, who is going to do actual road work in Buncombe County, then there will be given an impetus to road building all over the State, which will be of service.

It is a work of education which is to be done on the two "Good Roads Days" in November, and every institution of learning in the State should take part. The University has outlined its plan of work, and plans for a systematic use of the day should be mapped out by all the colleges and schools. Good roads are an aid to education as well as to agricultural, industrial, and mercantile success, and there should be full coöperation on the part of all people in North Carolina on these November days designated as North Carolina "Good Roads Days."

The *State Journal* of November 7th writes as follows:

Throughout the State there was quite a general observance of the 5th and 6th instant as Good Roads Days in response to the proclamation of Governor Craig. The Governor himself set the example by putting his own hand to the work in his home county of Buncombe. Clad in overalls he shoveled dirt to the great admiration of the large crowd which had gathered to witness the unusual performance. Many other officials and others in the higher walks of life entered heartily into the spirit of the occasion and worked manfully.

From every section of the State reports have come, not only of the great material value of the work done, but of the value of the spirit of coöperation which has been quickened and the great interest in better roads which has been aroused. Farmers, merchants, professional men, college students—men in every walk of life—laid aside their differences and met on the same plane to labor for the common good.

Good Roads Days, such as we have just had, have been held in several States with highly beneficial results, and it is safe to say that the cause of better public highways in this State will also receive a great stimulus.

The *News and Observer* of November 7th writes

The two days completed yesterday, set aside as Good Roads Days in North Carolina by proclamation of Governor Craig, has resulted in work being done on the roads in every part of the State.

Governor Craig led in actual road work and set the pace by his example. The two days have been made notable not alone by the work done, but by the increased interest given to the cause of good roads.

The work for good roads by volunteer movement this week has been fine. Next year the Good Roads Days should respond to an encore. With systematic State-wide plans there can be an improvement on the work done this year and the good roads spirit can be increased. What has been done is excellent. Let up keep at it till all North Carolina is linked together with good roads.

The *Durham Sun* of November 12th says:

Governor Craig announced to-day that he is receiving from every section of the State most gratifying reports of the work done on the two Good Roads Days, November 5th and 6th, and in a number of instances photographs have been sent showing the people engaged in the work. The Governor was especially gratified with the action of the faculty and students of the University and a number of other schools of the State in turning out for road work on a large scale.

"The people will never stop in this work until all the old roads are changed into fine highways. Clearly no stopping," declared the Gov. vernor.

A. STUDENTS OF LIVINGSTONE COLLEGE, WORKING THE ROADS AND STREETS, NOVEMBER FIFTH AND SIXTH.

B. INSTRUCTORS AND STUDENTS OF LIVINGSTONE COLLEGE WORKING ROADS IN ROWAN COUNTY.

The *News and Observer* of November 16th says:

One of the best results, the greatest result in fact, of the observance of Good Roads Days is in the advertisement which the good roads idea gets in that way. The benefits of good roads is more powerfully impressed upon the minds of North Carolinians to-day than it has ever been before.

SUMMARY OF WORK BY COUNTIES.

County	Township	Number of Men Who Worked	Subscriptions	Results of Work	Number Days of Work Done	Remarks.
Anson	Lilesville	259		½ mile road built	518	
	Wadesboro	Quite a number				Only indefinite information could be got. There are six other townships in Anson county, and in all some work done. Unable to ascertain amount.
Beaufort	Pantego	500		Great deal work done		All stores and factories closed in two towns in township. Gave impetus to good roads spirit, and much accomplished other than actual work.
	Other Tps.	200				
Bladen		Many citizens in all walks of life all over county.				
Buncombe		10,000			Estimated 20,000	The roads worked on were special roads over county.
	Biltmore			Permanent side walks built ¼ mile.		
Burke				Considerable work		
Cabarrus		1,500	About $350	Splendid work done	Estimated 3,000	Work done on school grounds by special committees in connection with children.
Carteret		300	30 teams	Two miles new road built, 25 miles old road improved.	600 60 (teams)	Most work done on Central Highway. Newport Tp. working roads every Thursday from 40 to 50 men and 10 to 20 teams.
Catawba		200	75 teams			
	Hickory	1,000	$130.75; entire road equipment includ-			

Catawba	Hickory	200 1,000	team 30.75; entire road equipment includ-			
			ing 40 mules and dump carts.			
	Conover section	100	25 teams and wagons			One community which was unprepared for work on November 5-6 did their work on the following days.
Chowan						Some work done.
Columbus		150	30 teams	Reshaped and patched 8 or 10 miles road.	200	
Craven		50	$34		100	Lack of definite system and competent supervisors prevented more and better work.
Cumberland		1,000	Shovels, road scapers, etc.	Improvement of streets and county roads.	2,000	$3,000 worth of work done.
	Cross Creek	1,000			2,000	
Currituck		1,500		Three miles graded, three miles repaired.		
Davidson		1,500	Plows, teams, wagons, road scraper, etc.	$1,000 improvement on roads of county.	3,000	
	Thomasville	30	Teams and tools		60	First Monday and Tuesday of December set apart as Good Roads Days, and will do additional road work at that time.
Duplin		500	Teams, plows, carts, road scrapers and tools.		1,000	
Forsyth		200 to 300			400 to 600	
Gates				$3,000 worth work done.		
	Mintonsville	250			500	
	Reynoldson	132			264	
	Gatesville	175			350	
Granville		350	Tools		700	
Guilford		2,000	Tools, road machinery, etc.		4,000	

SUMMARY OF WORK BY COUNTIES.—CONTINUED.

County	Township	Number of Men Who Worked	Subscriptions	Results of Work	Number Days of Work Done	Remarks
Haywood	Beaverdam			3½ miles of graded road.		
Jackson				Estimated $10,000 worth of work done.		
McDowell				One mile of new road on Central Highway built.		This includes a great deal of blasting and building walls.
Macon	Cartoopchage	42 men	Nine teams for one day	100 yards of sand-clay road		
	Highlands	All men in township	25 teams, scrapes, etc.	Four separate pieces of road. Estimated value, $500.	225	
Madison		*390	26 teams for two days	¾ mile Central Highway graded with no grade over 4½ per cent Road 18 to 20 feet wide. 800 feet new grade on Central Highway. ½ mile of new road on Mars Hill Highway. One mile new road in Pine Creek township.		
Moore		350	20 odd teams, tools, etc.	7½ miles graded and shaped up; 10½ miles graded and graveled or sand-clayed.		
New Hanover	Masonboro			¼ mile built by school children.		
	Cape Fear			Several miles im-		

New Hanover	Masonboro			clayed.	
	Cape Fear			¼ mile built by school children.	
				Several miles improved by colony of Hollanders.	
Randolph		2,000 men and boys each day.	150 teams	Eight miles graded and 1½ miles graveled.	4,000
Rockingham		500 men			300 (teams) 1,000
*This does not include students of Mars Hill Academy.					
Rowan		550	$1,000 prize money given by county commissioners.	Three miles of sand-clay road built; 10 miles scraped and graded; five blocks of Salisbury street improved.	1,100
Rutherford		500	20 two horse wagons. Two large road machines.	Three miles of new road built.	1,000
Wake	Raleigh			Two miles of road built.	
	House Creek			Three miles of road built.	
	Barton's Creek	50	Six mules, seven wagons	½ mile of road built	100
	St. Matthews'	Women worked as well as men.		½ mile of road built	
	Middle Creek			½ mile of road built	
Watauga		50	12 teams		100 24 (teams)
Wayne		250			500
Wilkes		275	40 teams and $50 in money.	40 miles old road improved. 3,000 feet of sand-clay road made.	550
Yadkin		13	One dump cart and two plows.		26
Yancey	Burnsville	60	Slag furnished by Black Mountain Railway.	1,000 feet turnpiked, and 100 feet surfaced with iron slag.	120
	Micaville		12 teams and wagons	250 feet sand-clayed.	

PUBLICATIONS

OF THE

NORTH CAROLINA GEOLOGICAL AND ECONOMIC SURVEY

BULLETINS.

1. Iron Ores of North Carolina, by Henry B. C. Nitze, 1893. 8°, 239 pp., 20 pl., and map. *Out of print.*

2. Building and Ornamental Stones in North Carolina, by T. L. Watson and F. B. Laney in collaboration with George P. Merrill, 1906. 8°, 283 pp., 32 pl., 2 figs. *Postage 25 cents. Cloth-bound copy 30 cents extra.*

3. Gold Deposits in North Carolina, by Henry B. C. Nitze and George B. Hanna, 1896. 8°, 196 pp., 14 pl., and map. *Out of print.*

4. Road Material and Road Construction in North Carolina, by J. A. Holmes and William Cain, 1893. 8°, 88 pp. *Out of print.*

5. The Forests, Forest Lands and Forest Products of Eastern North Carolina, by W. W. Ashe, 1894. 8°, 128 pp., 5 pl. *Postage 5 cents.*

6. The Timber Trees of North Carolina, by Gifford Pinchot and W. W. Ashe, 1897. 8°, 227 pp., 22 pl. *Postage 10 cents.*

7. Forest Fires: Their Destructive Work, Causes and Prevention, by W. W. Ashe, 1895. 8°, 66 pp., 1 pl. *Postage 5 cents.*

8. Water-powers in North Carolina, by George F. Swain, Joseph A. Holmes and E. W. Myers, 1889. 8°, 362 pp., 16 pl. *Postage 16 cents.*

9. Monazite and Monazite Deposits in North Carolina, by Henry B. C. Nitze, 1895. 8°, 47 pp., 5 pl. *Out of print.*

10. Gold Mining in North Carolina and other Appalachian States, by Henry B. C. Nitze and A. J. Wilkins, 1897. 8°, 164 pp., 10 pl. *Out of print.*

11. Corundum and the Basic Magnesian Rocks of Western North Carolina, by J. Volney Lewis, 1895. 8°, 107 pp., 6 pl. *Out of print.*

12. History of the Gems Found in North Carolina, by George Frederick Kunz, 1907. 8°, 60 pp., 15 pl. *Postage 8 cents. Cloth-bound copy 30 cents extra.*

13. Clay Deposits and Clay Industries in North Carolina, by Heinrich Ries, 1897. 8°, 157 pp., 12 pl. *Postage 10 cents.*

14. The Cultivation of the Diamond-back Terrapin, by R. E. Coker, 1906. 8°, 67 pp., 23 pl., 2 figs. *Out of print.*

15. Experiments in Oyster Culture in Pamlico Sound, North Carolina, by Robert E. Coker, 1907. 8°, 74 pp., 17 pl., 11 figs. *Postage 6 cents.*

16. Shade Trees for North Carolina, by W. W. Ashe, 1908. 8°, 74 pp., 10 pl., 16 figs. *Postage 6 cents.*

17. Terracing of Farm Lands, by W. W. Ashe, 1908. 8°, 38 pp., 6 pl., 2 figs. *Postage 4 cents.*

18. Bibliography of North Carolina Geology, Mineralogy and Geography, with a list of Maps, by Francis Baker Laney and Katherine Hill Wood, 1909. 8°, 428 pp. *Postage 25 cents. Cloth-bound copy 30 cents extra.*

19. The Tin Deposits of the Carolinas, by Joseph Hyde Pratt and Douglas B. Sterrett, 1905. 8°, 64 pp., 8 figs. *Postage 4 cents.*

20. Water-powers of North Carolina: An Appendix to Bulletin 8, 1910. 8°, 383 pp. *Postage 25 cents.*

21. The Gold Hill Mining District of North Carolina, by Francis Baker Laney, 1910. 8°, 137 pp., 23 pl., 5 figs. *Postage 15 cents.*

22. A Report on the Cid Mining District, Davidson County, N. C., by J. E. Pogue, Jr., 1911. 8°, 144 pp., 22 pl., 5 figs. *Postage 15 cents.*

23. Forest Conditions in Western North Carolina, by J. S. Holmes 1911. 8°, 116 pp., 8 pl. *Postage 15 cents.*

ECONOMIC PAPERS.

1. The Maple sugar Industry in Western North Carolina, by W. W. Ashe, 1897. 8°, 34 pp. *Postage 2 cents.*

2 Recent Road Legislation in North Carolina, by J. A. Holmes. *Out of print.*

3. Talc and Pyrophyllite Deposits in North Carolina, by Joseph Hyde Pratt, 190. 8°, 29 pp., 2 maps. *Postage 2 cents.*

4. The Mining Industry in North Carolina During 1900, by Joseph Hyde Pratt, 1901. 8°, 36 pp., and map. *Postage 2 cents.*

Takes up in some detail Occurrences of Gold, Silver, Lead and Zinc, Copper, Iron Manganese, Corundum, Granite, Mica, Talc, Pyrophyllite, Graphite, Kaolin, Gem Minerals, Monazite, Tungsten, Building Stones, and Coal in North Carolina.

5. Road Laws of North Carolina, by J. A. Holmes. *Out of print.*

6. The Mining Industry in North Carolina During 1901, by Joseph Hyde Pratt, 1902. 8°, 102 pp. *Postage 4 cents.*

Gives a List of Minerals found in North Carolina; describes the Treatment of Sulphuret Gold Ores, giving localities; takes up the Occurrence of Copper in the Virgilina, Gold Hill, and Ore Knob districts; gives Occurrence and Uses of Corrundum; a List of Garnets, describing Localities; the Occurrence, Associated Minerals, Uses and Localities of Mica; the Occurrence of North Carolina Feldspar, with Analyses; an extended description of North Carolina Gems and Gem Minerals; Occurrences of Monazite, Barytes, Ocher; describes and gives Occurrences of Graphite and Coal; describes and gives Occurrences of Building Stones, including Limestone; describes and gives Uses for the various forms of Clay; and under the head of "Other Economic Minerals," describes and gives Occurrences of Chromite, Asbestos and Zircon.

7. Mining Industry in North Carolina During 1902, by Joseph Hyde Pratt, 1903. 8°, 27 pp. *Out of print.*

8. The Mining Industry in North Carolina During 1903, by Joseph Hyde Pratt, 1904. 8°, 74 pp. *Postage 4 cents.*

Gives descriptions of Mines worked for Gold in 1903; descriptions of Properties worked for Copper during 1903, together with assay of ore from Twin-Edwards Mine; Analyses of Limonite ore from Wilson Mine; the Occurrence of Tin; in some detail the Occurrences of Abrasives; Occurrences of Monazite and Zircon; Occurrences and Varieties of Graphite, giving Methods of Cleaning; Occurrences of Marble and other forms of Limestone; Analyses of Kaolin from Barber Creek, Jackson County, North Carolina.

9. The Mining Industry in North Carolina During 1904, by Joseph Hyde Pratt, 1905. 8°, 95 pp. *Postage 4 cents.*

Gives Mines Producing Gold and Silver during 1903 and 1904 and Sources of the Gold Produced during 1904; describes the mineral Chromite, giving Analyses of Selected Samples of Chromite from Mines in Yancey County; describes Commercial Varieties of Mica, giving the manner in which it occurs in North Carolina, Percentage of Mica in the Dikes, Methods of Mining, Associated Minerals, Localities, Uses; describes the mineral Barytes, giving Method of Cleaning and Preparing Barytes for Market; describes the use of Monazite as used in connection with the Preparation of the Bunsen Burner, and goes into the use of Zircon in connection with the Nernst Lamp, giving a List of the Principal Yttrium Minerals; describes the minerals containing Corundum Gems, Hiddenite and Other Gem Minerals, and gives New Occurrences of these Gems; describes the mineral Graphite and gives new Uses for same.

10. Oyster Culture in North Carolina, by Robert E. Coker, 1905. 8°, 39 pp. *Out of print.*

11. The Mining Industry in North Carolina During 1905, by Joseph Hyde Pratt, 1906. 8°, 95 pp. *Postage 4 cents.*

Describes the mineral Cobalt and the principal minerals that contain Cobalt; Corundum Localities; Monazite and Zircon in considerable detail, giving Analyses of Thorianite; describes Tantalum Minerals and gives description of the Tantalum Lamp; gives brief description of Peat Deposits; the manufacture of Sand-lime Brick; Operations of Concentrating Plant in Black Sand Investigations; gives Laws Relating to Mines, Coal Mines, Mining, Mineral Interest in Land, Phosphate Rock, Marl Beds.

12. Investigations Relative to the Shad Fisheries of North Carolina, by John N. Cobb, 1906. 8°, 74 pp., 8 maps. *Postage 6 cents.*

13. Report of Committee on Fisheries in North Carolina. Compiled by Joseph Hyde Pratt, 1906. 8°, 78 pp. *Out of print.*

14. The Mining Industry in North Carolina During 1906, by Joseph Hyde Pratt, 1907. 8°, 144 pp., 20 pl., and 5 figs. *Postage 10 cents.*

Under the head of "Recent Changes in Gold Mining in North Carolina," gives methods of mining, describing Log Washers, Square Sets, Cyanide Plants, etc., and detailed descriptions of Gold Deposits and Mines are given; Copper Deposits of Swain County are described; Mica Deposits of Western North Carolina are described, giving Distribution and General Character, General Geology, Occurrence, Associated Minerals, Mining and Treatment of Mica, Origin, together with a description of many of the mines; Monazite is taken up in considerable detail as to Location and Occurrence, Geology, including classes of Rocks, Age, Associations, Weathering, method of Mining and Cleaning, description of Monazite in Original Matrix.

15. The Mining Industry in North Carolina During 1907, by Joseph Hyde Pratt, 1908. 8°, 176 pp., 13 pl., and 4 figs. *Postage 15 cents.*

Takes up in detail the Copper of the Gold Hill Copper District; a description of the Uses of Monazite and its Associated Minerals; descriptions of Ruby, Emerald, Beryl, Hiddenite, and Amethyst Localities; a detailed description with Analyses of the Principal Mineral Springs of North Carolina; a description of the Peat Formations in North Carolina, together with a detailed account of the Uses of Peat and the Results of an Experiment Conducted by the United States Geological Survey on Peat from Elizabeth City, North Carolina.

16. Report of Convention called by Governor R. B. Glenn to Investigate the Fishing Industries in North Carolina, compiled by Joseph Hyde Pratt, State Geologist, 1908. 8°, 45 pp. *Out of print.*

17. Proceedings of Drainage Convention held at New Bern, North Carolina, September 9, 1908. Compiled by Joseph Hyde Pratt, 1908. 8°, 94 pp. *Out of print.*

18. Proceedings of Second Annual Drainage Convention held at New Bern, North Carolina, November 11 and 12, 1909, compiled by Joseph Hyde Pratt, and containing North Carolina Drainage Law, 1909. 8°, 50 pp. *Out of print.*

19. Forest Fires in North Carolina During 1909, by J. S. Holmes, Forester, 1910. 8°, 52 pp., 9 pl. *Out of print.*

20. Wood-using Industries of North Carolina, by Roger E. Simmons, under the direction of J. S. Holmes and H. S. Sackett, 1910. 8°, 74 pp., 6 pl. *Postage 7 cents.*

21. Proceedings of the Third Annual Drainage Convention, held under Auspices of the North Carolina Drainage Association; and the North Carolina Drainage Law (codified). Compiled by Joseph Hyde Pratt, 1911. 8°, 67 pp., 3 pl. *Out of print.*

22. Forest Fires in North Carolina During 1910, by J. S. Holmes, Forester, 1911. 8°, 48 pp. *Out of print.*

23. Mining Industry in North Carolina During 1908, '09, and '10, by Joseph Hyde Pratt and Miss H. M. Berry, 1911. 8°, 134 pp., 1 pl., 27 figs. *Postage 10 cents.*

Gives report on Virgilina Copper District of North Carolina and Virginia, by F. B. Laney; Detailed report on Mica Deposits of North Carolina, by Douglas B. Sterrett; Detailed report on Monazite, by Douglas B. Sterrett; Reports on various Gem Minerals, by Douglas B. Sterrett; Information and Analyses concerning certain Mineral Springs; Extract from Chance Report of the Dan River and Deep River Coal Fields; Some notes on the Peat Industry, by Professor Charles A. Davis; Extract from report of Arthur Keith on the Nantahala Marble; Description of the manufacture of Sand-lime Brick.

24. Fishing Industry of North Carolina, by Joseph Hyde Pratt, 1911. 8°, 44 pp. *Out of print.*

25. Proceedings of Second Annual Convention of the North Carolina Forestry Association, held at Raleigh, North Carolina, February 21, 1912. Forest Fires in North Carolina During 1911. Suggested Forestry Legislation. Compiled by J. S. Holmes, Forester, 1912. 8°, 71 pp. *Postage 5 cents.*

26. Proceedings of Fourth Annual Drainage Convention, held at Elizabeth City, North Carolina, November 15 and 16, 1911, compiled by Joseph Hyde Pratt, State Geologist, 1912. 8°, 45 pp. *Postage 3 cents.*

27. Highway Work in North Carolina, containing a Statistical Report of Road Work during 1911 by Joseph Hyde Pratt, State Geologist, and Miss H. M. Berry, Secretary, 1912. 8°, 145 pp., 11 figs. *Postage 10 cents.*

28. Culverts and Small Bridges for Country Roads in North Carolina, by C. R. Thomas and T. F. Hickerson, 1912. 8°, 56 pp., 14 figs., 20 pl. *Postage 10 cents.*

29. Report of the Fisheries Convention held at New Bern, N. C., December 13, 1911, compiled by Joseph Hyde Pratt, State Geologist, together with a Compendium of the Stenographic Notes of the Meetings Held on the Two trips taken by the Legislative Fish Committee Appointed by the General Assembly of 1909, and the Legislation Recommended by this Committee, 1912. 8°, 302 pp. *Postage 15 cents.*

30. Proceedings of the Annual Convention of the North Carolina Good Roads Association held at Charlotte, N. C., August 1 and 2, 1912, in Coöperation with the North Carolina Geological and Economic Survey. Compiled

by Joseph Hyde Pratt, State Geologist, and Miss H. M. Berry, Secretary, 1912. 8°, 109 pp. *Postage 10 cents.*

31. Proceedings of Fifth Annual Drainage Convention held at Raleigh, N. C., November 26 and 27, 1912. Compiled by Joseph Hyde Pratt, State Geologist. 8°, 56 pp., 6 pl. *Postage 5 cents.*

32. Public Roads are Public Necessities, by Joseph Hyde Pratt, State Geologist, 1913. 8°, 62 pp. *Postage 5 cents.*

33. Forest Fires in North Carolina during 1912 and National and Association Coöperative Fire Control, by J. S. Holmes, Forester, 1913. 8°, 63 pp. *Postage 5 cents.*

34. Mining Industry in North Carolina during 1911-12, by Joseph Hyde Pratt, State Geologist, 1914. 8°, 102 pp., pl., figs. *Postage 20 cents.*

35. Good Roads Days, November 5th and 6th, 1913, compiled by Joseph Hyde Pratt, State Geologist, and Miss H. M. Berry, Secretary. 8°, 102 pp., 11 pl. *Postage 15 cents.*

36. Proceedings of the North Carolina Good Roads Association, held at Morehead City, N. C., July 31st and August 1st, 1913. In Coöperation with the North Carolina Geological and Economic Survey.—Statistical Report of Highway Work in North Carolina during 1912. Compiled by Joseph Hyde Pratt, State Geologist, and Miss H. M. Berry, Secretary. 8°, 127 pp., 7 figs. *Postage 10 cents.*

VOLUMES.

Vol. I. Corundum and the Basic Magnesian Rocks in Western North Carolina, by Joseph Hyde Pratt and J. Volney Lewis, 1905. 8°, 464 pp., 44 pl., 35 figs. *Postage 32 cents. Cloth-bound copy 30 cents extra.*

Vol. II. Fishes of North Carolina, by H. M. Smith, 1907. 8°, 453 pp., 21 pl., 188 figs. *Postage 30 cents.*

Vol. II. The Coastal Plain Deposits of North Carolina, by William Bullock Clark, Benjamin L. Miller, L. W. Stephenson, B. L. Johnson and Horatio N. Parker, 1912. 8°, 509 pp., 62 pl., 21 figs. *Postage 35 cents.*

Pt. I.—The Physiography and Geology of the Coastal Plain of North Carolina, by Wm. Bullock Clark, Benjamin L. Miller, and L. W. Stephenson.

Pt. II.—The Water Resources of the Coastal Plain of North Carolina, by L. W. Stephenson and B. L. Johnson.

Vol. IV. Birds of North Carolina. *In press.*

BIENNIAL REPORTS.

First Biennial Report, 1891-1892, J. A. Holmes, State Geologist, 1893. 8°, 111 pp., 12 pl., 2 figs. *Postage 6 cents.*

Administrative report, giving Object and Organization of the Survey; Investigations of Iron Ores, Building Stone, Geological Work in Coastal Plain Region, including supplies of drinking waters in eastern counties, Report on Forests and Forest Products, Coal and Marble, Investigations of Diamond Drill

Biennial Report 1893-1894, J. A. Holmes, State Geologist, 1894. 8° 15 pp. *Postage 1 cent.*

Administrative report.

Biennial Report, 1895-1896, J. A. Holmes, State Geologist, 1896. 8°, 17 pp. *Postage 1 cent.*

Administrative report.

Biennial Report, 1897-1898, J. A. Holmes, State Geologst, 1898. 8°, 28 pp. *Postage 2 cents.*

Administrative report.

Biennial Report, 1899-1900, J. A. Holmes, State Geologist, 1900. 8°, 20 pp. *Postage 2 cents.*

Administrative report.

Biennial Report 1901-1902, J. A. Holmes, State Geologist, 1902. 8°, 15 pp. *Postage 1 cent.*

Administrative Report.

Biennial Report, 1903-1904, J. A. Holmes, State Geologist, 1905. 8°, 32 pp. *Postage 2 cents.*

Administrative Report.

Biennial Report, 1905-1906, Joseph Hyde Pratt, State Geologist, 1907. 8°, 60 pp. *Postage 3 cents.*

Administrative report; report on certain swamp lands belonging to the State, by W. W. Ashe; it also gives certain magnetic observations at North Carolina stations.

Biennial Report, 1907-1908, Joseph Hyde Pratt, State Geologist, 1908. 8°, 60 pp., 2 pl. *Postage 5 cents.*

Administrative report. Contains Special Report on an examination of the Sand Banks along the North Carolina Coast, by Jay F. Bond, Forest Assistant, United States Forest Service; certain magnetic observations at North Carolina stations; Results of an Investigation Relating to Clam Cultivation, by Howard E. Enders of Purdue University.

Biennial Report 1909-1910, Joseph Hyde Pratt, State Geologist, 1911. 8°, 152 pp. *Postage 10 cents.*

Administrative report, and contains Agreements for Coöperation in Statistical Work, and Topographical and Traverse Mapping Work with the United States Geological Survey; Forest Work with the United States Department of Agriculture (Forest Service); List of Topographic maps of North Carolina and counties partly or wholly topographically mapped; description of special Highways in North Carolina; suggested Road Legislation; list of Drainage Districts and Results of Third Annual Drainage Convention; Forestry reports relating to Connolly Tract, Buncombe County and Transylvania County State Farms; certain Watersheds; Reforestation of Cut-over and Abandoned Farm Lands on the Woodlands of the Salem Academy nd College; Recommendations for the Artificial Regeneration of Longleaf Pine at Pinehurst; Act regulating the use of and for the Protection of Meridian Monuments and Standards Measure at the several county seats of North Carolina; list of Magnetic Declinations at the county seats, January 1, 1910; letter of Fish Commissioner of the United States Bureau of Fisheries relating to the condition of the North Carolina fish industries; report of the Survey for the North Carolina Fish Commission referring to dutch or pound-net fishing in Albemarle and Croatan sounds and Chowan River, by Gilbert T. Rude, of the United States Coast and Geodetic Survey; Historical Sketch of the several North Carolina Geological Surveys, with list of publications of each.

Biennial Report, 1911-1912, Joseph Hyde Pratt, State Geologist, 1913. 8°, 181pp. *Postage 7 cents.*

Administrative report, and contains reports on method of construction and estimate of cost of road improvement in Stantonsburg Township, Wilson County; report on road conditions in Lee County; report on preliminary location of section of Spartanburg-Hendersonville Highway between Tryon and Tuxedo; report of road work done by U. S. Office of Public Roads during biennial period; experiments with glutrin on the sand-clay road; report on Central Highway, giving Act establishing and report of trip over this Highway; suggested road legislation; report on the Asheville City watershed; report on the Struan property at Arden, Buncombe County; report on the woodlands on the farm of Dr. J. W. Kilgore, Iredell County; report on examination of the woodlands on the Berry place, Orange County; report on the forest property of Miss Julia A. Thorne, Asheboro, Randolph County; report on the examination of the forest lands of the Butters Lumber Company, Columbus County; proposed forestry legislation; swamp lands and drainage, giving drainage districts; suggested drainage legislation; proposed Fisheries Commission bill.

Samples of any mineral found in the State may be sent to the office of the Geological and Economic Survey for identification, and the same will be classified free of charge. It must be understood, however, that NO ASSAYS OR QUANTITATIVE DETERMINATIONS WILL BE MADE. Samples should be in a lump form if possible, and marked plainly on outside of package with name of sender, postoffice address, etc.; a *letter* should accompany sample and *stamp* should be enclosed for reply.

These publications are mailed to libraries and to individuals who may desire information on any of the special subjects named, free of charge, except that in each case applicants for the reports should forward the amount of *postage* needed, as indicated above, for mailing the bulletins desired, to the *State Geologist, Chapel Hill, N. C.*

NORTH CAROLINA GEOLOGICAL AND ECONOMIC SURVEY

JOSEPH HYDE PRATT, State Geologist

ECONOMIC PAPER No. 36

Proceedings of the Annual Convention of the North Carolina Good Roads Association, Held at Morehead City, N. C., July 31 and August 1, 1913, in Cooperation with the North Carolina Geological and Economic Survey

Statistical Report of Highway Work in North Carolina During 1912

Compiled by

JOSEPH HYDE PRATT, State Geologist, and Miss H. M. BERRY, Secretary

RALEIGH
EDWARDS & BROUGHTON PRINTING CO., STATE PRINTERS
1914

GEOLOGICAL BOARD

Governor Locke Craig, *ex officio Chairman* .... Raleigh.
Frank R. Hewitt .... Asheville.
Hugh MacRae .... Wilmington
Henry E. Fries .... Winston-Salem.
W. H. Williamson .... Raleigh.

Joseph Hyde Pratt, *State Geologist* .... Chapel Hill.

LETTER OF TRANSMITTAL

CHAPEL HILL, N. C., May 15, 1914.

To His Excellency, HONORABLE LOCKE CRAIG,
Governor of North Carolina.

SIR:—I beg to submit herewith for publication, as Economic Paper No. 36, a report giving the proceedings of the North Carolina Good Roads Association held at Morehead City, July 31 and August 1, 1913, together with a statistical report of highway work in North Carolina during 1912.

There has always been a close coöperation between the work of the North Carolina Geological and Economic Survey and the North Carolina Good Roads Association in carrying on an educational campaign for good roads throughout the State, and it is believed that the proceedings of this convention will be of interest and value to the citizens throughout the Sate. The statistics have been collected in coöperation with the United States Office of Public Roads, and are as complete as it is possible to give them with our present rather inadequate sources of information.

Yours respectfully,
JOSEPH HYDE PRATT,
State Geologist.

CONTENTS

FIGURES

PROCEEDINGS

OF THE

Annual Convention of the North Carolina Good Roads Association

HELD AT

MOREHEAD CITY, N. C., JULY 31 and AUGUST 1, 1913

In Cooperation with the North Carolina Geological and Economic Survey

---

Compiled by JOSEPH HYDE PRATT, State Geologist, and MISS H. M. BERRY, Secretary.

INTRODUCTION.

The North Carolina Good Roads Association was organized during the winter of 1901-2, as a result of a convention held in Raleigh, of the National Good Roads Association, the United States Office of Public Road Inquiries, the Southern Railway, and the principal Manufacturers of Road-Building Machinery in the United States. This meeting was called by Governor Aycock in the following message:

"Whereas the people of the State of North Carolina have pledged their best endeavors to the cause of education, the upbuilding of our State, and the development and utilization of her natural resources; and

"Whereas the farmers need better roads, both for their children to travel over daily on their way to the schoolhouses and for themselves and their families to use to reach their churches to worship Almighty God, as well as for the prompt and early delivery of their mail by the carriers of the United States Government and the transportation of their products and purchases; and the citizens living in towns and cities need good streets for the same purpose; and

"Whereas in those counties of our State where the greatest progress has been made in substantial good-road building there has been the greatest industrial advancement, as well as the largest increase in the value of farm lands, due to being thereby placed nearer to the towns and cities; and

"Whereas the National Good Roads Association of America, in coöperation with the Office of Public Road Inquiries of the United States Department of Agriculture, and the Southern Railway Company, will, during the week of February 10 to 15, 1902, in the city of Raleigh, give an exhibition of modern road building, to which all citizens who are interested in that commendable work are invited to come;

"Now, therefore, I, Charles B. Aycock, Governor of the State of North Carolina,, do hereby issue my proclamation calling a good road convention to be held in the city of Raleigh on Wednesday, February 12, and Thursday, February 13, 1902, to which are appointed delegates from the various sections of the State, requesting them and all other good citizens whose convenience will permit to attend said convention.

"Done at our city of Raleigh this the twenty-second day of January, in the year of our Lord one thousand nine hundred and two, and in the one hundred and twenty-sixth year of our American Independence."

CHARLES B. AYCOCK, *Governor.*

It will also be of interest here to quote the address of welcome made by Governor Aycock at this first Convention in which, with his usual wisdom and forcefulness of expression, he set out the reasons why North Carolina should expend her strength in the building of good roads.

It becomes my duty and pleasure this morning, as Governor of North Carolina, to extend to you all, the stranger as well as the citizen, a hearty welcome. I give this welcome to you not only on account of your personality, which would entitle you to a glad greeting anywhere, but particularly on account of the great work which you have assembled to consider and to aid in its progress and development—the work of good roads. The question of good roads touches us at every point. It measures the attendance upon school; we can calculate from the condition of the roads the number who go to church on Sunday; it touches our agricultural life; it meets us in the industries and in commerce; there is no interest in North Carolina which is not affected by it. The great strength of North Carolina has been its love of individual liberty, its devotion to the State. Its weakness has been its isolation. When this great State of ours was settled, our forefathers settled in scattered communities and Mr. Macon aptly expressed the feeling of our people when he said he did not want to live so close to his neighbor that he could hear his dog bark. In that way we lose the power of combination; we miss the strength which comes from unity; we lag behind in the race for wealth and commercial supremacy; and we lose ground in education. This is a rapid age, an age in which every man is on the move. We must do something, if we would keep up with it. The struggle for the good things of life is intense, and we cannot keep the pace with other States and peoples unless we bring to bear the whole power of all the people. We can never educate the children of North Carolina unless we shall have built such roads as bring them close together, whether they live within a few or many miles of each other. We live in an age which does not count distance by miles but by hours. If I should ask any man today how far it is to Washington, he would answer in the number of hours it takes to travel there. We must meet the conditions that confront us. The roads are the only thing in the State of which I am ashamed, because they are in a condition which is without excuse. Captain Galloway once said that there is a sand road in eastern North Carolina 8 miles long and 2 miles deep. The difference between the sand roads in eastern North Carolina and the clay roads of the middle and western parts of the State is that the latter are still longer and deeper. If we expect to get the power of combination and unity, we must make better roads. We have determined to educate all the children of the State. In order to attain that desirable end we must have larger school districts; in order to have these we must put the roads in such condition in the country that the children can attend school from longer distances. There is no interest in the State which is not vitally concerned in the building of public roads; and I extend to you gentlemen from a distance, and to the citizens of North Carolina, to all those who are here, the heartiest welcome, and bid you God-speed in your great work.

As this Convention was held largely under the auspices of the North Carolina Geological Survey, the State Geologist has from that time on acted as Secretary to this Association; and the work of the Association has largely been supplemented by the most active coöperation on the part of the Geological Survey.

The 1913 Annual Convention of the Association was held at Morehead City July 31 and August 1. The convention was called not only by the Good Roads Association but by the North Carolina Geological and Economic Survey, and the survey assisted very materially in the preparations for the convention. Invitations were sent to the mayors of cities, to the chairmen of the boards of county commissioners, to the presidents of the boards of trade and other commercial bodies requesting them to appoint delegates, these being in addition to the regular members of the Association. As the delegates were appointed, special notices were sent to them in regard to the convention. The proceedings of this convention are as follows:

PROCEEDINGS OF CONVENTION

THURSDAY, JULY 31, 10:30 O'CLOCK.

MORNING SESSION.

At ten thirty o'clock in the auditorium of the Atlantic Hotel at Morehead City, the annual convention of the North Carolina Good Roads Association was called to order by the President, Honorable H. B. Varner. He called on the Rev. Euclid McWhorter of the Methodist Church, who opened the convention with the following prayer:

Opening Prayer.

We thank Thee, Heavenly Father, for Thy blessings, for the peace and the quietude which we have enjoyed through the year, and we thank Thee for all the prospects which rise up in our bosoms, for all those things which stand out before us and beckon us on to greatness and usefulness, and to the acknowledgement of our powers in the amelioration of all the conditions about us. We thank Thee for material prosperity on every hand, and running parallel to it, moral and religious side of life, to which we must give praise. We thank Thee for every throb of patriotism. Help us, while we are building highways, opening our ports, and bringing the world into communication with all these things, that we may constantly live to create a high tone of morality and truth of character, that shall make us a city set upon the hill, to the light of which others shall come.

Help these men this morning as they talk about good roads, the bringing of towns closer together, and adding to the comfort and convenience of life, that they shall walk upon that highway which God has already made straight, the Highway of Holiness, upon which the redeemed of God shall walk. Give to these men joy and pleasure, and make their coming in our midst a pleasure to them, so that they may go home refreshed. Bless their families in their absence. Grant unto each of us peace, and save us, we ask in Thy name. Amen.

THE PRESIDENT: I regret very much to announce that it is impossible for the Governor to be here to deliver the address of welcome and to be with us on this occasion. He is considerably run down in his work, and had to take a rest. Therefore he went to the hills, and is now resting a few days. It gives me great pleasure, however, to present to you Hon. Charles L. Abernathy, of Beaufort, who will give the address of welcome in behalf of Morehead City and Carteret County.

Address of Welcome.

MR. CHARES L. ABERNATHY, SOLICITOR OF THE FIFTH DISTRICT.

Mr. President, Ladies and Gentlemen, and Members of the North Carolina Good Roads Association:—I came over here to be a spectator, not expecting to take any part in the speech-making. For some reason the Mayor of Morehead could not be here, and just why this Association should open up with a preacher and a Solicitor of the District just at this time, is one thing that I do not quite understand. I gladly welcome this Association here. We have a historic county. The first people came to this county about 1707. The Port of Beaufort was opened as a port of entry in 1722. This county is 95 miles long and about 15 miles wide, and you can reach any man's house in the county in a boat.

For a good many years our people did not believe in good roads. We could not get them interested in good roads, but since this great movement has swept over North Carolina, it has reached here, and we are proud to know that we are the terminus of that great highway which reaches from Ocean to Ocean. We have issued bonds in Morehead Township, and Newport Township. We have levied a special tax in Beaufort Township, and our people are greatly interested in the good roads movement. We are building this highway which is destined to be one of the greatest in this section of the world. When the harbor at Cape Lookout is opened up with the $3,500,000 appropriated by Congress through the instigation of Senator Simmons and John H. Small, we will have the greatest harbor on the Atlantic Coast; and, with a great harbor and good roads, we expect to see great development in this section.

We are proud to have so many of you here with us. We do not know just what we can offer you in the way of refreshments or amusements. We have an abundant supply of good artesian water. I can go this far but no further. Since the recent enactment of the Legislature by Senator Ward and others, we are living in a better age and a better time. We are glad to know that you people will come here and will be bountifully supplied with the good food of this hotel, that you will drink of our good artesian water, and that you will go home to your wives and your families no worse for the coming. (Applause.)

On behalf of the people of this good town of Beaufort, and Carteret County, I extend a welcome to each and all of you. I hope the day is not far distant in North Carolina when we will take the lead in good roads as well as everything else. I thank you.

THE PRESIDENT: I wish to thank Mr. Abernathy for his very warm welcome he has extended to us on behalf of Morehead City. I will ask Hon. John C. Drewry, of Raleigh, to respond on behalf of the Association.

Response on Behalf of the Association.

HON. JOHN C. DREWRY, OF RALEIGH.

Mr. President, Ladies and Gentlemen:—You will notice that my name is not on this program. Like my friend Abernethy, who has preceded me, I did not know until a little while ago that I had to make the response. I remember a story that was once told me by Senator Gore. He said he was introduced to an audience out west once, by a man who was unaccustomed to speaking in public. This friend got up and said: "Ladies and gentlemen, I am not in the habit of making public speeches, so I will not bore you with a speech. But I will introduce to you Senator Gore who will." (Laughter.) I suppose that was the view that President Varner of the Good Roads Association took, when he introduced me. I cannot understand why a man who is not in the habit of making a public address should have been chosen on this occasion, when we have so many shining lights present; so many eloquent men like Mr. Varner, Dr. Pratt and others, who are well posted on the subject of good roads, and it makes me feel like the old negro preacher who introduced one of his friends to his congregation one Sunday morning. He said: "Brethren and sisters; we have with us today a wonderful man, a man who understands the Bible. He can untangle many of the tangles, solve many of the problems contained in this good Book; he can make darkness light, and crooked things straight. In fact, he can unscrew the unscrutable things in this Book." (Laughter.)

We have with us today Mr. Varner, Dr. Pratt, Mr. Spoon and others, who can not only make crooked roads straight, but they can unscrew the "unscrutable" things that are contained in some of the roads of Wake County. (Applause.)

When you talk about good roads, I feel like my friend from the city who said that he had always had the good roads fever, but it had never broken out on him until he got an automobile. Now he was the darndest kind of fool on the subject. I am about the darndest goose on the subject of good roads in the State, and I am proud to say that I have just returned from an automobile trip through the Shenandoah Valley, up into Pennsylvania, New Jersey and New York, and I want to say, Mr. Varner, for the benefit of the

State of North Carolina, that while we went over some of the most beautiful highways, the best roads we saw in this entire trip were in Franklin County, North Carolina, and those are sand-clay roads. The credit for the building of those roads is due to one man, and that man is Mr. Sam Vann of Franklin County. He has done more for the building of good roads in that county and that section than any other man, and he has made an object lesson to all the people of the State. Mr. Leonard Tufts is another who has done much for the good roads cause. I hope Mr. Tufts is here today. We were in hopes he would be here so that he could tell us about some of the roads of Moore County.

While we want good roads we cannot get them without an effort. It requires an effort to get anything that is worth having, and that reminds me of a story that Zeb Vance used to tell on himself. He said that his servant came to him one day and said, "Governor, I am going to join the Presbyterian Church," and he asked him did he believe in the doctrines of the Presbyterian Church.

"Yassir, I believes in the doctrines of the Presbyterian Church."

"Well, do you believe in predestination?" said Zeb Vance.

"If dat's one of the doctrines, I believes in it."

"Well, do you believe in the doctrine of election?"

"Yassir; I believe in the doctrine of 'lection."

"Now, Sam, do you believe that I have been elected to go to heaven?"

"Well, you see, sah," says Sam, "you ain't never been 'lected to anything you ain't run fer." (Laughter.)

That is the way with good roads. We are never going to be elected to anything when we are not willing to make an effort to obtain it. It takes effort and money to build good roads, and we are moving in the right direction in the Good Roads Association of North Carolina.

I believe I was asked to respond to the address of welcome. We are very glad to be at historic Morehead. We would like to visit all the farmers in a boat. We want to take some boat rides here, and if we cannot get anything but water, we will take water, and most anything else we can get. We are delighted to be with you and enjoy the hospitality of the people of Carteret County. I thank you.

Report of Secretary.

A complete stenographic report of the proceedings of the Convention of the North Carolina Good Roads Association, which was held in Charlotte, August 1 and 2, 1912, is contained in Economic Paper No. 30, of the North Carolina Geological and Economic Survey, copies of which are here for distribution.

Six Good Road circulars have been printed and distributed since the last convention in coöperation with the North Carolina Geological and Economic Survey. One of these contained two county road laws, which were issued for the benefit of the members of the General Assembly desiring to have passed by their counties a desirable road law. One is a general road law providing for the construction and repair of the public roads, and the other is an act to authorize the county commissioners to submit to the voters of the county the question of issuing bonds to make and improve the public roads of said county.

The President and Secretary of the Association did considerable work during the session of the Legislature of 1913 in giving general information to the members in regard to road matters, and in working for State aid in the form of engineering assistance, use of State convicts on the public roads, and of State Security for county bonds. None of these bills, however, were passed.

The State Geologist is constantly receiving requests for road engineering assistance, which he is unable to supply on account of lack of funds; and, for this reason, it is believed that this Association can do no better work than to help bring about sentiment for State engineering assistance to counties.

A great many of the counties and townships proposing bond issues are rural and agricultural without large towns or cities, and these will be greatly benefited through a proper and economical expenditure of their road bonds; but they will be very greatly handicapped by unwise expenditure with poor results. The townships which are able to issue only a small amount of bonds find it hard to get any kind of a road engineer, because the job would not be a long one, and they would not be in a position to pay the salary commanded by an expert road engineer. There are enough instances of this kind in North Carolina to warrant the establishment of a State Highway Commission, or the furnishing of engineering assistance through the North Carolina Geological and Economic Survey. There are also numerous instances of counties and individuals subscribing money for constructing certain roads, this money to be supplemented by the county commissioners of the county, thereby raising enough money to build perhaps several miles of road, if they had competent engineering supervision. A great many requests of this nature have been received.

When a county issues bonds, it is now becoming more common for it to employ its own road engineer; but there are difficulties in the way of this, because a great many of the county laws have not provided for the administration of these funds in such a way as to eliminate it entirely from politics, and no first-class road engineer will permit roads to be located by county politics rather than by his transit and level rod. By the use of State engineers in this instance, the county politics could be eliminated and the roads located where they should go.

So that, I would recommend to this Convention that it work with all possible vigor, not only through its committees but through the individual members, for forms of State aid which have been advocated by the Association for many years:

For the maintenance of not only the surfaced highways but of the dirt roads of the county, through the use of the split-log drag.

For a law providing for the use of wide tires on the public highways, which will help to solve the maintenance problem.

And for the carrying on of a campaign of education until all the counties of the State have fallen into line with good roads throughout their borders.

The Secretary stated that in connection with this convention a number of letters and telegrams had been received from prominent people, expressing their regret at not being able to attend this convention, and these letters are incorporated in this report:

Telegrams.

WASHINGTON, D. C., July 30, 1913.

HENRY B. VARNER,
President, North Carolina Good Roads Association,
Morehead City, N. C.

Best wishes for successful convention. Your association cordially invited to send large delegation to American Road Congress, Detroit, September 29-October 1. (Signed) J. E. PENNYBACKER,
Secretary, American Highways Association.

SPEED, N. C., July 31, 1913.

DR. JOSEPH HYDE PRATT, *Morehead City, N. C.*

Regret very much that we can't be with you; however, urge the wide tire proposition as this is most important for the maintenance of good roads.
(Signed) B. F. SHELTON.

Letters.

WASHINGTON, D. C., July 14, 1913.

MR. HENRY B. VARNER, *Lexington, N. C.*

MY DEAR MR. VARNER: The President directs me to acknowledge the receipt of your letter of July 3rd, and to assure you of his hearty appreciation of your cordial invitation. He regrets that he is unable to accept for the reason that he is declining all invitations to attend public functions during his first year in the White House, in order that his time and attention may be devoted exclusively to his official duties.

With warm thanks in the President's behalf for your courtesy, and with an expression of his best wishes for a successful Convention, I am,

Sincerely yours,
(Signed) J. M. TUMULTY,
Secretary to the President.

WASHINGTON, D. C., July 14, 1913.

DR. JOSEPH HYDE PRATT, *Chapel Hill, N. C.*

MY DEAR MR. PRATT: Your letter of the 12th instant inviting me to attend the Annual Convention of the North Carolina Good Roads Association, to be held at Morehead City, July 31st and August 1st, and advising me as to the progress made in financing good roads in Western North Carolina since the Convention held at Charlotte last summer, has been received.

I appreciate this invitation very highly and should be very glad to accept if I could possibly arrange to do so. However, as I have made all arrangements for a short vacation with my family which will cover the dates of the proposed convention, it will be impracticable for me to be present.

If a suitable opportunity shall present itself during the convention, I shall thank you to express to those in attendance my great regret at being unable to be present, and to assure them of our continued interest in the good roads movement in North Carolina.

With sincere regards and best wishes, I am,

Yours truly,
(Signed) W. W. FINLEY,
President, Southern Railway Company.

WASHINGTON, D. C., July 29, 1913.

DR. JOSEPH HYDE PRATT, *Chapel Hill, N. C.*

MY DEAR MR. PRATT: I received your favor of recent date stating that my name had been placed on the program for Thursday afternoon and the same mail brought me a notice of a caucus of the Democratic Members of the House of Representatives to be held at two o'clock the afternoon of the 31st inst. You see this causes a direct conflict and it will be necessary for me to attend the caucus. I regret this very much as I was looking forward to attending your good roads meeting with much pleasure. Please make announcement when my name is reached on the program and kindly state why I am absent. (Signed) Yours very truly,

H. L. GODWIN,
Congressman from Sixth District.

WASHINGTON, D. C., June 30, 1913.

DR. JOSEPH HYDE PRATT, *Chapel Hill, N. C.*

DEAR DR. PRATT: I am in receipt of your kind favor of the 25th, inviting me to attend and address the Annual Convention of the North Carolina Good Roads Association at Morehead City, N. C., July 31st and August 1st. In reply will say that as I expect to be on the Pacific Coast at that time, I cannot accept.

As one feature of my plan is similar to the bill which efforts were made to enact in North Carolina, my only effort, if present at the convention, would be to impress upon the delegates present the importance of the other features. The principle of utilizing the superior credit of the government was adopted a number of years ago in the Irish Land Purchases Act, but I am informed that it has not been found very effective. That alone does not afford sufficient aid to form an inducement. Neither, in my opinion, will the adoption of the principle in road legislation be sufficient unless combined with something further that will arouse and enlist the activity of the states.

Maintenance is of no less importance than construction, and it seems to me that any plan for Federal or state aid in construction should include aid in maintenance. Otherwise, the policy would be short-sighted.

I was very much interested in your statement that during the past six months about a million and a half dollars have been raised in North Carolina by counties and townships in Western North Carolina, for road purposes. I assume that this was raised by bond issues, as that was the subject you were discussing. I should be interested in knowing how these bonds are generally issued and sold, the rate of interest, etc. It has been my opinion that bonds should be issued in small denominations and sold at par by popular subscription, rather than in large denominations by competitive bid. In the case of large bond issues, there is practically no competition. I believe it good public policy to encourage all citizens to invest their savings in public securities. Such investments make them better citizens by giving them a new interest in their county, state or nation.

I also think the educational feature of Federal or state aid is of great importance and for that reason have incorporated in my plan a provision for a National Academy of Highway and Bridge Engineering. Whether this institution be established or not, I believe state institutions should give such attention as is practicable to instruction along this line. In case a national school be established, the state institutions should give preparatory courses, leading to the special work of the National Academy.

With best wishes for the success of your convention,

Yours very truly,

(Signed) JONATHAN BOURNE, JR.

ASHEVILLE, N. C., August 13, 1913.

EXECUTIVE COMMITTEE, NORTH CAROLINA GOOD ROADS ASSOCIATION:

The Asheville Board of Trade, representing nearly seven hundred of Asheville's progressive citizens and business men, extend a very hearty and cordial invitation to the North Carolina Good Roads Association to meet at Asheville in 1914.

Asheville is the ideal Convention City of the South, and, as you know, organized the first good roads association south of the Mason and Dixon line, which association has been and is a live wire in spreading the gospel of good roads as well as actually building them.

It is a pleasure to announce that through the efforts of Col. Dell M. Potter, President of the Southern National Highway; the local North Carolina Division of that Highway and the Board of Trade, the American Automobile Association has agreed to log all the Southern Highway from Washington to the Pacific Coast via the highways as indicated at the February meeting in Asheville. This, as you know, names the Central Highway as the Eastern end of the Ocean to Ocean Highway.

Within less than a year, $1,447,000 in good road bonds have been voted by a few counties in Western North Carolina and the road fever is now at a high pitch.

Again urging you to accept our hospitality in 1914, we are,

Yours very truly,

(Signed) N. BUCKNER,

Secretary, Asheville Board of Trade.

WASHINGTON, D. C., August 12, 1913.

DR. JOSEPH HYDE PRATT, *Chapel Hill, N. C.*

MY DEAR DR. PRATT: I have always been kind of prejudiced against the fellow who said he would appear and didn't. Frankly, I thought that you had seen my face enough times down in North Carolina to welcome a change, and so didn't count upon being with you recently at the Morehead gathering. It would not have been possible in any event on account of my western trip, and so I didn't say that I would be with you. Apparently Mr. Diehl's letter, carbon copy of which reached me later, must have been misleading. If any apology is due I am going to hope that you will accept one from me, knowing that at all times I am ready to aid in every possible way in helping you out in North Carolina, in the future of which State I have utmost confidence.

With kindest regards, Yours very truly,

(Signed) A. G. BATCHELDER,

American Automobile Association.

THE PRESIDENT: The Treasurer, Mr. Joseph G. Brown, was not

able to be present on account of sickness in his home, and I will read his report:

Report of Treasurer.

To the North Carolina Good Roads Association:

Gentlemen: I beg to submit herewith report of receipts and disbursements:

Balance on hand, July 27, 1913	$ 39.04
Receipts	311.50
Total	$350.54
Disbursements as per vouchers	321.87
Balance on hand	28.67
Total	$350.54

Respectfully submitted,

(Signed) Jos. G. Brown,
Treasurer.

This report was audited by a committee of the convention and approved.

Following this some facts and figures were given by Dr. Pratt in regard to road legislation passed by the General Assembly of 1913, with a brief review of the road work accomplished in the State since the last convention:

Review of Road Legislation Passed by the General Assembly of 1913, With Brief Review of Road Work in the State Since the Last Convention.

A great many acts were passed by the General Assembly of 1913 relating to the building of roads through bond issues and by special tax. Some of these acts related to the county, as a whole, and others to townships. There is a great lack of uniformity in these bills, and variations in the methods of issuing bonds, some bond issues being authorized by election on a set date, some by election on petition of county commissioners; others to be directly issued by the county commissioners without any vote or petition, except the instruction of the General Assembly; and still others to be issued at the discretion of the county commissioners. In some cases, the election will be carried if the majority of the votes cast are in favor of bonds; in others, if the majority of the qualified voters cast their votes in favor of bonds. Some of the acts call for special road or highway commissioners to take charge of the road work, and others place the work under the county or township commissioners.

Of the bills passed there were twenty-seven general county bills providing for bond issues in various sums aggregating a total of $6,315,000. One hundred and five townships or road districts have been authorized to vote upon $2,762,500, and a general act applying to all the counties of the State, except four, provides that any township can issue bonds not exceeding

$50,000 with interest coupons at not exceeding five per cent, the elections to be called by the various Boards of County Commissioners upon petition of one-fourth the qualified voters of any township, and notice of thirty days shall be given thereof. In many cases, this act may work to the detriment of good roads. There is no question whatever but that the county should be the unit in road construction, and that the township should not issue township bonds for road work until the county has refused to do this. In the latter event it is right and proper that the individual township should not be kept back in its advancement on account of the county, but should have the right to issue township bonds.

About fifty-five counties have been included in special acts, and all the counties of the State except one (Anson) can take advantage of the general act for bond issues for road construction. In other words, practically the entire State is in a position now to provide funds for the building of roads through bond issues.

Below is given the amount of bonds which have been issued or voted since the General Assembly adjourned the first of March:

County.		*Amount of bonds.*
Brunswick:		
Two Townships	(Validated)	$20,000
Buncombe		50,000
Burke:		
Moganton Township		50,000
Carteret:		
Morehead and Newport Townships		13,000
Cleveland:		
No. 7 Township		50,000
Davie		175,000
Duplin:		
Two Townships	(Bonds legalized)	30,000
Edgecombe		200,000
Henderson		25,000
Hendersonville Township		50,000
Hooper's Creek Township		20,000
Edneyville Township		12,000
Jackson:		
Cullowhee Township		20,000
Dillsboro Township		15,000
Sylva Township		30,000
Lincoln		200,000
McDowell:		
Marion Township		50,000
Nebo Township		10,000
Old Fort Township		20,000
Macon:		
Franklin Township		100,000
Madison		300,000
Martin:		
Hamilton Township		40,000
Robersonville Township		50,000

Moore:	
Deep River Township	$12,500
Greenwood Township	10,000
Mineral Springs Township	10,000
Nash:	
Mannings Township	50,000
New Hanover	100,000
Pitt:	
Greenville Township	30,000
Polk	100,000
Rutherford	250,000
Stokes:	
Danbury Township	15,000
Meadows Township	40,000
Sauratown Township	50,000
Surry:	
Mt. Airy Township	80,000
Vance	200,000
Wayne:	
Goldsboro Township	100,000
Brogden Township	40,000
Yancey	150,000

As will be seen from the above, $2,737,000 have been voted or validated for the building of good roads in twenty-five counties and thirty townships during the past five months. The question that now comes up is: Will this money be spent to the best advantage of the counties and township? Would it not be more economical for the State to furnish an engineer who could probably attend to the work of several counties or townships?

Below is given a brief digest of road work done in the State during 1912, which is shown by statistics collected by the North Carolina Geological and Economic Survey in coöperation with the U. S. Office of Public Roads:

Total amount of money raised by special tax for road work (expended for maintenance, construction, and interest and sinking fund on bond issues)	*$1,118,942
Amount of bonds issued during 1912	†965,000
Number of County bond issues	13
Number of Township bond issues	32
Number of Counties using convicts on public roads	37
Approximately the number of convicts used during 1912	1,500
Number of Counties leasing convicts to other counties	37

ROAD MILEAGE.

Number of miles of public roads in State	48,870
Number of miles of macadam (water-bound) built during 1912	71¾
Average cost of macadam per mile	$3,150
Number of miles of sand-clay road built during 1912	742½
Average cost per mile of constructing sand-clay road	$730

*This does not include all the poll tax, accurate figures for which we have not been able to secure. In some counties there is also a special dog tax.

†These bond issues have been by the counties or townships.

Number of miles of gravel road built during 1912	250
Average cost per mile of building gravel road	$1,000
Number of miles of specially surfaced road built during 1912 (tar, asphalt, or bituminous macadam)	21¼
Number of miles of dirt road graded during 1912	642½
Total number of miles of road built and surfaced during 1912	1,061¼
Total number of miles improved, including surfaced and graded road, during 1912	1,728
Number of miles of unimproved road in the State	43,767

It will be seen from the above that the mileage of macadam road as built in the State is very small in comparison with the sand-clay and gravel road, and that the sand-clay is getting to be more and more the road which can be built to the best advantage in most of our counties, particularly in the rural sections of the county. Wherever the sand-clay road has not given satisfaction, it will be found that it was not properly built, and the point that we wish to stress is that such a road cannot be built by an amateur. It requires skill and experience to build this kind of road; and, when first built, if properly maintained, it is practically indestructible. It will be noted that we still have a large mileage of unimproved road in the State,—about 43,767 miles—which is undoubtedly taxing the citizens of the State to the extent of $10,000,000 to $12,000,000. To get rid of this enormous burden and at the same time get our money's worth of the bond issues and special tax money, etc., which will be spent all over the State is the problem now facing us; and to solve it two factors must be eliminated; first, politics in the administration of the road funds; and second, inexperience in the location and building of the roads. These two factors enter largely into the problem of any county and township, so much so that engineers will throw up their work rather than locate roads against their judgment.

One State engineer could readily do the work of one, two, or even four counties. His work would be subject to the approval of his Department, which would be a guarantee of efficient work; local politics would be eliminated in the location of roads (a most important consideration); competent engineers would be available, whereas at the present time the demand is infinitely greater than the supply; and the chances for the wise and economical expenditure of the $9,000,000 of bond money now being considered by the various counties and townships increased at least seventy-five per cent.

That the county officials are realizing the need for expert advice and assistance in their road building is a most encouraging sign, and this is all the more reason why the State should meet the demand. At the present time the Geological Survey has twenty-five applications on file for road engineering assistance, which it is unable to supply, simply because, with the meagre appropriation now given for this work, it is not possible to employ a staff of engineers; and this need can not be met unless the State provides a sum sufficient to meet the needs of such a department.

It seems to me if the State is to continue as a State, and not as a collection of counties and townships, there is no more important or urgent service she can render her individual units than to see to it that these sums of money (representing in many cases a real sacrifice in some of the poorer sections) are properly, efficiently, and advantageously expended; and a State appropriation necessary to do this, of say $50,000 annually to start with, is very small in view of the immense benefits and savings to the counties and townships which would undoubtedly result.

The President: Next on the program is an address by Hon. Chas. H. Davis, of Massachusetts, and although he has sent three or four representatives of the National Highways Association, we feel very much disappointed that he could not come in person to deliver the admirable address. He has prepared for the North Carolina Good Roads Convention and has gone to the trouble and expense of having it printed his address on "Good Roads Everywhere," and it is for distribution. I want every member of this Association to have a copy of this address because it relates solely to North Carolina and he has illustrated his address with some views of North Carolina, and has also prepared a map showing the various highways of North Carolina. I wish Mr. Davis could have been here to have received the commendation and appreciation of this Convention for the great work he is doing for *good roads everywhere.* He wants to see good roads not only in North Carolina and in Massachusetts, but *everywhere.* He is doing a magnificent work.

Below is given Mr. Davis's address:

Good Roads Everywhere.

Charles Henry Davis, President National Highways Association.

"See America first!" During the year 1912 more than 100,000 tourists crossed the water to "do" Europe—the Galleries of Italy, the Cathedrals of England, Paris, and all the other places which they were obliged to visit because it was the proper thing to do—while "doing" Europe.

But what part of the trip was most enjoyed by the great majority? Certainly not the hot, stuffy galleries, nor the dark and gloomy cathedrals. The vast majority will tell you, if they tell you honestly, that it was out-of-doors where the most enjoyment and recreation were found,—the mountains, Switzerland, the Italian Lakes, the Rhine, Wales, the fords of Norway.

Europe caters to tourists—especially American tourists. Everything is provided for their comfort—for a consideration. Much of the population of Switzerland derive their living from American tourists.

The State of North Carolina possesses scenery the equal of any in the world. Its mountain-peaks are among the loftiest east of the Rockies. Their slopes are covered with a more varied fauna and flora than are found in most other sections of the country. Rhododendron, azalea, ferns, galax leaves, balsam, and spruce grow in utmost profusion. Brooks, waterfalls, mirror lakes, abound everywhere. The air is invigorating; trout-fishing is excellent.

But why are these facts not known? Why do not pleasure-seekers flock to the Carolina Mountains—and see America first? Why do so many endure the tortures of seasickness, the discomforts of foreign customs, to journey to the distant Alps when equal or superior attractions are at their threshold? Why does not the money which these tourists so lavishly distribute accrue to the people of this country and to the State of North Carolina?

An answer is found in roads. Good roads abound in Europe. Highways built primarily for scenic purposes are common in Switzerland, France, and Germany, and most of the other countries of Europe. In America they are so limited as to be almost negligible.

Through the efforts and influence of Dr. Joseph Hyde Pratt, State Geologist, and his many co-workers, there has been formed an association, known as the Appalachian Highway Company, whose purpose is to build a scenic highway through the heart of the mountains of western North Carolina. This road, which is now under construction, is known as the "Crest of the Blue Ridge Highway," and will, when completed, be about 353 miles long, extending from Marion, Va., to Cornelia, Ga., nearly all of which lies within the borders of North Carolina. At the north this highway will eventually connect with the Bristol-Washington Highway, which continues through Roanoke and the beautiful Shenandoah Valley to the National Capital. On the south it will continue by the National Highway to Atlanta, thus affording a through route from Washington into the heart of the South, which is probably unexcelled anywhere in the world.

But great as the effect of this highway will be in bringing tourists, automobilists, and others into North Carolina, with the many benefits to the people of that State, financial and otherwise, it will be far surpassed by the cheapening of transportation and consequent agricultural development adjacent to the road.

The soil in the mountain country is most productive. There are excellent and productive farms along all the valleys, in the coves, and even on the very top of the mountains. All the produce from these farms must be hauled to the railroads by teams. The present roads are of the worst—during the spring rains the farm wagons are commonly up to the hub in mud.

The "Crest of the Blue Ridge Highway" will drain practically all of Watauga and Ashe counties, and a considerable share of Mitchell, Caldwell, and McDowell counties, and will at first be the only good road in this region. Certainly, its future value to agricultural development is assured.

North Carolina has made great progress in good road construction during the last ten years. No State in the Union has more varied conditions to contend with in highway construction. Extending five hundred miles from the coast westward, it embraces within its borders all varieties of topography, from the lowlands of the coastal plain to the steep mountain ranges of the western part of the State. Furthermore, North Carolina is largely an agricultural State and has no very large centers of population, trade, or accumulated wealth upon which to draw a large revenue for highway construction. The burden falls upon the rural districts. In spite of this, the movement for Good Roads Everywhere has spread all over North Carolina, and many excellent intercounty and interstate roads are now constructed or in the process of construction.

But, notwithstanding all this most praiseworthy work, there are still far more than 90 per cent of the public roads of North Carolina which remain unimproved. Likewise, in the United States as a whole, less than 10 per cent of the roads are improved. Therefore let us illustrate the case of North Carolina by reference to our great National problem as a whole.

To have Good Roads Everywhere throughout these United States will mean more to this nation than any other development since our Declaration of Independence. During all ages it has been of primary importance to provide a people with means of intercommunication. People, like water, must move or stagnate. They must run and play like the brook itself or become sluggish and dull—to themselves as well as to others. Of the seven modes of intercommunication—water, roads, postal, railroad, telegraph, telephone, and wireless—only one, roads, is free to all the people of the earth. Roads are the most universally used and are therefore the most beneficial to the greatest number of people. The importance of Good Roads Everywhere is paramount—their benefits are all-embracing.

It has been estimated that more than five billion tons of freight pass over our highways per annum. The present average haul is a little under ten (10) miles; the cost, about twenty-three (23) cents per ton mile. This cost should not exceed eight (8) cents per ton mile on a good road. In other words, at least one dollar and a half ($1.50) could and should be saved on every ton moved on our highways. Thus the annual saving from good roads is almost beyond comprehension.

Seven and one-half billions of dollars per annum! This would build fifteen (15) Panama Canals a year; fifteen hundred (1,500) dreadnaughts a year; it would reproduce all of the 250,000 miles of railroads in the United States within a period of three (3) years. It represents one quarter of the entire annual wealth produced by this great nation!

But this is only one of the enormous financial savings which would be brought about by Good Roads Everywhere. They would increase farm values; reduce wear and tear of vehicles, harness, and horses; reduce the investment cost of extra horses and vehicles; and bring numerous other benefits measurable in dollars and cents. But staggering as these financial benefits are proven to be, even greater still are those whose worth cannot be reduced to a money value; namely, social, moral, and educational. To take the latter point as an illustration:

There are eighteen million (18,000,000) children who endeavor to attend school. There are over thirty million (30,000,000) who should attend school. Why don't they? Largely because during much of the school term a considerable part of the two million (2,000,000) miles of our roads is impassable. This is shown by the fact that only nine tenths of one per cent (0.9%) urban white population of the United States of native parentage is illiterate, while rural illiteracy is six hundred (600) per cent greater in the same class of inhabitants. How can we have or get good schools in the rural districts if we have not the good roads to reach them at all times and in all seasons?

The relation of good and bad roads to illiteracy is indicated by the following table:

	Native Whites of Native Parentage / Total Population (1910)	Per Cent Improved Roads (1909)	Per Cent of Illiterate Native Whites of Native Parentage (1910)		
			Total	Urban	Rural
NEW ENGLAND: Maine, New Hampshire, Massachusetts, Rhode Island, Connecticut.	2,135,801 / 6,552,681	22.2	0.7	0.5	1.2
SOUTH ATLANTIC: Delaware, Maryland, Virginia, West Virginia, North Carolina, South Carolina, Georgia, Florida	5,397,864 / 12,194,895	6.0	8.0	2.2	9.8
PACIFIC: Washington, Oregon, California	1,684,658 / 4,192,304	14.2	0.4	0.3	0.6
WEST SOUTH CENTRAL: Arkansas, Louisiana, Oklahoma, Texas	4,101,510 / 8,784,534	5.6	5.6	1.4	6.8

This table does not of course include foreign born, native born of foreign parentage, or negroes, all of which are excluded for obvious reasons. Illiteracy is eleven (11) times greater in the South Atlantic States than in New England, while the percentage of improved roads (such as they are) is about one-fourth. Similar figures for the Pacific and West South Central are: fourteen (14) times greater illiteracy, while the percentage of improved roads is less than half as much. The increase in illiteracy in rural New England is only one hundred and forty (140) per cent above the urban population, while in the South Atlantic States this increase is nearly three hundred and fifty (350) per cent, due to the lower percentage of improved roads. This difference is slightly greater in comparing the other two groups in the table.

The children of today are the electors, the representatives, the senators, the judges, one of them the President, of tomorrow. The population is increasing by leaps and bounds. If education means liberty, and if poor roads mean illiteracy or worse, have we a right *not* to build good roads, even if they would not pay for themselves well within the generation which builds them?

Such indisputable facts and figures can be multiplied indefinitely to show the paramount necessity of Good Roads Everywhere. We have been unprogressive, but now as a nation we are waking up to these facts. The people of the nation are ready. Public sentiment is strong. What we need is a definite, logical plan to bring about Good Roads Everywhere—speedily, economically, uniformly.

Let us turn to the history of highways in this country. In the early days road-building was largely confined to the efforts of local communities—the villages, towns, and cities. The town road officials directed these improvements, sought the appropriations therefor, and controlled the work and expenditures. But this caused the growth of a disjointed system of roads. One town spent more money and built better roads than the adjoining town.

Thus jealousies were aroused between the local communities until finally a larger unit, the county, took over the more important routes and built roads of uniform construction, connecting the various portions of the county in a much more comprehensive and efficient manner. But soon the same difficulties developed upon a larger scale. No attention was paid to intercounty highways, and, consequently, roads developed which did not properly connect the various parts of the State; hence the creation of State Highway Commissions and State Highways. There were also other reasons for this. Larger appropriations could be obtained from the State. Bonds could be issued by the State at a lower rate of interest. Uniformity of construction and maintenance could be secured. Accentuation in town and county road improvement was not the least of the beneficial results obtained.

But now we are confronted with still larger problems—the development of good roads throughout the nation and connecting all parts of the United States. Should we not apply the lessons learned by the experience of the past? Can effective interstate highways be obtained efficiently, speedily, and economically through the disjointed efforts of the several states, each working independently, no matter how excellent their individual efforts may be? And can Federal "Aid" to these separate States produce anything but the present chaos—poor roads, impassable roads, roads beginning nowhere, ending nowhere—and at the cost of millions of dollars annually? No! What we need is National Highways. Highways beginning somewhere, ending somewhere. Highways constructed according to some definite plan and along uniform lines throughout the whole United States. Highways backed by the people of the whole Nation, coöperating and working together for the greatest benefit to all. It is no longer a local problem. It is a national problem, and can be met only by the whole Nation working together as a unit.

National Highways built, owned, maintained, and controlled by the National Government under the direction of a National Highways Commission constitutes the one and only logical plan to bring about a unified and therefore effective system of highways throughout the entire country.

The National Highways Association has devised a plan, and the only plan yet advanced, for a comprehensive and unified system of Good Roads Everywhere in these United States.

This system of National Highways of not exceeding 50,000 miles (only 2% of our mileage) is so located as to serve over sixty (60) per cent of our population. At the high figure of $20,000 per mile this system would cost $1,000,000,000. A lot of money? Yes. But the United States Government gave $1,000,000,000 to our privately owned railroads to help build them. Can not it afford to spend an equal amount in building our highways? Would not this do more good to more people, a thousand times over, than lining the pockets of a few favored individuals at the expense of the many? To say nothing of the fact that such expenditures would in a very few years be returned a hundred-fold to the whole people in the multitude of savings thus brought about.

The argument, advanced by many, that we want market roads is undoubtedly sound. We do want them; but how are we to get them? That we want good roads from farm to railroad is equally sound. How are we to get them? Does this argue against National Highways? Quite the opposite. The same argument was advanced in the early development of railroads. The farmer of one State believed he did not want to reach another State. He thought he wanted short pieces of railroad to reach nearby centers. Did he get them? Were they the first to be built? Not at all. The Pennsylvania Railroad pushed on to Pittsburgh and the West, long before its many present branches were built. The New York Central and Lake Shore grew to Chicago after the same manner. Likewise the Northern, Union, and Southern Pacific and all the other great Western railroads. The branches developed after the trunk lines were built, and were supported by and acted as feeders to these trunk lines. It must be the same with roads. They, being also means of communication, must follow the same law. If the farmer waits for the reversal of this law he will die "in the mud." But, on the other hand, a system of National Highways will encourage and accentuate the building of Good Roads Everywhere—market roads, roads from farm to railroad, and all other local and branch roads, whether built by State, county, city, township, or town, for the collecting and distributing medium of these National Highways.

Such a system of National Highways will, at first, be paid for mostly by the large, rich centers of population. The greatest immediate and lasting benefit will accrue to the rural districts that will furnish the least toward their building. The greatest increase in real estate values will come to the rural districts. The decreased cost of hauling farm products will benefit them also. Enormous sums will be spent in country communities that otherwise would be diverted elsewhere. And this is as it should be; for the cities derive wealth automatically from the rural districts and should be willing to return it automatically through highway building, from which they in turn will benefit as much.

Such, in brief, is the plan of the National Highways Association. Magnificent in its conception! Definite! Logical! Effective! If it can be put into effect it will mean more than all the navies of the seas; it will be more valuable than a dozen Panama Canals; it will be more important than anything ever done by any Government since the dawn of this Nation. In a word, it will mean an increased measure of happiness for every resident under our Stars and Stripes.

To favor, foster, and further the development of National Highways in the length and breadth of these United States of America will secure the benefits —social, moral, commercial, industrial, material, educational, and personal— in the progress and uplift of the American people which follow in the train of easy and free intercommunication and transit from the great rural productive areas of the Nation to the great centers of population and distribution, and will "bind the United States together in a common brotherhood, and thus perpetuate and preserve the Union."

Following this was an address by Capt. Langdon, of the United States Army, as follows:

The Military Value of Good Roads.

By Captain Russell C. Langdon.

Mr. President, Ladies and Gentlemen of the Good Roads Convention:—I thank you for the opportunity of saying a few words on the subject of the "Military Value of Good Roads."

Being on duty in your State as the representative of the War Department in the instruction and inspection of your militia troops, it naturally strikes me that you are increasing the defensive potentiality of North Carolina by improving your roads.

We live in an age when *universal peace* is being talked of all over the world. And yet since the foundation of The Hague Tribunal there has not been a year in which thousands of lives have not been sacrificed in battle. While we all earnestly desire peace, and while the world is undoubtedly coming nearer to its ideal, we must not be blind to actual facts, and to use a familiar saying, we must "make haste slowly."

We will all admit that our commercial activity brings us into close competition with powerful neighbors. We are attempting to enforce a doctrine of international diplomacy which as been tolerated but not accepted in the chancelleries of Europe.

We teach our children the fallacy that a patriotic but untrained American is the equal of several of the best soldiers of Europe. And yet we permitted Great Britain to invade Maryland in 1814, and burn our capitol in Washington. We have permitted Mexican bandits to invade our soil time and again. We allowed Canadians to invade one of our states with an armed force in 1863. We saw Spain execute Americans without a trial in the Virginius affair at Santiago.

Great Britain, Germany, France, and even Spain can each place upon our shores right here in Morehead City more troops than we can place here in the same length of time. In short, I counsel all of you to read Homer Lea's splendid book, "The Valor of Ignorance," in order to get an idea of America's unpreparedness.

We cannot depend upon railroads for the movement of troops because of the small amount of rolling stock on hand. To move one regiment of infantry of war strength with all of its animals and wagons requires the following rolling stock: About forty tourist cars, fourteen baggage cars or freight cars, eight flat cars and thirteen horse cars.

But we have neither the troops nor the rolling stock in anything like adequate numbers. Even if the railroads had sufficient tracks and rolling stock, we must have a network of good, hard, serviceable roads over which our infantry, cavalry, artillery, baggage wagons, ammunition wagons, etc., can move to the threatened point. It may be said that the good roads would aid the invaders just as much as they would aid us. Were the enemy to possess the detailed information necessary to enable him to select the best roads for his advance, this would in a very limited sense be true. Upon giving the matter a little consideration we can readily see that to successfully resist an invader we must meet him *before he has a chance to use our roads.* Furthermore, we must move troops from many directions in order to converge upon him. Hence, we would always use more roads than he.

But it is not alone in a defensive war that we need roads. To place our troops where they can best entrain or embark for a foreign war requires good roads, for our railroad service may be crippled or it may not have adequate facilities at the point of departure.

This leads us to consider the men who have to march upon these roads. A large proportion of them will be our militia soldiers.

Before closing I want to say a word in behalf of the citizen soldiers of your state, as this subject, besides being constantly in my mind, is naturally brought up in yours when I speak of war.

North Carolina has splendid material in her militia soldiers. But they need better opportunities for training. They greatly lack suitable armories. Due to poor roads, it is impossible for them, in many cases, to reach adequate maneuver grounds without great waste of time. They are wage earners, and time is precious with them.

We are merely preparing for the defense of our country, and for the attainment of that honorable and stable peace, which with us should always be the one aim of war.

Why State Convicts Should be Used on the Public Roads.

By H. B. Varner, President.

I find that my name is on the program to make a speech on the subject "Why Convicts Should be Used on the Public Roads." I have been so busy with road campaigns, and with my duties as Chairman of the Central Highway Trustees, that I have made no preparation whatever.

In the beginning I want to say that I do not blame the men who are profiting by the present system of the State giving away its convict labor, and I do not blame them to fight to hold on to it—that's human nature. Most any of us would kick and raise a great row and use all the influence possible before we would surrender such a soft snap as receiving $358 per day in the way of convict labor from the State, without giving anything of value in return. These gentlemen who are promoting these railroad projects are splendid fellows, it is true, but there are lots of good fellows in this State who are just as much entitled to this bonus from the State as these men are.

Some of the newspapers have been criticizing my action along this line, because I have been trying to do something for the good of the State with the State's convicts. At the present time, as you all know, I presume, the State convicts are being worked on the State's farm, and on the various railroads of the State. Now, when I mention that they have been worked on the railroads, do not get the idea that they are being hired out to these railroads, that the railroads are taking care of them, and are paying the State something for their services. This is a mistake. They are being employed *not* by real railroads, but by lumber railroads, and roads promoted for personal gain by a favored few. The promoters of these projects get bills logrolled through the Legislature, providing that the State shall furnish convicts to these roads, that the State shall board them, keep them, and take care of them in every way, and that the State will take in payment stock in the railroads, and we have to-day in the Treasury of the State something over $400,000 in stock of this character. The State has paid the board for these convicts, which is something like 66 cents per day each. They have gone down in the Treasury and have taken the hard-earned tax money of the people and paid this expense, and have done this work on these railroads, and have taken in payment stock that is absolutely worthless. A few days ago I saw the Chief Clerk of the Treasury Department in a meeting, and I asked him what was the value of this stock. He said it was absolutely worthless. I knew it was worthless, but I wanted to have it authoritatively. We are throwing away this convict labor; we are giving it away, not for the good of the people of a few counties, but to enrich promoters. We are giving away $358 of convict labor each day, which amounts to $104,700 every year. At the same time we could hire out every convict in the State to real railroads, and get $1.50 a day cash for their work. Now, if we are going to work the convicts on the railroads, we ought to hire them out to railroads that will pay us cash, and thereby wipe out the deficit in the State's Treasury.

As Chairman of the State Prison Board, I made a report to the Governor of the State, expressing these sentiments, and to-day I am being denounced by certain newspapers, who seem to be more interested in the welfare of the men who are securing this convict labor than they are in the welfare of the State. I want the people to understand this proposition, and when they do, I am sure they will instruct their members of the Legislature what to do. This policy of giving away our convict labor must be stopped, and will be stopped. The convicts ought not to be worked in competition with the farmers; they should be worked on the public roads, and build wagon roads and let the counties or road districts pay the actual expenses of working these convicts, so that it would not be a drain upon the State Treasury. We would be encouraging road building and helping the counties build up North Carolina, and make it the good State it ought to be.

This is my idea. The State of Georgia is putting all of her convicts on the public roads and building market roads to the towns, and the result is that Georgia is going far ahead of all southern states in road building and general development along all lines. Dr. Pratt and myself and a number of other good roads advocates spent some time with the General Assembly during January of this year, trying to advise the legislators about this convict proposition, but the legislators seemed to think they knew more about it than we did, and refused to heed the request of this Association in regard to the State's convicts being put on the roads. It was due to the fact that so much lobbying was done and that the legislators did not understand the proposition that these convicts are allowed to be put on these railroads. We ought to stop this fraud and begin building roads and do something for the good of the State. I do not believe my friend, Senator Ward, would vote for this policy to continue if he understood it, because he wants to vote right. There were acts passed by the recent General Assembly calling for nearly 2,000 convicts to work on various railroads and other projects to be paid for in worthless stock—chips and whetstones—absolutely throwing the convict labor away. We go down in the State Treasury and take out something like $1.50 per day and get in return absolutely nothing but worthless stock.

We ought to take some steps at this convention in regard to this matter. Now, at the last Good Roads Convention, there was lobbying done in favor of continuing the policy by men connected with the State government. Men were there muddying the waters. I am not running for any office. If I was, I probably would not talk this way. Certain newspapers gave out that I was thinking about running for Congress, and some one thing and some another. I am not wanting office at present, thank the Lord. I would rather help "bust" up this infamous convict system than to hold any little office. This is the greatest office I have ever held, an office of service to the

State, working without reward or the hope of reward, except the consciousness of knowing that I am doing my duty to the people of the State, aiding in my feeble way in the elevation and the betterment of mankind. It is a pity, indeed, that a man cannot attempt to do anything of this kind unless he is charged with running for an office.

What I want is to stop giving away this convict labor, and put them on the public roads. And then you will see North Carolina go forward in road building and general development along all lines, and she will stand in the forefront of all the states of the Union.

I thank you very much for your attention.

DISCUSSION.

Mr. Bennehan Cameron, of Durham County: Mr. Chairman, in view of your remarks, I think there are two or three points that will permit of discussion. You stated that you did not know how Senator Ward voted; I have got that confidence in him and in his desire to vote for the welfare of North Carolina that makes me feel that he voted right. And in connection with that I want to take this opportunity here in this presence to thank Senator Ward for the great and many kindnesses he performed for the roads cause in the legislature.

We got him to play a very important part in connection with the bill asking for coöperation of the states of Tennessee and Arkansas and other states in the line of our Transcontinental Highway, and I take this opportunity to express to him in a public way my indebtedness to him for that work.

I am sure he voted right in this other matter.

Dr. Pratt: I would like to say a few words in connection with what work the State convicts should do. We have made a pretty careful study of the convict question, and the Survey has made the study, not only in this State, but it has spent considerable time in studying the convict labor question in a great many states. It is becoming the unanimous opinion that the best use that can be made of them is by working them on the public roads, both from a moral and physical standpoint, and condition of the convict. There is hardly a State in this country which is now looking upon the convict as collateral out of which the State shall try to make just as much as it can. We are beginning to look upon the convict as a man, and that we must in our treatment of the convict do what we can to make him a better man when he gets through his sentence, realizing that he must again become a citizen of the community from which he was convicted. And we believe by working the convict on the public road we are doing more toward the upbuilding of his life than any other work that we could put him on. We know of instances in Virginia where the convicts have received, at the end of their term of sentence, good positions, some of them as road builders, some as farmers; and some in the squads have gotten positions from farmers living along the roads on which they have worked.

When a man commits a crime against society, I know of no better way for him to pay the penalty than to work him on the public roads, in which society, as a whole, is interested. We do not now look upon the convict as collateral out of which the State can make so much money. We lose sight of this in our zeal to make of him a better man and enable him to be a better citizen of society, when his sentence is over.

Mr. Douglass, of Wake County: I am in favor of memorializing this second session of the Legislature. I think, as you do, that it is an urgent matter, and it ought to be attended to. I have never examined into this matter and do not know whether the contracts are binding or not, but I move that we appoint a committee of three to investigate this matter for a few hours and see what we can do along the line of taking the convicts off of these railroads, and putting them on the public roads.

PRESIDENT: All in favor of appointing a committee of three to investigate this question of memorializing the next session of the Legislature in trying to get the convicts off these railroads and putting them on the public roads, will please say "Aye," all opposed, "No." Carried unanimously.

PRESIDENT: I will appoint as that committee, Mr. W. C. Douglass, of Wake, Chairman; R. R. Cotten, of Pitt County, and William Dunn, of Craven County.

Mr. Cameron: I move that a resolution be passed that it is the sentiment of this Association that such a Highway Commission should be established by the Legislature. Motion carried.

EVENING SESSION.

THURSDAY, JULY 31, 8 P. M.

The evening session was held in the Red Men's Hall, as it was felt that a number of the Morehead City people would attend here, who were unable to get down to the hotel.

The first speaker of the evening session was Mr. W. L. Spoon, of the United States Office of Public Roads, who spoke as follows:

Sand-Clay and Earth Road Maintenance.

BY W. L. SPOON, HIGHWAY ENGINEER, U. S. OFFICE OF PUBLIC ROADS.

The problem of road maintenance antedates the construction of the road. This statement may surprise you, but it is nevertheless a fact, and too frequently entirely overlooked in the preliminary and final surveys and location, to say nothing of the actual construction. Too often locations are made as if it would never rain after the road is built. The construction of the road, bridges and culverts take into consideration no possible accidents due to rain and storm water. As a result the bridge foundations undermine, the throat is too small, and in consequence not only the bridge is wrecked or totally washed away, but the approaches on one or both sides torn away beside. An ounce of know-how preventative in such a case would be far better than the many pounds of expensive cure in subsequent maintenance.

The importance of right locations and proper provision for storm water cannot be too strongly urged, for it is my observation that the great burden of maintenance is not due to travel but to the destructive effect of rain storms. Hence the question of repair lies primarily in the hands of the locating and constructing engineer, and the expense of subsequent upkeep will be largely determined by his decisions. It has been truthfully said over and over again that drainage is the fundamental in road building and right maintenance. The side, the top and the bottom of the road all need proper drainage. The side ditch should have fall enough to free it of standing water in every place, and yet not enough to cause a gully to wash. It should be for the road and not a farm drain for receiving all the terrace and ditch water from adjacent fields. If farmers will do the unwise thing of dumping their terrace water into the public road ditch, then they should not object to giving enough additional land space to care for their water until it reaches the natural drain and there it should be carried across the road in a culvert and disposed of along the line of natural drainage. Some legislation along this line might not be amiss.

Too frequently side ditches are understoood to mean the all of drainage. The crown or transverse curvature as shown in Figures 1 and 1a, are

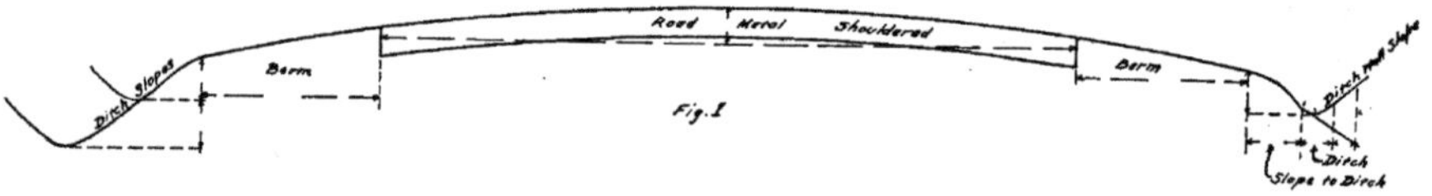

Fig. 1

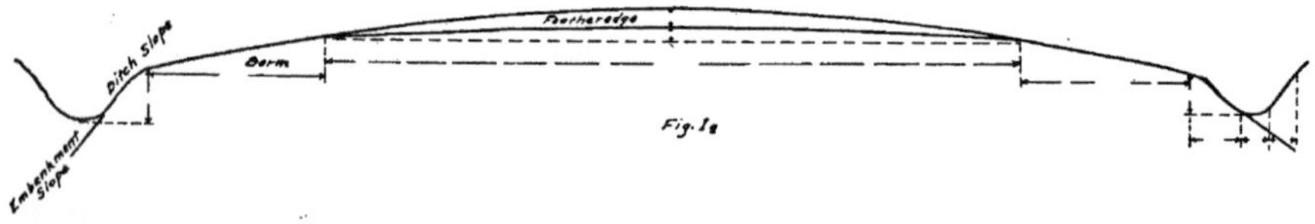

Fig. 1a

essential to the proper maintenance. If the crown is lost and the road becomes rutted the water soon converts the small wheel track to a veritable ditch in the place where the wheel should run. It is a well established fact that the steeper the grade the sharper must be the crown in order to more quickly convey the storm water to the side ditches. Beside the crown, under drains are necessary to carry off seepage from springy conditions. Such drainage is necessary if the minimum difficulty and expense is to be had in maintenance.

The difficulties of drainage will be greater in clay than sand, greater when level or very broken. In level countries it is difficult to get the water away from the road; often the road has to be built up, while in hilly sections care has to be taken to keep the road ditch from eating up the road and the adjacent farm lands. All these questions enter primarily into the problem of road selection and forcibly emphasize the vital importance of right locations and the necessity for the greatest skill and experience in making such locations from a maintenance standpoint.

By reference to Figures 2-3, two types of soil construction will be seen, both of which are on clay foundations. Fig. 2 shows a bed cut out in the

Fig. 2.

clay conformable to the finished crown, having an even thickness and shoulders. It is well to notice two possibilities of failure of this type not likely to occur in Fig. 3. The first one is the shoulders of clay form an

Fig 3.

impervious water trough and tend to supersaturate the topsoil cover, thereby causing it to fail either from prolonged rainy weather or from hard freezing. Furthermore, the topsoil is of uniform thickness and will wear through in the centre earlier than at the sides, thus breaking through to the clay base and consequent mud holes earlier than is likely to occur in a road of the form of Fig. 3, where the top of the sub-grade is finished level and the crown formed of the topsoil. These two figures make the points clear and need no further discussion. It is also clear that the road easiest to maintain is the one with these elements of weakness eliminated. This will not only prove a more durable type of contruction but cheaper, because the hand work of cutting the curved and shouldered base shown in Fig. 2 is very expensive. Dressing the base in Fig. 3 is quite easy and a machine proposition, hence much less expensive. Notice these two types are on a clay base with a soil top.

Fig. 4.

In Fig. 4 a new type of road construction is encountered. This is not an infrequent occurrence, and a specific remedy is easy of application. It will be noticed that the top has a loose sand, beneath it a sand-clay hard pan, and beneath that deep sand. This may be converted into the form shown in Fig. 5 by simply plowing deeply through the hard pan and then fully mixing and pulverizing it with harrows and plows. Care and good judgment, however, must be used in not bringing up too much of the sand from beneath the hard pan. The loose surface sand usually combines with the sand-clay hard pan, and the two make a proper mix. Caution, however, must be taken to observe the depth of the water table and never plow into it. One should also observe the character of the hard pan and its depth, particularly its clay percentage, and bring up only enough of the clay hard pan to harden the top loose sand. After the plowing and harrowing has been done a proper crown may be pulled by a road machine or split log drag, and the finished road have the form shown in Fig. 5. This is an easy way of

Fig. 5

repairing a road of the form shown in Fig. 4. Afterwards the maintenance is simply a matter of using the split log drag occasionally, the same as in maintaining either Fig. 2 or 3. Really the whole problem of maintenance in the case of a soil or sand-clay road is reduced to a very few simple operations, hauling a little material and replenishing washed places and dragging.

The repair of a clay road has its annual return with the regularity of the seasons and is a perpetual tax which levies twice each year and never fails to collect promptly and to the last mite of your time, your patience, your money, and your soul as you slowly drag through a winter's mud, and when the springtime has come and the mud dries, you are tossed to and fro in your haste over holes and mounds, ruts and wrenchers, until in desperation you again pay an unwelcome and unwilling tax to "round" up the road again. Each year this round repeats itself until men rise up and declare they will be free from mud slavery. In most cases the relief is near at hand,—sand, sandy soil, or gravel may often be found either on the hill top or beside the running brook only waiting for wiser men to recognize its value and use it. Such a repair to a clay road will be of lasting benefit, while brush and red clay only fill mud holes with future troubles. There is no possibility of maintaining a clay road if much heavy travel goes over it in the winter. Ditches may be deep as wells and within three feet of the edge one not infrequently sees mud hub deep. The tough clays hold water like a jug and only travel is needed to do the rest when protracted rains come. Maintenance without first applying sand, gravel or stone is out of the question and to discuss it idle talk.

Before closing this discussion it may not be amiss to say a few words about macadam roads. The automobile has introduced a new difficulty, and one, the macadam road, unaided by some binder other than the stone and stone dust, seems unable to successfully meet. At best the macadam road is too expensive except for thickly settled communities possessed of more than the average agricultural wealth. Then when the life of the macadam road is reduced to one-half its expected life because of the auto traffic, the greatest alarm is felt and rightly so because it is a matter of no small account to make repairs on a macadam road and properly maintain it. By reference to Fig. 6 a method of macadam construction is shown that has proven to a marked degree its ability to withstand traffic for at least ten to fifteen years. This method perhaps would not be a successful north as it is south, because of frost there. In the figure referred to the all-important shoulder drain is shown and these should be put in as often as every two stations, and especially at all depressions. This will keep the base free from water sobbing. In putting down the first course roll it thoroughly, but use no stone dust in this course. On top of the first course put about one and one half inches of the stickiest red or other clay possible. Spread it evenly as possible. Then apply number two stone and roll and wet and roll till firm. Roll good.

Fig. 6

Sprinkle and roll until almost a face, using no stone chips up to this time in either course. After all disposition to creep has disappeared from under the roller, a thin application of sandy soil placed over the road and left for rain, with travel blocked off until after the rain comes and washes it into the interstices of the top course of stone; then apply a covering of stone chips and roll and sprinkle and roll and finish. The application of soil need not be more than an inch or an inch and a half, but it must be good, dry, sandy soil, easily pulverized and easily washed into the voids by the rain. No sprinkling cart can take successfully the place of falling rain in this last or soil application. After the rain and before the roller, apply the stone chips or dust as a final dressing. This is far superior to "drowning" the road with stone chips, bottom and top course. Stone chips may, with water, give a sort of temporary bond and help the "roller man," but it

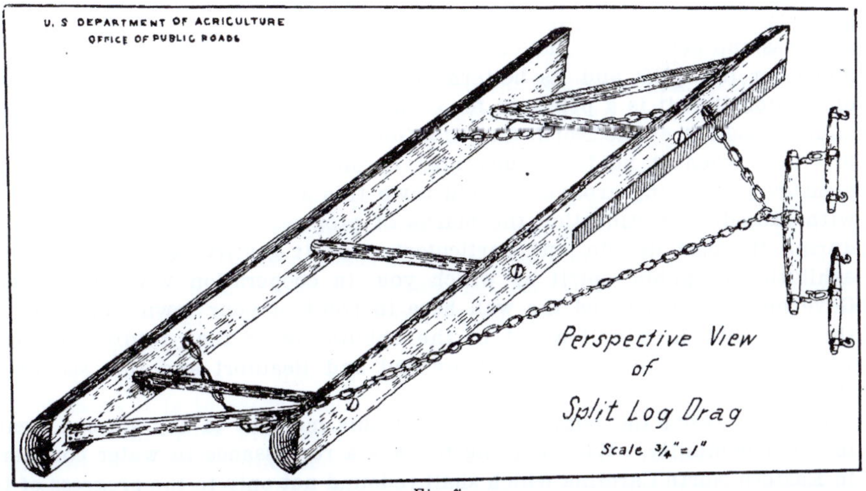

Fig. 7

inevitably ravels under auto travel. The above method is now standing heavy auto travel and has stood travel for more than ten years with very little ravel. Aside from an asphaltic binder this is the nearest to a successful macadam for auto traffic. The maintenance of such a road is materially reduced in cost, and comfort to man and beast enhanced. If you have occasion to build a macadam road again try this receipt and watch results.

In conclusion, let me say that last of all and best of all for the great mass of public roads in the rural districts is the sand-clay road, or the soil

from human pen, in any of the Republics of South America, and yet you would not have a great Republic like ours. Why? Because they are different people. The natural resources do not make a great State. For centuries the wonderful resources of South Africa lay dormant. The savages roamed among them unmindful of what God, in his goodness, had bestowed upon them. Not until the Hollander and the Englishman, with their basic ideas of civilization and progress, set foot upon the soil of South Africa were these natural resources begun to be utilized for the benefit of the world. It is the folk which make a community. The kind of community, the kind of State, and the kind of Government depend upon the kind of folk—the kind of folk that do things, that help their fellows, that uplift humanity, that make the world better, that substitute contentment for unhappiness. Ah! the kind of folk who have seen the vision of life, and have dedicated themselves in part to human service. For more than a century in North Carolina we forgot the lesson which we owed to the children of our State.

A great many people talk about the old times. I would rather live the year 1913 in North Carolina than to have lived forty years in the good Old State in antebellum times. Why do I say it? Because in this year of grace, in this beginning of the twentieth century, there is a greater chance for the average boy and girl, and the average man and woman in North Carolina. Equality of opportunity! A chance for all! Each with his talent, his ability, his energies, and ambitions has opportunity to carve for himself in Life's activities that niche to which his abilities and his energies entitle him. For more than a century, I say, we forgot the obligations which we owed to the training of every child in North Carolina.

One of the things about which we love to speak in this day is the progress we are making in public education. How we love to ring upon audiences that pregnant statement of a public school building every day in the year; of the hundreds of thousands of dollars which we are devoting to public education, increasing from year to year; of the thousands of communities in our State which have voluntarily levied upon themselves local taxes for the maintenance of schools! Why the change? What brought it about? Because in these communities in our State there are men and women who have seen the vision; have learned their duty, and resolved, themselves, to dedicate a part of their time and their talents for the maintenance of public schools, for the giving of a chance to every girl and boy within their borders. It is the spirit of service with which the people are inoculated which makes possible the success of these movements that make for the public weal. So that, if we are to have good roads; if we are to continue the improvement of our public schools; if we, in our respective communities, are to bring forth those things that make for the communities' wheel of progress and contentment, and make life better and worth living, we must increase the opportunity of those men and women who have consecrated themselves to public service. Whose duty is it to engage in this work of service? Primarily, it is the duty of everyone; but, particularly, it is the duty of the men and women who know, who have been trained, have had the benefit of education, who have gone about in the world, who have seen the result of the spirit of service in progressive communities. Particularly does it devolve upon them to be followers and leaders in all these movements that make for the public uplift. To whom it has been given, it is expected, and woe unto the man or woman, who, having seen this vision of service and having realized what their duty is toward their community and their State, fails to enlist in the common cause for community and State growth.

I talked with a young man within the past month, who had graduated at one of our colleges (as a matter of fact, the University of North Carolina), and I asked him something about his future plans in life. It so happened he had decided to adopt law as his vocation. I talked to him for an hour as I wanted to see, as he viewed the horoscope of life, what he had in view; whether the ego played too all important part, or whether he realized that he owed a duty to his community and State. After talking with him one hour, the only idea that I received from him was that he wanted to be a successful lawyer with a large practice and a large income. I say, and I say it with emphasis, that the young man who attends the University or any of our denominational colleges, who lives within its portals for four years before graduation and who has not conceived that he has an obligation to the people of his community and his State, and must perforce contribute some of his talents for the benefit of the public; then, I say, that man is only half educated and half trained. I think the University of Wisconsin is the greatest University in the United States. A college or university which confines its teaching to the academic curriculum, simply training the mentality of the boy, and sending him out a bundle of selfishness and compressed ego is a misnomer. I like the University of Wisconsin because their professors in the courses of that University take into consideration all matters touching on the activities which affect the welfare of the State of Wisconsin—road building, school betterment, public health, the value of coöperation in all of the vocations of life. And they tell me that a boy cannot spend three or four years there (if he is a normal boy) and not emerge with some idea and conception of his duty to his community, his State and his country. I want to see the time when the University of North Carolina and the other colleges in North Carolina shall in a large degree identify themselves with all these activities in the State, which make for the betterment of the State and the uplift of its citizenship.

With your permission, I will detain you just a little while longer to give you two or three crude ideas about what I consider are some of the problems in road building in North Carolina along the lines which Professor Spoon has suggested—the psychological side of the subject. To repeat what I have said before, we cannot get good roads in Carteret County, we cannot get them in any county in North Carolina, except through the *folk*. North Carolina is as yet an agricultural State. That is the dominant industry. We have no large cities. And for myself I not only am content with that condition, but I am hopeful that it may always continue so. Not that I would in the slightest retard the movement of manufacturing. I would like to see more of the raw products, which we produce in this State, converted into a more valuable production, thereby employing more labor and adding to the wealth of the State. But never do I wish to see a decline in the urban movement which shall take away certain virility from the farms, and stop the progress we are now making for agricultural betterment in this State.

How are we going to get these roads? Ladies and Gentlemen, it is simply a matter of educating the people of certain communitites and counties in the State. The greatest obstacle with which we have to contend in this State is ignorance. The worst feature about an ignorant man is that nine times out of ten he thinks he knows it all. In all these communities, for instance, where we have sought to levy a local tax for schools or roads, or issue bonds, it is not the intelligent or the owners of property and wealth, who are the more difficult to convince. Now and then you will find a man of wealth who lives only for himself, but they are exceptional. The one whom it is most difficult to reach and to move is the man who pays the least taxes. It seems to be the concomitant of ignorance. With intelligence we have the willingness to learn. The only way we can overcome this handicap of ignorance is by the process of education. The spoken word, the written word, both applied with patience, with fidelity, with persistence, and with good humor. Never does it pay to lose your temper when you are dealing with an ignorant man. With patience and good temper we will greatly recruit the ranks of the progressives of which we already have a goodly company in every county and community of the State. That process of education can only be accomplished by those men and women who have already seen the vision and have dedicated themselves to public service. Wherever two or three men are gathered together in a community who are willing to dedicate themselves to the success of the common cause of the public good, those men, few though they be, may rely upon the proposition that, if with persistence and courage, they pursue their cause, in the face of all obstacles triumph shall come to them.

Another obstacle in this movement for public roads is the indisposition of so many of our citizens to burden themselves with taxation. Now, there is a reason why our people, as a rule, dislike bond issues. There is a similar reason why they dislike increased taxes. We must remember that for many years (how far back I do not know) the public men in North Carolina have in political campaigns inveighed against taxation and bond issues. It seemed in the past that a political party could find no worse thing to say about the other party than that they had increased the taxes; and if, perchance, one political party of a State or county had issued bonds, that was regarded as a heinous crime, and entitled the political party responsible for its outcome to be outcast. The result has been to permeate the minds of our people with a prejudice against taxation and bond issues. Now upon that I will say this, and say it with due emphasis, that taxation and bond issues, provided they are for necessary public purposes, which public purpose will live and serve as a public betterment, and provided the proceeds of the bonds and the revenue derived from the taxes are honestly expended, are public blessings. (Applause.) And the men who go about in North Carolina without rhyme or reason inveighing against bond issues, inveighing against taxation are nine times out of ten veritable demagogues, seeking to advance their selfish interests in public opinion. There never was a community which made any progress upon which was not imposed a burden as a penalty and the price of that progress. There are these limitations: The taxation must be for a public purpose. It must advance public interest and serve for human betterment; it must be honestly collected; it must be wisely, efficiently, and honestly expended. And it is the duty of every community and every citizen of that community, in accordance as God has blessed them to contribute to that burden which makes for public betterment.

The demagogue in North Carolina is the hardest man to meet. He always comes out in the guise of a patriot. He prates about his love for the people. He poses as the very adamantine obstacle to those who would impoverish the State. He talks about his love for them, and how he would sacrifice himself to save them. There is only one satisfactory outcome of such a character and that is that eventually he comes to his own and is repudiated by the very men whose confidence he has forfeited and whom he has deceived. (Applause.)

Ladies and Gentlemen, there is another feature about the man of service and that is that he must be willing to stand criticism. The man who has not learned to accept criticism and ask himself the question: "Is that criticism deserved?" and if it is deserved, apply it to his own heart and profit by it, that man has not grown to the stature of manhood yet.

As a boy, one of my favorite diversions was attending school commencements. How I did love to hear the Commencement orators talk! I remember well when I was at Old Trinity how I would find time to follow them around to hear them speak. But this impression was made upon my mind that every speaker, political or Commencement, deemed it his bounden duty to pronounce a panegyric upon North Carolina and North Carolinians, and the applause just rang when he talked about the glories of North Carolina and the virtues of North Carolinians. And the result of all that has been to deaden our sense of introspection, to deaden our disposition to look into our own hearts as citizens and see whether we come up to the standard of manhood and womanhood; and besides that, it has made us impatient of critics of ourselves in North Carolina.

I think I can say with perfect candor that if a man or woman in North Carolina is consecrated to public service and stands for those things which make for the growth and betterment of North Carolina, I will give him carte-blanche to criticize us all he wants to.

I read some criticisms of a distinguished son of North Carolina, Walter H. Page, now Ambassador of the United States at the Court of St. James. I read it in *Charity and Children*, published by one of my personal friends and one whom I love. I want to say in this public way that this criticism is undeserved. I have read the book upon which the criticism is based, and since the criticism, I have read it again. I do not stand for some of the things that are in the book. I do not expect everybody to stand for all the sentiments I have expressed. I only try to be honest in my opinions and brave in their expression. But I do say that all those movements with which and by which we are growing in stature every day,—the redemption of the obligation which we owe to the children of North Carolina in giving to every boy and girl a chance; the building of public roads; the betterment of public health; the coöperation of men and women together; the joining of hands for the common good; line upon line and precept upon precept, have the great talents of Walter H. Page been devoted to this movement which has done most for the good of our State and our people. Wherever brains and intelligence, civilization and righteous conviction to public duty are recognized, Mr. Page is placed among the foremost, and for one I am proud that he is a son of North Carolina.

Ladies and Gentlemen, you do not know how grateful I am to you for the patience and the courtesy you have exercised this warm evening. I have simply rambled along. I hope I have told the truth; I have tried. I have concealed nothing that was in my mind. Not wishing to speak with egotism, for my intentions are far from it, I believe the best policy for a man who serves the people in a public capacity to follow is to always scrupulously and with courage and candor to tell the truth as he sees it; and the man who, by the confidence of his fellow citizens, has been placed in a public position, whether it be township constable, county officer, State Legislator or Senator, Member of Congress, Governor or President, and who attempts to keep his ear to the ground so closely that he may find that which is popular and will not sacrifice popularity to personal truth is not worthy of the confidence of the people.

May we each in our capacity, each with the talent with which we have been blessed, each with the training which we have received, each with our ideals of public duty, be able to return to our homes from this meeting resolved to consecrate ourselves in the future, even more than in the past, to the building of Good Roads in North Carolina, and to every movement which makes for the public welfare, for human betterment and in human service.

The President then announced the appointment of the following committees:

Committees.

RESOLUTIONS.

W. C. Douglass, of Wake County.
William Dunn, of Craven County.
R. R. Cotten, of Pitt County.
James A. Wellons, of Johnston County.
J. E. Cameron, of Lenoir County.
W. A. Blair, of Forsyth County.

NOMINATIONS AND NEXT MEETING PLACE.

John C. Drewry, of Wake County.
A. P. Gilbert, of Durham County.
John E. Moore, of Northampton County.

MEMBERSHIP.

G. D. Canfield, of Carteret County.
Senator Ward, of Craven County.
W. S. Fallis, of Henderson County.

MORNING SESSION.

FRIDAY, AUGUST 1, 10:00 O'CLOCK.

PRESIDENT: I am very sorry that we have not a larger crowd to open our session, but most of our folks are out fishing. We will now continue where we left off last night, and I will ask Mr. W. S. Fallis to talk to you about the Maintenance of Highways. He is the man who built the roads in Franklin County about which you have heard, and which are considered the best sand-clay roads in the State. Ask him any questions you wish, and I am sure he will be glad to answer them.

Maintenance of Highways.

MR. W. S. FALLIS, ROAD ENGINEER.

Mr. President, Ladies and Gentlemen of the Convention:—I thank Mr. Varner very much for his kind words in connection with my work in Franklin County. I will be glad to have you, gentlemen, ask me any question, and I will do my best to answer them.

There was one question that Mr. Spoon did not take up in his talk last night, and that was the road deterioration which man puts on the roads himself. This part of the deterioration is occasioned by the narrow tires of wagon and other horse-drawn vehicles; and this is one of the most detrimental features to a sand-clay road, where the traffic is heavy. As a general thing heavy farm traffic does not do a great deal of damage to the sand-clay roads; but the occasional heavy load, such as the hauling of sand and lime with the narrow-tired vehicles is extremely detrimental to the roads. Narrow tires, with excessive loads, are very much heavier per linear inch than any road roller which you can put on the road. It weighs 450 pounds where the ordinary wagon weighs from 300 to 400 pounds and will run up to 700 pounds per linear inch.

This is one reason why in the construction of the sand-clay roads we do not use the road roller. The province of the road roller is in macadam work principally to knit together the stones in the road, so the road will have as few voids as possible. Now, this is not true in building the sand-clay road. The narrow tires act like a knife, gradually cutting into the sand-clay; and, during wet spells of weather, especially in those sections where the drainage is poor, the narrow tires cut through the sand-clay down into the mud beneath and turn it up. One thing we need is to pass a wide-tire-road-law, which will help to maintain the sand-clay road instead of causing it to deteriorate. There is no use in building a sand-clay road, and then let these destructive agencies work against it all the time.

Mr. Cotton: Do you use steel shovels?

Mr. Fallis: We use steel shovels sometimes in mixing the sand and clay.

Question: What is the cost of putting the topsoil on?

Answer: From $250 to $500 per mile, depending on how far you have to haul the sand or clay. In a portion of Franklin County we can get top soil cheaper than that, but the grade work runs the cost up.

Mr. Cameron: We have on the Quebec-Miami Highway a condition that I would like to get a little light on. For years we have had a road that was never known to be anything but excellent, but that road was just ridged up on the natural surface of the ground. In laying out the Quebec-Miami Highway we concluded that we would go in on a better grade. Now to get that grade, we had to take in the top of the knolls and also go into the little bottoms; then grade down the knolls and put the dirt into the bottoms, which I do not consider very good engineering.

Mr. Fallis You should do your grade work and disregard the character of the materials you remove in the grade work, and then get your surfacing materials.

Mr. Cameron: Why was it necessary to cut through these little knolls at all, when you are entirely on a 3 per cent grade in going over them?

Mr. Fallis: I would not be able to answer that without being on the ground.

Question: How would it do to build these roads by contract? After the road has been surveyed, have the work done by contract, subject to the inspection of a road engineer. I think we ought to be able to get a contractor to build these roads just like a building. The difference is that when you have a contractor who knows his business and you have an engineer to see that he is doing the work according to specification; then when we get the work, we get what he is paid to do.

Mr. Fallis: It is a good plan to have a board of business men who are not petty politicians, then let them hire a competent road engineer, and give him entire charge of the location, construction, and maintenance of the roads, letting his expenditures be subject to the approval of the board.

Question: I would like to get some ideas as to whether there is any science in the mixing of the sand and clay in building this type of road.

Answer: There is considerable science in it, and it is a hard matter to get a foreman who knows just how to mix the sand and clay.

Question: Will any kind of sand and clay make a good sand-clay road?

Answer: Not just any kind. You need a good sharp sand and a plastic clay.

Mr. Fallis: There is another feature in the building of the sand-clay road which is of importance, and that is the grass proposition on each side of the road. You do not want to disturb this, because it will help protect the road and keep it from washing. In considering the question of maintenance of the sand-clay road, you should build your road not less than 30 feet wide. Some people object to building a road 30 feet wide, but it is absolutely necessary if you expect to maintain it at a minimum cost.

There is another feature about road work which I have not had the opportunity to discuss at any Convention, and that is the relation of the engineer to the county, and his authority in handling the road work of the county. The road work is so often handled by a County Commission, and this County Commission is frequently a political body who have certain obligations they wish to pay to the people of their county in the location of the roads. The first thing that must be considered in road building is the proper location, which includes the proper grading. I am very much in favor of having the grades as low as 3 per cent on all roads, unless physical conditions are such that it is absolutely impossible and prohibitive on account of the cost of construction. Now, the ultimate success of an engineer's work in a county is directly dependent on the authority he has in making his locations. If the roads are mislocated, your money is absolutely wasted, so that nothing should stand in the way of the proper location of a road. If you put your road work in the hands of a political body who have political debts to pay, and who feel that they have to locate a road around by a certain man's house, because he happens to be a man that controls a great many votes; then your road will be a failure. The success of the sand-clay roads in Franklin County was based absolutely on that principle. When I took charge of the work, they told me that where I thought the roads should be located, there the roads should go. In the 75 miles we built in that county, not a single change was made in any of my locations. The result is the maintenance of these roads is not a question at all. It has cost about $5 a mile per year for maintenance, and the roads are in just as good condition to-day as they were the day they were finished. This is the result of the engineer having absolute authority in making locations. I would like to impress on this Convention that whenever you get an engineer into your county, give him this authority and permit him to make the proper locations of your roads.

The roads in Franklin County were built by a foreman who, without an exception, is one of the best in the State; and it is a mistake to get any other kind. His knowledge of how to handle dirt is the reason why we got such good results in mileage. We built some 75 miles of road out of $60,000, and the bulk of this cost is in the grade work.

Report of Committee on Nominations and Next Meeting Place.

The Committee on Nominations of Officers and place of meeting report their recommendation that the present officers and members of the Executive Committee be reëlected, and that the name of Mr. J. E. Cameron, of Kinston, be substituted for the late R. M. Phillips, of Greensboro, and that the place of meeting in 1914 be left to the decision of the Executive Committee.

(Signed) JOHN C. DREWRY,
Chairman.

It was announced that the Committee on Resolutions would report later.

THE PRESIDENT: We have with us today a man who is a warm good roads advocate, and who has done much in his section for the good roads cause. I am sorry that we have not a larger audience to hear him. After you hear him you will realize that I have underestimated him. I have the honor to present to you Hon. Jesse Taylor, Vice-President of the National Highways Association, and President of the Ohio Good Roads Federation.

Address.

BY HON. JESSE TAYLOR, PRESIDENT OHIO GOOD ROADS FEDERATION.

Mr. Chairman, Ladies and Gentlemen, and Fellow Highwaymen:—As far as I am concerned, it is wholly unnecessary for the Chairman of this meeting to apologize for those who are absent; for I assure you, if I were a fisherman, I would not be listening to anybody speak. I do not care if it is a road question; it is a dry, old question; but down here in North Carolina (and I imagine in Ohio) that any of us could get very warm over it, if we talked about it very long. I see something different in North Carolina from what I have observed in many other States, and I want to congratulate you people down here that you have someone (and I imagine it is Dr. Pratt) in charge of your road work, who has sense enough to get road engineers who can stand up before an audience and say things without reading a paper. I have attended road meetings in Ohio at which there were thousands of engineers who were wholly unable to answer the simplest question propounded in these meetings; and, if they did answer them, they would always have to refer to some paper. But I have found down here in North Carolina that the engineers have ability, and when there is an inquiry made he can stand on his feet and answer it. I saw something else demonstrated in this meeting. I saw last night an engineer from the Office of Public Roads, Washington, D. C., who could stand on his feet and tell you what he thought about roads right "off the bat." If anything makes me tired, it is to go to a road meeting and find men, who are paid from $3,000 to $6,000 per year, who have to confine themselves to a manuscript. I do not see that down here in North Carolina. The President of this Association who is also Chairman of the State Prison Board was not afraid to get busy, do what he thought was right, and not give a darn. I find that in many states to the north of us it is the most difficult thing you ever saw to induce a Member of Congress of the United States to attend any sort of meeting like this, where somebody might jam some question into him, which he would not want to answer or commit himself about. But I witnessed last night what I have seldom seen before, and that was one of the leading Congressmen of the State who could stand up before the folk and tell them what he thought about the road question, as John Small did last night. I know what Varner said is true. I never saw Congressman John Small before, but never has any Congressman looked so good to me as he did last night; and I want to congratulate you people of North Carolina that you have a Congressman who has the sand to come home, and tell the folk what he thinks. I believe he will tell you the truth about the situation. I believe it is true that he is the Congressman that is doing more for North Carolina than any other member you have sent up to Washington, and I hope there may be some opportunity to boost John H. Small for the upper house. Elbert Hubbard said: "Instead of hitching your wagon to a star, why not just get in touch with the good roads movement?" I think the people of North Carolina have got in touch with the good roads movement. I think the people of Ohio are already in touch with the good roads movement.

The New England States have expended millions of dollars in the building of highways, and Governor Sulzer of New York stated that the people set out to expend $50,000,000 on the construction of highways in the state of New York, and someone stole one third of it; and I believe he was telling the truth. Now, what we all want; what the people of New York want; what the people of Texas want; what the people in the Rocky Mountains want, is *Good Roads Everywhere*. We want roads that reach from one city to another. We want roads that connect up all the States. We want roads that will bring the country women into town; that will carry the children to the schools; that will permit the farmers and their families to go to church on Sunday, to market their produce every day in the week; and we want roads that will let the children attend the schools every day during the school term. We want to break up the loneliness and desolation of rural life.

Last summer, it fell to my lot at a Chautauqua to follow an eminent divine, who was paid $250 to go there and devote one hour of his time to the discussion of his side of the divorce question. He stated that he believed that when we were once "tied up," we should always be "tied up." I followed him to talk on roads, for which I did not get a cent. I say this, and I say it with all due respect to the great Doctor and with due respect to his knowledge of the affairs of this world of ours, were I a lonely woman living on the back end of a bad road and had a great big horny-handed husband who would not hitch the horse or mule to a split-log drag and smooth that road and let me and my family out into the outside world and get into social communication with my neighbors, I would get me a horse or mule or anything else, and I would go to the nearest court and sue that brute for a divorce. The majority of women confined in the insane asylums of the State of Ohio come from the rural districts. The majority of the women in the insane institutions are there because of the loneliness of their lives on the farms. If you are not interested in this road question from the standpoint of the farmer who wants to lessen the distance to the nearest market; if you are not interested in it from the standpoint of the betterment of humanity; then every man in North Carolina and every man in this great Union of ours should be interested in the uplift of rural life, so as to do away with this awful condition that comes to a majority of the women on account of loneliness. If there is anything in this road question that appeals to me, it is the woman on the back end of a bad road.

Here, in North Carolina, you tell me, you engineers that are here (and I have heard about it elsewhere), that you can build sand-clay roads for $300 to $600 per mile, and that you can maintain these at from $10 to $30 per mile per year. Why, don't you know up in Ohio if we had that chance; if Indiana, New York, or any other of the Northern States had the sand and clay and could mix them as you do, and could build roads for from $300 to $500 per mile as you can, every road of the eighty-eight thousand miles in Ohio would have been a sand-clay road years and years ago. In Ohio, we have a muddy, black, clay condition in many places and a dry condition in other places; and our roads are costing us from $5,000 to $8,000 per mile. Furthermore, a brick bitulithic costs us from $15,000 to $20,000 per mile. No matter where you go, either in the North or the South, the story which has been told that we can have good roads without money is a delusion and a snare, and a dream of some fanatic. If you want good roads in North Carolina, in Ohio, or in any part of this Union, make up your minds that they are going to cost money, and make up your minds that you must have a system of some kind and leave politics out of it. The only way to do is that way Mr. ———, who is a rich man and who has traveled much and seen conditions as they exist in other countries, who came back home a year ago and said: "I intend to rout out all the dirty politics and nasty grafters." And he went at it and did it. You can do it. You, Colonel Cameron, and any others in this Association for any county in North Carolina which has an auxiliary Association to the North Carolina Good Roads Association. Clean up the situation, root out the dirty politicians, so that any money you spend will go into the building of the roads and not into the pockets of these men. Then, and not until then, can we have the condition which should exist in our road affairs. Why I get mad, mad as mad can be, when I see the men in our State wasting the money on the public roads.

Twenty-three years ago I was sent to the plains of Western Kansas on account of ill-health, believing I was a consumptive. I lived on the plains three or four years; and, while in that country, I had the opportunity to travel over the plains of Kansas one day and saw along the road in front of us a man mowing down sunflowers, and I said to the man, "What are you doing?" and he said, "I am working the roads." A short time after when I was in Southern Missouri, I saw a man prizing up stumps and I asked him what he was doing. His reply was that he was working the roads. Another time I saw some men marching along the roads with axes on their shoulders, and by and by we saw them engaged in cutting knots off the trees. I asked them what they were doing and they replied, "We are working the roads." Soon after that we saw a road machine and eight horses pulling on a road grader. The man on the front seat guiding the team, and the man in the back with a great big whip, and every man cussing and swearing. The man with me said, "What in the H——l are you doing?" and he said, "We are working the roads." The time has come when we must have some sort of system! Why bless your souls, I would be willing to bet money that a train could not run into here next Sunday morning, were it not for the fact that the section men are kept on the track to watch and see that it is clear! Something would happen. Here we are spending thousands and thousands of dollars on the roads and expect God Almighty to look after the maintenance of them. You have here in North Carolina places to accommodate people in winter and summer. President Davis said that during 1912 more than a hundred thousand tourists crossed the water to European countries and here in North Carolina, although it is hot here now, they tell me that in certain seasons of the year, there is no more delightful place to be found anywhere. They tell me that back here in these mountains you have the loftiest peaks east of the Rockies. You can accommodate people winter and summer, because for the fellow who is hunting for the cool breezes of the sea coast, you have your seaside resorts down here in the east. And here you are a great State with all the conditions that tourists desire allowing 100,000 people to go abroad each year, who might be coming into your State and spending their money here. Did they build that great system of roads in Germany without money? Did they keep their roads in splendid condition without money? No, sir. In England and the European countries, the average cost to haul per ton per mile is 9 cents, while over here it is 23 cents. The U. S. Secretary of Agriculture says that the difference in the cost of hauling over poor roads in excess of what it costs to haul over good roads during one year is enough to build the Panama Canal. Our tourists go abroad and they enjoy riding over those great systems of highways in England, France, and Germany. Now, there are no better engineers in France than there are in North Carolina. There are no better teachers in France than there are in North Carolina. There are no better statesman than John H. Small. There are no better road materials in France, Germany, or Switzerland than there are in North Carolina.

There are many Government officials who think that the Government should take a hand in this matter and create a system and devise a plan for the building of great National Highways, and then taking care of the roads after they are constructed. How should they be kept? They should have them under a patrol system. Every six or seven miles there should be men whose duty it is to look after a section of the public highways, and whether it be a sand-clay, a macadam, or whatever kind of road it may be, to see that the road is made better every year, better next year than this year, and better fifty years from now; because of the fact that it is patrolled once every day of the year and kept in proper condition. Then and then only will we have a system of roads in North Carolina such as you want.

We never will have a system of roads in Ohio such as we will all want until this great Federal Government of ours lets down the bars, and we all coöperate with each other; and the Federal Government with the states. Then we will have a great National system of highways, a great State system of highways, and a great county system of highways, all properly taken care of every day in the year. Now, I am not an engineer; I am a farmer. Last winter I was with a bunch of road enthusiasts and one of these was called upon to make a speech in which he said that he did not understand the building of roads, but he knew good roads when he saw them. He said, "We have earth roads, gravel roads, brick roads, slag roads; and we have a lot of roads we call 'macadam' without the 'mac' in front of them."

Now, out in Colorado they are taking their convicts, and, instead of hiring them out to corporations, they are putting them on the public roads. I have traveled over that great scenic highway in the Grand Canyon, Colorado, and I have seen that great highway which was built by convicts. At most any place you stop your machine, you can look down 5,000 feet to the right and 5,000 up to the left. About ten miles west of Canyon City, we looked up as directed by the guide and beheld 28,000 feet to the top of that rock. And this beautiful road was built by convicts, employed on the honor system.

During the last campaign we, in Ohio, had a three-cornered scrap, and the real progressive of the crowd was one of Mr. Small's crowd, Jimmy Cox. One of the first things he said was, "I am in favor of a system of roads," and the Legislature proceeded to obey Jim and lay out a system of highways, and the Highway Commissioners, as directed by the law and encouraged by Governor Cox, has laid out a connected system of roads which connects county seat with county seat, commercial center with commercial center; so that in Ohio we will have a system of 9,000 miles, over which 80 per cent of all the traffic in Ohio will go. I have been told that a system of roads making 20 per cent of all the mileage in Ohio hauls the majority of the trade in the State; and I am told that 20 per cent of the highways of the United States hauls 90 per cent of the products of the United States.

Now, we have in our State a system of road building, and the Federal Government should appropriate a sum to help out the States in building national highways. It has been proposed to appropriate $50,000,000, which will bring into Ohio $3,500,000 annually, 25 per cent to be expended under the direction of the Governor and the other under the State Commission, and we hope the first road to be constructed in Ohio is the Old Cumberland Road. The people of Ohio, Indiana, Illinois, and Missouri want that old road built, and we, in Ohio, have determined that it shall be built. Now, last year, Congress appropriated $500,000 as Federal aid, and they said to the States they would divide up equally, $75,000 to each, and they must put up 2 to 1. Indiana could not put it up, for they had no Highway Commission. Illinois had no Highway Department, and no funds from which they could take the necessary amount; neither had Missouri. All the states were shy of provisions to meet the Federal Government; but our Governor Jim Cox wrote a letter to the Postmaster-General saying, "We will take all the money that the Federal Government will give to Ohio. Yea! four to one, and if necessary, six to one."

Now, you people in North Carolina, what you want is a system. What you want is what John Small told you last night,—go home and talk to the folk, and tell the people that North Carolina wants to organize a State Highway Department with Dr. Pratt as the head, and give him a real job.

In regard to working the convicts, we do not propose to send the convict out on the public roads without compensating him for the work he does. I believe there are a lot of good fellows in our penitentiary. There are some who are born criminals. We cannot avoid them. We do not want this last class turned loose on the public. But there are thousands of men in our penitentiaries who were sent there for some small offense, which possibly they could not avoid. Some of them are there for something done while under the influence of intoxicating liquor. The Prison Board should not retain from these convicts the entire amount which their labor is worth. They should hold back a certain per cent to accumulate for them, when their term is up, and send, say 10 per cent, home for the support of their families. I am in favor of having a law by which you can arrange to take care of the families of these men in the penitentiaries, and so treat the convict that when he is turned out, he can be returned to society as a citizen and not an outcast. This is what we call human betterment.

Now, why does that fellow come from Ohio to North Carolina to say something at a road meeting, would be the proper inquiry. Why does he do it? Now, I want to say to you they tell me that every farmer in the State of Iowa who does not own an automobile, possesses a Ford. I belong to that class of citizenship who have for years thought that the horse is the only thing to ride behind, but for the last year I have become convinced that the horse has got to go back to the soil, so far as his use for pleasure is concerned. We people are living in a different age. In Ohio, the people used to ride horseback. But that was long ago, and to-day they cannot buy an automobile fast enough to suit them. They want to go 50 to 80 miles an hour. I heard one man say he bet $20 to 50 cents that that fellow Taylor was sent down here by the Standard Oil Company. Over in Indiana the chairman of a meeting introduced me, and they would not allow me in the hall until I certified to them that I was not drawing a salary from the Barber Asphalt Company or the Austin-Western Company. I want to assure the people here that I don't even possess a Ford. I have a few horses left that I am going to press into service. I am just an ordinary everyday crank, who got to turning an idea over in his head. The thing that started me in the road movement was an old road that passed through the farm of my father-in-law. Now, he had helped to build the roads in Green County, Ohio.

About fourteen years ago, I was connected with a little bank in the city in which I live, and we had some money loose, so we invested in some land seven miles from the town. We could not get the corn to market, so I started out to fix the road to town. I was engineer, foreman, and everything in the building of that road. I tried my best to get the authorities to fix it, and went to one or two young attorneys, but was unable to get it done, so I went at it myself. Just three months after that road was built I was offered $25 per acre more than what I paid for it. Nothing happened to increase the value of that land but that little road, and I said to myself if the building of a little old cheap road on a cheap farm will jam up the price like that, then I am for roads. And, if I can do anything for our neighboring townships, and if I can find time and any place to help the people realize the value of good roads, I am willing to do everything I can to accomplish this. My wife over there goes along with me, and she is now one of the biggest good road cranks in the United States. If I go into a neighborhood and see the fences and barns and houses, I can pretty soon tell you what kind of roads they have. Take me through a country that has prosperous farms, well-built houses, good schools, and churches, and I will tell you at once that they have good roads there. Take me into a neighorhood where you have bad conditions everywhere, and I will show you by the roadside a shiftless population nine times out of ten. Go with me into the country where they have good roads, and I will show you happy mothers, kids with smiles on their faces, prosperous homes, and farmers sitting by taking advantage of every crop report, with his telephone at his ear phoning into the market places to ascertain the latest prices, with his sulky plow and other modern machinery on his farm. When you people in North Carolina make an effort to get us Northern people to come and buy your farmland, the Yankee will ask you three questions:

First: Have you a rural route?

Second: Is there a telephone?

Third: Has it a good road to market?

The time has come in this country when, if you want to sell land to people that count, it is necessary to answer these three questions in the affirmative. The time has come when you cannot expect immigration into North Carolina, until you get roads for the people to drive over. The time has come when you cannot expect the New Yorker to invest his money in this section until you make the farm products worth producing by providing an easy means to market. The time has come in Ohio when we cannot expect the men who have moved away from us to other States to come back and cast their lot with us again, unless we have good roads for them to use. The time has come when, throughout this nation, men will not move into a locality where there are no good roads. Time was, when

I was a kid, that the road we used was built and paid for by my grandfather; but now the time has come when the county, the State, and the Nation must take part in building these roads. Time was when nobody used these roads except people living adjacent to them; but that has changed. The automobile has made the travel nation-wide. Time was when I hated for my father and my mother to announce to me that I had to put on my shoes and go to church. Eleven miles and a half meant two hours on a hot summer's day, to drive from our place to the town. About seven years ago Mrs. Taylor and I and her father made this eleven miles and a half in an hour, and now the distance can be covered in 20 minutes.

The whole thing has changed; changed in Ohio; changed in North Carolina; changed all over the world. To-day, I am told we have five automobiles for every mile of improved road in the United States. And they are ruining this country, if one would listen to what many have to say about it. It is not the farmer altogether who is wearing out the road. The automobiles have a very wearing effect, particularly on macadam roads, but the automobile brings us into close touch with the people all over the country. To-day we hear of someone going from Cincinnati; here goes another from Cleveland; here goes one from Birmingham, Ala.; and a day or two ago, I heard of one going from Los Angeles, Cal., on his way to the Atlantic Coast. What doing? Improving your road? Not on your life! Wearing out the old road.

I am opposed to the old method of working the roads. I believe that if I own land abutting the road and use that road entirely that I ought to pay 10 to 15 per cent of the cost of the road. But I believe that since travel has become not township, not county, not state, but *Nation-wide*, I believe the time has come when the State should be taxed to contribute to the upkeep and construction of a system of highways. We, in Ohio, are doing it, and have laid a levy on probably every automobile in the State. In New York, Pennsylvania, Ohio, and every other State where people are beginning to realize the effect of automobiles on the roads, they are saying, "Boys, you must contribute toward the upkeep of these roads." In some places they are putting on a horsepower tax, and there is not a State in this Union where men live and own automobiles, who will oppose and not see the justice of this kind of a tax. The automobile tax in Ohio will bring us $900,000 per year, which goes into the road fund. Last year we had 57,000 automobiles registered in the State, and now we have 76,000, and everybody is still buying a machine. Mr. Small, I want to congratulate you on being able to bring to these people down here three or four million dollars for the improvement of that Inland Waterway. I am not one of those who is for breaking down or abusing a policy for the construction of such a waterway. I am not one of those who is for doing away with the policy in the Philippine Islands; but let us build us a good system of public highways for the Philippinos! In doing this, however, let us not forget the homefolks! I do not say anything against anybody for voting for the building of these roads, and I hope John Small voted for them. I believe in it. We spent $400,000 in building roads in Alaska, and I believe in it. We spent $1,300,000 in the construction of wagon roads in the Canal Zone. We expended $87,600 from the Federal Treasury in the construction of roads in the Island of Guam, and I am glad of it. I do say it is not right to take from the

Federal Treasury moneys to spend in the construction of roads in the Philippines, in Alaska, in the Island of Guam, unless we recognize the fact that the Federal Government should also spend money in the building of great systems of public highways for the folks at home. I love the people that live in North Carolina a thousand times better than I love a black Philippino. I think more of the beauties and the glories of an automobile ride over the roads in North Carolina than I would in Alaska. And what we want, and all the people want, is to have a man like John Small, who will stand up for the folks and some day, somehow, sometime, give us the means for building the great public highways for the use of the folk at home. Sometime somebody, through the Committee of the House, is going to get up on the floor of the House; and, when it comes up for discussion, in a sane and sensible way, discuss the question of Federal aid in the building of great through highways. What we want and what we must have is a system of *Good Roads Everywhere*. We don't want the Government to say to the people, "Take the money and do with it what you 'darn' please"; but we want them to send engineers to select the locations, plan out the highways, and say here is the way and here are the engineers for building your roads. Supervise it from the time the engineer goes out until the highway is completed, and be as liberal in appropriating from the Federal Treasury as possible. What we want is a system of National Highways taken charge of by officials of the Federal Government. Men in the Federal Government take charge and build for us a great system of waterways, then why not build highways? You have the natural resources; you have the scenery; then why do they not bring you in the revenue commensurate with the value? Because you have no good roads leading to them. Good roads will bring you better people, better homes, better churches, and better schools. They will bring you happy mothers, a better citizenship, and they will mean the uplift of your civic centers. And the North Carolina Good Roads Association will, if it keeps on growing, in ten years' time be a body which will mean the uplift of your entire State.

I thank you for your attention.

Following this a rising vote of thanks of the Association was given to Mr. Taylor.

Following this a paper was given by Professor A. H. Blanchard, Professor of Highway Engineering of Columbia University, New York City.

The Third International Road Congress, London, 1913.

BY ARTHUR H. BLANCHARD, PROFESSOR OF HIGHWAY ENGINEERING IN COLUMBIA UNIVERSITY, AND CONSULTING HIGHWAY ENGINEER, NEW YORK CITY.

"Stop, Look and Listen," the characteristic sign which attracts the attion of the traveler at crossings of highways and railways throughout the United States, contains advice of inestimable value to those interested in the development of highways. As a pertinent citation of its application, the work of the Third International Road Congress is worthy of careful study in order that the mass of information collated through the medium of reports, discussions, conclusions and exhibitions may be drawn upon to furnish ideas which may be used in the development of highway engineering in this country.

To-day the world appreciates the admirable work instituted by the French Government in 1908, through the medium of its famous Department of Roads and Bridges, in calling to Paris highway engineers and officials from all over the globe for the purpose of mutual exchange of opinions pertaining to the administration, construction, and maintenance of highways. At this convention, the First International Road Congress, steps were taken to form the Permanent International Association of Road Congresses.

The Association includes in its membership national governments, state governments, municipalities, associations and societies, companies manufacturing materials and machinery, and individual members. According to the 1913 report of the Executive Committee of the Association, the membership on May 31st included 32 national governments, 256 corporate bodies and 944 private members. The dues of these members for the year ending May 31, 1913, were $21,520, of which $14,980 were subscribed by national governments.

Of particular interest to the citizens of the United States are the regulations relative to the affiliation of national governments, the pertinent portions of the regulations pertaining to the two controlling bodies of the Association, the Permanent International Commission and the Permanent Council, are as follows:

"The Permanent International Commission is composed of members belonging to the various countries represented in the Association. Each country has the right to one representative for each $200 of its total annual subsidy. Provided, however, that the number of representatives from any one country shall not exceed fifteen and that any country which pays not less than $50 shall have the right to appoint one delegate.

"The Permanent Council is composed of representatives chosen from among the members of the Permanent Commission: One for each country whose annual subsidy does not exceed $100; two for each country whose annual subsidy exceeds this amount, and is less than $2,000; three for each country whose annual subsidy exceeds $2,000."

It is unfortunate that our national government stands alone among the great governments of the world in not having affiliated with the Permanent International Association. Our neighbors, Cuba and Mexico, are among those who have lead us in officially expressing the interest of their national governments in the improvement of highways.

Since 1908 the subject of affiliation has been under consideration in the United States and since the Second International Road Congress held in Brussels in 1910, an active campaign has been waged to secure the adherence of the United States. In order that the United States may take its proper and dignified place in the world progressive movement conducted under the Association, it appears the duty of every Association interested in good roads to pass resolutions memorializing the Congress of the United States to take the necessary steps to become a member of the Permanent International Association of Road Congresses.

During the sessions of the Third International Road Congress held in London in June, 1913, it was decided to accept the invitation extended by the German Government to hold the 1916 Congress in Munich. Since the Brussels Congress there has been a tacit understanding that the Fifth International Congress should be held in the United States in 1919. It is, of course, obvious that unless the United States becomes a member prior to 1916, it will be practically impossible to carry out this very desirable program, desirable not only from the standpoint of the citizens of the United States, but also from the standpoint of highway engineers and officials in all the countries of the world.

A brief outline of the scheme upon which is founded the work of an International Road Congress will give some idea of the large amount of available information relative to every phase of highway engineering which is disseminated among highway engineers and officials throughout every land. The Permanent International Commission about two years in advance of a Congress meeting decides upon a series of topics which it considers of vital importance and upon which a large amount of investigative work is in progress. Another series of topics is selected pertaining to subjects upon which thought has not crystallized as definitely as in the case of the first set of subjects but information in regard to which will serve as the basis for future concentrated and coöperative work. The first set of topics is defined as Questions, the second set as Communications. The Executive Committee of the Association then notifies the national representatives in various countries of the list of Questions and Communications and requests that in each country a Reporter or a group of Reporters be designated to prepare a comprehensive review on each Question and upon each Communication, the viewpoint in each case being national. The reports are delivered to the Executive Committee some six to nine months prior to the meeting of a Congress, are printed in the three official languages of the Association, English, French and German, and distributed before the opening of the Congress to all members of the Association. In the country in which a given Congress is held General Reporters on each Question are appointed to review all reports submitted, to summarize the practice indicated and to draft a set of conclusions which represent the majority opinion relative to various essential phases of each subject. These general reports are supposed to be distributed prior to the meeting of a Congress. The business sessions of the various sections of a Congress are devoted to a consideration of the conclusions submitted by the General Reporters. Naturally many amendments are proposed before the Conclusions are finally adopted by the section particularly interested in a given subject. The conclusions as reported by the various sections are submitted at the final general meeting of a Congress where they are considered for final adoption. The discussions, conclusions, general work of the Congress, and a description of the excursions, entertainments and the exhibition are published as the Proceedings of the Congress.

At the Third International Congress a total of 140 reports were presented by Reporters from nineteen national governments, nine Questions and ten Communications composing the program. Nine general reports by British engineers were prepared relative to the Questions. The meetings of the Third Congress were well attended, the total attendance being between 2,500 and 3,000. The Congress was so conducted that the proceedings of the various sessions, although carried on in the three official languages of the Congress, English, French and German, were interesting and instructive. By having present expert interpreters, those in attendance were made acquainted with the remarks of members from all countries without any material delay in the progress of the meetings.

The Exhibition was divided into four divisions: Road materials and machinery; traffic; models, maps, drawings, and publications; and historical data. The first division comprised 42 exhibits of the principal types of material and machinery employed in Great Britain and on the Continent.

The practical influence of the Congress on the development of administration and organization of highway departments and the improvement of roads and pavements will depend to a marked degree upon the extent of the adoption of the principles and recommendations contained in the conclusions of the Congress. The conclusions, although expressing in many instances the fundamentals of modern highway engineering practice, nevertheless will repay careful digestion by every American interested in good roads. Unfortunately American engineers and highway officials have not universally adopted many of the fundamental principles laid down at the International Road Congresses. Among the 83 conclusions adopted at the Third Congress, which are of especial interest to those having charge of highway work in the United States, are the following:

First Question.—Planning of New Streets and Roads.

"As a general principle, it is better that new main roads be constructed to pass outside rather than through towns, and that, where an existing main road passing through a town is unsatisfactory for through traffic, it is often better in preference to widening an existing narrow main road through the centre of a town, new roads should be planned according to the principles of the science of town planning."

Second Question.—Types of Surfacing to be Adopted on Bridges, Viaducts, Etc.

"On short bridges in town or country, it is desirable that the surfacing should be the same as that on the adjoining streets or roads."

Third Question.—Construction of Macadamised Roads Bound with Bituminous (Including Tarry and Asphaltic) Materials.

"Confirming the conclusions adopted in 1910 by the Second Congress (Brussels, Second Question), which called attention to the advantages of a dry foundation and a sound subsoil, the Congress especially insists upon the great importance of efficient foundations in the case of road crusts bound with bituminous (including tarry or asphaltic) binders for the following reasons:

" 'The road crust being expensive, it is important to give it a base which will increase its life.

" 'As the weight, speed and intensity of the traffic continually tend to increase on roads considered worthy of such a crust, it is best to provide a foundation which has been so constructed as to secure for the crust the best possible conditions of resistance to wear.'

"It is agreed that it is absolutely necessary to carry out repairs, in the case of all bituminous (including tarry and asphaltic) road crusts, immediately the necessity for them arises.

"The complete renewal rendered necessary by wear must be carried out immediately; the depth of the road crust is below a given limit of safety, or when its waterproofing qualities have become so poor that the road will unduly suffer from climatic conditions.

"In the mixing method, the stone must always be dry, and if necessary it must be heated.

"One must never employ road rollers which are too heavy.

"Sufficient information is now available to enable engineers to select and specify bituminous binders which will have no prejudicial effect upon public health, fish life, or vegetation; but which, on the contrary, will conduce to conditions of considerable hygienic advantage."

FOURTH QUESTION.—WOOD PAVING.

"Hard woods give varying results according to local circumstances, and it does not appear desirable to recommend them for roads with intense traffic in large cities, unless some means are devised to effectively prevent the rapid destruction of the joints and the resulting destructive effect on the concrete below."

FIFTH QUESTION.—METHODS OF LIGHTING.

"Every vehicle, whether standing or moving, should carry or show a light of sufficient power at night which can, except when specially authorized, be seen from the rear as well as from the front of the vehicle.

"Every motor car must carry after nightfall, two lighted lamps in front and one at the back; if it is able to move at a high speed, it must be fitted in front with a headlight of sufficient illuminating power to light up the road or path for at least fifty yards to the front. In inhabited places where the ordinary lighting is sufficient to allow motorists to see their way and to be easily seen, the light of the headlights must be limited to that of the ordinary lamp.

"One and the same color should be universally adopted as the color for danger signals.

"It is desirable that each Government should do away as soon as possible with colored lights on automobiles."

SEVENTH QUESTION.—REGULATIONS FOR FAST AND SLOW TRAFFIC ON ROADS.

"That all regulations for the control of road traffic should be based on the principle of allowing the speed practicable for each different kind of vehicle consistent with public safety, general convenience, and the normal wear of the road."

EIGHTH QUESTION.—AUTHORITIES IN CHARGE OF THE CONSTRUCTION AND MAINTENANCE OF ROADS. FUNCTIONS OF CENTRAL AUTHORITIES AND LOCAL AUTHORITIES.

"A principle that can be laid down as of universal application is, that the unit of highway administration shall be sufficiently large and command sufficient resources to employ and adequately remunerate a competent staff."

NINTH QUESTION.—FINANCE OF THE CONSTRUCTION AND UPKEEP OF ROADS. PROVISION FOR REVENUES.

"The expenditure on the maintenance and improvement of roads which are used mainly by long distance traffic, unless such expenditure is borne wholly out of the National Revenues under a system of State Administration of roads (which system is practicable and suitable in the case of some roads in some countries) should be mainly paid for out of National Revenues, whether or not such roads are locally administered and maintained, subject, where local administration prevails, to the supervision of a central government authority both as to efficiency and expenditure.

"It is desirable to abolish, so far as possible, all tolls on public roads, but it is equitable that vehicles which, on account of their weight or weight combined with speed or any other exceptional circumstances connected with either the vehicle or use of the road, cause special damage to roads beyond the wear and tear of the ordinary traffic of any district, should be subject to special taxation the proceeds of which should be earmarked for expenditure on roads.

"Borrowing money for new road construction and for the periodic renewal of the surface coating of a road is consistent with sound financial principles, provided that the loan period in the case of loans for renewals, is kept well within the life of the surface coating."

Even a brief summary of the work of the Third International Road Congress should not be closed without reference to the hospitality and elaborate series of entertainments and excursions provided by our British cousins and the officials of the Permanent International Association of Road Congresses.

Following this is a report of the Special Committee in regard to the use of State Convicts on the Public Roads:

Report of Committee on State Convict Labor.

WHEREAS, It appears to the North Carolina Good Roads Association in convention assembled at Morehead City, N. C., on this 31st day of July, 1913, that, under the existing laws of the State of North Carolina persons imprisoned in the State Prison at Raleigh have for a long while been and are now being hired to certain persons, firms and corporations engaged in grading, building and constructing certain railways or railroads in the State of North Carolina, and as a consideration for the services performed by said convicts, in the grading, building and construction of said railroads or railways, said persons, firms or corporations pay no sum or sums of money into the Treasury of North Carolina, but in lieu thereof, and as the only consideration for such services performed by said convicts, said persons, firms or corporations issue certain certificates of stock in said railroads or railways to the State of North Carolina.

AND WHEREAS, It further appears to this Association that a majority of the stock in said railways or railroads which has been heretofore and which continues to be issued to the State of North Carolina for the services of said convicts is absolutely worthless;

AND WHEREAS, It further appears to this Association that the convicts which are being placed with and hired to said persons, firms and corporations are greatly needed and could be used more profitably and to a better advantage in the construction and maintenance of the public roads and highways in the various counties of the State of North Carolina,—

It is, therefore, Resolved:

1. That the General Assembly of North Carolina, which has been called to meet in Raleigh, N. C., on the 24th day of September, 1913, by His Excellency, Locke Craig, Governor, be and is hereby earnestly requested to enact such laws and to pass such resolutions as will effectively withdraw all convicts which have been heretofore placed with or hired to any person, firm or corporation engaged in grading, building, or constructing any railroad in this State, where the services of said convicts is to be paid for in stock or bonds or any other interest in such railroad or railroads, and to prohibit the further placing or hiring of convicts to any person, firm or corporation; and to provide for the working of said convicts upon the highways which are known and designated as such of the various counties of the State of North Carolina which are now in existence or which may be hereafter established.

2. That the Secretary of this Association be and he is hereby authorized

and directed to have this resolution printed and copies thereof mailed to each and every member of the General Assembly of North Carolina, within thirty days from the passage thereof.

Respectfully submitted,
(Signed) W. C. Douglass, *Chairman*,
R. R. Cotten,
Wm. Dunn,
Committee.

Mr. Beard: I would like for that committee to state further that the farms belonging to the State shall be sold and the convicts put on the public roads.

Mr. Douglass: I believe that this Association ought to continue the report of its Committee on Resolutions to a called meeting to be held at Raleigh about the 24th day of September. We are willing to meet at some central point as a committee, if your Association will have a special meeting to pass upon these resolutions about the time of the meeting of the Legislature at Raleigh.

Mr. Cotten: I endorse the selling of the State farms, but it may not be a good thing to undertake this at this time.

Mr. Wood: This special session of the Legislature is called for particular work with regard to freight rates, and it will probably take the full twenty days for this work.

Following this there was considerable discussion with regard to the right of the State to repudiate the contracts now in force with the railroads.

Mr. Douglass: I move that this Association have an adjourned meeting to be held at Raleigh during the special session of the Legislature; and that a report of the Committee on Resolutions be handed in at that meeting.

Motion passed.

AFTERNOON SESSION.

Friday, August 1, 2:30 o'clock.

The first number on the program for the afternoon session was a paper by Mr. T. F. Hickerson, Associate Professor of Civil Engineering, University of North Carolina, as follows:

Duties of the Highway Engineer.

By T. F. Hickerson, Associate Professor of Civil Engineering, University of North Carolina.

The rapid progress of the better roads movement throughout the country requires the services of highway engineers of thorough training and wide experience to solve the increasing problems of road building in the best and most economical way.

The old idea, that "anybody can build a road," is almost obsolete now, though many fail to realize the variety and complexity of the problems that are involved in the location, construction and maintenance of roads and pavements that will meet the demands of modern traffic conditions.

No important road should ever be located without a careful consideration of alignment, grades, and drainage, as well as economy of construction. It is desirable that the curves and tangents should be laid out with the same degree of accuracy as those of a railroad. A survey for a road may mean anything from a reconnaissance or walking trip to an accurate instrumental survey, but it can rarely be considered entirely satisfactory until data are obtained for the plan, profile and cross sections to be shown on paper with estimates of yardage based upon an attempted equalization of cuts and fills.

The task of selecting the location, size, and type of culverts and bridges occurs on every road. A knowledge of hydraulics is often required, instead of some rule of thumb method, to determine what size of waterway will safely carry the flood waters from a given watershed. A familiarity with the qualities and prices of the various kinds of culverts is necessary.

The engineer should be competent to design bridges of both concrete and steel and to find out definitely whether existing structures are safe under the strain of heavier traffic.

He should know the most economical methods of moving dirt, stumps, and rock under various conditions.

All such matters as width of road, slope of the banks, crown of the road surface, shrinkage of material, grade stakes, guard rails, retaining walls, curbs, gutters, expansion joints, etc., demand attention on roads and pavements.

The engineer should know the characteristics and relative proportions of the materials and every detail connected with the construction of sand-clay, gravel, top-soil, macadam, concrete, and bituminous roads, as well as the numerous kinds of city pavements.

A knowledge of the properties and wearing qualities of the asphalts and tar products used largely on the first class highways of today as dust preventives and rock binders presents a wide field for study in itself. There is a difference of opinion as to how much of a chemist a highway engineer should be, but it seems necessary that he should be able to make tests and select intelligently the best type of bituminous product for the case at hand.

The engineer should be familiar with the relative merits and defects of the various kinds of road appliances, be it a road drag or the most elaborate rock crusher.

He should be able to write contracts and specifications clearly and concisely and understand the relations which should exist between himself and the contractor.

He should be able to give the approximate cost of everything pertaining to highway construction. Also he should know enough about bonds and sinking funds to give advice as to the proper financing of roads and pavements.

In order that a highway engineer may be fully equipped to understand all the duties of his profession, he should have had a four years' course in civil engineering at some college of repute and preferably a fifth year of research work on strictly highway engineering problems.

Many of the universities and technical schools have recently established special courses in highway engineering, among them being the University of North Carolina, which institution in connection with the North Carolina Geological and Economic Survey hopes to supply engineers for every county in the State.

It is unreasonable, of course, to expect the average young engineer, fresh from college, to fill the most responsible positions before they have gained a wider experience. In fact, they must first try to secure subordinate positions with older engineers for a length of time depending entirely upon their ability.

It is to be hoped that highway engineering as a profession will become more generally recognized and that salaries will be adequate to induce the best men to continue their work of bringing the highways of the country to the highest degree of perfection.

Following this the President announced that he would hear reports from engineers and representatives from counties and townships, who were present at the meeting:

Report of Highway Engineers.

Mr. W. S. Fallis, Road Engineer for Franklin, Catawba, and Vance Counties.

I have worked in two or three counties, and I believe I will start with the work in Catawba County. In one township in this county, we have a $50,000 bond issue and an outfit of some 30-odd mules, and have located perhaps 15 or 16 miles of road and built 8 miles.

In Franklinton Township, Franklin County, we have issued bonds to the amount of $60,000. We have built 75 miles of road, and just about finishing the work now.

In Youngsville Township, they have issued $40,000 in bonds and have built 30 miles of road, which will be finished in a year's time.

In Louisburg Township, they have issued $40,000 in bonds and have built 30 miles of road. There is still some work to be done. Louisburg Township has employed convicts altogether, and we are not only using the convicts as laborers, but are using the "trusties" as guards: We take a man that has been put in for a light offense and who has shown himself worthy, and make a guard out of him.

I have just taken charge of the work in Vance County. They have one outfit and expect to have four more. They have a bond issue for $200,000.

Mr. N. C. Hughes, Road Engineer for Halifax County.

Mr. Chairman and Gentlemen of the Convention:—I have only been in Halifax County since the first of June, which is just about two months. Prior to my having gone with these people, the road work that was going on in the county was supervised by the Magistrates of the county. We are subject to the orders of the county commissioners, and also the road force was augmented by a chain gang that was handled by a very efficient superintendent. But since this new Highway Board came into operation they appointed a superintendent and engineer and placed him over the entire work. The amount of money that was expended prior to June 1st I am not in a position to give the facts for the reason that these different Magistrates and county officials expended the money in such a manner that it was absolutely impossible to get on to what was done with the money. Right now we are trying to get the thing in a more systematized shape, and we hope in the near future to get things in pretty good shape.

The first thing that the Highway Board did was to authorize a survey made of the whole county, which we hope is going to mean a great deal to the county. This survey showed not only the main lines of road and the country roads but also the township lines, main creeks, the size and dimensions of the branches, and a report on the condition of same. It showed the country churches, schoolhouses, and sawmills. The money has been expended very poorly, and the least estimate of the road as I find it is about $2,200 a mile. That included some metal culverts that were put in, but it did not include some of the concrete culverts. One culvert cost $1,500 and another $450.

The method we are now pursuing is by means of a chain gang, which handles the dirt by shovel work. They are taking the clay from the side of the road, and distributing it with shovels. Recently we have augmented this force with teams. The amount of work that we can do with that chain gang, since I have been with them, shows up to be about a mile of road per week of sand-clay road. That does not mean the cutting of new rights-of-way. It means the digging for the clay and mixing at a cost of $350 to $400 per mile. In the upper part of the county where there is clay and gravel, I should think, although I am not in a position to say positively, that we can build sand-clay roads close around $450 a mile, including the small drainage.

In the upper part of the county, where it is all clay and gravel, the cost will be increased, because there will have to be a lot of grading.

Mr. Woodard, Chairman of the Board of County Commissioners of Wilson County.

We are building some roads by main strength and awkwardness. We have no engineer. We have a pretty good superintendent of our chain gang, and he has built some pretty good roads. We have built 25 miles of road, or rather we have converted 25 miles of old narraw road into 25 miles of good road. First we broke it up with a plow, and where we had too much clay, we put sand; and where we had too much sand, we put clay, and ran a smoothing harrow over it. After the first big rain we find that we have built good hard roads. I find by this method we have good roads for 6 or 7 months. I began in December in the winter to build my first road. As I said, we have 25 miles, and expect to continue in this way.

Mr. Fallis was engineer for our county and built 25 miles of macadam which has stood pretty well up to the present time, but is now beginning to unravel, and I am now looking for some method of repairing this road, that Mr. Fallis built for us.

Mr. R. P. Coble, Road Engineer for Lee County.

We started work in Lee County last fall, the first of September, with fifty mules, and divided them into two outfits of 25 mules each: one clearing force is clearing enough for both outfits, and the other does the grading of the road. At the present time we have about 25 miles of road graded and surfaced in the county. We have built the roads 30 feet wide and they are surfaced either with sand-clay or gravel. Most of the work there is rather light, but in some instances we are striking some pretty heavy work. Up to the present time we have spent about $40,000, which includes equipment which cost between $18,000 and $20,000. I believe if the work goes on as it is at the present time, we will get 90 miles out of the $100,000 bond issue. We would have gotten 100 miles, if we had not had to take out for the bridges.

We have one thing there we have to fight against. The people in Moore County are building a very cheap road. They think because Moore County can build cheap roads, they ought to be able to do the same thing. Moore County has a subsoil, which Lee County has not. That has been somewhat overcome, and the people are pretty well pleased with the roads.

Mr. J. C. M. Valentine, Road Engineer for Rutherford County.

I have been in Rutherford County about 3 or 4 months. We have a bond issue of $250,000 and a special tax, with which we hope to grade and surface 250 miles of road. We have a convict force of from 20 to 30 men and twenty mules. We have not quite gotten to the honor system, but I have taken the stripes off of them, and I am gradually approaching the honor system. We find it necessary, in order to make time, to contract some of the work. I think one of our engineers said it was not profitable to contract work, but it is the only way we can fulfill the expectations of our people in the county. I prepared specifications and the bids have been so close, that I am sure we are not paying too much for it. It seems to me that since the Government and the railroad corporations are contracting work, there is no reason why we should not contract work. Wherever the work is heavy enough to justify it, we let it out by contract. We are doing both ways, however. The only thing about that is we cannot afford to let work by contract if it is too light.

We invested in a road machine and a traction outfit, which cost us something less than $5,000 delivered in the county, and it is the best investment the county ever made. I do not know of any cheaper way of doing grading than with a traction engine, followed by a road plow.

We have not been at it long, but on the whole the outlook is satisfactory.

Representative from Greene County.

I am sorry I cannot report any improved roads in the county. Now there is a campaign on to vote a $180,000 bond issue. We have 9 townships in the county, and they are voting by townships, $20,000 each, and it is very likely the majority of them will carry it. In one township, it is doubtful. If we do, we expect to build 500 or 750 miles. It is my task to get an estimate as to what the roads will cost, and to draw up specifications. I find it a very difficult proposition. I would appreciate any assistance in the way of information on this subject. I have asked several, but they were unable to assist me.

Mr. J. E. Moore, of Northampton County.

Our county commenced the work of building roads in 1904. We levied a tax of 20 cents on the $100 and 16⅔ cents on the poll and $1 road tax or free labor, which brought us in $2,000, making in all from $12,000 to $14,000 a year. We bought some road equipment and teams, and went over the roads as best we could, rounded them up, and for the first four or five years the roads were greatly improved; but since then the thing has stood still. We have only made over and touched up those roads. We got in a good fund from a Dispensary, which gave us about $4,000.

In 1910 one of our townships, Rich Square, withdrew from the county and issued bonds to the amount of $30,000. The Supervisor and Commissioner are here today, but I will simply say that they have been doing some very good work, and have built four miles of 30-foot road and it has been properly located. I think that road will be a demonstration to our people.

I think the representative people of the county are strongly in favor of better roads. They are thoroughly aroused to the importance of it, and for myself I have been on the Board almost continuously, with the exception of two years. We have had many troubles on account of inefficient management. Of course, I am not a road man. I am only one of the commissioners.

I have written to Dr. Pratt and Mr. Varner in regard to getting us a man, but we have failed so far. We cannot get a man at the price we ought to pay with the funds that we have to use. We have about 575 miles of road in Northampton County and eight townships besides Rich Square, and now with the increased valuation of property, we raise about $14,000 or $15,000 to expend on the public roads. We have never had an efficient man in charge of the road work. I am sure that I can say here today that I know half of our money, which has been about $150,000, has been thrown away by inefficient management. And the people are getting dissatisfied along that line. They do not mind paying taxes, but they want to see the money spent right. Of course, if we were to put up an election to vote on bonds there today, I believe it would be voted down, but I wrote to the Office of Public Roads at Washington City, and asked them to send me a man to build a demonstration road. They promised to send me one in August to build the road. I do not think the day is far distant that we will begin to make progress along this line. The people are anxious for better roads, and they want to see something for their money. They shall either have it or I will get off the Board, and let someone else have my place.

We bought a traction engine, but we did not succeed very well with it. It would sink in the dirt, and tear up our little bridges. They were not strong enough to carry it over. So we sold it to Rich Square Township, and they seem to be succeeding very well with it. They have not had competent men to take care of it, and consequently it has been out of commission for some time.

I also wrote to the U. S. Office of Public Roads and asked them to send me a man to look at the situation in our county. They sent us a man and he went over the situation carefully and told us that we could build roads at a very reasonable cost. The trouble is we have a bad country to drain and we have to do a great deal of ditching. We have sand, but is not convenient. Our sand beds are along the streams. You have to haul it two or three miles, and the hauling is very expensive.

A number of reports of road work in the counties were received from engineers and county officials who were unable to be in person at the convention. These are given as follows:

Mr. James C. Wellons, of Johnston County.

We are trying to build some roads in our county by taxation, I am sorry to say. I do not think that we ought to do it. I think we ought to build roads in every county in North Carolina by a bond issue. We have four townships in the county which have voted special taxes, and these townships are building fairly good roads. We have no civil engineer. We have got some of our roads in very good shape, and the amount of money that we get from this special tax is just enough to keep everybody in the township dissatisfied with road building. It is sort of a patch work and that is all we can do there, or, in my judgment, anywhere with the old method. I have been hoping somebody would tell us how to get our farmers interested in the building of public roads.

I have been listening, Mr. Chairman, to get an answer to my question. In my county it is not the people who live in the towns and villages, but the farmers who are disinterested. I want to ask the Chairman of this Convention what to do with the farming element.

Mr. Varner: Distribute literature around and educate them.

Mr. Wellons: No, I think I will take the suggestion of the lady to my right, and make them buy automobiles. It seems to me the biggest thing the North Carolina Good Roads Association can do is to do something or devise some means by which we can interest the farmers of North Carolina. I believe the merchants, the lawyers, the educators, and the professional men all over the State are exceedingly interested. I don't believe you can ever build roads by voting a special tax; but how are we going to get them to vote bonds. Mr. Chairman, I am going to make this suggestion for what it is worth, that this convention before it adjourns, take some action on the question of the establishment of a Good Roads Commission in this State composed of three men or as many men as we ought to have, these men to send all over the State men who can educate the people to bond issues rather than taxation.

You cannot build good roads by special tax, because of the fact that you have not got enough money to build them.

I believe the road movement has reached that point in North Carolina that we ought to have a Good Roads Commission in this State composed of three men or one man, or as many men as we ought to have, and let these men take charge of the road work, and systematize it. So that the money that we have for road construction will no longer be spent in patch work, but we will get results from our expenditures.

Question: Why is the bond issue better than a special tax?

Mr. Wellons: You cannot build good roads by a special tax, because of the fact that you do not get enough money at one time to build them to advantage. It is building by retail rather than by wholesale. I believe in building the road good, then giving ten miles of it to one man, and appropriate so much money for the purpose of maintaining that road, and he will go over it whenever seasons are such that he can do it and keep it in repair; instead of the old method of doing a little patch work between one place and another as is being done under the special tax system, which soon gives you a road all to pieces.

Mr. Varner: I would like to supplement Mr. Wellons' remarks along this line and say that it is a great mistake to build roads by special tax. We have a good example of this in Mecklenburg County. They have been forty years building their roads and it has cost them $4,000,000. Now the county of Guilford watched Mecklenburg under the influence of good roads and they decided to have them at once. They voted a bond issue of $300,000, and built their roads, which increased their taxable property twice in ten years.

This was followed by a speech by Mr. James C. Bryan, of New Bern, against the bond issue method which, however, was not reported.

Mr. Cameron: I move that those who favor the policy of bond issues for building good roads rise.

There was only one vote against it, and that was Mr. Bryan.

Mr. Cameron: I move that a resolution be passed that it is the sentiment of this Association that a Highway Commission be established by this Legislature.

Motion carried.

Reports Sent in by Letter.

ALAMANCE COUNTY.

BURLINGTON, N. C., July 30, 1913.

Mr. J. H. Pratt, Morehead City, N. C.

DEAR SIR: On account of sickness I cannot be at the Good Roads Convention, but will say in regard to the road work at the present we are grading, putting down some sand, repairing macadam roads and dirt roads. We put down a little macadam last year.

Trusting that the Convention may be a success, I am

Yours very truly,

(Signed) G. A. FOGLEMAN.

CRAVEN COUNTY.

NEW BERN, N. C., July 30, 1913.

Dr. Joseph Hyde Pratt, Chapel Hill, N. C.

DEAR SIR:—Last year the road tax was levied by townships, each township spending its own money as suited its own ideas. This year the county is spending a tax of 15 cents on the $100 levied throughout the county under my supervision and we have voted for next year a 20 cent tax, an increase of 5 cents over the past year. This will be spent the same as the present year.

We are using what is needed to maintain the roads and using the remainder to rebuild and improve the leading market roads. We are using the patrol system of maintenance.

The county is making an effort to pay for the road construction as they go. Our grading is light. The principal cost of securing good roads in this county arising in securing proper drainage.

The county is making a decided stand for good roads, and the citizens are unanimously in favor of using every effort to secure good roads.

Yours very truly,

(Signed) R. E. SNOWDEN.

CUMBERLAND COUNTY.

FAYETTEVILLE, N. C., July 23, 1913.

Dr. Joseph Hyde Pratt, Chapel Hill, N. C.

DEAR SIR:—I regret very much that it is impossible for me to attend the Good Roads Association to be held at Morehead City, July 31st, and August. 1st. The County Commissioners have charge of our roads now, and will in October levy a direct road tax of about twenty-five cents, which will give us thirty or forty thousand each year for road building. I am very anxious that the commissioners employ an expert road builder to do their work, and want to enlist your aid in bringing this about. I have arranged for Mr. D. K. Taylor, one of the county commissioners to be present at the meeting. I want to ask, if you can find time, that you talk with Mr. Taylor and let him know that you can assist him in finding the right man to build our roads. I think he is inclined to employ a cheap man, which is false economy.

Again, expressing regret that I can't be with you, I remain

Yours very truly,

(Signed) T. G. MCALISTER

DURHAM COUNTY.

DURHAM, N. C., July 30, 1913.

Dr. Joseph Hyde Pratt, Chapel Hill, N. C.

DEAR SIR:—The policy of the county is to build roads radiating from Durham as a center to the adjoining counties. All improved roads are 30 feet wide.

The Central Highway has been completed except one mile, the road force is at work on this extension, which is expected to be completed in about 60 days. Our road force and equipment consists of: 79 convicts, 36 head of stock, 18 wagons, 12 wheel scrapes, 6 drag scrapes, 5 road machines, 2 rollers, (1 stem, 1 gasoline), 2 traction engines, 1 scarifier, 2 rock crushers and bonds, 1 road sprinkler, 3 wagon scales, 1 automobile for superintendent of roads, 2 steel cages for convicts, 2 portable camphouses.

Stock is protected by tents. Convict force is divided into three camps, two for construction and one for repair. Our commissioners are paying more attention to the repairing of roads.

Durham County has no road bonds outstanding and none under consideration. The road tax is 20⅓ cents on the one hundred dollars property valnation.

We spent from June 30, 1912, to July 1, 1913, on road construction, $28,418.73; on construction of bridges, $5,110; on maintenance of bridges,

$1,123.15; and spent for general maintenance of roads, $10,367.61. Total, $45,019.49.

Miles of macadam road	127
Miles of gravel road graded	15
Miles graded ready for macadam or gravel	15
Miles of road open to travel not improved	193
Total mileage	700

Yours very truly,
(Signed) J. M. POLLARD, *Superintendent.*

GASTON COUNTY.

MT. HOLLY, N. C., July 28, 1913.

Dr. Joseph Hyde Pratt, Chapel Hill, N. C.

DEAR SIR:—I regret very much that I will be unable to attend the Convention at Morehead this year. In Gaston County we have about 90 miles of macadam roads and 20 miles of sand-clay, or soil roads, and are building at the rate of about 18 miles per year. At the present time we are building the sand-clay road altogether only where we had rock corded previously, and in localities where we cannot find the right kind of material for surfacing. We are not repairing any macadam roads except to keep the dirt part surfaced up to rock and the rock top dressed where sand is plentiful. We have not decided what method to pursue, when they have to be rebuilt. The method we are using toward keeping the sand-clay road in repair is just to fill up the holes and the gutters that occur on the sides of the road with the same kind of material the road was built of, and smooth it with a steel drag. Land values adjacent or near an improved road have increased so as to be almost prohibitive for farming purposes.

In the last few years land has doubled and in some cases near towns tripled in value. I consider good roads has had more to do with increasing values than any other cause.

(Signed) T. L. WARE,
Superintendent of Roads.

IREDELL COUNTY.

STATESVILLE, N. C., July 30, 1913.

Dr. Joseph Hyde Pratt, Chapel Hill, N. C.

DEAR SIR:—

Total number of miles of road graded	160
Total number of miles entirely completed	137

Most grades are from 2 to 2½%; 4% is fixed as the maximum grade, but there are only few 4% grades.

The above represents only topsoil roads, as they are the only kind being constructed in Iredell County. When the system is finished, there will be at least 200 miles, or perhaps more, of modern topsoil roads.

Iredell County has about 30 miles of macadam roads, and is now facing the serious problem of what to do with them, as the macadam roads have deteriorated pretty badly, and Iredell County is now figuring out plans of how to maintain those macadam roads, and get them in first-class shape.

The work that has so far been done with topsoil roads proves very conclusively that topsoil or sand-clay roads are much better suited for our conditions than macadam.

MAINTENANCE.

Contracts have been let pretty much all over the county for maintenance of the roads that have been finished, at the rate of $10 per mile per annum. The contractor is required to give a $200 bond and to go over his section of the road with a split log drag after every rain, and as often as necessary, and twice per annum is required to go over it with a road machine, but the contractor must furnish his own teams. The work done by the contractor must be approved by a member of the board of county commissioners.

After the roads are all completed, it is proposed to divide the entire system up into different sections, and maintain several small forces of hands in those different sections, whose duty it will be to maintain the roads. We favor the employment of a County Inspector of roads, whose duty it will be to go over and constantly inspect the roads in the entire county, and see to it that the necessary work is done on it. We feel that it is money that would be well spent.

BRIDGES.

As the roads are built, permanent bridges are constructed. These bridges have concrete piers, steel girders or beams, and are therefore permanent constructions. Over some of the larger streams, larger and more expensive bridges have been built, with trusses, but all the bridge work is of a permanent character.

STOOD WINTER WELL.

That portion of the topsoil roads in Iredell County completed in 1912, passed through last winter and stood the weather very satisfactorily, and we are perfectly satisfied that the topsoil road is the best for our conditions, and with proper maintenance we feel that they will last indefinitely. We are satisfied the maintenance will be comparatively low.

EQUIPMENT.

The county owns 100 mules and equipment consisting of road machines, scrapers, drags, etc. The investment in this equipment is about $35,000. More satisfactory work has been produced, and at a lower cost with the equipment owned by the county than where the work has been let by contract, and the county feels it made a good investment in its mules and equipment. Twelve outfits are now at work in the county, located in different portions of it, and the roads are being pushed as fast as possible to the county line.

Only two outfits are doing contract work in the county. The improved roads radiate from the two towns of Statesville and Mooresville in every direction. There are seven highways leading out of Statesville in different directions, and a number out of Mooresville, and the roads, when completed, will give Iredell County a very complete system.

SOME FIGURES SHOWING COST.

Some very careful figures were kept, and a section of road 27.87 miles long, showed an average cost per mile, including bridges, of $1,573.28. After deducting the cost of bridges, which was 8,186, it left the average cost per mile for the completed road, $1,283.

FREE LABOR VS. CONVICT.

A comparison as to the cost of building roads by convict and free labor shows the following results. The period of time in this particular instance was from February 22, 1913, to May 31, 1913.

The grade on the road where the convicts were used was not as heavy as where free labor was employed.

On a stretch measuring 2.20 miles, the cost per mile, with convict labor was $1,480. On a stretch of 3 miles, with free labor, the cost per mile was $1,006.

The convict labor was employed on the Houstonville road, and free labor on the Wilkesboro road. There was somewhat more dirt to remove on the Wilkesboro road, on account of the grades being heavier.

Yours very truly,
(Signed) G. E. French.

MADISON COUNTY.

Marshall, N. C., July 30, 1913.

Dr. Joseph Hyde Pratt, Chapel Hill, N. C.

Dear Sir:—Madison County has by far the hardest link in the Central Highway to build. It is more than thirty miles the nearest way through the county, and the road for a considerable part of the way will have to be blasted from the solid rock. There will be several miles on which the rock work alone will cost the county something like ten thousand dollars a mile. Mr. Clingman, one of the State's engineers, has surveyed the road on a grade nowhere greater than 4½%. It follows the crests of the mountains overlooking the French Broad River and when completed will be one of the most picturesque roads in the country.

Until 1880 there was a stage road from Tennessee along the French Broad River into Asheville. This was the main highway from Western North Carolina into the State of Tennessee. When the railroad was built through Madison County it took over the stage road and used it as a road bed. Since this time no other road has been built along the river because of the immense expense of building it through the Smoky Mountains.

I am informed that the railway company paid the State of North Carolina for taking the stage road. The railway company today pays taxes on more than a million dollars worth of property in Madison County. This line of railroad has helped to build Western North Carolina and has brought untold wealth into the State. The State has shared these benefits along with us and it can do no less than furnish a camp of convicts to help build the highway through Madison County.

The last Legislature passed an act authorizing and directing that the county of Madison be furnished not less than twenty-five convicts to build not less than fifteen miles of road in lieu of the old stage road. The act directed that the convicts be at work in Madison not later than June 1, 1913. At the same time an act was passed directing that convicts be placed on a road in Buncombe and Henderson counties (known as the Hickory Nut Gap Road) not later than July 1, 1913. The Council of State has directed that fifty convicts be sent to the Hickory Nut Gap Road, but has made no provision for Madison County.

When the act was passed giving State aid to Madison County, it so encouraged the advocates of good roads that they carried a $300,000 bond issue for the improvement of the roads of the County. At the June meeting of the Madison County Highway Commission $50,000 of bonds were sold, on a bad market, and private individuals agreed to make good the loss, that we might have money available to supplement the work of the State convicts. When it was learned that fifty convicts has been given to the Hickory Nut Gap Road and none given to Madison County, our people became so discouraged that there is a demand now being made on the Highway Commission to sell no more bonds. It is true that the amount of labor done by the convicts would be only a small item in building a highway through Madison County, but the greatest good would come from the encouragement to the people in knowing that the State of North Carolina was coöperating with them.

The present taxable value of Madison County is five million dollars. If the Central Highway is completed through the county and made the center of a system of good roads, it will mean that in a very few years the taxable value will be doubled and that this increased value will add to the wealth of North Carolina. It appears to be a short-sighted policy to hire out the convicts to private individuals and railroads at so much per day when by working them on the public roads we could add to the wealth of the State so much more rapidly. No man ever accumulated any considerable wealth at daily wages and I know of no reason why it should be different with a State.

At a session of the Greater Western North Carolina Association in Asheville on July 24, 1913, the claims of Madison County were presented and resolutions were passed requesting the Council of State to send convicts to Madison at the earliest possible moment. This Association is composed of the counties of Buncombe, Henderson, Transylvania, Haywood, Jackson, Polk, and Madison. It is one of the strongest organizations in Western North Carolina and the fact that Madison's neighboring counties endorse the action of the Legislature tends to prove the justness of our cause.

If Madison County fails to receive its convicts promptly, I fully believe that road building here will be set back a number of years.

Yours very truly,

(Signed) Guy V. Roberts.

ORANGE COUNTY.

Chapel Hill, N. C., July 30, 1913.

Dr. Joseph Hyde Pratt, Chapel Hill, N. C.

Dear Sir:—A Good Roads Commission was appointed and a Superintendent was elected in May in accordance with the provisions of the Bond Act. In June surveys were begun for the series of improved roads proposed by the commission. The first road projected was the one across the county from the Durham County line to the Alamance line.

About the time this survey was finished the commission, finding they would be forced to wait until another session of the Legislature to have the bonds validated before selling them, had the surveying work suspended. The Superintendent was put in direct charge of the repairs of existing roads. He spent a large portion of the time making minor relocations where the roads were so badly situated that repair was impracticable. In the meantime some work was done on mapping and computations of the survey already made, and one double span heavy beam bridge was put in on the road between Chapel Hill and Durham.

In January and February the surveying work was continued. Owing to dissatisfaction among the people along the route, several surveys were made over a part of the distance from Hillsboro to the Durham line before a final location was made. The people who are to be benefited by the road have thus delayed the work by bringing long complaints and petitions before the Commission.

Actual construction was begun about the 10th of June on the Hillsboro-Durham section. Work was begun at the Hillsboro end, which involves the roughest part of the grading. To date there have been two miles practically graded to final shape and the culverts and bridge abutments put in. The headwalls to the culverts are not yet built.

The contract for the section from Hillsboro to the Alamance County line was made July 18th with a firm in Portsmouth, Va. Their forces arrived July 29th to begin work. This branch will be pushed to completion as rapidly as possible.

The survey has been practically completed across the County by way of Chapel Hill and White Cross, so that estimates will be ready in a short while for letting this road. Two other surveys are to be started within the next week, one leading northwest from Hillsboro, the other north from Efland to Cedar Grove.

The Commission has hired the entire equipment of one contractor with which to carry on the surfacing work. This will be done by a force under the supervision of the Highway Superintendent. Gravel, topsoil and sand-clay will be used for surfacing, according to the relative convenience of the different materials along the route and the nature of the foundation upon which they are to be used.

Since December there has been surfaced a stretch of about one-half mile by farmers' teams. The material used was gravel and sand from the bank of Eno River. Part of the material was put on before the winter rains and has become thoroughly mixed and compacted. Even that part which was put on in the spring after the rainy season has compacted in very good condition. It has exceeded the expectations of those who used it for the first few weeks after the work was begun. It seems to be difficult to convince the people of this section of the country that a sand-clay road can be built to stand the winter weather. This will certainly serve as a vindication of this kind of road for Orange County citizens.

While considerable time has been lost in waiting for the Legislature to validate the bonds, we are planning now to push the work as rapidly as possible and get as much road built before winter comes as we can handle.

Respectfully submitted,

(Signed) R. T. Brown,
Highway Superintendent.

POLK COUNTY.

The absent delegation from Polk County begs to report that for over half a century Polk County floundered over her red clay roads, and forded her streams, strenuously opposing more improved methods; until 1908, the thrifty village of Tyron bonded itself and built about a mile of macadam under supervision of a road engineer from the U. S. Department of Agriculture. Following this object-lession the township issued bonds and built two miles of macadam to Lynn. These roads have proven the desirability of good roads to the extent that this spring Polk County, without oppsition issued $100,000 in bonds for good roads, sold them at par, and cash is now in our banks ready for business. An expert road engineer is now laying out the more important roads where work will begin at once and be rushed to a finish. Our people are now enthusiastically determined to improve our roads, and with this in view we beg to invite other counties in the State to be neighborly and come over and observe the changed conditions in Polk.

(Signed) George B. Cobb.

ROCKINGHAM COUNTY.

Reidsville, N. C., July 30, 1913.

Dr. Joseph Hyde Pratt, Chapel Hill, N. C.

Dear Sir:—Here in Rockingham County, in the centre of the Piedmont section of North Carolina, I believe that the road problem is more complicated than in almost any section of the State. With our numerous streams and sundry separate sheds, we are confronted with requirements in road building which are hard to meet. We are forced to build many parallel roads near each other on account of the difficulty across our valleys from one ridge to the other. We also have four or five towns skirting the county which forces the building of more roads than if we had one common centre toward which all main roads would point. These conditions force us to maintain nearly fifteen hundred miles of roads. Our soil is easily washed and becomes muddy very easily.

I think I am expected to give some of the history of the road building and road sentiment in the county which has had to meet so many complex and knotty problems with its roads. Here in Rockingham County, we originally worked our roads (or rather did not work them) by warning in all the able-bodied men between the ages of eighteen and forty-five to go over our roads some two or three times a year, under the direction of an overseer. Under this system all the little work was done very grudgingly and very sparingly and we had very narrow, winding roads.

The Legislature of 1897 passed a bill abolishing this old and antiquated system and substituted the working on our roads of all of the county's convicts whose terms were less than ten years, and provided that all of the county commissioners could levy taxes for road building and road maintenance not to exceed 25 cents on the hundred dollars valuation of property and 75 cents on the poll. We are building and maintaining roads under the provisions of this bill now. We work our convicts all the time on road building and keep up our maintenance work with hired labor. We have also arranged to work the convicts from several other nearby counties that have no arrangements for working their convicts. In the fifteen years that we have been working under our present system we have made some considerable improvement in our roads. In this time we have, including our re-located and re-graded roads, built or improved approximately seven hundred miles of road and have built fourteen miles of good macadam road and several miles of sand-clay roads. For repair work we keep three road machines with eighteen mules on the roads all the year, suitable for such work. We usually with these forces get over all the roads in the county at least once a year. Our roads are not perfect but improved and we hope soon to make much greater improvements. For the last five or six years we graded all the roads which we improved at all, to a standard grade and width which places them practically ready for macadam or sand and clay. We insist even on our hills to keep our grades below five per cent. We have just enough six per cent grade to not want any more that steep.

In 1898, the first year our law became operative, the commissioners levied a tax of 8⅓ cents and bought six mules to begin work. We now work from thirty to forty mules all the time. This rate of 8⅓ cents was adhered to till 1903 when it was advanced to 16⅔ cents and maintained there until 1907 when we decided to begin building macadam roads by taxation and advanced the rate to 25 cents which is the limit. We failed by a very small margin to carry a bond issue for half million dollars for permanent road work on a large scale, but with the growing sentiment in that direction we hope to carry this bond issue soon. It was not a lack of road sentiment which lost it before. Our people would not stand for a movement for any step backward or any curtailment of our present work.

This is a little of the history of the road work in a county full of difficulties and I hope soon to be able to make a much better report.

Yours very truly,

(Signed) S. B. Dameron.

WILKES COUNTY.

Maple Springs, N. C., July 29,.1913.

Dr. Joseph Hyde Pratt, Chapel Hill, N. C.

Dear Sir:—There has been but a little change in the roads in Wilkes County for several years. Public spirited men in five townships have made some excellent grades around bad hills, but the townships and public have done but little. Our present road law serves, generally, to keep the roads repaired and but little permanent improvement is being made.

There is a growing sentiment to vote bonds and construct permanent roads.

Respectfully yours,

(Signed) C. R. Triplett.

The President: Mr. Small has some remarks to make, and we will now hear from him.

Honorable John H. Small.

Mr. President, Ladies and Gentlemen:—I will promise to be brief and make only a few comments which have been provoked by the interesting proceedings which we have had here to-day. The address of Professor Blanchard upon the International Association of Road Congresses touched upon a very important phase of this problem in its international aspect, and it brought new light to me. He referred to an International Association known as the International Navigation Congress. The United States Government is a member of that Congress, and its last session was held in the city of Philadelphia one year ago. I had the opportunity and privilege of attending its sessions for about a week, and anyone interested in water transportation could not fail to be deeply impressed by the information which was set forth there by delegates from practically every civilized country. We are accustomed to refer to Europe as the "home of good roads." This idea has found too ready lodgment in our land. No man can read some of the current history of England, France, Germany, Ireland, Norway and Sweden without being impressed by the fact that we have something to learn from those countries in the progressive movements which are now taking possession of us for the betterment of our people. We have just sent to Europe a National Commission to study rural credits, which has just returned and will, in a few weeks or months, submit their report to the Secretary of Agriculture. Dr. Houston told me a day or two ago that he had arranged for Mr. Knapp and Dr. Carver to go to Europe and study these questions of agricultural credits. I asked Dr. Pratt a moment or two ago if the address of Professor Blanchard would be published, and if so, I will do all in my power to have the United States Government become a member of this International Association just as it has become a member of this International Navigation Congress, because none of them, no matter how important they may be, can transcend in importance, to the people of North Carolina, our nation and country, this question of building highways.

Another thought which has been provoked, Mr. President. I was very much impressed, as we all were, by the address of Hon. Jesse Taylor, of Ohio. I am delighted that he came among us. I hope he will come again and bring Mrs. Taylor and the old gentleman. I have enjoyed his presence and his fine, inspiring and uplifting talk. Now, for fear that a wrong conception may be taken of his address, I want to take this occasion to give this expression. First, I am impressed with the idea of the Federal Government and the States undertaking to build a systematized series of National Highways, and the appointment of a commission to determine where the highways shall be built, and to consider all the elements that enter into that problem of building highways; and then build them according to the report of the finest talent which can be placed upon them by the Commission to study that great problem. The idea is a revelation to me. My thought had all along been Federal coöperation with the States, appropriating so much money to be expended in the States in coöperation or in conjunction with certain money appropriated by the States and the local communities. Now, this is all right in its sphere, as I will refer to in a moment. But this idea of the Federal Government itself building great national highways and interstate highways which shall bind us all together in stronger ties; stronger than they have perhaps ever been before; stronger possibly than our great interstate lines of railroads; stronger than has been consummated by the telegraph and telephone of our admirable postal service. I am in favor, I say, of the United States building a national system of highways; and there is nothing in the Constitution, nothing in our theory of government which militates against this idea. But let us remember that that does not in the slightest degree minimize the necessity of states, counties, and townships doing their share and having their system for the building of roads. (Applause.) This is one thought that I wished to bring to you.

Now, in North Carolina, as in other States, we may have a state fund and each county have funds, and it would be entirely proper and wise for Congress to have a separate appropriation for coöperation with States and counties. I simply wish to differentiate that idea from the original idea of National Highways.

Now, Mr. President, just a few more words along the line which is running in the minds of many of our delegates here; that is, how we are going to impress the consciences and arouse the conviction and the sense of duty of the folks, and as Mr. Wellons says, in North Carolina the *farmers*, because they are 75 per cent and more of our population.

We stand at the threshold of better public roads in North Carolina, and to my mind, the primary essential is that we shall have a Highway Commission, a Commission accompanied by sufficient appropriation to pay a man of ability at the head of it. By the way, we cannot get any more appropriate man at the head of this Highway Commission than that man who is now, with finest ability, simply acting upon his own inspiration and sense of civic duty, and love for his job—Dr. Pratt. We should have an appropriation sufficient to pay him and also employ one, two or three highway engineers, or as many highway engineers as we require, and among those, one or two to go among the folks, and talk the "Gospel of Good Roads." How many public schools are there in North Carolina levying taxes? Nearly 2,000, are there not? How is it that it has been possible to induce 1,500 rural districts in North Carolina voluntarily to go to the polls and levy a tax for public schools upon themselves? It is because we have been sending missionaries; because we have been sending the inspired St. John the Baptist into these various sections and talking education to these people. We must have a systematized organization, a Highway Commission, clothed with power and fortified with sufficient appropriation to furnish these missionaries to go among the people; engineers who can go here and there where the people desire them to give them information and educational talks about how to build their public roads. Why has not North Carolina that Highway Commission? There is absolutely no excuse except the lethargy of our people. I am ashamed of my State and the condition which I am going to portray to you in just one moment.

In my Congressional District, I have *ten* calls for a highway engineer, and I have to go to the Office of Public Roads and beg for an engineer. I am ashamed that this great State of North Carolina with all its pride of history, and its pride in itself, that it should be dependent upon the Federal Government in order to obtain the services of a highway engineer to meet the demands of our people. I cannot conceive why our last two Legislatures have failed to provide a Highway Commission. There are some things which a State cannot afford to deny itself. No community is so poor that it can afford to fail to provide an opportunity for the training of every child in that community, and the State of North Carolina is not so poor that it cannot provide this Highway Commission. If we, who are here, would return to our respective counties, and interview our members of the General Assembly and the State Senators and let them know the demands of the people, we would get that Highway Commission, and we won't get it until then. If we get this Highway Commission with a live man at the head of it, ready to create sentiment, and ready to respond to sentiment when it is created, we will reach the civic consciences and arouse the convictions of the farmers of North Carolina. I have faith in our farmers; I have been among them, and know them; and when you put before them a man in whom they have confidence, they are not niggardly; they are not narrow; neither are they parsimonious. All you have to do is to appeal to their better nature, to their pride as citizens. Let us organize this Highway Commission, let it send its missionaries among the people, and it will be one of the strongest factors we can create to solve for us this question of "More roads and better roads." This education of the people will afford a ready solution of whether we shall build roads by issuing bonds or whether we shall build them out of a special tax. If they want the roads quickly, and ordinarily you will find they do, then it is better to issue bonds. If the county has sufficient taxable property that will yield a sufficient sum out of a current tax to carry on the road work as it should be carried on, you must first create an intelligent sentiment and appreciation of the importance of public roads with a fair and intelligent idea of how best to build the roads; then the question of taxation will straighten itself.

Just this, and I am done: I was talking with quite a distinguished member of a Trust Company, which deals largely in all classes of drainage bonds, municipal bonds, county bonds, and irrigation bonds of various kinds. He gave me this idea, and it impressed me. More and more in the future there is going to be what is technically known as "amortization" of these bond issues. Reducing this to plain English, bonds payable not all at one time, but payable during a series of years. And I am inclined to think when we consider a bond issue of say $100,000, it will be best to issue it in lots of say $10,000. Then gradually increase until they are all paid at stated periods at the end of say thirty years, as the case may be. They will be more salable, and we will avoid the one objection to bond issues payable all at one time. That is to say, a county issuing $200,000 payable thirty years from now, it may be assumed that when they fall due, they will not be paid in cash but they will be liquidated at the end of thirty years by issuing new bonds; unless in the meantime you have a sinking fund, and it is not always practicable to create a sinking fund for successive periods of five or ten years. I think this worthy of the consideration of any county or township which takes up the matter of issuing bonds.

I thank you for this opportunity.

Resolutions.

Resolved, That it is the sense of the North Carolina Good Roads Association that, in the interest of highway improvement in this country, the United States Government should become a member of the Permanent International Association of Road Congresses, as Great Britain, France, Germany, Russia, Italy, and other great countries of the world have; and be it further

Resolved, That copies of these resolutions be sent to the Secretary of State, the Secretary of Agriculture and the Postmaster-General.

Dr. Pratt: I move that the thanks of the Association be extended to Mr. Canfield.

Motion passed.

Dr. Pratt: I move that the thanks of this Association be extended to the city of Morehead and to the Committee on Arrangements for what they have done to make this convention the success that it has been.

Motion passed.

Report of Nominating Committee.

The Nominating Committee reported as follows in regard to the officers for the coming year:

President—H. B. Varner, Lexington.

Secretary—Joseph Hyde Pratt, Chapel Hill.

Assistant Secretary—Miss H. M. Berry, Chapel Hill.

Treasurer—Joseph G. Brown, Raleigh.

Vice-Presidents—J. L. Patterson, Roanoke Rapids; R. L. May, Trenton; M. C. Winslow, Selma; P. H. Hanes, Winston-Salem; P. B. Beard, Salisbury; F. M. Shannonhouse, Charlotte; E. C. Chambers, Asheville; A. B. Skelding, Wilmington; H. E. Stacy, Rowland.

Executive Committee—H. B. Varner, Lexington; Joseph Hyde Pratt, Chapel Hill; Joseph G. Brown, Raleigh; G. D. Canfield, Morehead City; Frank H. Fleer, Thomasville; William Dunn, New Bern; Dr. C. P. Ambler, Asheville; Wade Harris, Charlotte; James A. Wellons, Smithfield; D. A. McDonald, Carthage; R. R. Cotten, Bruce; J. E. Cameron, Kinston; John C. Drewry, Raleigh; Leonard Tufts, Pinehurst.

AMALGAMATION WITH THE NATIONAL HIGHWAYS ASSOCIATION.

It was decided by the Association that the Executive Committee should decide upon terms of amalgamation with the National Highways Association, and this committee has agreed upon the amendment of the Constitution of the Association, the following being the new regulations governing the North Carolina Good Roads Association, North Carolina Division of the National Highways Association:

Regulations

OF THE

NORTH CAROLINA GOOD ROADS ASSOCIATION

North Carolina Division of the National Highways Association.

ARTICLE I.

NAME.

Section 1. The name of this organization shall be the "North Carolina Good Roads Association."

ARTICLE II.

PURPOSES.

Section 1. The purpose of this Association is to act as the North Carolina Division of the National Highways Association and shall exist:

To favor, foster and further the establishment, development and maintenance of the National, State, County and Township Highways and "Good Roads Everywhere."

To secure the social, moral, commercial, industrial, material, educational and personal benefits in the uplift of the citizens of North Carolina, which follows in the train of easy and free intercommunication and transit between the great centers of population and the great productive areas of the State.

To disseminate knowledge and increase interest relative to the ethical and economic value of our public roads.

To aid all efforts for their improvement.

To advocate wise, equitable and practical Road Legislation.

To urge the adoption of a comprehensive and efficient plan of administration that will improve, maintain and unify as one complete system the public thoroughfares of the country—to the end that we may secure:

A national Highway System.

A State Highway System.

A County Highway System.

A Township Highway System.

Each a distinct unit, yet all integral factors of a complete system of "Good Roads Everywhere."

To insist that Road officials faithfully perform the duties of their respective offices.

To secure integrity of expenditure and skill in construction and maintenance in all classes of road building and road improvement.

ARTICLE III.

HEADQUARTERS.

Section 1. The official headquarters of this Association shall be located and maintained in the town of Chapel Hill, North Carolina.

ARTICLE IV.

MEMBERSHIP.

Section 1. All persons, firms or corporations who may be members of record and are in good standing in the North Carolina Good Roads Association on or after the 28th day of July, 1913, shall be members of the North Carolina Good Roads Association, North Carolina Division of the National Highways Association, and shall thereby be members of the National Highways Association and have all the rights, privileges and obligations as provided by the Constitution and By-laws thereof.

All persons, firms or corporations who shall pay to the Secretary the annual dues of any class for one year in advance shall be a member of the North Carolina Good Roads Association, North Carolina Division of the National Highways Association.

The members shall be divided into the following nine (9) classes:

(1) *Patron Members*—who shall pay a life membership fee of one thousand ($1,000) dollars.

(2) *Life Members*—who shall pay life membership fee of five hundred ($500) dollars.

(3) *Corporate Members*—Corporations who shall pay an annual fee of fifty ($50) to five hundred ($500) dollars.

(4) *Collective Members*—Individuals, firms or corporations who shall pay an annual fee of twenty-five ($25) to two hundred ($200) dollars.

(5) *Sustaining Members*—who shall pay an annual fee of ten ($10) dollars.

(6) *Contributing Members*—who shall pay an annual fee of five ($5) dollars.

(7) *Highway Members*—who shall pay an annual fee of two dollars and fifty cents ($2.50).

(8) *Union Members*—who shall pay an annual fee of one ($1) dollar.

(9) *Scout and Camp-fire Members*—who shall pay an annual fee of fifty (50) cents, and who shall not exceed eighteen (18) years of age. Scout and Camp-fire members shall not have voting or property rights, but shall have the right of free entrance and free speech.

Section 2. All dues shall be a continuing obligation in the class designated, unless the membership is discontinued by death, resignation or by order of the Board of Trustees of this Association.

Section 3. All dues shall be paid annually in advance, and shall be due and payable each year during the month from which the membership dates. Members three months in arrears shall not be allowed to resign without payment of dues for the current year. Members in arrears may be dropped from the membership list by order of the Board of Trustees of this Association.

Section 4. Members shall not be liable for any dues or assessments other than the payment of annual dues as herein provided. The officers of this

Association and its Board of Trustees shall not have power to contract any debts or liabilities of any kind, which in the aggregate are in excess of funds available for the use of the Association, for which the Association or its membership individually or collectively can be held responsible.

ARTICLE V.

VOTING PRIVILEGES.

Section 1. Members of the Association shall be entitled to participate in the proceedings of its meetings and vote upon all questions that may come before it. Voting by proxy shall not be allowed.

ARTICLE VI.

MEETINGS.

Section 1. The annual meeting of this Association shall be held each year at such time and place as may be determined by the Board of Trustees. Fifteen days' notice shall be given to all members of the time and place where such meeting is to be held. At such annual meeting the Association shall transact such business as may be brought before it by the Board of Trustees.

Section 2. Special meetings of this Association may be held at any time and place when called by its Board of Trustees, of which at least ten days notice shall be given to all members of the time and place wherein a special meeting should be held.

Section 3. Every notice calling a special meeting shall state the question proposed to be considered, and no question of which due notice has not been given shall be considered at any special meeting unless approved by a unanimous vote of all the members of the Board of Trustees present.

Section 4. A majority of all Members registered as being in attendance at any annual or special meeting of this Association shall constitute a quorum for the transaction of business.

ARTICLE VII.

BOARD OF TRUSTEES.

Section 1. The business of this Association shall be managed by a Board of Trustees. This Board shall consist of fifteen (15) members, elected by the Association at the meeting at which these regulations are adopted upon the concurrent nominations by the Board of Trustees of the National Highways Association. Other members of the Board may be added from time to time by a vote of two thirds of the members of the Board with the concurrence of the Trustees of the National Highways Association. Members of the Board shall hold office until removed as hereinafter provided. Vacancies on the Board shall be filled in the same manner as upon an original election.

Section 2. The Board of Trustees shall meet upon the call of the President, the Chairman, or any two (2) members of the Executive Committee, or any seven (7) members of the Board.

Section 3. The members of the Board of Trustees present at any meeting of which three days' written notice has been given each member, shall constitute a quorum for the transaction of business.

Section 4. The Board of Trustees shall give directions as to the general policies of the Association. They shall hear reports of the Executive Committee and transact such other business as they may determine. They shall have custody of all property of the Association, supervision of all its expenses, appoint all committees and all officers, not otherwise provided for, but subject to the approval of the Trustees of the National Highways Association; and they shall have general supervision and control over all work carried on by the Association and its officers. The Board of Trustees may cause a call to be made upon the general public for voluntary subscriptions to a fund in aid of the general work of the Association, or for any specific purpose it may at any time be engaged in promoting.

ARTICLE VIII.

OFFICERS AND EXECUTIVE COMMITTEE.

Section 1. The officers of the Association shall be a President, a First Vice-President, a Chairman of Board of Trustees, a Secretary and a Treasurer, and such Vice-Presidents and other officers as the Board of Trustees may from time to time determine. The office of Secretary and Treasurer may be held by the same person.

Section 2. The Executive Committee shall consist of five (5) members of the Board of Trustees, one of which shall be Chairman of the Board of Trustees, elected by the Board, and ad-interim meetings of the Board of Trustees shall have all the powers thereof.

Section 3. The officers of the Association shall be nominated by the Trustees of the National Highways Association and elected by the Board of Trustees of the Association. They shall hold office until removed as hereinafter provided. Vacancies occurring in any office or member of the Executive Committee shall be filled in the same manner.

Section 4. Any officer, Trustee or member of the Executive Committee may at any time be removed by a majority of the Board of Trustees subject to the approval by the Trustees of the National Highways Association.

ARTICLE IX.

VACANCIES AND REMOVAL FROM OFFICE.

Section 1. When a vacancy occurs or is about to occur in the office of President, Secretary, Treasurer or Executive Committee of this Association, the Board of Trustees of this Association shall at once notify the Board of Trustees of the National Highways Association and by the concurrent action of that Board such vacancy shall be filled.

ARTICLE X.

DUTIES OF OFFICERS.

Section 1. The President of this Association shall be the Chief Executive officer of this Association and shall preside at all meetings thereof.

Section 2. In the absence of the President, the First Vice-President shall act in his place and stead, provided, that in the absence of both the President and First Vice-President, the Chairman of the Board of Trustees shall perform the duties of the President.

Section 3. The Secretary shall keep the records, shall receive and receipt for all moneys paid to the Association, shall keep a correct list of all members and minutes of the Association and of the Board of Trustees, and send all notices required by this Constitution or by the direction of its officers. He shall draw all orders upon the Treasurer for the payment of money, which orders shall be approved by the President. He shall receive and record all applications for membership, dues and other receipts of the Association, and account for the same to the Treasurer. He shall furnish corporate surety bond as required by the Board of Trustees, at the expense of the Association. He shall serve all notices and perform all duties necessary to the proper conduct of the business affairs of the Association, and shall perform such additional duties as may be assigned him by the Board of Trustees. He shall make a written report annually, and whenever directed by the Board of Trustees, of the work of the Association, accounting for all funds received and disbursed.

Section 4. The Treasurer shall receive from and receipt to the Secretary for all moneys from the Secretary belonging to the Association and deposit the same in a bank or trust company approved by the Board of Trustees, and disburse same upon proper voucher signed by the Secretary and approved by the President. He shall keep an accurate account of the finances of the Association subject at all times to inspection of the officers of the Association and furnish corporate surety bond at the expense of the Association.

ARTICLE XI.

Section 1. The Constitution and By-laws of the National Highways Association and the rules of the Trustees thereof, which may be adopted by them from time to time, are hereby accepted as binding upon this Association as the North Carolina Division of the National Highways Association, provided that the National Highways Association, or the Trustees thereof, shall have no power or authority to levy any tax or assessment upon this Association, except by and with the approval of the Trustees of the North Carolina Good Roads Association, North Carolina Division of the National Highways Association.

ARTICLE XII.

AMENDMENTS.

Section 1. This Constitution may be altered or amended at any annual or special meeting upon the written recommendations of the Board of Trustees by a vote of three-fourths of the members of the Association present. Before such amendments shall be considered in force they shall receive the concurrence of the Trustees of the National Highways Association.

DELEGATES TO THE CONVENTION.

A register was kept of the delegates, and the following thirty-eight counties were found to be represented at this convention:

Alamance, Ashe, Anson, Beaufort, Cabarrus, Carteret, Craven, Davidson, Davie, Duplin, Durham, Edgecombe, Forsyth, Franklin, Greene, Guilford, Halifax, Harnett, Jones, Johnston, Lee, Lenoir, Martin, Mecklenburg, Moore, Nash, New Hanover, Northampton, Onslow, Orange, Pamlico, Pitt, Rowan, Rutherford, Sampson, Wake, Wayne, and Wilson.

The States of Ohio, North Carolina, New York, Virginia and Kentucky were represented at this convention.

The following 143 delegates were registered:

Will Ward Duffield	Harlan, Ky.
R. R. Cotten	Bruce, N. C.
Guelda Elliott	Chapel Hill, N. C.
H. B. Varner	Lexington, N. C.
John E. Moore	Jackson, N. C.
Miss H. M. Berry	Chapel Hill, N. C.
D. A. McDonald	Carthage, N. C.
Wm. Dunn	New Bern, N. C.
A. P. Gilbert	Durham, N. C.
W. L. Spoon, U. S. Sr. H. Egn.	Burlington, N. C.
Jesse Taylor	Jamestown, Ohio.
Arch H. Huston	Columbus, Ohio.
R. P. Coble	Sanford, N. C.
J. M. Cates, Roanoke Bridge Co.	Burlington, N. C.
R. E. Snowden, County Engineer	Craven Co.
Joseph Hyde Pratt	Chapel Hill, N. C.
John C. Drewry	Raleigh, N. C.
B. E. Rice	Norfolk, Va., N. S. R. R.
W. C. Douglass	Raleigh, N. C.
Bennehan Cameron	Statesville, N. C.
M. McDarmains	Faison, N. C.
H. J. Faison	Faison, N. C.
N. C. Hughes	Weldon, N. C.
Clyde A. Douglass	Raleigh, N. C.
W. L. Arendell	Morehead City, N. C.
F. H. Foy	Polloksville, N. C.
K. B. Johnson, Wake Co.	Cardenas, N. C.
H. P. McPherson	Cameron, N. C.
M. C. Lasitter	Snow Hill, N. C.
E. E. Hanks	Charlotte, N. C.
John E. Currie	Carthage, N. C.
M. C. Winston	Selma, N. C.
Walter F. Woodard	Wilson, N. C.
Lawrence Brett	Wilson, N. C.

Major Loftin ....Mt. Olive, N. C.
Elias Vander Horst ....New York City.
F. Buck ....Trenton, N. C.
F. E. Cook ....Greensboro, N. C.
O. Martindale ....Wilmington, N. C.
H. T. Davis ....Goldsboro, N C.
R. A. Burnett ....Wilmington, N. C.
J. P. Herring ....Wilmington, N. C.
C. M. Wade ....Morehead City, N. C.
Clarence Smith ....Dunn, N. C.
B. P. Gentry ....Dunn, N. C.
J. R. Peterson ....Clinton, N. C.
J. H. Arnold, The Texas Co. ....Norfolk, Va.
J. K. Warren ....Trenton, N. C.
J. B. Pollock ....Trenton, N. C.
H. B. Tomlinson ....Smithfield, N. C.
L. H. Champion ....Clayton, N. C.
J. E. Cameron ....Kinston, N. C.
Frank Parker ....Salemburg, N. C.
R. C. McNeill ....Sanford, N. C.
D. D. Buie ....Sanford, N. C.
J. B. Willis ....Jacksonville, N. C.
T. F. Hickerson ....Chapel Hill, N. C.
Vernon Simpson ....Smyrna, N. C.
C. T. Scott ....Jacksonville, N. C.
A. F. Davis ....Davis, N. C.
K. B. Stewart ....Newport, N. C.
L. H. Lyon ....Wilmington, N. C.
R. C. Langdon, Capt. U. S. Army ....Brooklyn, N. Y.
Mrs. R. C. Langdon ....Brooklyn, N. Y.
W. F. Outland ....Woodland, N. C.
John H. Small ....Washington, N. C.
Geo. Y. Thomason ....Salisbury, N. C.
P. M. Bissut ....Salisbury, N. C.
R. P. Parker ....Parker, N. C.
E. L. Mattocks ....Maysville, N. C.
Robt. A. Sanders ....Smithfield, N. C.
John F. Sanders ....Clayton, N. C.
L. W. Tucker ....Greenville, N. C.
W. E. Proctor ....Grimesland, N. C.
Thos. O. H. Dupre ....Greenville, N. C.
G. A. Walton ....Jacksonville, N. C.
Wm. A. Blair ....Winston-Salem, N. C.
D. H. Blair ....Winston-Salem, N. C.
John Fries Blair ....Winston-Salem, N. C.
J. E. Alexander ....Winston-Salem, N. C.
H. Montague ....Winston-Salem, N. C.
J. B. Blades ....New Bern, N. C.
G. R. Small ....Newport, N. C., Route 2.
S. C. Camper ....Beaufort, N. C.

C. N. Mason	North Harlowe, N. C.
E. R. Loftin	Kinston, N. C.
J. Beale Johnson	Cardenas, N. C.
A. B. Skelding	Wilmington, N. C.
M. F. H. Gouverneur	Wilmington, N. C.
H. de W. Rapalje	Wilmington, N. C.
P. B. Beard	Salisbury, N. C.
Glaucus A. Bryant, C. E.	Wilson, N. C.
Geo. P. Galvin, Mgr. Car Metal Product Co.	Wilmington, N. C.
J. B. Taylor	Kinston, N. C.
Foy	New Bern, N. C.
James Wellons, Jr.	Smithfield, N. C.
Mrs. Jesse Taylor	Jamestown, Ohio.
Mrs. Archibald H. Huston	Columbus, Ohio.
W. H. Garner	Newport, N. C.
T. G. Gould	Newport, N. C.
J. B. Blades	New Bern, N. C.
D. B. Oglesby	Newport, N. C.
Mrs. Lawrence Brett	Wilson, N. C.
Milford W. Haynes	Tarboro, N. C.
Jas. A. Wellons	Smithfield, N. C.
J. E. Hall, Atlas Portland Cement Co.	Lynchburg, Va.
Orin Weeks	Kinston, N. C.
Wm. Hayes	Kinston, N. C.
G. D. Canfield	Morehead City, N. C.
Mrs. Wm. Dunn	New Bern, N. C.
J. P. Cook	Concord, N. C.
Mrs. J. P. Cook	Concord, N. C.
Arthur Blanchard, Columbia University	New York City, N. Y.
A. Turner Grant, Jr.	Mocksville, N. C.
L. H. Cutler	Jessama, N. C.
Mrs. L. H. Cutler	Jessama, N. C.
Franc L. Ives	Rocky Mount, N. C.
J. H. Turlington	Clinton, N. C.
N. A. Graham	North Carolina.
W. C. Steele	Mount Olive, N. C.
Chas. L. Abernethy	Beaufort, N. C.
R. L. May	Trenton, N. C.
H. W. Little	Wadesboro, N. C.
J. C. M. Valentine, Highway Engineer	Rutherford, N. C.
H. L. Gibbs	Oriental, N. C.
A. D. Ward	New Bern, N. C.
James A. Bryan	New Bern, N. C.
A. M. Hall	Orange, N. C.
W. S. Fallis	Franklinton, N. C.
Geo. M. March	Wilson, N. C.
R. R. Eagle	New Bern, N. C.
J. B. Pollock	Trenton, N. C.
G. D. Canfield	Morehead City, N. C.
R. B. Bailey	Woodleaf, N. C.

H. G. Monk ....Trenton, N. C.
L. W. Tinker ....Greenville, N. C.
W. E. Proctor ....Grimesland, N. C.
J. W. Martin ....Tarboro, N. C.
C. T. Munford ....Greenville, N. C.
C. T. Munford, Jr......................................Greenville, N. C.
James E. Patrick ....Farmville, N. C.
C. F. Sapp ....Rich Square, N. C.

Special Meeting

OF THE

NORTH CAROLINA GOOD ROADS ASSOCIATION.

HELD AT

Raleigh, N. C., September 24, 1913.

The meeting was called to order by the President, H. B. Varner, at 11 o'clock, who stated:

"This is an adjourned meeting of the North Carolina Good Roads Association. We decided at the Morehead City meeting to meet here on the 24th of September for the purpose of deciding whether or not we shall make an attempt to have any special legislation passed by the special session of the Legislature; and the main purpose for which we are assembled here today is to receive the report of the Resolutions Committee, and see what we can do to get the General Assembly to establish a Highway Commission. We want to establish that, and we want to discuss it very thoroughly, and decide whether it is wise to try and do it at this time. If so, we want to appoint a committee to bring it to the attention of the Legislature."

Mr. Wellons, of Smithfield: Mr. Chairman, Mr. Cotten and myself met with Mr. Douglass this morning. He called us together yesterday afternoon, but we were so busy that we were unable to get together. Mr. Douglass, who is very busy today, asked us to present the report.

The following is the report presented by this committee:

"*Resolved*, by the North Carolina Good Roads Association in session in the city of Raleigh this September 24, 1913,

"That we do declare in favor of Federal roads; in favor of Federal aid to same. We further declare in favor of State roads, and State aid to the same; and in favor of county roads to be built under the supervision of the proper county authorities.

"We declare in favor of a State Highway Commission and urge the General Assembly now in session to create said commission. We declare it to be the sense of this Association that it is unalterably opposed to the present system of working State convicts on the railroads or any other private enterprise. We favor the working of our State convicts on the public roads of the State the same to be done under the supervision and direction of the State Highway Commission. We favor and ask the present General Assembly now in session to enact a law making such appropriations as shall be deemed wise for the purpose of furnishing to the different counties of the State such engineering assistance as may be needed. We favor the issuing of bonds to build roads for counties in the place and stead of having special taxes for the building of township roads. We urge the county commissioners of the several counties in the State to give their special attention to the building of better roads in their respective counties. And we further urge that the county commissioners set apart at least one day in the year to be devoted exclusively to the roads in their counties.

"*Resolved*, that this Convention appoint a committee to prepare bills in accordance with these resolutions to be presented to the General Assembly to be enacted into law at this present session."

Motion was then made that the resolution be adopted.

DISCUSSION.

Dr. Pratt: Before the motion is put to the house, I would like to ask whether, if we adopt these resolutions, as they stand, it will mean that we are going to have drawn a sufficient number of bills to include the various subjects mentioned in the resolution and if we think that several bills can be put through at this special session; or whether we shall adopt one particular bill, the creation of the Highway Commission, and try for that one thing; or whether we shall try to get through several bills as outlined by the resolution.

Mr. Wellons: It was the sense of the committee that we declare this to be the wishes of the North Carolina Good Roads Association, and that we then arrange for such committees as we deem wise to press such matters as we might think best at this session of the legislature. I am of the opinion that the best thing to do would be to pass that resolution, but not undertake to get them all through at this session. It seems to me that the Highway Commission bill is the most important of all, and we ought to take this one particular feature and center our efforts in getting the Legislature to give us that one thing. I believe this is the sense of the committee.

Dr. Pratt: Then this simply represents a set of resolutions we favor, and we will decide on just one thing that we will try to get through the Legislature.

Mr. Mills: I would not like to vote for these resolutions, because it says that this Association is unalterably opposed to the present system of working the State convicts on the railroads. I think this is a very far-reaching proposition. I will say right here that I am to a small extent interested in working the convicts on the railroads, and I want you to understand that I am not saying what I am saying for personal reasons.

I believe that you will make a mistake if you take the convict off the railroads. Our State is running behind every year on account of its income, and you might say we are running behind on account of the stock they are getting from the railroads. How was it many years ago when we built all the railorads in the State? The stock was worth very little then. Moreover that stock was never worth anything until a very few years ago. In fact there is no stock which in the beginning is worth very much. If you hold it until the railroad gets on its feet and begins to make money, it will become valuable. I think the State taxes the North Carolina Railroad about $50,000 per year, so you see you not only get your stock but you get taxes back into the State Treasury. If you take your State convicts to build county roads, your roads will soon wear out and the State gets no benefits.

Now I will say for Wake County (and their system is a very good one) that we have 50 to 70 convicts on our roads, and we are improving them. In this county they are using the county convicts on the public roads. I feel that it is a bad proposition for us to say to the State that you shall not lease any more convicts to the railroads. If the county wants good roads, let them put their own county convicts on the roads like Wake County, or else hire their labor.

Mr. J. J. Laughinghouse: I was a member of the Legislature that granted these convicts to the building of the Elkin road. I agree with Mr. Mills most thoroughly, because I realize, after visiting different camps in North Carolina, that you get with ten men and 20 mules more work than with 75 convicts. I have seen that demonstrated fully in Iredell County. You cannot afford to work a man at $1.50 a day, when mules and machinery will do more for 75 cents per day; and no progressive road building is being carried on in this State except by machinery and mules. I used to feel exactly as you feel, who have not any experience along this line and I thought the convict ought to be put on the public roads; but, when in my capacity as Superintendent of the State Prison, I visited squads in Iredell County and saw them doing more work with ten men and twenty mules, I changed my mind about the use of convicts. The man who does not benefit by observation and demonstration is not a fair-minded man. I have seen that thing demonstrated fully. Taking these points into consideration, I am coming down to the same point that Mr. Mills made: I can say to you today, and I think I can prove it by my friend, Mr. Cheatham, over there, that the value that the Elkin road will bring to the State and the appreciated value of the property contiguous to it will put into the treasury of North Carolina not only 10 per cent but 15 per cent of the value of this stock. I wish to say emphatically that if the State does not get a cent for these bonds, it will be handsomely paid. What would have been the result of the State of North Carolina if she had not gone ahead and built the North Carolina Railroad? You know the State would never have been developed one-tenth as much as it has been developed. I think when the State of North Carolina develops a section of the State and puts it in such position so that it will become prosperous and contribute toward its own wealth and the wealth of the State, we have done a grand thing for the State of North Carolina;

and I believe if the people of the State were consulted along this line they would agree with me. I am a good roads man. I am in favor of good roads. I wish every county in North Carolina could issue a $100,000 in bonds to build good roads; but I am opposed to putting 75 men out on the road to do what ten men and good roads machinery can do at half cost. When I see what is being done in Iredell County and other counties with machinery, I say it would be absolutely wrong in principle. I will take the three counties of Ashe, Alleghany, and Watauga. They are no good as far as North Carolina is concerned. They do their trading in Virginia; but when this railroad is developed they will then become a part of the State of North Carolina, as the railroad will make it possible for them to get in touch with other parts of our State. And I think the State of North Carolina has made it sufficiently interesting for Mr. Mills and his friends to work toward the building of a railroad. Mr. Cheatham and his brothers, father, and friends worked every way possible to get the Southern Railway to do something toward the development of this section, but they could never get a thing done until the State put convicts there.

Mr. Varner: I want to say, gentlemen, this is not a railroad meeting but a good roads meeting.

Dr. Pratt: I do not agree with Mr. Laughinghouse in some of the points he has made in regard to the question of convict labor. But as this point is brought out in the resolutions we are considering, I believe we should discuss it fully and freely; so that we may know each other's ideas. In the first place I want to make the point that if it is a feasible proposition to work convicts in grading railroads, and they can be worked to advantage in grading a railroad, it is just as feasible, cheap and economic a proposition to work these same convicts in grading the public road. The principle of grading is the same. The railroad can use machinery in grading just as well as a public road. In our public road work they are using a great deal of machinery in grading so far as they can do it to advantage in grading our roads. We can also use every convict to advantage in grading the public roads as well as the railroads, and we have contractors who can take county convicts and use them in grading the road under contract; and, therefore, I do believe that we can use the convict to grade a country road to as good advantage as in grading a railroad. I don't believe there is a man in this room who would not agree that the construction of a railroad in any part of North Carolina is a splendid thing, not only for the particular section through which that railroad goes but it is a good thing for the State at large. But another question comes up, and that is whether it is the function and duty of the State of North Carolina to assist a private enterprise; and, if so, why single out one enterprise in preference to some other private enterprise? In other words, is it the function of the State of North Carolina to assist in the development of a private corporation, and in this particular case the building of railroads? Now, a comparison has been made as to the original work that North Carolina did in building railroads. I agree that North Carolina did a splendid thing when she built the North Carolina railroad; but North Carolina, as I understand it, controlled that railroad. She did not build it for someone else; she built it for herself. She has leased it recently, and, as I understand it, she controls the stock; and has recently leased or sold outright part of the railroad from Asheville towards the Tennessee line, so that what she has done really in building this railroad was done for herself; and was not contributing and taking stock with someone else in a privately owned and controlled railroad. I admit that it is frequently a splendid thing for a community, and probably some railroads could not have gotten started if the State had not helped them with convicts or otherwise, as in the case of the three counties mentioned by Mr. Laughinghouse. I am very familiar with the conditions in each of these three counties; and there are perhaps no three counties in the State which need a railroad more in order to accomplish that development than these, and will undoubtedly mean a great deal to this section, and also to the income of the State. But even with all these conditions as they are, I do not believe it is the function of the State to subsidize these railroads with something that belongs to the State, as a whole. I think it has been the opinion of the Good Roads Association that where the State has entered into a perfectly valid contract with any railroad regarding the convicts they were not going to propose the breaking of that contract; but I think it has been expressed in many of our meetings and conventions that the Association, as a whole, is opposed to leasing convicts from now on for use in railroad building. It has been voted by the majority at our conventions that the Association shall go on record as opposed to the State's furnishing convicts to private corporations. The reason the railroads were mentioned particularly was because most of the convicts have been leased to railroads.

Mr. Mills: I want to correct you in saying the railroads are private corporations. They are certainly controlled by private individuals but they serve a public function.

Dr. Pratt: I take that back. Of course the railroad is a public corporation owned by private individuals. I will put it this way: We are doing it for a private enterprise. For this reason I have been opposed to the question of working the State convicts for any enterprise of that sort.

Mr. Wellons: I want to say this. Some of the arguments which have been produced this morning are a complete argument to my mind in favor of the resolution, and that is with these State convicts we want to do the most good to the most people. If the building of a railroad in one section will enhance the value of that property in that community and thereby be of great assistance to the State of North Carolina, why is it not more eminently true that if you put these convicts to work upon the public roads of the State you build public roads and benefit more people and enhance the valuation of property in more sections than if you confine that to one particular section? As I see the matter, the time has come (I know it was true and wise for our forefathers to build the North Carolina railroad, but the times are not now as they were then), the time has come when the State of North Carolina demands public roads over which her people may travel. Now, the question is how are we of the present day to get them? To my mind the best way is to build these roads with the State convicts. Now, I don't mean that we can go to the county of Wayne or Guilford or any other and use their convicts. That resolution provided for a State Highway Commission, which would look after the building of roads with these convicts; and it further provides that the convicts shall be worked on the *State roads*. I think no better way can be devised than that these convicts under this State Highway Commission be used in the building of State roads all over the State. If the counties want them; if the county of Wayne, for illustration, desires the services of State convicts, let it employ these convicts and pay them just as they would for other day labor.

I have had some experience in working convicts on a road in the county of Johnston where they have a road district through which the roads are being built by convicts, and I know that it is pretty costly to do that; but I know also that the counties and townships in North Carolina which are building the best roads and are building them the fastest are those which are using the convicts. We have not time to go into the minute details of this system, but if you hire men to come and work on the roads they will get there at 7 o'clock and quit before night. They won't work. If you try to make them work, they quit, and the result is you have your machinery and your mules, etc., paying the hired labor just the same, and yet you cannot force the men to do a day's work. If you have the convicts you can build the roads. You can get more work done. And, Mr. Chairman, it seems to me that it is the wisdom of this Association to declare in favor of the working of convicts on the public roads of this State. There is enough wisdom in the Legislature to prepare a bill, throw around it safeguards, so that the State will reap full benefit from the use of these convicts.

I am opposed to working convicts on any private enterprise. I am in favor of placing the services of the State convicts in building the roads of the State of North Carolina, and give us what we ought to have,—a system of good roads all over the State.

Mr. Royall: I want to endorse what Mr. Wellons has so well said. If it is a good investment for the State to use its convicts in railroad building, it is a better investment to use them on the public roads; because, as I understand it, the convicts are hired to the different counties, so that the State will certainly get an income from these counties. I believe it is a matter of record that a great deal of the work that has been done on the railroads, for which the State has received bonds or stock, has amounted to nothing. The stock has been valueless and therefore it has been a contribution of the State to the railroads. We are all glad to see the advent of the railroads; but it seems to me that the advent of the railroads has been ahead of the advent of the county roads; and, therefore, it behooves this State to turn its attention to the county roads. Take the county convicts and put them on the county roads, and for the same amount of money expended, you will get better results because you will cover a greater territory. The amount of advance in property in building the railroads applies just as strongly to building good county roads. If you will take the portion of the Central Highway through Wake County, you will find an advance in property along the lines of that highway as great in comparison as along the line of the Southern Railway.

As I was coming down yesterday afternoon I passed by some property which less than six months ago was being offered at $16 an acre, and I was told that today it was sold for $300 an acre. It seems to me the railroads have made advance ahead of the county roads, and I think it is the part of wisdom to pass that resolution.

Resolution passed. (Two votes against it.)

Dr. Pratt: It seems to me it would be well to discuss here briefly the question as to whether or not it is going to be the right thing to introduce a bill at this General Assembly. If we do, we must get a committee appointed to draft the bill and see that it is introduced.

Mr. Drewry: It seems to me that we can hardly decide this morning, because we do not know what is going to be taken up at this General Assembly. I think it would be well to appoint a committee of say, five, who, if it is found advisable, will introduce the bill and investigate and act along the lines that wisdom dictates at the time the matter comes up.

Mr. Royall: I think the suggestion is a proper one. I think it would be better to appoint a committee and let them take up the matter. While I am on my feet, I want to say I think we should press the matter in this Legislature of getting a Highway Commission bill passed.

Mr. Drewry: I think the matter ought to be pressed as rapidly as possible, and that is why I made the suggestion.

Mr. Cameron: I would like to state that I am in favor of railroads myself. But I ride on the county roads a great deal more than I do on the railroads, and I am heartily in accord with working the convicts on the county roads. I have endorsed the counties building roads and using their convicts, and also gathering convicts from neighboring counties. As I started to say, it seems that this Legislature is being assaulted as to railroads, and I do not know whether it would be a proper time for us to start on this question or not; but I think if we can get this matter before the people and get them to thinking, they will send men to the Legislature next time to carry out this idea. I am sure of this because the people I have come in contact with are well alive on this question, and if they are given an opportunity to express themselves they will vote for good roads and for convicts to build these roads.

Mr. Varner: I want to say a few words in justice to Mr. Mills. I want to say the State Prison Board several months ago made an investigation of all its railroad projects in North Carolina, and it was our opinion that there were none of these railroads worthy of State aid with the exception of the Elkin & Alleghany Railroad. While we do not approve of the policy yet, if the State is going to aid any railroad in North Carolina, it ought to aid this one; because it is being built for some good purpose. I do not approve of the policy that he is advocating, and he would not either if he were not president of that road; but I want to say that he is representing a railroad. It is the only one in the whole business, as I have formerly said, that is worth anything, and these others are all alleged railroads and not railroads at all; nothing but lumber roads.

Mr. Mills: I want to say that I am a good roads enthusiast. I believe in good roads. Our County Commissioners in Wake County have one or two days every month in which they consider roads in this county.

Mr. Drewry: If there is nothing more to come before the house now, I would like to state that it has been agitated and suggested that the Governor of the State appoint two days as Good Roads Days. It seems to me that this Good Roads Convention ought to take that matter up and suggest to the Governor setting aside certain days to be known as "Good Roads Days." I move that this Association put itself on record as favoring that proposition, and that the Governor be requested to designate certain days and call upon everybody in North Carolina to get out and work at least two days on the public roads of the State. I believe it is a good thing and a step in the right direction.

Mr. Varner: I would like for you to discuss this matter very freely in regard to the Governor's appointing these Good Roads Days. I would like for you to suggest about when these Good Road Days ought to be. When do you think it would suit the people of the different sections of the State?

Mr. Royall: Mr. Chairman, I think we are getting just a little ahead. We were discussing the matter of the State Highway Commission.

President: Gentlemen, you have before you the motion of Mr. Drewry that a committee of five or more be appointed to take in hand the preparation of a bill to be introduced in behalf of the North Carolina Good Roads Association. What do you think about it?

Motion seconded.

President: It has been moved and seconded that the Chair appoint a committee of five or more as a Legislative Committee to prepare bills to introduce into the Legislature, if they think it is the wise thing to do.

Motion carried.

President: Now, in reference to the Good Roads Days, what is the best time? How about the latter part of October or the first of November?

Mr. Mills: I should think it would be a good time about Fair time.

Mr. Varner: We want to try and get out 200,000 people on the roads. It will take sometime to work the publicity campaign. These days ought to be selected when the farmers are not so busy.

Mr. Cotten: You will find the roads are getting bad by the first of November, and that it is not a very good time to work on them.

Mr. Varner: We can stir up all kinds of enthusiasm and walk around and look at them. The fact that the Governor will make such a proclamation will call the attention of the people of the State to the roads and it will be an advertisement of the State that will be worth thousand of dollars to the State.

Mr. Royall: I would like an expression from Dr. Pratt. It seems to me that it is a backward step in good roads building to have everybody—inexperienced and otherwise—fooling with the roads. I remember I took a trip with Dr. Pratt, and he was criticizing the building of roads by the old labor system. To go out now and work on the roads by that same old way without proper supervision would be, to my mind, not intelligent road building. The only way I can see would be for Dr. Pratt to send out instructions as to what the people should do on these days.

Dr. Pratt: I would say that I have had an interview with Governor Craig in regard to this question of the feasibility and practicability of calling "Good Roads Days," when we will try to get all the people of North Carolina out to do something toward bettering the roads. We discussed as to whether we could make a success of it, and decided that each township would have to be organized, so that the road officials would have control of what work was to be done and how it was to be done; and, in case men are not able to work, a substantial subscription would be accepted in lieu of their labor. Now, at this time of the year I believe we can put in to advantage some work in clearing out the ditches of old roads, clearing rights-of-way for new roads and grading them up. If we could have a number of new roads located and this labor expended on these roads, it would undoubtedly be of great service. It would not be a good plan, however, to disturb the surface of the roads at this time of the year; for, if we did, we would do them more harm than good. If we do organize our counties, our townships, our communities, and our districts, it will take considerable time of course; so that, if we do, and the county commissioners, road superintendents, road supervisors, or engineers should work out a plan as to where the work should be done, it will undoubtedly result in great benefit to the State. It should not mean that any man should go out in front of his place and dig a little in the road. And I would like to repeat that the very best that we can do is to thoroughly organize our section, plan out the work, have the tools ready, clear the right-of-way, and grade on a new road; and that the only work that can be done to advantage on the old roads is in clearing out the ditches, and throwing the material out on the opposite field and not on the road. It is very seldom you find anything washed into a ditch that will benefit the road.

Question: What do you think of those roads we have already surfaced and got them drained, and they have grown up with grass on the sides to the ditches?

Dr. Pratt: In a great many countries the roads have grass growing along from the side ditches for a certain distance toward the center of the road to keep the dirt from washing; but where you have a good 30 or 40-foot width for your road, this is a good plan and I do not object at all if the grass is mowed down. But we must bear in mind that we want every part of our road available for use. We want the road so crowned from the center to the ditches that it is possible for it to drain off at any time.

Question: With all that grass growing from six to eight feet, we cannot drag the road very well.

Mr. Cotten: Of course, all this would not be helped by the Governor's Proclamation. I think the moral effect of this proclamation would be good. There will be certain localities which will undoubtedly do some work. It would be an education in itself I am perfectly satisfied, and I think it would be wise to pass a resolution and ask the Governor to make the proclamation. Motion seconded.

PRESIDENT: It has been moved and seconded that this Association urge the Governor to issue a Proclamation naming two days as Good Roads Days in North Carolina during the first part of November, and assuring him of our hearty coöperation in this work.

Mr. Hanes: What is the intention of the two days?

PRESIDENT: The object is to get the people thoroughly aroused for good roads, as they were out in Missouri. In other words, to wake up the people.

Mr. Hanes: The question is, are you not setting these days too late, when the weather will be cold and bad.

Resolution adopted.

Mr. Wellons: I would like to get someone here to tell me how to get the farmers in my county interested in good roads. As a rule the farmers are against good roads.

PRESIDENT: The only answer I have heard is to put text-books in the schools, and sell them automobiles.

Mr. Cotten: The farmers in my county are all in favor of good roads.

Mr. Wellons: I do not mean the better class of farmers. I am talking about those little fellows who do not pay any taxes and own a one-horse farm, or live on one as a tenant.

Mr. Mills: Do you expect every man to work two days on the roads?

Mr. Hanes: If the farmers were to get to owning automobiles, then they would want good roads. In my county, they are beginning to use them. I see automobiles on our front streets offering vegetables for sale long before the wagon brigade can get in. But the good roads question will grow in itself and it is a thing you cannot hurry.

I began the good roads work in Forsyth fifteen years ago. I got the Southern Good Roads train to stop at Raleigh and build a sample of good roads on the day that the Good Roads Association was organized. Since that time we have begun to build good roads in many sections of the State. I hope to see the time when we will have good roads, both macadam and sand-clay, connecting every principal town with every section of our county.

Dr. Pratt: There is a report I want to make if you are through with the general business, and that is the report of the committee that took up the question of effecting an amalgamation with the National Highways Association. This has been done, the constitution having been framed to meet the requirements and trustees appointed; and we are now the North Carolina Good Roads Association, North Carolina Division of the National Highways Association. The trustees are as follows:

Joseph Hyde Pratt, Chairman, Chapel Hill, N. C.
H. B. Varner, Lexington, N. C.
Frank H. Fleer, Thomasville, N. C.
F. L. Seely, Grove Park Inn, Asheville, N. C.
William Dunn, New Bern, N. C.
John C. Drewry, Raleigh, N. C.
James A. Wellons, Smithfield, N. C.
E. C. Chambers, Asheville, N. C.
G. D. Canfield, Morehead City, N. C.
W. A. Erwin, Durham, N. C.
Leonard Tufts, Pinehurst, N. C.
Joseph G. Brown, Raleigh, N. C.
M. F. H. Gouverneur, Wilmington, N. C.
F. M. Shannonhouse, Charlotte, N. C.
Hugh Chatham, Winston-Salem, N. C.

We have submitted to the National Highways Association the Constitution and By-Laws of the North Carolina Good Roads Association, which have been approved, and we are now formally amalgamated with the National Highways Association.

There is one change which has been made, and that is in the dues of the Association, which I think it is best to read. You remember the dues in our Association have always been $1 a year. In the National Highways Association, there are dues which run up as high as $25,000, of which they have one or two. Membership is divided into nine classes, as follows:

Patron members	$1,000.00
Life members	500.00
Corporate members	500.00
Collective members ......$25 to	200.00
Sustaining members	10.00
Contributing members	5.00
Highway members	2.50
Union members	1.00
Scout and Camp-fire members	.50

We are to employ an Organizer—a man who can go all over North Carolina talking good roads. That we get from our amalgamation with the National Highways Association. Membership in the North Carolina Good Roads Association carries with it membership in the National Highways Association, so that the membership fee of $2.50 will cover them both.

Mr. Varner: One thing that Dr. Pratt did not make plain is that all this money goes into the Treasury of the North Carolina Good Roads Association for the promotion of good roads in this State.

Resolution adopted.

The President appointed the following committee as a Legislative Committee:

John C. Drewry, Chairman; James A. Wellons, George C. Royall, Dr. A. Cheatham, M. L. Shipman, H. B. Varner, *ex officio* Chairman.

Members present at this meeting were as follows:

John Mills, Raleigh, N. C.
John C. Drewry, Raleigh, N. C.
James A. Wellons, Smithfield, N. C.
D. A. McDonald, Carthage, N. C.
J. E. Cameron, Kinston, N. C.
George C. Royall, Goldsboro, N. C.
Frank Nash, Hillsboro, N. C.
John Johnson, Hillsboro, N. C.
Joseph G. Brown, Raleigh, N. C.
Joseph Hyde Pratt, Chapel Hill, N. C.
H. B. Varner, Lexington, N. C.
Fred Olds, Raleigh, N. C.
R. R. Cotten, Bruce, N. C.
B. C. Beckwith, Raleigh, N. C.
W. H. Williamson, Raleigh, N. C.
George L. Becton, Wilmington, N. C.
Fleming Ramsaur, Kings Mountain, N. C.
J. S. Atkinson, Elkin, N. C.
J. C. Click, Elkin, N. C.
W. G. Wilson, Wilson's Mill, N. C.
Miss H. M. Berry, Chapel Hill, N. C.
P. H. Hanes, Winston-Salem, N. C.
W. S. Sanders, Smithfield, N. C.
J. E. Erwin, Morganton, N. C.
Dr. B. B. Williams, Ridgeway, N. C.
J. J. Laughinghouse, Greenville, N. C.
R. M. Cheatham, Elkin, N. C.

STATISTICAL REPORT

OF

Highway Work in North Carolina During 1912

The report of highway work in North Carolina during 1911 took up in considerable detail a history of the road work of the State, status of work in the several counties, descriptions of the methods of building roads, as well as tables giving detailed statistics, and certain suggested legislation. The present report will deal only with the statistical data, given principally in the form of tables. These statistics were collected in coöperation with the United States Office of Public Roads, and show the counties or townships which have issued or sold bonds; those which have levied a property, poll or labor tax, and the property valuation of the counties; the mileage of public road by counties; the number of miles of macadam, sand-clay, gravel, specially surfaced or graded public roads in each county; the cost of constructing the surfaced roads; the statistics relating to the use of convicts on the public roads. These figures were obtained chiefly from county and road commissioners of the various counties.

Methods of Financing.

Two methods are employed in the counties and townships of North Carolina to finance the building of public roads; *i. e.*, by direct taxation on property, on the poll, or special tax, as a dog tax or automobile tax; and the issuance of bonds. Interest has grown to such an extent in road building that in many localities money has been given by individuals for the building of certain stretches of road, and also subscriptions in the form of teams and labor. The amount derived from this source is not known, but from press notices, it is known that such donations have been made.

Direct Taxation.

There is given in Table I the assessed valuation of personal and real property in the various counties of the State; the special tax levied for road work, whether by county or township; the total amount raised by such a levy, and how this amount is spent; the rate on the $100 worth of property, and the rate on the poll; and under labor tax, there is given the number of men subject to such tax, the number of days required, and the age limit.

TABLE I—REVENUE BY TAXATION DURING 1912.

County	Assessed Valuation Personal and Real 1912 Lists	How Levied, County or Township?	Special Tax. Name of Township	Amount Raised by Tax (Property and Poll)	How Spent, Construction or Repair?	Rate of Property and Poll Tax: Rate on $100 Worth of Property	Rate of Property and Poll Tax: Rate of Poll	Number of Days Required	Labor Tax Age Limits	Number of Men Subject to Tax
Alamance	$8,224,380	County		$ 13,707	Repair dirt and other roads.	$ .16⅔	$ 1.25	3	21–45	†2,000
Alexander	2,258,447	Township	Ellendale	898	Repair and construction	.25	.75	4	18–45	1,650
Alleghany	1,218,501							On old roads 8 On new roads 6	18–45	†400
Anson	4,843,752	County		1,500	Repair and construction	.25		6	18–45	1,800
Ashe	3,081,533	County		1,200	Repair	*.10		6	18–45	1,000
Avery	2,133,170							6	18–45	1,000
Beaufort	7,069,562	Townships	Chocowinity, Washington, Long Acre and Bath	10,000	Repair; mostly thrown away	.20	2.00	6	18–45	†3,000
Bertie	5,658,267	County		10,000	Construction	.20		4	18–45	3,500
Bladen	4,072,531	Township	Brown Marsh	1,000	Interest on bonds and repair	.13	.39	6	21–45	†1,500
Brunswick	4,332,237	Townships	Smithville, Town Creek, Lockwoods Folly and Shallotte	2,033	Interest on bonds and construction	.81½ .10	2.13 .30	6	18–45	2,000
Buncombe	20,381,634	County and Township	Black Mountain	47,860	Repair and construction	.20		4	18–45	3,250
Burke	3,408,767	County		5,248	Bridges, repair and construction	.15	.45	6	18–45	†1,500
Cabarrus	7,470,179	County		27,000	Repair and construction	.30				
Caldwell	3,882,496							6	18–45	†2,500
Camden	1,492,000							6	18–45	700

†Estimated.

*A tax of $1 on each dog after all the sheep killed by dogs are paid for; balance to roads.

Carteret	2,769,804	1 Township	Beaufort	400	Repair		.05			6	8445	800
Caswell	2,561,221	Townships	All	3,000	Repair		**.10			4	1845	1,800
Catawba	6,730,597	County		10,000	Repair		.20		(or $100	4	2445	1,200
Chatham	5,568,879	County		,303	Repair		.10 .15			4	21-45	3,000
Cherokee	3,854,040	Townships	Valleytown, Murphy, Marble District	5,781	Interest on bonds		.20 .35 .15		In Murphy tp. Outside Murphy and Valleytown Tps.	6 8	18-45	†500
Chowan	2,868,442	Townships	1st, 2nd, 3rd and 4th.	4,000	Repair		.10 .20	.30 .60				
Clay	945,581	County		3,309			.35			4	18-45	†500
Cleveland	7,850,215	Townships	No.2, No. 4, and No. 6	10,000	Repair and construction		.10		In other tps.	2	18-45	2,000
Columbus	6,382,987	County		11,000	Repair and construction		.10	.30		6	21-45	†3,500
Craven	8,512,304	County		17,500	Repair and construction		.15	.45				
[illegible]	7,934,130	County		9,511	Construction		.09			6	18-45	3,750
Currituck	2,157,457									6	18-45	2,000
Dare	884,468									6	18-45	1,000
Davidson	8,440,337	7 Townships	Alleghany, Abbott's [illegible]k, Lexington, Thomasville, Boone, [illegible]on Grove and Silver Hill	10,000	Repair and construction		.20	.40	When no special tax	6	21-45	†600
Davie	3,784,5?0									6	18-45	†1,400
Duplin	5,884,929	Township	Warsaw	3,070	Interest on bonds		.20	Warsaw Tp. .60		6	18-45	2,000
Durham	21,961,875	County		55,958	Repair and construction		.20⅓					
Edgecombe	8,951,528	County		20,500	Repair and construction		.25					

**Also dog tax.

REVENUE BY TAXATION DURING 1912

County	Assessed Valuation Personal and Real 1912 Lists	How Levied, County or Township?	Special Tax. Name of Township	Amount Raised by Tax (Property and Poll)	How Spent, Construction or Repair?	Rate of Property and Poll Tax: Rate on $100 Worth of Property	Rate of Property and Poll Tax: Rates of Poll	Number of Days Required	Labor Tax Age Limits	Number of Men Subject to Tax
Forsyth	19,503,664	County		$ 75,000	Repair and construction	$ .33⅓	$			
Franklin	5,791,178	3 Townships	Louisburg, Franklinton, Youngsville	27,460	Construction	.30 .35 .25	.90 1.05 .75	When no special tax 6	18-45	500
Gaston	10,693,841	County		36,966	Repair and construction	.25	.75			
Gates	2,663,339							6	18-45	1,000
Graham	1,377,938	County		3,500	Repair and construction	.25⅓		4	18-45	500
Granville	6,253,390	County		21,709	Repair and construction	.25		4	18-45	2,000
Greene	3,998,858							6	18-45	†1,200
Guilford	18,580,102	County		32,085	Repair and construction	.15		2	21-45	4,200
Halifax	11,112,579	County		23,000	Repair	.20	.60	6	18-45	3,500
Harnett	6,772,481	Township	Averysboro	5,000	Repair and construction	.30		6	21-45	400
Haywood	6,402,467	County		10,884	Repair and construction	.17		6	18-45	1,000
Henderson	5,523,207	County		12,500	Bridges, repair and construction	.20		6	21-45	2,000
Hertford	4,025,279	5 Townships	Winton, Harrellsville, Ahoskie, St. John's, Maney's Neck	†5,000	Repair	.05 .15	.15 .30 .45	6	18-45	1,500
Hoke	3,058,835	County		5,000	Interest on bonds	.15	.45			
Hyde	1,711,228	2 Townships	Swan Quarter, Fairfield	678	Repair	.20		6	18-45	800

Iredell	9,425,915	County	----	†22,000	Interest and sinking fund		.23		.69	----	----	----	----
Jackson	2,904,295	Townships	All	6,000	Repair		.10 .25	----	----		5	18-45	2,000
Johnston	10,886,190	Townships	Smithfield, Clayton and Selma	10,000	Repair and construction		.30	----	----		6	18-45	3,000
Jones	2,280,850	7 Townships	All	3,421	Repair		.15		.45		2	21-50	700
Lee	3,425,820	County	----	9,500	Repair and construction		.20		.60	----	----	----	----
Lenoir	5,867,070	County	----	12,958	Repair and construction		.20	----	----	----	----	----	----
[illegible]ln	4,192,733	Townships	All	8,000	Repair		.20		.60	----	----	----	----
McDowell	2,769,884	County and Township	Marion	10,000	Repair	County Marion Tp.	.10 .40	----	----		6	18-45	1,000
Macon	2,598,961	Township	----	8,000	Repair		.25 .40	----	----		4	21-45	1,700
Madison	3,638,946	County	----	6,000	Repair and construction		.15	----	----		6	18-45	2,000
Martin	4,920,693	Township	Williamston	2,000	Interest on bonds		.20		.60		6	21-45	†1,700
Mecklenburg	21,356,996	County and Township*	----	†70,000	Repair and construction		.30	----	----		4	21-45	†2,000
Mitchell	2,108,152	County	----	11,000	Repair and grading		.50	----	----		4	21-45	800
Montgomery	4,276,000	Townships	All	5,000	Repair		.10	----	----		4	18-45	†1,300
Moore	7,065,186	3 Townships	Carthage, McNeill's, Sand Hill	9,800	Repair and construction		.25		.75		6	18-45	800
Nash	9,915,591	Road Districts	N. Whitakers, Ferrell's, Baileys, Mannings, Jacksons, Rocky Mt.	†29,000	Repair and construction	Rocky Mt. District County	.20 .30		.60 .90	----	----	----	----
New Hanover	13,382,878	----	----	----	----	----	----	----	----		4	21-45	900
Northampton	6,095,671	County	----	14,000	Bridges and repairs		.20	----	----		3	21-45	2,500
Onslow	4,295,631	----	----	----	----	----	----	----	----		4	18-45	1,200

†Estimated. *All townships levy a maintenance tax of 10 cents.

REVENUE BY TAXATION DURING 1912.

County	Assessed Valuation Personal and Real 1912 Lists	How Levied, County or Township?	Special Tax. Name of Township	Amount Raised by Tax (Property and Poll)	How Spent, Construction or Repair?	Rate of Property and Poll Tax: Rate on $100 Worth of Property	Rate of Property and Poll Tax: Rates of Poll	Number of Days Required	Labor Tax Age Limits	Number of Men Subject to Tax
Orange	4,280,276	County		$ 13,840	Interest, sinking fund and repair	$ .30	$			
Pamlico	1,890,440	County		3,780	Repair and for bridges	.20		4	21–45	1,000
Pasquotank	5,105,377	County		11,650	Repair	.15	.45			
Pender	3,003,674							8	18–45	†1,400
Perquimans	2,746,089	[illegible]	All	6,314	Filling swamps and tiling roads	.15	.45	6	18–45	†800
Person	3,605,698	County		5,408	Repair	.15				
Pitt	8,279,906	County		12,420	Repair and construction	.15	Not over .50	6	18–45	3,500
Polk	1,925,099	County and Township	Tryon	Co., 1,500 Tp. 4,812	Repair and construction	County .25 Township .30		4	21–45	1,000
Randolph	7,220,352	County		6,772	Repair	.08⅓		4	18–45	2,500
Richmond	7,526,400	County		18,340	Repair	.30	.90			
Robeson	12,193,566	County		28,000	Repair	.25				
Rockingham	9,773,043	County		25,500	Repair and construction	.20	.60	3	21–50	1,000
Rowan	11,086,039	County		27,715		.25		4 (or $2.50)	21–45	500
Rutherford	5,682,505	3 Townships	Union, Sulphur Springs and High Shoals	3,100	Repair and construction	.20 .10	.30 .60	6	18–45	3,000
Sampson	5,922,885	County		5,923	Interest on bonds	.10		6	21–45	2,500
Scotland	4,239,289	Townships	Stewartsville, Williamson, Laurel Hill and Spring Hill	14,130	Interest on bonds and repair	.18⅓ .28⅓ .33⅓ .38⅓				

Stanly	4,862,615	County		5,000	Repair	.09	.27	4	21-45	1,500
Stokes	3,924,432							6	18-45	2,000
Surry	6,645,501	Township	Mt. Airy	5,000	Repair and construction	.30		6	18-45	2,500
Swain	2,381,578	County		5,000	Repair and construction	.10		4	18-45	800
Transylvania	2,596,687	County		3,500	Repair	.15		5	18-45	†500
Tyrrell	2,04[illegible]97	Townships	Alligator and Scuppernong	2,400	Repair	.10	.30			
Union	7,744,786	County and Township	Monroe	9,200	Repair and construction	.10 .22	.30 .66	6	18-45	†3,500
Vance	7,458,408	County		11,000	Repair	.11				
Wake	20,575,153	County and Townships **	Cedar Fork, Cary, Holly Springs, Middle Creek and Panther Branch	72,944	Repair and construction	.25 .10				
Warren	4,675,894	8 Townships	Roanoke, Six Pound, Haw Tree, Smith Creek, Nut Bush, Warrenton and Judkins	10,000	Repair	.25				
Washington	2,792,815	County		8,720	Repair	.20	.60	6	18-45	†900
Watauga	2,402,798							On old road 8 On new road 4	18-45	†1,100
Wayne	9,880,549	County		11,000	Repair and construction	.10				
Wilkes	4,878,823	County		6,000	Repair	.10		10	18-45	2,000
Wilson	8,600,207	County and Township	Wilson	30,800	Repair and construction	.25 .22½	.67 .75			
Yadkin	3,159,524							6	18-45	1,200
Yancey	1,684,719	County		2,435	Repair	.15		6	18-45	2,000
Totals	$609,525,102			$1,158,442						$125 050

**Special dog tax amounting to $3,408. †Estimated.

A review of this table shows that forty-eight counties have levied a special tax for road work, the tax being levied for the whole county. There is raised by this tax about $782,841, the greater proportion of which is spent in connection with the labor tax in repairing the dirt roads of the county. As a rule, this money is not spent under the direction of a competent road engineer, but is apportioned among the townships and used to employ people living along the road, unskilled in road building, to work at such times when their crops are not needing them. Twenty-nine counties have from one to eight townships issuing special road tax, amounting to $179,485. There are seven counties in which there is a county road tax and certain townships having a special road tax, aggregating $167,116. One county is divided into road districts, which have issued $29,000 in bonds. This makes a total of $1,158,442, as the amount reported raised by special tax for roads in the whole State. Of this amount $74,777 is used to pay interest on bond issues, and $1,083,665 is spent in repair of dirt roads and construction of new improved roads. Seventy counties have a labor tax, and these reported an aggregate number of 125,050 men subject to this tax, who work on an average of five and three-seventh days each during the year, making a total of 678,842 days of labor that were put on the roads in these counties during 1912. Valuing this labor tax at one dollar per day, it is equal to $678,842 spent on the roads by the seventy counties referred to above. Of the fifteen counties which had this labor tax exclusive of any other tax, only five reported any improved roads, which demonstrated very conclusively the inefficiency of this method. All of the counties or townships which reported improved surfaced roads have either a special tax or bond issue or both for building them.

This form of raising revenues for building roads has not proven the most successful one, because the amount of money thus raised annually is too small to admit of the county or township employing a road engineer; and, unless the road work of the county or township is systematized and put in the hands of a skilled man, the money is spent to little advantage in the location and construction of new roads, the laying out of a system of roads, or the maintenance of dirt roads. Most of the counties of North Carolina are rural, having no large cities from which a large revenue can be derived by special tax, and to raise enough money to carry on road work systematically and effectively would be too much of a burden on the individual citizen.

Revenue by Bond Issue.

The next table (II) gives the counties and townships voting bonds during 1912, the amount of bonds issued to January 1, 1913, the amount sold to January 1, 1913, and date of sale (when same could be obtained).

TABLE II—REVENUE BY BOND ISSUE DURING 1912.

	Amount of Bonds Issued to January 1, 1913	Amount of Bonds Issued During 1912	Amount of Bonds Sold to January 1913	Date of Sale	Kind of Bonds, County or Township	Names of Townships
Alamance	$ 400,000	$	$ 400,000	1908	County	
Alexander						
Alleghany	50,000		50,000		Township	
Anson	50,000	50,000			Township	Wadesboro
Ashe						
Avery						
Beaufort						
Bertie	25,000		25,000	$5,000, 1907 20,000, 1911	Township and County	
Bladen	10,000		10,000	1908	Township	
Brunswick	35,000		35,000	1908 & 1911	2 Townships	
Buncombe	20,000		20,000	1907	Township	Black Mountain
Burke						
Cabarrus	145,000	105,000	40,000	1911	County	
Caldwell						
Camden						
Carteret						
Caswell						
Catawba	100,000	100,000	50,000	1912	2 Townships	Hickory and Newton
Chatham						
Cherokee	262,000	187,000	262,000	1907 & 1911	2 Townships	Valleytown and Murphy and Marble Dist.
Chowan						
Clay						
Cleveland	125,000	25,000	75,000	25,000, 1910 25,000, 1911 25,000, 1912	2 Townships	No. 4 and No. 6
Columbus						
Craven						
Cumberland						
Currituck						
Dare						
Davidson	100,000		100,000		Township	Lexington
Davie						
Duplin	65,000	65,000	65,000	1912	Townships, Districts	Warsaw Tp. Rose Hill Tp. Faison Tp. Calypso Dist. Wallace Dist.
Durham						
Edgecombe						
Forsyth						
Franklin	110,000	75,000	110,000	1909 & 1911	Townships	Franklinton, Louisburg and Youngsville
Gaston	300,000		300,000	1905 & 1908	County	
Gates						
Graham						
Granville	160,000	40,000	160,000	1903 & 1909	County	
Greene						
Guilford	300,000		300,000	1905 & 1909	County	
Halifax						

TABLE II—REVENUE BY BOND ISSUE.—CONTINUED.

	Amount of Bonds Issued to January 1, 1913	Amount of Bonds Issued During 1912	Amount of Bonds Sold to January 1913	Date of Sale	Kind of Bonds, County or Township	Names of Townships
Harnett	$	$	$			
Haywood	50,000	50,000	50,000		Township	Waynesville
Henderson						
Hertford						
Hoke	50,000		50,000	1911	County	
Hyde						
Iredell	400,000	400,000	125,000	1912	County	
Jackson						
Johnston						
Jones						
Lee	115,000	100,000	115,000	1912	County and Township	Sanford
Lenoir						
Lincoln						
McDowell	5,000		5,000		Township	Marion
Macon						
Madison	20,000	10,000			Township	Mars Hill
Martin	40,000		35,000	1911 & 1912	Township	Williamston
Mecklenburg	300,000		300,000		County	
Mitchell						
Montgomery						
Moore	32,000		32,000	1910 & 1911	3 Townships	McNeill, Carthage and Sand Hill
Nash	70,000	20,000	30,000	1907 & 1912	Districts	Rocky Mt., N. Whitakers
New Hanover	200,000		200,000	1902, 1905, 1907 & 1911	County	
Northampton						
Onslow						
Orange	290,000	250,000	40,000	1908	County and Township	Hillsboro
Pamlico						
Pasquotank	10,000		10,000	1905 & 1906	County	
Pender						
Perquimans						
Person						
Pitt						
Polk	12,000		12,000	1911	Township	Tryon
Randolph						
Richmond	100,000	100,000	100,000	1905, 1907 & 1909	7 Townships	
Robeson						
Rockingham						
Rowan						
Rutherford						
Sampson	50,000	10,000	50,000	1909, 1910, 1911 & 1912	County	
Scotland	130,000	130,000	130,000	1909 & 1911	4 Townships	Stewartsville Williamson Laurel Hill Spring Hill
Stanly						
Stokes						
Surry	5,000	5,000	5,000	1912	Township	Mt. Airy

TABLE II—REVENUE BY BOND ISSUE.—CONTINUED.

	Amount of Bonds Issued to January 1, 1913	Amount of Bonds Issued During 1912	Amount of Bonds Sold to January 1913	Date of Sale	Kind of Bonds, County or Township	Names of Townships
Swain	$	$	$			
Transylvania						
Tyrell						
Union						
Vance	20,000		20,000	1904	County	
Wake						
Warren						
Washington						
Watauga						
Wayne						
Wilkes						
Wilson	100,000		100,000	1905 & 1910	Township	Wilson
Yadkin						
Yancey						
	$4,001,000	$1,682,000	$3,456,000			

A review of this table shows that up to January 1, 1913, thirty-seven counties had issued bonds; that of these thirty-seven counties, thirteen voted or issued bonds during 1912, amounting to $1,682,000; that eleven of these bond issues were made by the county, as a whole; that thirty-six townships issued bonds; in two instances a county bond issue was supplemented by a township bond issue; and four road districts reported bond issues.

Up to January 1, 1913, there were issued by counties and townships, $4,100,000 in bonds for road construction. Of this amount $3,456,000 have been sold, and there were issued during 1912, $1,682,000.

Road Mileage in North Carolina.

Table III gives the estimated total mileage of public roads by counties; number of miles of macadam, sand-clay, gravel, etc., built to date; and the number of miles of each of these kinds of road constructed during 1912, together with the average cost of constructing the various forms of surfaced road. There is also given the number of miles of unimproved dirt roads in each county.

TABDE III—ROAD MILEAGE

County	Number of Miles of Public Road in County (Estimated)	Macadam		Sand-Clay		Gravel		Specially Surfaced		Kind	Number Miles Dirt Road Graded During 1912	Number Miles Dirt Road Unimproved	Average Cost Per Mile of Constructing			
		Number Miles in County	Number Miles Built During 1912	Number Miles in County	Number Miles Built During 1912	Number Miles in County	Number Miles Built During 1912	Number Miles in County	Number Miles Built During 1912				Macadam	Sand-Clay	Gravel	Grading
Alamance	800	47½	½	11	4			6½	6	Asphalt	6	729	$	$	$	$
Alexander	500											500				
Alleghany	350											350				
Anson	550	25		34		30					10	451			$1,500	
Ashe	500											500				
Avery	600					2	2					598				
Beaufort	400			2							4	394				
Bertie	850			1		400	*150					449		*250		
Bladen	200			3								197				
Brunswick	360			30	10							330				
Buncombe	600	83	15	33	18						12	472	4,000	600		400
Burke	500			2½							6	491½				500
Cabarrus	350	20				10		30		Asphalt macadam	6	284				2,500
Caldwell	600	6		4	1						3	587		1,000		300
Camden	90										10	190				
Carteret	50			10	5							140		1,000		
Caswell	50	2										498				
Catawba	40			10	10						12	428		800		
Chatham	60											600				
Cherokee	90	13	3					2				385				
[illegible]an	85			1							2	182				
Clay	60											160				
Cleveland	60			22	12							578		1,200		800

*Soil.

Columbus	800			2								798		**750		
Craven	495	2		20	5			2	2	Bituminous Sand-Clay	2	469				
Cumberland	400			45	20							355		500		
[illegible]	200			1¾	1						20	178¼				175
Dare	70											70				
Davidson	700	3		6	2							691				
Davie	300			3							13	284		1,000		400
Duplin	900			30	30						30	840		500–400		75
Durham	600	123	8			11	4				10	456	4,500		1,800	1,500 to 3,000
Edgecombe	750			8							25	717				
Forsyth	800	84	4	12	12			9		Tar macadam	15	680 *				
Franklin	500			146	46	150						204		800		
Gaston	500	97	12	9	5							394	3,500	2,500		
Gates	300											300				
Graham	250										3½	246½				
Granville	700	4		110	10							586		1,400		
Greene	400											400				
Guilford	900	120		52	12		1	18		Asphalt	18	691		1,800		
Halifax	750			8		75	50					667		300		
Harnett	800			43	18							757				
Haywood	200	25									14	161				1,600
Henderson	800			17	2							783				600
Hertford	600											600				
Hoke	200			100	100							D0		250		
Hyde	250											250				
Iredell	400	30		76	70							294		†		‡
Jackson	400											400				
Johnston	800			150	50	15						635		1,000		
Jones	400			4								396				
Lee	225			5	4	3	3				7	210		600	900	
Lenoir	600			7½	6	10	10	2	2			580½				
[illegible]	400			3	1½						3	394		2,000		
McDowell	350	6									5	339				
[illegible]	750											750				

**Sand-Asphalt, $1,000 per mile. †By county force, $1,3_5; by contract, $2,254. ‡Contract, $1,754; County, $915.

TABLE III—ROAD MILEAGE—Continued.

County	Number of Miles of Public Road in County (Estimated)	Macadam		Sand-Clay		Gravel		Specially Surfaced		Kind	Number Miles Dirt Road Graded During 1912	Number Miles Dirt Road Unimproved	Average Cost Per Mile of Constructing			
		Number Miles in County	Number Miles Built During 1912	Number Miles in County	Number Miles Built During 1912	Number Miles in County	Number Miles Built During 1912	Number Miles in County	Number Miles Built During 1912				Macadam	Sand-Clay	Gravel	Grading
Madison	300			5	5						6	289	$	$	$	$
Martin	400			22	7							378				
Mecklenburg	1,000	304	14			18		22	10		14	642	3,500			
Mitchell	500											500				
Montgomery	300			35	15							265		50		
Moore	600			275	75							325		350		
Nash	800			75	25						250	475		300		
New Hanover	125	60	5	5							5	55	3,500			575
[illegible]	675											675				
Onslow	350											350				
Orange	300	10				10					5	275				
Pamlico	200											200				
Pasquotank	225											225				
Pender	500											500				
Perquimans	200											200				
Person	600											600				
Pitt	1,000			17	12						60	923		600		40
Polk	300	3										297				
Randolph	400					14	14					386			800	
Richmond	450			210	10	28	3					212		400	400	
Robeson	900			45	20						20	835		300–400		
Rockingham	600			10	5							590				
Rowan	400	125	10	38				12				225	1,000			
Rutherford	600			1¼		3	3					595¾				
Sampson	800			105	15							695		450		
Scotland	300			175	25							125		300		

Stanly	550											550				
Stokes	400											400				
Surry	350			6	6							344		800		
Swain	300										4	296				800
Transylvania	200											200				
Tyrrell	200											200				
Union	900	4		1	1						*2	894	1,200			500
Vance	400											400				
Wake	1,000	5		21	1	110	10	1¼	1¼	Concrete	40	822¾		300	500	
Warren	400											400				
Washington	250			6	6							244				
Watauga	300											300				
Wayne	1,000			135	60	25						840		150		
Wilkes	800	¼	¼									799¾	4,000			
Wilson	600	30		1								569				
Yadkin	300											300				
Yancey	200											200				
Totals	48,870	1,231¾	71¾	2,210	742½	914	250	104¾	21¼		642½	43,767				

*100 miles graded in all.

A review of this table shows that the total mileage of public roads in North Carolina is 48,870, of which there are 1,231¾ miles of macadam, 2,210 miles of sand-clay, 914 miles of gravel, 104¾ miles of specially surfaced road (concrete, bituminous macadam, etc.), making a total of 4,460½ miles of improved or surfaced road in the State. Of this mileage 71¾ miles of macadam were built during 1912, 742½ miles of sand-clay, 250 miles of gravel, and 21¼ miles of specially surfaced road, making a total of 1,085½ miles of improved or surfaced road built during 1912. In addition to this improved road, there were reported 642½ miles of road graded. The average cost of constructing a macadam road was $3,150 per mile; of sand-clay, $837.50; of gravel, $983.34; and of grading, $897.50.

Convict Labor in Road Construction.

Convicts are sentenced to work on the public roads of the various counties by the judges of the Superior Court. These are misdemeanor as well as long-term convicts. The next table gives the average number of convicts reported during the year by counties using them, and the average cost of maintaining these convicts (including board, guards, etc.).

TABLE IV—USE OF CONVICTS IN ROAD WORK IN NORTH CAROLINA DURING 1912.

	Average During Year	Leased to Other Counties	County or Counties to Whom Leased	Average Cost of Maintaining
Alamance	15			$
Alexander				
Alleghany				
Anson	35			
Ashe				
Avery				
Beaufort	26			.50 per day
				.30 to
				.35 per day
Bertie	6			
Bladen				
Brunswick		Lease	Columbus	
Buncombe	70			.68 per day
Burke		Lease	McDowell	
Cabarrus	25			30.00 per month
Caldwell		Lease	Gaston	
Camden		Lease	Pasquotank	
Carteret				
Caswell		Lease	Rockingham	
Catawba		Lease	Cleveland	
Chatham		Lease	Anson and Union	
Cherokee		Lease		
Chowan				
Clay		Lease	Haywood and Buncombe	
Cleveland	No. 6 Tp. 30			
Columbus	30			
Craven	22			300.00 per year
Cumberland	25			.75 per day
Currituck		Lease	Pasquotank	
Dare		Lease	Pasquotank	
Davidson				
Davie		Lease	Forsyth	
Duplin		Lease	Sampson	
Durham	85			.32 per day
Edgecombe	25			.40 per day
Forsyth	90			.55 to
				.60 per day
Franklin	One Tp. 20			
Gaston	50			
Gates		Lease	Pasquotank	
Graham		Lease	Buncombe	
Granville	15			1.00 per day
Greene				
Guilford	35			.40 per day
Halifax	25			.75 per day
Harnett	14			18.00 per month
Haywood	26			.28 per day
Henderson	35			12.00 per month
Hertford		Lease	Halifax	
Hoke				
Hyde				
Iredell	20			No record
Jackson		Lease	Haywood and Buncombe	
Johnston	40			1.00 per day
Jones		Lease	Lenoir and Edgcombe	
Lee		Lease	Union	

TABLE IV—CONTINUED.

	Average During Year	Leased to Other Counties	County or Counties to Whom Leased	Average Cost of Maintaining
Lenoir	25			$ (No record)
Lincoln		Lease	Cleveland and Gaston	
McDowell	Marion Tp. 25			
Macon		Lease	Haywood	
Madison		Lease	Buncombe	
Martin		Lease	Edgecombe	
Mecklenburg	114			.65 per day
Mitchell		Lease		
Montgomery				
Moore		Lease	Union	
Nash	Rocky Mt. Road Dist. 24			.46 per day
New Hanover	Outside of quarry 35			.67 per day
Northampton		Lease		
Onslow				
Orange		Lease	Durham	
Pamlico		Give them	Craven and Edgecombe	
Pasquotank	34			15.00 per month (approximately)
Pender		Lease	Sampson	
Perquimans		Give them	Pasquotank	
Person	5			1.00 per day
Pitt	35			.50 per day
Polk		Lease	Henderson	
Randolph		Lease	Guilford	
Richmond		Lease	Anson and Union	
Robeson	25			1.00 per day .25 to .40 per day
Rockingham	30–35			
Rowan	30			
Rutherford		Lease		
Sampson	12			150.00 per year
Scotland		Lease		
Stanly		Lease	Town of Albemarle	
Stokes				
Surry		Lease	Forsyth	
Swain		Lease	Haywood	
Transylvania	6			.45 per day
Tyrrell		Lease	Beaufort	
Union	50			.40 per day
Vance		Lease	Granville	
Wake	60			.50 per day
Warren	One Tp.			
Washington	5			.85 per day
Watauga		Lease		
Wayne	40			.60 per day
Wilkes		Lease	Iredell	
Wilson	26			1.10 per day
Yadkin		Lease	Forsyth	
Yancey		Lease	McDowell	

A review of this table will show that only about 1,350 convicts were reported as the average number which were being worked in the various counties during 1912; yet it is believed that a much larger number were worked than this report would indicate. These convicts are under the direct supervision and care of the boards of county commissioners or boards of road commissioners of the counties to which the prisoners are sentenced or leased. Forty-three counties lease their convicts to other counties to be worked on the public roads. The average number worked in the counties per year varied from 6 to 114.

The average cost of guarding, feeding, clothing, housing, etc., of the convicts varied as reported by the different counties from 42 to 72 cents per convict per day.

The work of the convicts on the public roads is equal to, and, in many instances, more effective than that of paid labor. Many of the counties report that the work on the public roads improves the health of the convict, and it is undoubtedly true that where the camps are supervised and maintained in a sanitary way that both the physical and moral effect upon the convict is good.

Summary.

The following gives in brief what we have spent during 1912, and what have been the results:

EXPENDITURES.

Total amount of special tax (including poll, etc.) for road work during 1912	$1,158,442
Amount paid for interest and sinking fund on bond issues	74,777
Amount from special tax used in road construction and maintenance	$1,083,665
Estimated amount of bond issues used in road construction and maintenance	800,000
Valuation of free labor	678,842
Estimated value of convict labor	250,000
	$2,812,507

RESULTS.

71¾	miles of macadam at an average cost of $3,150 per mile	$226,012
742½	miles of sand-clay at an average cost of $837.50 per mile	621,844
250	miles of gravel road, at an average cost of $984 per mile	246,000
21¼	miles of specially surfaced road	60,000
	Total for improved roads	$1,153,856

This leaves approximately $1,658,651 spent in maintaining the dirt roads.

From the condition of the majority of dirt roads of North Carolina it can readily be seen that the great proportion of this million and a half dollars is spent to little or no advantage, and is practically thrown away. This is principally due to the present haphazard and unbusinesslike methods of spending this money. With, however, the establishment of a State Highway Commission with competent road engineers to furnish to the counties; the placing of the county road work on a systematic basis, and the establishment of a system of maintenance by county or townships or road districts, this large sum of money will be used to advantage, and every citizen of the State will feel satisfied with the conduct of road affairs.

TOLL ROADS OF NORTH CAROLINA.

The Jefferson Turnpike.

The Jefferson Turnpike (J. E. Finley, President, North Wilkesboro), extends from North Wilkesboro, Wilkes County, to Jefferson, Ashe County, a distance of forty miles. The State aided in the construction of this road and owns considerable of the stock. The rates are:

For one-horse buggy or a two-horse wagon........	25 cents
For two-horse wagon	30 cents
For automobiles	25 cents

at each gate. There are two gates, one about eight miles and the other fifteen miles from North Wilkesboro.

The road is not in very good repair. Address H. W. Horton, North Wilkesboro.

The Lenoir-Blowing Rock Turnpike.

The Lenoir-Blowing Rock Road is owned by the Lenoir-Blowing Rock Turnpike Company, of Lenoir, N. C., and extends from Lenoir, Caldwell County, to Blowing Rock, Watauga County, a distance of forty-three miles. There are two toll gates, one four miles and the other twelve miles from Lenoir. The rates of toll are as follows:

	Between Lenoir and Patterson		Between Lenoir, Ft. Mountain and Richlands		Between Lenoir and Blowing Rock	
	Tires 4" and Over		Tires 4" and Over		Tires 4" and Over	
Horse and rider	$.10	$---	$.10	$---	$.15	$---
One-horse vehicle	.12	----	.15	----	.30	----
Two-horse vehicle	.15	.10	.20	.15	.40	.20
Three-horse vehicle	.20	.15	.25	.15	.50	.30
Four-horse vehicle	.30	.20	.35	.20	.60	.35
Six-horse vehicle	.35	.25	.40	.25	.75	.40
Each additional horse	.05	.05	.05	.05	.05	.05
Automobile	.25	----	.35	----	.50	----
Bicycle	.10	----	.10	----	.15	----
Horses and mules	.05	----	.05	----	.10	----
Cattle	.03	----	.01	----	.05	----
Sheep and hogs	.01	----	.01	----	.02	----

This road is kept in good condition and can be readily traveled by automobiles.

The Blowing Rock-Boone Turnpike.

The Blowing Rock-Boone Turnpike extends from Blowing Rock, Watauga County, to Boone, Watauga County. The distance is ten miles. There is one toll gate and the rates are as follows:

Two-horse team ....20 cents.
Four-horse team ....30 cents.
Automobiles ....25 cents.

The road is kept up in pretty good condition and automobiles can travel it except in very wet weather.

The Yonahlossee Road.

The Yonahlossee Road belongs to the Yonahlossee Road Company, and extends from Blowing Rock, Watauga County, to Linville, Avery County, a distance of twenty-two miles. There are two toll gates, one eight and one-half and the other seventeen miles from Linville. The rates of toll for the whole distance are as follows:

Toll for cattle, sheep or swine....................02 cents.
Toll for one person, on horseback, one way....................10 cents.
Toll for one-horse buggy, one way....................20 cents.
Toll for two-horse buggy, one way....................30 cents.
Toll for two-horse surry or carriage, one way....................30 cents.
Toll for automobile one way ....50 cents.
Toll for one-horse wagon, one way....................20 cents.
Toll for two-horse wagon, one way....................30 cents.
Toll for three-horse wagon, one way....................40 cents.
Toll for four-horse wagon, one way....................50 cents.

ECONOMIC PAPERS.

1. The Maple Sugar Industry in Western North Carolina, by W. W. Ashe, 1897. 8°, 34 pp. *Postage 2 cents.*

2. Recent Road Legislation in North Carolina, by J. A. Holmes. *Out of print.*

3. Talc and Pyrophyllite Deposits in North Carolina, by Joseph Hyde Pratt, 1900. 8°, 29 pp., 2 maps. *Postage 2 cents.*

4. The Mining Industry in North Carolina During 1900, by Joseph Hyde Pratt, 1901. 8°, 36 pp., and map. *Postage 2 cents.*

Takes up in some detail Occurrences of Gold, Silver, Lead and Zinc, Copper, Iron, Manganese, Corundum, Granite, Mica, Talc, Pyrophyllite, Graphite, Kaolin, Gem Minerals, Monazite, Tungsten, Building Stones, and Coal, in North Carolina.

5. Road Laws of North Carolina, by J. A. Holmes. *Out of print.*

6. The Mining Industry in North Carolina During 1901, by Joseph Hyde Pratt, 1902. 8°, 102 pp. *Postage 4 cents.*

Gives a list of Minerals found in North Carolina; describes the Treatment of Sulphuret Gold Ores, giving Localities; takes up the Occurrence of Copper in the Virgilina, Gold Hill, and Ore Knob districts; gives Occurrence and Uses of Corundum; a List of Garnets, describing Localities; the Occurrence, Associated Minerals, Uses and Localities of Mica; the Occurrence of North Carolina Feldspar, with Analyses; an extended description of North Carolina Gems and Gem Minerals; Occurrences of Monazite, Barytes, Ocher; describes and gives Occurrences of Graphite and Coal; describes and gives Occurrences of Building Stones, including Limestones; describes and gives Uses for the various forms of Clay; and under the head of "Other Economic Minerals" describes and gives Occurrences of Chromite, Asbestos, and Zircon.

7. Mining Industry in North Carolina During 1902, by Joseph Hyde Pratt, 1903. 8°, 27 pp. *Out of print.*

8. The Mining Industry in North Carolina During 1903, by Joseph Hyde Pratt, 1904. 8°, 74 pp. *Postage 4 cents.*

Gives descriptions of Mines worked for Gold in 1903; descriptions of Properties worked for Copper during 1903, together with assay of ore from Twin-Edwards Mine; Analyses of Limonite ore from Wilson Mine; the Occurrence of Tin; in some detail the Occurrences of Abrasives; Occurrences of Monazite and Zircon; Occurrences and Varieties of Graphite, giving Methods of Cleaning; Occurrences of Marble and other forms of Limestone; Analyses of Kaolin from Barber Creek, Jackson County, North Carolina.

9. The Mining Industry in North Carolina During 1904, by Joseph Hyde Pratt, 1905. 8°, 95 pp. *Postage 4 cents.*

Gives Mines Producing Gold and Silver during 1903 and 1904 and Sources of the Gold Produced during 1904; describes the mineral Chromite, giving Analyses of Selected Samples of Chromite from Mines in Yancey County; describes Commercial Varieties of Mica, giving the manner in which it occurs in North Carolina, Percentage of Mica in the Dikes, Methods of Mining, Associated Minerals, Localities, Uses; describes the mineral Barytes, giving Method of Cleaning and Preparing Barytes for Market; describes the use of Monazite as used in connection with the Preparation of the Bunsen Burner, and goes into the use of Zircon in connection with the Nernst Lamp, giving a List of the Principal Yttrium Minerals; describes the minerals containing Corundum Gems, Hiddenite and Other Gem Minerals, and gives New Occurrences of these Gems; describes the mineral Graphite and gives new Uses for same.

10. Oyster Culture in North Carolina, by Robert E. Coker, 1905. 8°, 39 pp. *Out of print.*

11. The Mining Industry in North Carolina During 1905, by Joseph Hyde Pratt, 1906. 8°, 95 pp. *Postage 4 cents.*

Describes the mineral Cobalt and the principal minerals that contain Cobalt; Corundum Localities; Monazite and Zircon in considerable detail, giving Analyses of Thorianite; describes Tantalum Minerals and gives description of the Tantalum Lamp; gives brief description of Peat Deposits; the manufacture of Sand-lime Brick; Operations of Concentrating Plant in Black Sand Investigations; gives Laws Relating to Mines, Coal Mines, Mining, Mineral Interest in Land, Phosphate Rock, Marl Beds.

12. Investigations Relative to the Shad Fisheries of North Carolina, by John N. Cobb, 1906. 8°, 74 pp., 8 maps. *Postage 6 cents.*

13. Report of Committee on Fisheries in North Carolina. Compiled by Joseph Hyde Pratt, 1906. 8°, 78 pp. *Out of print.*

14. The Mining Industry in North Carolina During 1906, by Joseph Hyde Pratt, 1907. 8°, 144 pp., 20 pl., and 5 figs. *Postage 10 cents.*

Under the head of "Recent Changes in Gold Mining in North Carolina," gives methods of mining describing Log Washers, Square Sets, Cyanide Plants, etc., and detailed descriptions of Gold Deposits and Mines are given; Copper Deposits of Swain County are described; Mica Deposits of Western North Carolina are described, giving Distribution and General Character, General Geology, Occurrence, Associated Minerals, Mining and Treatment of Mica, Origin, together with a description of many of the mines; Monazite is taken up in considerable detail as to Location and Occurrence, Geology, including classes of Rocks, Age, Associations, Weathering, method of Mining and Cleaning, description of Monazite in Original Matrix.

15. The Mining Industry in North Carolina During 1907, by Joseph Hyde Pratt, 1908. 8°, 176 pp., 13 pl., and 4 figs. *Postage 15 cents.*

Takes up in detail the Copper of the Gold Hill Copper District; a description of the Uses of Monazite and its Associated Minerals; descriptions of Ruby, Emerald, Beryl, Hiddenite, and Amethyst Localities; a detailed description with Analyses of the Principal Mineral Springs of North Carolina; a description of the Peat Formations in North Carolina, together with a detailed account of the Uses of Peat and the Results of an Experiment Conducted by the United States Geological Survey on Peat from Elizabeth City, North Carolina.

16. Report of Convention called by Governor R. B. Glenn to Investigate the Fishing Industries in North Carolina, compiled by Joseph Hyde Pratt, State Geologist, 1908. 8°, 45 pp. *Out of print.*

17. Proceedings of Drainage Convention held at New Bern, North Carolina, September 9, 1908. Compiled by Joseph Hyde Pratt, 1908. 8°, 94 pp. *Out of print.*

18. Proceedings of Second Annual Drainage Convention held at New Bern, North Carolina, November 11 and 12, 1909, compiled by Joseph Hyde Pratt, and containing North Carolina Drainage Law, 1909. 8°, 50 pp. *Out of print.*

19. Forest Fires in North Carolina During 1909, by J. S. Holmes, Forester, 1910. 8°, 52 pp., 9 pl. *Out of print.*

20. Wood-using Industries of North Carolina, by Roger E. Simmons, under the direction of J. S. Holmes and H. S. Sackett, 1910. 8°, 74 pp., 6 pl. *Postage 7 cents.*

21. Proceedings of the Third Annual Drainage Convention, held under Auspices of the North Carolina Drainage Association; and the North Carolina Drainage Law (codified). Compiled by Joseph Hyde Pratt, 1911. 8°, 67 pp., 3 pl. *Out of print.*

22. Forest Fires in North Carolina During 1910, by J. S. Holmes, Forester, 1911. 8°, 48 pp. *Out of print.*

23. Mining Industry in North Carolina During 1908, '09, and '10, by Joseph Hyde Pratt and Miss H. M. Berry, 1911. 8°, 134 pp., 1 pl., 27 figs. *Postage 10 cents.*

Gives report on Virgilina Copper District of North Carolina and Virginia, by F. B. Laney; Detailed report on Mica Deposits of North Carolina, by Douglas B. Sterrett; Detailed report on Monazite, by Douglas B. Sterrett; Reports on various Gem Minerals, by Douglas B. Sterrett; Information and Analyses concerning certain Mineral Springs; Extract from Chance Report of the Dan River and Deep River Coal Fields; Some notes on the Peat Industry, by Professor Charles A. Davis; Extract from report of Arthur Keith on the Nantahala Marble; Description of the manufacture of Sand-lime Brick.

24. Fishing Industry of North Carolina, by Joseph Hyde Pratt, 1911. 8°, 44 pp. *Out of print.*

25. Proceedings of Second Annual Convention of the North Carolina Forestry Association, held at Raleigh, North Carolina, February 21, 1912. Forest Fires in North Carolina During 1911. Suggested Forestry Legislation. Compiled by J. S. Holmes, Forester, 1912. 8°, 71 pp. *Postage 5 cents.*

26. Proceedings of Fourth Annual Drainage Convention, held at Elizabeth City, North Carolina, November 15 and 16, 1911, compiled by Joseph Hyde Pratt, State Geologist, 1912. 8°, 45 pp. *Postage 3 cents.*

27. Highway Work in North Carolina containing a Statistical Report of Road Work During 1911, by Joseph Hyde Pratt, State Geologist, and Miss H. M. Berry, Secretary, 1912. 8°, 145 pp., 11 figs. *Postage 10 cents.*

28. Culverts and Small Bridges for Country Roads in North Carolina, by C. R. Thomas and T. F. Hickerson, 1912. 8°, 56 pp., 14 figs., 20 pl. *Postage 10 cents.*

29. Report of the Fisheries Convention Held at New Bern, N. C., December 13, 1911, compiled by Joseph Hyde Pratt, State Geologist, together with a Compendium of the Stenographic Notes of the Meetings Held on the Two Trips taken by the Legislative Fish Committee Appointed by the General Assembly of 1909, and the Legislation Recommended by this Committee, 1912. 8°, 302 pp. *Postage 15 cents.*

30. Proceedings of the Annual Convention of the North Carolina Good Roads Association held at Charlotte, N. C., August 1 and 2, 1912, in Cooperation with the North Carolina Geological and Economic Survey. Compiled by Joseph Hyde Pratt, State Geologist, and Miss H. M. Berry, Secretary, 1912. 8°, 109 pp. *Postage 10 cents.*

31. Proceedings of Fifth Annual Drainage Convention held at Raleigh,

N. C., November 26 and 27, 1912. Compiled by Joseph Hyde Pratt, State Geologist. 8°, 56 pp., 6 pl. *Postage 5 cents.*

32. Public Roads are Public Necessities, by Joseph Hyde Pratt, State Geologist, 1913. 8°, 62 pp. *Postage 5 cents.*

33. Forest Fires in North Carolina during 1912 and National and Association coöperative Fire Control, by J. S. Holmes, Forester, 1913. 8°, 63 pp. *Postage 5 cents.*

34. Mining Industry in North Carolina during 1911-12, by Joseph Hyde Pratt, State Geologist, 1914. 8°, pp., pl., figs. *Postage cents.*

35. Good Roads Days November 5th and 6th 1913 compiled by Joseph Hyde Pratt State Geologist, and Miss H. M. Berry, Secretary. 8° pp. pl. *Postage cents.*

36. Proceedings of the North Carolina Good Roads Association, held at Morehead City, N. C. July 31st and August 1st, 1913, in Coöperation with the North Carolina Geological and Economic Survey. Statistical Report of Highway Work in North Carolina during 1912. Compiled by Joseph Hyde Pratt, State Geologist, and Miss H. M. Berry, Secretary. 8°, pp., 7 figs. *Postage cents.*

VOLUMES.

Vol. I. Corundum and the Basic Magnesian Rocks in Western North Carolina, by Joseph Hyde Pratt and J. Volney Lewis, 1905. 8°, 464 pp., 44 pl., 35 figs. *Postage 32 cents. Cloth-bound copy 30 cents extra.*

Vol. II. Fishes of North Carolina, by H. M. Smith, 1907. 8°, 453 pp., 21 pl., 188 figs. *Postage 30 cents.*

Vol. III. The Coastal Plain Deposits of North Carolina, by Wm. Bullock Clark, Benjamin L. Miller, L. W. Stephenson, B. L. Johnson and Horatio N. Parker, 1912. 8°, 509 pp., 62 pl., 21 figs. *Postage 35 cents.*

Pt. I.—The Physiography and Geology of the Coastal Plain of North Carolina, by Wm. Bullock Clark, Benjamin L. Miller, and L. W. Stephenson.

Pt. II.—The Water Resources of the Coastal Plain of North Carolina, by L. W. Stephenson and B. L. Johnson.

Vol. IV. Birds of North Carolina. In press.

BIENNIAL REPORTS.

First Biennial Report, 1891-1892, J. A. Holmes, State Geologist, 1893. 8°, 111 pp., 12 pl., 2 figs. *Postage 6 cents.*

Administrative report, giving Object and Organization of the Survey; Investigations of Iron Ores, Building Stone, Geological Work in Coastal Plain Region, including supplies of drinking-waters in eastern counties, Report on Forests and Forest Products, Coal and Marble, Investigations of Diamond Drill.

Biennial Report, 1893-1894, J. A. Holmes, State Geologist, 1894. 8°, 15 pp. *Postage 1 cent.*

Administrative report.

Biennial Report, 1895-1896, J. A. Holmes, State Geologist, 1896. 8°, 17 pp. *Postage 1 cent.*

Administrative report.

Biennial Report, 1897-1898, J. A. Holmes, State Geologist, 1898. 8°, 28 pp. *Postage 2 cents.*

Administrative report.

Biennial Report, 1899-1900, J. A. Holmes, State Geologist, 1900. 8°, 20 pp. *Postage 2 cents.*

Administrative report.

Biennial Report, 1901-1902, J. A. Holmes, State Geologist, 1902. 8°, 15 pp. *Postage 1 cent.*

Administrative report.

Biennial Report, 1903-1904, J. A. Holmes, State Geologist, 1905. 8°, 32 pp. *Postage 2 cents.*

Administrative report

Biennial Report, 1905-1906, Joseph Hyde Pratt, State Geologist, 1907. 8°, 60 pp. *Postage 3 cents.*

Administrative report; report on certain swamp lands belonging to the State, by W. W. Ashe; it also gives certain magnetic observations at North Carolina stations.

Biennial Report, 1907-1908, Joseph Hyde Pratt, State Geologist 1908. 8°, 60 pp., 2 pl. *Postage 5 cents.*

Administrative report. Contains Special Report on an examination of the Sand Banks along the North Carolina Coast, by Jay F. Bond, Forest Assistant, United States Forest Service; certain magnetic observations at North Carolina stations; Results of an investigation Relating to Clam Cultivation, by Howard E. Enders, of Purdue University.

Biennial Report, 1909-1910, Joseph Hyde Pratt, State Geologist, 1911. 8°, 152 pp. *Postage 10 cents.*

Administrative report, and contains Agreements for Co-operation in Statistical Work, and Topographical and Traverse Mapping Work with the United States Geological Survey; Forest Work with the United States Department of Agriculture (Forest Service); List of Topographic maps of North Carolina and counties partly or wholly topographically mapped; description of special Highways in North Carolina; suggested Road Legislation; list of Drainage Districts and Results of Third Annual Drainage Convention; Forestry reports relating to Connolly Tract, Buncombe County; Transylvania County State Farm, certain Watersheds, Reforestation of Cut-over and Abandoned Farm Lands, on the Woodlands of the Salem Academy and College; Recommendations for the Artificial Regeneration of Longleaf Pine at Pinehurst; Act regulating the use of and for the Protection of Meridian Monuments and Standards of Measure at the several county-seats in North Carolina; list of Magnetic Declination at the county-seats, January 1, 1910; letter of Fish Commissioner of the United States Bureau of Fisheries relating to the conditions of the North Carolina fish industries; report of the Survey for the North Carolina Fish Commission referring to dutch or pound-net fishing in Albemarle and Croatan sounds and Chowan River, by Gilbert T. Rude, of the United States Coast and Geodetic Survey; Historical Sketch of the several North Carolina Geological Surveys, with list of publications of each.

Biennial Report, 1911-1912, Joseph Hyde Pratt, State Geologist, 1913. 8°, 118 pp. *Postage 7 cents.*

Administrative report, and contains reports on method of construction and estimate of cost of road improvement in Stantonsburg Township, Wilson County; report on road conditions in Lee County; report on preliminary location of section of Spartanburg-Hendersonville Highway between Tryon and Tuxedo: report of road work done by U. S. Office of Public Roads during biennial period; experiments with glutrin on the sand-clay road; report on Central Highway, giving Act establishing and report of trip over this Highway; suggested road legislation: report on the Asheville City watershed; report on the Struan property at Arden, Buncombe County; report on the woodlands on the farm of Dr. J. W. Kilgore, Iredell County; report on examination of the woodlands on the Berry place, Orange County; report on the forest property of Miss Julia A. Thorn, Asheboro, Randolph County; report on the examination of the forest lands of the Butters Lumber Company, Columbus County; proposed forestry legislation; swamp lands and drainage, giving drainage districts; suggested drainage legislation; proposed Fisheries Commission bill.

Samples of any mineral found in the State may be sent to the office of the Geological and Economic Survey for identification, and the same will be classified free of charge. It must be understood, however, that *no assays or quantitative determinations will be made.* Samples should be in a lump form if possible, and marked plainly on outside of package with name of sender, post office address, etc.; a *letter* should accompany sample and *stamp* should be enclosed for reply.

These publications are mailed to libraries and to individuals who may desire information on any of the special subjects named, free of charge, except that in each case applicants for the reports should forward the amount of *postage* needed, as indicated above, for mailing the bulletins desired, to the *State Geologist, Chapel Hill, N. C.*

NORTH CAROLINA GEOLOGICAL AND ECONOMIC SURVEY

JOSEPH HYDE PRATT, State Geologist

ECONOMIC PAPER No. 37

FOREST FIRES IN NORTH CAROLINA DURING 1913

AND

STATE FOREST FIRE PREVENTION IN THE UNITED STATES

BY

J. S. HOLMES, Forester

RALEIGH:
E. M. Uzzell & Co., State Printers and Binders.
1914.

GEOLOGICAL BOARD.

Governor Locke Craig, *ex officio* Chairman .... Raleigh.

Frank R. Hewitt .... Asheville.

Hugh MacRae .... Wilmington.

William H. Williamson .... Raleigh.

Henry E. Fries .... Winston-Salem.

Joseph Hyde Pratt, State Geologist .... Chapel Hill.

LETTER OF TRANSMITTAL.

CHAPEL HILL, N. C., July 1, 1914.

To His Excellency, LOCKE CRAIG,

Governor of North Carolina.

SIR:—There has just been completed by the North Carolina Geological and Economic Survey the collection and tabulation of statistics regarding forest fires in North Carolina during the past year. We have also obtained information regarding what other States are doing toward protecting their forests from fire and the results accomplished. I would, therefore, submit for publication as Economic Paper, No. 37, of the Reports of the North Carolina Geological and Economic Survey the report on the *Forest Fires in North Carolina During 1913* and a *Summary of State Forest Fire Prevention in the United States.* This report will give information that should be of value in the framing of an efficient forest policy for North Carolina.

Yours respectfully,

JOSEPH HYDE PRATT,

State Geologist.

35017

CONTENTS.

FOREST FIRES IN NORTH CAROLINA DURING 1913.

By J. S. HOLMES, Forester.

INTRODUCTION.

In making his annual report for 1913, the Chief Fire Warden of the Washington Forest Fire Association summarizes the essentials of forest fire prevention so satisfactorily that they might fitly form a text for this report. He says: "This has been a successful season, made so by a combination of circumstances, in having (1) favorable weather; (2) three strong patrol organizations working in unison; and (3) the coöperation of the public."

He goes on to say: "By strengthening the patrol force from year to year, and continuing to deal fairly with the public, we can hope to make each season a successful one, even though the weather be not favorable." That is, in Washington and other States where fire prevention is a policy of the people, they are planning to make the weather a negligible quantity, something that does not count. Here in North Carolina, on the other hand, the weather is the only factor upon which we can depend in dealing with fires.

The contrast is startling and alarming. With 600 fires, the members of the above association lost only one million feet of timber out of 250 billion feet protected; while with about the same number of fires North Carolina lost sixty times as much timber out of a total estimated stand in the State of less than one-sixth of that protected by the Washington Forest Fire Association. Yet our last year's season was comparatively favorable, probably quite as favorable as that of Washington. It was not the weather, but the lack of any system of patrol and the indifference instead of the coöperation of the public, which made our proportionate loss of timber nearly 400 times as great as theirs.

Fortunately, in North Carolina there is a very decided growth of public opinion in favor of fire prevention which will undoubtedly soon result in securing definite assistance from the State.

THE WEATHER.

It is undoubtedly true that the weather has more to do with the prevalence and seriousness of fires in North Carolina than any other one thing. Local weather conditions must be watched as closely as the more

FOREST FIRES IN NORTH CAROLINA DURING 1913.

By J. S. HOLMES, Forester.

INTRODUCTION.

In making his annual report for 1913, the Chief Fire Warden of the Washington Forest Fire Association summarizes the essentials of forest fire prevention so satisfactorily that they might fitly form a text for this report. He says: "This has been a successful season, made so by a combination of circumstances, in having (1) favorable weather; (2) three strong patrol organizations working in unison; and (3) the coöperation of the public."

He goes on to say: "By strengthening the patrol force from year to year, and continuing to deal fairly with the public, we can hope to make each season a successful one, even though the weather be not favorable." That is, in Washington and other States where fire prevention is a policy of the people, they are planning to make the weather a negligible quantity, something that does not count. Here in North Carolina, on the other hand, the weather is the only factor upon which we can depend in dealing with fires.

The contrast is startling and alarming. With 600 fires, the members of the above association lost only one million feet of timber out of 250 billion feet protected; while with about the same number of fires North Carolina lost sixty times as much timber out of a total estimated stand in the State of less than one-sixth of that protected by the Washington Forest Fire Association. Yet our last year's season was comparatively favorable, probably quite as favorable as that of Washington. It was not the weather, but the lack of any system of patrol and the indifference instead of the coöperation of the public, which made our proportionate loss of timber nearly 400 times as great as theirs.

Fortunately, in North Carolina there is a very decided growth of public opinion in favor of fire prevention which will undoubtedly soon result in securing definite assistance from the State.

THE WEATHER.

It is undoubtedly true that the weather has more to do with the prevalence and seriousness of fires in North Carolina than any other one thing. Local weather conditions must be watched as closely as the more general influences. Even in a period when showers are general there are some localities that get little or no rain. Winds are often more or less local. When a drought and a wind come together a very serious fire hazard is created, which, combined with the carelessness or sometimes the viciousness of the individual, is apt to bring about a state of destruction such as visited the Linville region in the spring and Polk County in the fall of 1913.

According to the reports of the United States Weather Bureau, we had no extensive dry spells last year. The annual precipitation for the State was slightly above the normal and was well distributed, though there was considerable variation between certain places, Highlands having nearly three times as much rain as Asheville or Marshall, and Weldon having less than two-thirds the rainfall of Lumberton or New Bern.

The two driest months were April and November, and these were the times our severest fires occurred. After abundant rains through January and February, the first week in March was quite dry. Fires occurred in both eastern and western North Carolina, but general rains on the 10th prevented any extensive damage. April was a month of light rainfall, though around the middle of the month good rains were general. Again at the end of the month light rains were reported from nearly all stations. It was not, however, until towards the 10th of May and in some places nearly the end of the month that soaking general rains came which finally extinguished the forest fires, which had been so frequent and disastrous through this period. The late summer and fall was wet up till about the 10th of November, with light rains around the 15th. From then on to the end of the month the weather was dry, especially in the western part of the State, where some devastating fires occurred, especially along the eastern slope of the Blue Ridge.

The following table shows by percentages the months and seasons in which fires are most likely to occur. It is based not only on the records showing when fires did actually occur, but also on the opinion of correspondents all over the State as to what is the most dangerous season. It is seen that the two fire seasons, spring and fall, are even more strongly emphasized the past year than in former years.

TABLE 1.—RELATIVE MONTHLY AND SEASONAL FIRE RISK IN 1913 AND AVERAGE FOR THREE YEARS, IN PERCENTAGES.

	1913.	Average.		1913.	Average.
March	19	17			
April	31	24	Spring	64	54
May	14	13			
June	3	5			
July	2	6	Summer	6	16
August	1	5			
September	2.5	5			
October	8	7	Fall	21	23
November	10.5	11			
December	5	4			
January	0.5	1	Winter	9	7
February	3.5	2			

FIRE DAMAGE.

The information from which the following tables have been compiled has been voluntarily furnished by nearly 700 correspondents all over the State. Only seven counties this year were unrepresented, though less than half the townships of the State have been reported for.

It should be kept in mind that the figures given do not purport to be exact. They are more or less careful estimates made by well informed and impartial citizens of the special townships for which they are reporting. These correspondents receive no compensation for their services other than the knowledge that they are thereby helping the movement which will make their State a better place to live in. They cannot therefore be expected to travel all over the township, or to investigate personally each fire. Their estimates are, however, made with care and with due regard to the facts in the case as far as they can be ascertained. There can be no doubt that the figures are conservative and represent less rather than more than the actual damage in nearly every case.

TABLE 2.—FOREST FIRES IN NORTH CAROLINA DURING 1913—COMPARATIVE STATEMENT—SUMMARY OF REPORTS FROM CORRESPONDENTS BY REGIONS.

	Mountain.		Piedmont.		Coastal Plain.		State.	
	1913.	Average for Previous Four Years.	1913.	Average for Previous Four Years.	1913.	Average for Previous Four Years.	1913.	Average for Previous Four Years.
Total number of townships in region	166	166	454	450	370	364	990	980
Number of townships reporting	82	61	251	173	133	124	466	358
Number of replies received	115	66	413	171	156	112	684	351
Number of forest fires reported	126	180	258	228	167	246	551	654
Total area burnt over, in acres	100,350	167,708	151,796	98,015	71,298	174,758	323,444	440,480

TABLE 2.—FOREST FIRES IN NORTH CAROLINA DURING 1913—COMPARATIVE STATEMENT—SUMMARY OF REPORTS FROM CORRESPONDENTS BY REGIONS—CONTINUED.

	Mountain.		Piedmont.		Coastal Plain.		State.	
	1913.	Average for Previous Four Years.	1913.	Average for Previous Four Years.	1913.	Average for Previous Four Years.	1913.	Average for Previous Four Years.
Total standing timber destroyed, in M feet, board measure	7,471	28,623	28,439	7,911	23,904	21,224	59,814	57,75
Value of timber destroyed, in dollars	$ 30,693	$ 71,879	$ 74,088	$ 27,456	$ 66,041	$ 58,268	$170,822	$ 157,60
Area of young growth destroyed, in acres	56,659	48,265	67,691	26,078	25,572	45,425	149,922	120,16
Value of young growth destroyed, in dollars	$ 76,435	$ 66,985	$193,225	$ 29,776	$ 48,828	$ 76,279	$318,488	$ 175,56
Value of forest products destroyed, in dollars	$ 39,612	$ 78,361	$ 34,786	$ 66,390	$ 84,966	$ 87,736	$159,364	$ 232,48
Value of improvements destroyed, in dollars	$ 10,120	$ 17,642	$ 29,615	$ 23,242	$ 17,800	$ 26,759	$ 57,535	$ 67,69
Total damage reported, in dollars	$156,860	$236,120	$331,714	$148,390	$217,635	$250,422	$706,209	$ 634,94
Number of lives lost	----	----	3	----	----	2	3	
Cost to private individuals to fight fire	$ 4,116	$ 6,922	$ 4,439	$ 4,999	$ 9,386	$ 7,627	$ 17,941	$ 19,54

TABLE 3.—FOREST FIRES IN NORTH CAROLINA DURING 1913. SUMMARY OF REPORTS FROM CORRESPONDENTS BY COUNTIES.

MOUNTAIN REGION.

County.	Total Number of Townships in County.	Number of Townships Reporting.	Number of Replies.	Number of Fires.	Total Area Burnt Over, in Acres.	Merchantable Timber Destroyed, M.	Value of Timber Destroyed.	Area of Young Growth Destroyed, in Acres.	Value of Young Growth Destroyed.	Value of Products Destroyed.	Value of Improvements Destroyed.	Lives Lost.	Cost of Fighting Fi...
Alleghany	8	1	1	1	40	20	$ 100	10	$ 50	$ 150	$ 100	----	$..
Ashe	15	1	1	2	700	500	----	700	----	----	300	----	[illegible]
Avery	7	5	7	8	15,800	2,250	5,725	6,200	23,000	----	5,000	----	[illegible]
Buncombe	13	4	5	4	1,300	40	200	400	----	200	----	----	
Cherokee	6	2	3	----	500	10	15	75	100	200	75	----	
Clay	5	4	9	12	15,900	800	1,900	6,600	21,300	2,200	1,375	----	[illegible]
Graham	3	3	3	8	5,500	600	1,010	5,500	5,250	1,250	----	----	
Haywood	13	6	7	8	1,700	300	1,500	900	1,120	5,000	----	----	[illegible]
Henderson	8	7	9	4	850	2	10	----	----	----	20	----	
Jackson	15	4	5	5	2,400	5	5	100	500	700	50	----	
Macon	11	6	7	4	25	----	----	----	----	----	----	----	
Madison	16	10	10	10	30,550	374	2,360	25,334	4,605	8,012	100	----	[illegible]
Mitchell	9	5	7	2	100	100	350	----	----	2,500	----	----	---
Swain	5	2	3	7	11,000	70	200	6,000	13,000	17,000	1,000	----	1,[illegible]
Transylvania	9	7	12	39	7,600	250	6,750	3,840	2,700	1,300	----	----	[illegible]
Watauga	12	9	13	4	510	100	218	150	410	----	----	----	
Yancey	11	6	13	8	5,875	2,050	10,250	850	4,400	1,100	2,100	----	
Totals	166	82	115	126	100,350	7,471	30,693	56,659	76,435	39,612	10,120	----	4,[illegible]

TABLE 4.—FOREST FIRES IN NORTH CAROLINA DURING 1913. SUMMARY OF REPORTS FROM CORRESPONDENTS BY COUNTIES.

PIEDMONT REGION.

County.	Total Number of Townships in County.	Number of Townships Reporting.	Number of Replies.	Number of Fires.	Total Area Burnt Over, in Acres.	Merchantable Timber Destroyed, M.	Value of Timber Destroyed.	Area of Young Growth Destroyed, in Acres.	Value of Young Growth Destroyed.	Value of Products Destroyed.	Value of Improvements Destroyed.	Lives Lost.	Cost of Fighting Fire.
Alamance	13	12	21	1	40		$	40	$ 100	$	$		$
Alexander	8	7	10	6	520	10	275	517	320	200	200		5
Anson	8												
Burke	12	6	6	10	86,000	20,550	52,200	31,000	86,000	4,500	5,000		1,250
Cabarrus	12	7	20	1	25	4	20			2,000			
Caldwell	12	2	5	5	2,000	200	1,200	500	1,000	1,000			100
Caswell	9	6	7	1	2								
Catawba	8	7	15	1	3		5						
Chatham	14	7	9	4	503	25		510	10		800		
Cleveland	11	7	8	2	200	110	520	100	100				10
Davidson	17	6	8	2	75	60	100	10	50	200	6,000		
Davie	7	7	23	2			250						
Durham	6	2	2	1	10			10					
Forsyth	14	8	15	2	3			3	15				
Franklin	10	5	7	18	2,200	195	1,360	590	2,500	3,200	2,000		100
Gaston	6	3	7	6	126	500	16	300	225				
Granville	9	7	10	3	24		45						2
Guilford	18	10	11	2	15		250	5	7				
Iredell	16	5	12	3	150	200	200	50	200	300	500	1	50
Lee	7	3	4										
Lincoln	5	2	2										
McDowell	11	4	6	10	7,018	2,000	5,200	3,518	15,036	236	1,200		566
Mecklenburg	15	11	19	3	30	15	150						
Montgomery	11	8	9	2	2,020	55	135	1,000	200	100	250		20
Moore	9	8	12	15	6,050	50	100	4,420	8,100	16,000	5,900		825
Orange	7	3	6	5	60			60	160				
Person	9	4	4	2	49			49	475				
Polk	6	6	13	27	28,080	1,101	2,200	12,000	72,400	1,600	1,200		600
Randolph	19	6	9										
Rockingham	11	5	7	2									
Rowan	14	10	16	5	500	102	175	300	650	900	500		210
Rutherford	12	7	6	14	6,850	2,120	2,350	5,700	2,300	575	3,100		120
Stanly	8	1	1	2	60	7	30	20	200	500			
Stokes	8	2	4										
Surry	14	12	21	8	194	100	650	55	700	1,550	250		100
Union	9	5	6										
Vance	9	5	8	2	15								10
Wake	19	2	2										
Warren	12	8	15	34	4,740	35	3,315	5,900	500	550			100
Wilkes	21	17	34	19	4,105	910	2,952	924	1,802	750	1,015		316
Yadkin	8	8	13	8	129	90	390	110	175	825	1,700		55
Totals	454	251	413	258	151,796	28,439	74,088	67,691	193,225	34,786	29,615	1	4,439

LE 5.—FOREST FIRES IN NORTH CAROLINA DURING 1913. SUMMARY OF REPORTS FROM CORRESPONDENTS BY COUNTIES.

COASTAL PLAIN REGION.

County.	Total Number of Townships in County.	Number of Townships Reporting.	Number of Replies.	Number of Fires.	Total Area Burnt Over, in Acres.	Merchantable Timber Destroyed, M.	Value of Timber Destroyed.	Area of Young Growth Destroyed, in Acres.	Value of Young Growth Destroyed.	Value of Products Destroyed.	Value of Improvements Destroyed.	Lives Lost.	Cost of Fighting Fire.
ıfort	6	4	4	2	2,100	50	$4,150	10	$ 50	$------	$------	----	$----
ie	9	7	12	11	7,771	1,875	7,650	4,150	550	5,200	2,650	----	3,225
len	15	2	2	------	------	------	------	------	------	------	------	----	------
ıswick	6	------	------	------	------	------	------	------	------	------	------	----	------
den	3	1	1	------	------	------	------	------	------	------	------	----	------
eret	9	1	1	------	------	------	------	------	------	------	------	----	------
van	4	3	3	1	------	------	------	------	------	------	------	----	------
mbus	14	8	15	17	17,100	730	1,680	2,833	2,533	6,500	1,300	----	1,025
en	9	4	4	3	2,000	500	1,500	------	------	2,000	------	----	------
berland	11	4	3	4	4,025	5,000	5,000	500	1,000	6,000	400	----	325
ituck	5	2	3	3	300	------	------	150	300	500	------	----	------
	5	------	------	------	------	------	------	------	------	------	------	----	------
lin	13	3	3	2	40	100	150	30	------	200	------	----	50
ecombe	14	2	2	2	100	10	40	10	50	90	100	----	15
s	7	------	------	------	------	------	------	------	------	------	------	----	------
ne	9	2	2	------	------	------	------	------	------	------	------	----	------
fax	12	1	1	3	1,200	100	150	1,200	3,500	2,000	1,000	----	100
ıett	13	8	11	11	2,100	200	1,300	150	1,500	7,700	2,800	----	------
ford	6	2	2	------	------	------	------	------	------	------	------	----	------
ə	5	1	1	1	150	10	25	------	------	1,000	500	----	100
e	4	1	1	------	------	------	------	------	------	------	------	----	------
ston	17	6	8	11	300	40	120	100	500	200	150	----	100
s	7	1	1	1	1,000	------	------	------	------	------	------	----	------
ir	12	6	6	7	860	90	375	675	300	11,035	455	----	90
in	10	------	------	------	------	------	------	------	------	------	------	----	------
	14	6	6	16	3,520	532	1,056	2,467	5,770	5,506	800	----	1,426
Hanover	4	------	------	------	------	------	------	------	------	------	------	----	------
hampton	9	6	7	1	20	2	10	10	25	------	------	----	------
ow	5	3	3	5	2,500	200	750	1,100	600	1,025	------	----	25
lico	4	3	4	6	2,300	1,100	1,900	700	1,500	15,000	------	----	1,000
uotank	6	------	------	------	------	------	------	------	------	------	------	----	------
ler	10	5	5	15	4,300	450	2,300	8,500	24,800	3,600	6,400	----	220
uimans	5	3	2	5	2,300	2,000	10,000	650	1,700	1,500	150	----	25
	11	4	4	2	1,000	500	1,500	500	2,500	------	------	----	------
mond	7	1	1	2	500	------	------	------	------	------	------	----	------
son	19	9	12	15	11,210	10,020	25,060	650	1,190	110	------	----	600
ɔson	16	9	11	7	22	25	125	12	60	------	------	----	------
and	4	2	2	4	3,100	100	100	------	------	300	------	----	------
ell	5	------	------	------	------	------	------	------	------	------	------	----	------
ington	4	3	3	2	1,000	100	500	1,000	200	200	------	----	------
ıe	12	7	7	3	280	70	200	100	------	10,300	100	----	1,010
n	10	3	3	5	200	100	400	75	200	5,000	1,000	----	50
Totals	370	133	156	167	71,298	23,904	66,041	25,572	48,828	84,966	17,800	----	9,386

TABLE 6.—FOREST FIRES IN NORTH CAROLINA DURING 1913. COMPARATIVE STATEMENT OF AVERAGES BY REGIONS FOR 1913 AND FOR FOUR PREVIOUS YEARS.

	Mountain, 1913.	Average for Previous Four Years.	Piedmont, 1913.	Average for Previous Four Years.	Costal Plain, 1913.	Average for Previous Four Years.	State, 1913.	Average for Previous Four Years.
Percentage of townships reporting	49	37	55	38	36	34	47	36.5
Average area of each fire, in acres	796	1,036	588	447	427	707	587	673
Average damage by each fire, in dollars	$ 1,240	$ 1,506	$ 1,286	$ 648	$ 1,303	$ 1,024	$ 1,282	$ 968
Average area burnt over per township reporting, in acres	1,223	*2,042	1,605	*576	536	*1,565	694	*1,189
Average damage per acre burnt, in dollars	$ 1.56	$ 1.18	$ 2.19	$ 1.52	$ 3.05	$ 1.45	$ 2.18	$ 1.34
Average damage per township reporting, in dollars	$ 1,913	$ 3,871	$ 1,322	$ 858	$ 1,636	$ 2,020	$ 1,515	$ 1,774

*For the years 1912, 1911, and 1910. No township figures for 1909.

From the above tables it is seen that though the damage from forest fires was considerably less in 1913 than in the previous year, yet the loss was above the average for the past five years, and this in the face of not specially unfavorable weather conditions.

This somewhat abnormal damage is no doubt due in part to the 30 per cent increase in the number of townships reporting. Too much stress, however, must not be laid on this fact, as the increase in the number of replies came largely from the Piedmont region, over the greater part of which serious fires are rare.

The growing realization of the value of unmerchantable young growth is perhaps the chief reason for the apparently high money loss. Whereas in 1911, the first year any general estimate was placed on destroyed young growth, the loss from this one cause amounted to only 25 per cent of the total damage, in 1912 it comprised 33 per cent, while in 1913 it has increased to 45 per cent of the total estimated damage. An instance of the growing recognition of the destructiveness of woods fires comes from Transylvania County. A farmer there claimed $300 reduction in the tax valuation of his place because 300 acres had been burnt over. This reduction was granted by the county commissioners. The county therefore lost several dollars in taxes every year from that one fire, besides the much more serious loss sustained by the farmer.

In North Carolina the destruction of mature timber is only a small part of the fire damage, because the usual surface fires, unless occurring late in the spring, do not kill the larger trees. For this reason the value of the reproduction and young growth destroyed necessarily assumes large proportions.

The very serious annual loss from forest fires can perhaps best be brought out by a comparison. The average loss from fires in North Carolina for the past five years has been about $650,000 a year. This is equivalent to a tax levy of 36 cents on the $100 on all the land in the State, or a tax of 13 cents on the $100 on all property, real and personal, now listed for taxation. How quickly would this fire tax be done away with if it came in the form of a regular tax levy! Yet the fire tax is paid year after year by the people of North Carolina without a murmur. One or two per cent of the amount lost, if properly spent by the State, would reduce the fire damage one-half the first year, and not only save much valuable property belonging to our citizens, but insure the future well-being of our State.

CAUSES OF FOREST FIRES.

The relative importance of the different causes of forest fires in North Carolina, as given in the following table, does not vary very widely from that shown by the investigations of previous years. The carelessness of the individual was responsible for a still larger proportion of fires, 46.5 per cent coming under this general heading, compared with 45 per cent in 1912, and 42 per cent the previous year.

TABLE 7.—CAUSES OF FOREST FIRES IN NORTH CAROLINA IN 1913 BY REGIONS, COMPARED WITH THE PREVIOUS FOUR YEARS, IN PERCENTAGES.

	1913.				Average for Previous Four Years, State.
	Mountain.	Piedmont.	Coastal Plain.	State.	
Farmers burning brush, grass, rubbish, etc.	14.5	18.5	6	13.5	11
Hunters	25.5	8.5	3.5	10.5	12
Cigars, cigarettes, matches, etc.	3.5	3	2.5	3	2.5
Carelessness	12.5	17.5	26.5	19.5	19
Railroad locomotives, sparks from	2	17.5	20	15	19
Logging locomotives, dummy engines, etc.	9		13	6	7.5
Sawmills, etc.	2	10.5	5	7	4
Traction engines		4		1.5	.25
Accidental, caught from burning buildings, etc.			1.5	.5	.5
To improve the range		1	4	1.5	3.5
Set by chestnut-gatherers, root-diggers, etc.	2	2		1	1
Without object, to see it burn	2	1		1	4
Malice or incendiary	12.5	6.5	2.5	7	7
Unknown causes	9	9	13	10.5	7
Lightning			2.5	1	1
Loafers, trespassers, etc.	3.5	1		1	.5
Campers	2			.5	.25

Farmers and hunters seem to be the chief offenders. The former were said to be responsible for nearly one-fifth of the fires occurring in the Piedmont region. Careless handling of fire in burning brush, stumps, rubbish, grass, and leaves when too dry or when the wind is too high, most commonly in the spring, is not confined to the small renters, but is a fault of many of our best land-owning citizens. Allowing boys or other irresponsible persons to burn in dry weather is on a par with letting children play with loaded guns.

In nine cases out of ten hunters are not the owners of the land over which they hunt, and whether they are bird hunters from the town or opossum hunters from the adjoining plantation, they apparently feel little or no responsibility about the occurrence of fires. The recent amendment to the camp-fire law, making hunters responsible for camp-fires left unextinguished, seems as yet to have had no appreciable effect, as no prosecutions of hunters have been reported. The new amendment to the old law, though an improvement, is not sufficient. Men will not prosecute their neighbors for what appears to be simply carelessness. Grand jurymen, who are the only State officials who can take the initiative in such investigations, have not the time or the opportunity to look up the evidence in forest fire cases. Such work must be done at the time of and immediately succeeding the fire. Township forest wardens, responsible directly to the State, whose special duty it is to prevent, extinguish, and investigate forest fires, are the only officials who can control this nuisance.

IMPROVING THE RANGE.

The Coastal Plain region is the only part of the State where the practice of starting fires for the purpose of furnishing early feed for cattle is common. One reports that the chief cause of fires is "burning the woods for pasture for cattle," while another says: "Out in the back-woods, where there is not much timber, the woods are set on fire and burnt off for grazing purposes." It is in just such places, "where there is not much timber," that the young timber growth is needed to fill up the openings and provide for a second-growth forest. The total assessed value of cattle grazing on these open-range lands is 15 cents per acre, and yet for this pittance young timber is destroyed which would yield ten times this revenue, not only to the owner of the land, but also to the community at large.

LIGHTNING.

Electrical storms were more frequent and severer during the summer of 1913 than for many years. Throughout the State many trees and houses were struck and much live stock was killed. Yet so far as can be ascertained, only two forest fires were caused by lightning, and these were in the adjoining counties of Cumberland and Harnett. This is in strong contrast to reports from the western States, where—in California, for example—half the fires on the National Forests were started by lightning. In that State more fires were set in this way on the National

Forests alone than were reported for the whole State of North Carolina. We are fortunate in having so few fires which are unpreventable.

INCENDIARY.

Malicious setting fire to the woods in order to destroy property or to conceal crime is comparatively rare in North Carolina. The last report showed that 7 per cent of the replies gave this as the chief cause of fires. In 1912 18 per cent of the Mountain fires and 10 per cent of the Piedmont fires were said to have been of incendiary origin; while this year the number has come down to 7 per cent, which is the average for the past five years.

One rather remarkable feature of this year's report is that the majority of the reported incendiary fires occurred in one county, and that most of the remainder were in three other counties in the same immediate region. In 1912 Transylvania suffered more from forest fires than any other county in the State, the reported loss running up into the hundreds of thousands of dollars. In 1913, though the total reported damage was less than in Polk, the number of fires was greater than in any other county, Polk having about two-thirds as many. In six out of seven townships in the former county incendiarism was assigned as the chief cause of fires, while in three out of six townships in Polk the same cause was given. These two counties seem to have had more incendiary fires than all the rest of the State put together. Some were set by "blockaders to disguise their stills," but the greater part were probably started with the idea of getting even for some real or fancied grievance. The fact is generally lost sight of that while the owner of the land loses by fire the value of his stumpage, the community loses twice as much in the value of the labor it would take to manufacture that timber and put it on the market.

PROSECUTIONS.

Under the present law practically the only action that can be taken against one who sets out fire is personal prosecution. Such action is almost never taken against individuals, chiefly because a private citizen objects to making a personal matter of what is really the concern of the community or of the State.

The weakness of the present situation is illustrated by conditions in Transylvania County, which is not very different from other parts of the State. This county reports 39 fires, most of which were of incendiary origin. One correspondent, when asked if any one had been prosecuted for setting fires, replies: "No! No!! No!!! and I should like to know why." The reason is that our forest laws are antiquated and machinery for their enforcement is entirely lacking. Even in Polk County, where, since the severe fires of last November, the citizens have organized a Forestry Club, have employed a forest warden, and offered a reward for evidence sufficient to convict any one of setting fires, no one has yet been punished. However, such an active and decided step will undoubtedly tend to prevent many fires in the future.

The sum total of prosecutions in North Carolina for 1913 seems to be five. Three of these were civil suits for damages, all of which were still pending at the end of the year. Iredell has the distinction of being the only county, out of eighty reporting forest fires, in which individuals were prosecuted and punished for setting fires. Although "just a small fine" was imposed, the good effect of this example will no doubt be felt far beyond the county lines.

Railroads usually pay damages, where a claim is made, without letting the matter go to court. Five cases of settlement for damages by railroads were reported for 1913, and no doubt there were others that were not heard of.

Such a remarkable lack of prosecutions must mean one of two things: either the average citizen is indifferent to fires, or else the procedure is absolutely inadequate. The first is not the case, judging from the correspondents, many of whom speak strongly against the people who purposely or carelessly set fire to the woods. From the east as well as the west come such expressions as, "Hunters, villains, idiots"; "Carelessness and cussedness, cussedness mostly"; while only one or two of the whole number of correspondents attempt feebly to defend the practice. The sentiment against burning is well-nigh universal amongst land-owning North Carolinians. It must be, then, that our present laws are not strong enough or comprehensive enough to furnish adequate protection.

PRESENT FOREST FIRE LAWS.

Only two sections of North Carolina law, dealing respectively with setting fires in the woods and leaving camp fires unextinguished, are of State-wide application. These two laws were printed in full in Economic Papers 25 and 33, but are again copied here for convenience of reference:

SECTION 3346. **Woods.** If any person shall set fire to any woods, except it be his own property or, in that case, without first giving notice in writing to all persons owning lands adjoining to the woodlands intended to be fired, at least two days before the time of firing such woods, and also taking effectual care to extinguish such fire before it shall reach any vacant or patented lands near to or adjoining the lands so fired, he shall, for every such offense, forfeit and pay to any person who shall sue for the same, fifty dollars, and be liable to any one injured in an action, and shall moreover be guilty of a misdemeanor.*

*Revisal of 1905.

SECTION 3347. **Woods, from Camp Fires.** If any wagoner or other person encamping in the open air shall leave his camp without totally extinguishing the camp fires, or hunter who shall set fire to any tree, stump, or other combustible matter and leave without totally extinguishing such fire, he shall be guilty of a misdemeanor, and upon conviction thereof shall be fined not exceeding fifty dollars or imprisoned not exceeding thirty days.†

These two laws are good as far as they go, but they were enacted many years ago when conditions were very different from what they are today. During the past five years, while the State has lost upwards of three million dollars by fires, these laws have probably not been invoked half a dozen times.

CONCLUSIONS.

For the purpose of information and comparison, and with the hope that the woodland owners of North Carolina may be led to demand that protection from forest fires which is their right and which the citizens of other States enjoy, the remainder of this report is devoted to some account of what other States are doing to reduce the fire menace.

Last year's report (Economic Paper 33), besides giving the report on Forest Fires in North Carolina during 1912, contained some account of Federal Forest Protection in the United States as well as recent developments in coöperative fire control. Under the former heading were taken up in a general way fire protection on the National forests and National forest fire laws, together with a brief account of what the other departments of the Government are doing to help in the work of protection. Coöperative fire control was briefly taken up as offered to the various States by the Federal Government under the Weeks law. The splendid work being done by the various timberland owners' protective associations was outlined and the beginnings of railroad coöperation considered.

The conclusion was reached that in order to successfully control forest fires both organization and coöperation are essential. Organization must originate with and be maintained by the State, and the State must act first. As soon as an organization is started, full coöperation can be secured from the Federal Government under the Weeks law. In States containing National forests, such as North Carolina, assistance can also be secured from the Forest Administration. Experience has shown that the coöperation of timberland owners and lumbermen, and then of the railroads and other corporations, will quickly follow the State's initiative. The State, however, *must* take the lead.

---

†Revisal of 1905, as amended in 1913.

STATE FOREST FIRE PREVENTION IN THE UNITED STATES.

THE LAKE STATES.

For many years what is known as the Lake Region was the center of the lumber industry in this country. For the past two or three decades, however, the output of lumber from these three States (Minnesota, Wisconsin, and Michigan), which have supplied the white pine of commerce, has been declining, until now the production of lumber is of yearly decreasing importance. For many years some of the worst forest fires of the country have raged through the cut-over lands as well as the virgin forests of these States, causing untold loss of property and the sacrifice of hundreds of lives. Since the inauguration of efficient fire protection, however, the annual damage has been greatly reduced.

MINNESOTA.

Minnesota has an approximate area of 52,000,000 acres. According to the estimate of the State Forester, of the 28,000,000 acres of forested land in the State, about 13,000,000 acres will eventually be cleared for farming. The remaining 15,000,000 acres, because of its character, will probably always remain in forest.

This State has for many years been one of the foremost in fire protective legislation. As early as 1895 what were then advanced forestry laws were passed. These have been amended and added to from time to time, until in 1911 the present law, which is perhaps the best in the United States, was enacted. This was again amended and greatly strengthened in 1913.

An Early Fire Law.—The forest law as passed in 1895 and amended in 1903 provides:

(1) For a forest commissioner, who shall be supreme in all matters relating to the preservation of forests and for the prevention and suppression of forest fires.

(2) For a fire warden system consisting of the supervisors of townships, the mayors of cities, and the presidents of village councils in what are called organized townships, and wardens appointed by the forest commissioner in an organized territory.

(3) The appointment of a chief fire warden by the forest commissioner to be in supreme charge of the fire fighting and administer the

forest fire laws of the State. During dry and dangerous seasons the chief fire warden was to use such means under his command as he might deem necessary to prevent or suppress fires, his expenses to be paid by the State, with the proviso, however, that his total expenses in one year should not exceed $5,000.

(4) It was the duty of fire wardens to take precautions to prevent the setting of forest and prairie fires, to patrol in dry seasons and, when necessary, to employ one or more extra patrols, to warn against careless use of fire, to control forest fires, to call for assistance, in emergencies, on any able-bodied male person over 18 years of age, who, if refusing to go, was liable to a fine of not exceeding $100.

(5) Both the chief fire warden and the fire wardens under him were given the powers of arrest without warrant for any violation of the forest laws, and were required to institute suits against offenders. It was their duty also to inquire into the cause of each fire in their district and report to the chief fire warden. Compensation was fixed at $2 per day, together with necessary expenses, and $1.50 per day for assistants hired by the wardens.

(6) One-third of the total cost of fire protection, outside of the salary of the chief fire warden, was paid by the county and two-thirds by the State.

(7) Strong provisions against setting forest fires, either willfully, negligently, carelessly, or maliciously, were incorporated in the law.

(8) The total appropriation for carrying out this scheme of fire protection was $5,000 for payment of wardens and their expenses, and $1,000 for prosecuting offenders.

It was found by experience that this law was inadequate in several particulars, notably in the unequal protection furnished by the various organized townships and in the inadequacy of the appropriation. The present law, which was passed in 1911 and strengthened by the Legislature in 1913, is in many respects the best State law now in force in this country. Several important sections will therefore be quoted in full so that a basis of comparison may be had for the laws of other States.

The strongest and most essential features of the Minnesota law are the appointment of a competent and well paid forester who has supreme control of all fire preventive measures, including a fire warden system composed of men whose chief, and in many cases only, duties are to act as fire wardens; a strong law for the inspection and control of railroad engines, and a law which puts into the hands of the State Forester the power to make and enforce regulations for slash disposal.

ORGANIZATION OF STATE FOREST SERVICE.

State Forestry Board.—"There shall be a State Forestry Board of nine members, composed of the director of the Forestry School and the dean of the Agricultural College of the University of Minnesota, and seven others appointed by the Governor for a term of four years and until their successors qualify. Two of said members shall be appointed upon the recommendation of the regents of the University, and one shall be appointed upon the recommendation of each of the following bodies: The State Agricultural Society, the State Horticultural Society, and the State Game and Fish Commission: *Provided* suitable persons be recommended by them to the Governor not later than January 31st of the year in which such terms expire. All vacancies shall be filled the same as the original appointments. The members now in office shall hold through the terms for which they were respectively appointed. So far as practicable, all such appointees shall be appointed with reference to their knowledge of and interest in the planting and cultivation of trees in prairie regions, the preservation of natural forests, the reforesting of denuded lands and the protection of the sources of streams."

Chief among its duties, the law provides that the State Forestry Board "shall have the management of the forest reserves and of all other property acquired therefor, supervise all matters of forest protection and reforestation and have charge of all moneys appropriated therefor or accruing therefrom, including the forest reserve fund and the forest service fund."

State Forester.—"The board shall appoint a State Forester who shall be a trained forester, at a salary not to exceed four thousand dollars ($4,000) per annum, and he shall be allowed necessary traveling and field expenses incurred in the conduct of his official duties. The office of the State Forester shall be at the State capital, and the board is hereby authorized to employ such office assistants as may be necessary and to fix their compensation. The State Forester, with the approval of the State Forestry Board, may appoint an assistant forester and such other employees, outside of the office assistants, as may be necessary in carrying out the provisions of this act, and fix the amount of their compensation. The State Forester shall execute all rules and regulations issued by the State Forestry Board pertaining to forestry and forest protection within the jurisdiction of the State; have charge of the work of protecting all forests and lands from fire; shall investigate the origin of all forest fires and prosecute all violators of this act; shall prepare and print for public distribution an abstract of the forest fire laws of Minnesota, together with such rules and regulations as may be formulated by the State Forestry Board. He shall prepare printed notices calling attention to the dangers from forest fires, and cause them to be posted in conspicuous places, and shall furnish same to the railroad companies, whose duty it shall be to post them in such places as he may direct."

District Rangers.—"As soon as practicable after this act shall take effect, the State Forester may, with the approval of the State Forestry Board, create and establish patrol districts, including all lands of both State and private ownership, upon which there is a probability of forest and brush fires starting, and establish rangers over the said districts.

"Under the direction of the State Forester, the district rangers are charged with preventing and extinguishing forest fires in their respective districts, and the performance of such other duties as may be required by the State Forester.

"They may arrest, without warrant, any person found violating any provisions of this chapter, take him before a magistrate and there make complaint. When the district rangers shall have information that such violation has been committed, they shall without delay make similar complaint, and have the same prosecuted. The district rangers shall not be liable for civil action for trespass committed in the discharge of their duties."

Fire Patrolmen.—"At any time district rangers, with the approval of the State Forester, may employ suitable persons to be known as fire patrolmen permanently to remain upon and patrol such territory, State or private, as may be assigned to them as long as may be required to prevent and extinguish any fire. Each such patrolman so employed shall be supplied with the necessary equipment. The State Forester and the district ranger may, and if they are absent and fires are actually burning in the forest, the fire patrolmen may summon any male person of the age of 18 years and upwards to assist in stopping the fires, and may incur any other necessary and reasonable expense for the same purpose, but shall promptly report the same to the district ranger.

"Any persons summoned by any official of the State who is physically able and refuses to assist shall be guilty of a misdemeanor, and shall be punishable by a fine of not less than $5 and not more than $25."

Payment for Fighting Fire.—"The wages and expenses of men summoned or employed to fight forest fires actually burning shall be fixed and paid for by the State Forester and the labor reckoned and paid for by the hours of labor performed, which shall not exceed the rate of 25 cents per hour employed: *Provided*, no pay shall be given for fighting fire within one mile of the residence of such person, unless employed by the State Forester or his assistants."

Road Overseers to Extinguish Fires.—"Every road overseer or assistant of a road overseer or other local officer having charge of the highway, who finds that any person has left a camp fire burning in his district, shall extinguish the same, and take prompt measures to prosecute the person or persons who so left such fire."

Negligently Setting Fires.—"Whoever under any circumstances sets fire must exercise care and precaution in proportion to the danger.

"Whenever a fire set by any person or corporation spreads to and destroys property belonging to another, it shall be *prima facie* evidence that the party so setting such fire is guilty of negligence in setting the same and allowing it to spread."

County Attorney to Prosecute.—"Whenever an arrest shall have been made for violation of any of the provisions of this chapter, or whenever information of such violation shall have been lodged with him, the county attorney of the county in which the offense was committed shall prosecute the accused with all diligence and energy."

Auxiliary Patrol Force.—"The State Forester may appoint supervisors, constables, and clerks of towns, mayors of cities, and presidents of village councils fire wardens for their respective districts, and it is hereby made their duty to do all things necessary to protect the property of such municipalities from fire and to extinguish the same.

"All towns, villages, and cities are hereby authorized and directed to take necessary precautions to prevent the starting and spreading of forest or prairie fires and to extinguish the same, and are hereby further authorized to annually levy a tax of not more than five mills upon a taxable property of such municipalities, which, when collected, shall be known as the 'Fire Fund,' which shall be used in paying all necessary and incidental expenses incurred in enforcing the provisions of this act."

Appropriation.—"There is hereby appropriated from the general revenue funds of the State out of any moneys not otherwise appropriated, the sum of $15,000 for the fiscal year ending July 31, 1911, $75,000 for the fiscal year ending July 31, 1912, and $75,000 for the fiscal year ending July 31, 1913, which shall be credited to the Forest Service, to be used therefor as provided in this act."

RAILROADS; REGULATIONS AND DUTIES.

The railroad law gives large powers to the State Forester, but fixes responsibility so clearly yet impartially that it has the effect of securing the active and hearty coöperation of the railroads in fire prevention. This is the object of the law and the avowed policy of the State Forester. Chapter III of the State Forester's annual report for the year 1913 is perhaps the best discussion of railroad fire prevention ever published in this country.

Because of the exceptional efficiency of the Minnesota railroad fire law, it is here given in full:

STATE FORESTER TO PROVIDE MEASURES FOR IMMEDIATE CONTROL OF FIRES.

"When, in the judgment of the State Forester, there is danger of the setting and spreading of fires from locomotive engines, he shall order any railroad company to provide patrolmen to follow each train throughout such fire patrol district or districts as he deems necessary to prevent fires. When the State Forester has given a railroad company notice to provide such patrol after trains, the said railroad company shall immediately comply with such instructions throughout the territory designated; and upon its failure so to do, the State Forester may employ patrolmen with the necessary equipment to patrol the rights of way of said railroad, and the expense of the same shall be charged to the said railroad company, and may be recovered in a civil action in the name of the State of Minnesota, and in addition thereto the said company shall be guilty of a misdemeanor.

"The State Forester may prescribe such other measures which are considered by him to be essential for the immediate control of fire.

Duties of Railroads.—"It is also made the duty of any railroad company, acting independently of such State Forester, to patrol its right of way after the passage of each train when necessary to prevent the spread of fires and to use the highest degree of diligence to prevent the setting and spread of fires to cause the extinguishment of fires set by locomotives or found existing upon their respective rights of way, and for any violation hereof such railroad company, its officers and patrolmen, shall be guilty of a misdemeanor, and be punished by a fine of not less than fifty dollars ($50) nor more than one hundred dollars ($100) and costs, and in addition thereto such railroad company shall be liable for all expenses and damage caused or permitted by it, to be recovered in civil action.

Ash-pan and Spark Arrester.—"Every company operating a railroad for any purpose shall equip and use upon each locomotive engine a practical and efficient ash-pan and spark-arresting device, which the master mechanic shall cause to be examined, and the same shall be examined by the master mechanic or some employee each time before leaving the roundhouse, except when snow is on the ground.

Record of Examination of Locomotives.—"A record shall be kept of such examinations in a book to be furnished by the railroad company for the purpose, showing:

"1. The place and number of each engine inspected.

"2. The date and hour of day of such inspection.

"3. The condition of the said fire protective appliance and arrangements; and

"4. A record of repairs made to any of the fire protective appliances. The said book to be open for inspection by the State Forester or other authorized officer appointed by him.

"The master mechanic or employee making such examination shall be held responsible for the good condition of the same, but without relieving the company from its responsibility hereunder.

State Inspection Authorized.—"Any locomotive inspector appointed by the State Forester is authorized to inspect any locomotive, donkey, traction, or portable engine and all other engines and boilers operated in the vicinity of forest, brush, or grass lands, and to enter upon any property for such purpose or where he may deem it necessary in order to see that all the provisions of this act are duly complied with.

Right of Way.—"Every such company shall keep its right of way clear of combustible material, logs, poles, lumber, and wood, except ties, material for shipment, and other materials necessary for the maintenance and operation of the road, from March 15th to December 1st. During particularly dry and dangerous periods the State Forester may prohibit any and all burning along part or all of railroad right of way for a definite period.

Fire-breaks Along Right of Way.—"Every railroad company shall establish and maintain such fire-breaks along the route of its railway as can be constructed and maintained at not excessive expense. The intention shall be to adjust the protective measures to the local conditions, and to make the expense proportionate to the fire risk and the possible damage.

Other Engines.—"Except when snow is on the ground, no donkey, traction, or portable engine or other engines and boilers except locomotives shall be operated in the vicinity of forest, brush, or grass lands, which do not burn oil as fuel, except they be provided with a practical and efficient ash-pan and spark-arresting device.

Deposit of Live Coals and Ashes.—"No company shall permit any of its employees to leave a deposit of fire, live coals, or ashes in the immediate vicinity of woodland or lands liable to be overrun by fire, and every engineer, conductor, or trainman discovering a fire adjacent to the track shall report the same promptly to the agent at the first telegraph or telephone station reached by him, whose duty it shall be as representative of such company to at once take necessary steps to put out such fire.

Posting Warning Placards.—"Every such company shall give its employees particular instructions for the prevention and extinguishment of fires, and shall cause warning placards, such as are approved by the State Forester, to be conspicuously posted at every station in the vicinity of forest, brush, and grass lands; and, when a fire occurs on the right of way of its road, shall immediately concentrate such help and adopt such measures as shall be available for its extinguishment.

"Every railroad company shall make such reports to the State Forester as are deemed necessary by him of fires occurring on or adjacent to their respective rights of way.

Combustible Material Close to Railroad.—"Whenever any combustible material shall be left in the proximity of any railroad, either without proper fire protection or so as to constitute a fire menace to other property, it shall be the duty of the owner of such material, upon being notified in writing by the State Forester or any forest ranger as to the nature and extent of the protection required, to forthwith comply with all the terms of such notice so as to properly protect or remove such material.

Penalty.—"Any company or corporation violating any provision of this section shall be deemed guilty of a misdemeanor, and on conviction thereof shall be fined not less than fifty dollars ($50) and not exceeding one hundred dollars ($100) and costs of prosecution for each offense, and any railroad employee or other individual violating the same shall be guilty of a misdemeanor, and shall be punished by a fine of not less than twenty-five dollars ($25) nor more than one hundred dollars ($100) and costs of prosecution, or by imprisonment in the county jail not exceeding ninety (90) days."

DISPOSAL OF SLASH.

Powers of Forester and Rangers as to Slashings.—"Where and whenever in the judgment of the State Forester or district ranger there is or may be danger of starting and spreading of fires from slashings and débris from the cutting of timber of any kind and for any purpose, the State Forester or district ranger shall order the individual, firm, or corporation by whom the said timber has been or is being cut to dispose of the slashings and débris as he may direct. Where conditions do not permit the burning of the slashings and débris over the entire area so covered, the State Forester may require the person, firm, or corporation by whom the timber was cut to dispose of such slashings and débris in such a way as to establish a safe fire line around the area requiring such protection, the said fire line to be of a width and of a character satisfactory to the State Forester.

Expense of Burning Slash Can Be Collected by State as Mechanics Lien.—"When any such branches, slashings, or débris are left unattended contrary to the instructions of the State Forester or district ranger, the State Forester, the district ranger, or patrolman may go upon the premises with such force of men as may be necessary, and burn such branches, slashings, and débris, and the expense thereof shall be a lien upon the land on which they are situated, and also upon the logs and other timber products cut upon said land, and enforced as liens are enforced for the improvement of real estate or personal property.

Clearing for Right of Way or Roadbed.—"Any person or corporation who cuts or fells trees or bushes of any kind in clearing land for roadbed or right of way for any railroad, highway, or trail shall in the manner and at the time as above prescribed burn the slashings and all combustible material except fuel and merchantable timber.

Clearing for Agricultural Purposes.—"Any person or corporation who cuts or fells trees or bushes of any kind in clearing land for agricultural or pasturage purposes, or who in any way clears land, is prohibited from setting fire to the slashings, brush, roots or excavated stumps or other combustible material on such land and letting the fire run; the material must be disposed of pursuant to the regulations of the State Forester.

Contractors to Pile and Burn Slash.—"Any contractor who enters into a contract for the construction of a public road, and which contract involves the cutting or grubbing of woods, standing timber, or brush from any part of the right of way of such road, shall pile all the slashings and débris cut or grubbed from the roadbed or right of way in the middle of such right of way, and shall burn and dispose of such slash and débris without damage to adjoining timber or woods, which burning shall be done in a manner and at a time satisfactory to the State Forester."

COMMENT.

Only one season has passed since the above law has gone into force, and so it is too soon to compare it with the deficiency of previous years. The State Forester, however, is enthusiastic about the improved conditions and administration of the law. In summing up the work of the State Forest Service for the season, he says:

"The season just ended has undoubtedly been the worst fire season that has been experienced since the present Forest Service has been organized, although there were less fires reported this year than in the previous years.

"Every effort was made during the year to prevent fires. The field force under the direction of the district rangers was about the same as in previous years. Approximately sixty patrolmen were employed by the State during the spring and fall, when the danger of fire was the greatest. This number was decreased during the summer months, when weather conditions were such as to decrease the fire danger. The Federal Government furnished an average of eighteen men per month. The various railroads maintained during the dangerous seasons a large force of patrolmen, who were engaged solely in the work of fire prevention. Quite a number of townships again employed patrolmen in their respective towns; the lumber companies had on duty during the entire year a large number of men who took every precaution in guarding against fires. Aside from the above, there were a number of special patrolmen such as National Forest Service officers and men employed by the Indian Service.

"The railroads have shown a marked improvement in their coöperation for fire prevention. In 1912, 44 per cent of the fires were set by railroads, while in 1913 only 20 per cent are charged to railroads.

"The number of patrolmen, the length and location of their beats, were determined by the ranger of each district. The rangers are intimately acquainted with the territory which they control, understanding the relative 'fire danger' of the different localities. In deciding upon the number of patrolmen needed, several things are considered: the number of trains per day; condition of engines in regard to fire protective devices; conditions of right of way and of adjacent land, whether covered with timber or grass; and proximity to towns, sawmills, or stored products such as ties, posts, or logs.

"Slash disposal is now a regular part of logging in Minnesota. The loggers in the last year spent in the neighborhood of $300,000 in burning brush, or approximately 10 cents a thousand on the cut of three billion feet of timber. The slash resulting from pine cuttings was practically all burned and fire lines of different kinds were burned around spruce and cedar cuttings. Only a very limited amount of lopping was done, and this mostly in areas of hardwood."

WISCONSIN.

The forest fire laws of Wisconsin have until recently been well ahead of the other Lake States; in fact, three or four years ago it was generally supposed that they were about the best State laws in the country. Their administration was in the hands of the State Forester, who was responsible to a representative forestry commission. One or more fire wardens were appointed by the forester in each township where the need for them existed, and these were paid for the time actually employed by them in preventing and suppressing fires at a rate not to exceed 25 cents per hour. All bills for services for wardens and those employed by them were paid by the township in which the work was done up to an amount not to exceed $100 a year in such township.

Lake States Forestry Conference.—After the two most disastrous fires of 1908 and 1910, not only in Wisconsin, but also in Minnesota and Michigan, it was realized by these States that their present laws were inadequate to cope with the forest fire situation. In December, 1910, a conference was called at St. Paul at which representatives of the three States came together to discuss the situation and the working out of a better system of fire prevention. This conference was an unusually strong and representative one, headed by the Governors of Minnesota and Wisconsin, members of the legislative committees on forestry from the Lake States, and also lumbermen, foresters, etc. The sense of the meeting was that "the old system of doing nothing until the fire occurred had always and everywhere proved to be little better than no system at all, and that the only sensible, practical plan was to concentrate the efforts of each State to building up the best possible system of fire prevention." After a two days meeting they passed a series of strong resolutions, among which are the following:

Adequate Patrol System Recommended.—"First. That the forest fire protection of each State and such other branches of State work as may be deemed best to combine with it be placed under the control of a nonpartisan commission empowered, as fully as possible under the constitutions of the different States, to carry on the work, and under civil service rules. Such commission should represent all the interests involved as far as possible, and we recommend that such commission place the work in charge of a chief forester who should be a professional graduate forester, and that the commission employ such trained foresters and other assistants as may be necessary; define their duties and fix their salaries; said employees to be engaged under such civil service regulations as the commission may prescribe.

"Second. *Resolved,* That it is the sense of this conference that the present forest fire warden service of Michigan, Wisconsin, and Minnesota is totally inadequate to meet the existing fire hazard to both life and property, and that forest protection service, to become efficient, must be greatly extended. To this end we recommend an adequate forest patrol system, maintained by the State, organized and operated by the commission referred to."

Subsequent to this meeting Minnesota greatly strengthened her forestry laws (see pages 19-27) until now she has perhaps the most efficient fire preventive system in the country. Wisconsin was not so fortunate, however.

Fire Protection Made a Local Affair.—"A bill was introduced in the Wisconsin Legislature of 1911 to provide for a State forest fire patrol, but the Legislature refused to appropriate State funds for this purpose, and the legislative committee changed the bill so that all lands benefited by the patrol would pay a special tax of 2½ cents per acre, per annum. The timberland owners refused to agree to this amendment, with the result that the bill was killed. Wishing to accomplish something, the Legislature passed a law providing that town chairmen should act as town fire wardens, and the road supervisors should be deputy town fire wardens. The idea of this law was to place the responsibility for and the cost of fighting fires directly upon the local community where they occurred.

Weakness of New Law.—"This law is only a makeshift, and is especially weak and inefficient for the following reasons:

"1. Some of the best men in the towns are elected as town chairmen and road supervisors, but because they are good men it does not naturally follow that they have the strength and endurance or the knowledge of how to fight forest fires. The impression seems to prevail that any one can fight forest fires. Almost any fairly able-bodied man can assist very materially, but the men in charge of the work must know the country thoroughly, and, more important still, must know just where and how to attack the fires. Experienced woodsmen should be in charge of the fire warden system in each town, and not simply some good man who happens to hold an office and upon whom it is easy to assign another duty by law.

"2. The towns that have the most timber are always, for that very reason, either without any settlers at all or else both settlers and roads are very few. Such towns, as a rule, have no road supervisors, and as a result, where the fire warden system should be the strongest it is in fact the weakest, and *vice versa.*

"3. The town chairmen and road supervisors almost never take any action until the fire actually occurs. In other words, the present law makes the same old mistake of providing for fighting fires, but not preventing them. Prevention is the watchword of any successful fire warden system, and this has been proved in every State from the Atlantic to the Pacific. No city of any size would think of being without a fire department, and no town containing a large area of timberlands should be without a strong fire warden system which would devote its efforts in the first place to preventing fires."

RAILWAYS.

The strongest feature of the present law and the one which will best repay careful study by North Carolinians is that which provides efficient State inspection for spark arresters and for fire preventive devices on railway locomotives, donkey, traction, and portable engines. The following synopsis of the work of this law given by the State Forester in his report for 1911-'12 is quoted almost in full because of the importance of this subject. Railroad inspection in some parts of Canada may be somewhat more complete and effective, but Wisconsin has certainly one of the strongest and most workable laws in the United States:

Spark Arresters.—"Between March 1st and December 1st all logging locomotives, donkey, traction, or portable engines which are operated in, through, or near forest, brush, or grass land, and which do not burn oil as fuel, must be equipped with screens or wire netting on top of the smokestack, and so constructed as to give the most practicable protection against the escape of sparks and cinders. 'The term logging locomotive as used in this act shall be construed to mean any locomotive operated on a railroad, branch line or division, the chief or main business of which is the transportation of logs, lumber, or other forest products.' The great value of this provision of the law will be at once apparent to any forester, as it compels every locomotive which is operated through the forests to be equipped with the oldest, simplest, and yet by far the most effective device for preventing the escape of sparks or cinders. namely, a screen or hood over the smokestack. Locomotives that are operated on main through lines and that make long runs could not be equipped in this way, for with the smokestack covered with a hood the front end of the engine would clog up with cinders, and then of course the engine could not steam or pull its load. Therefore the law provides that 'all locomotives operated on any railroad other than a logging railroad shall be equipped with the most practicable spark arresters so constructed as to give the greatest possible protection against the escape of sparks and cinders from the smokestacks thereof, and each such engine shall be provided with the most practicable device to prevent the escape of the coals from ash-pans and fire boxes, and such devices between March 1st and December 1st shall at all times be maintained in good repair.'

Railroad Locomotive Inspectors.—"The law provides that the superintendent of motive power or equivalent officer on each railroad shall designate an employee of such railroad at each division point and roundhouse, who shall examine each locomotive each time it leaves the division point or roundhouse between March 1st and December 1st, and such employee shall be held responsible for the proper carrying out of the provisions of this section, but without relieving the company from its responsibility hereunder. This provision of the law has proved very effective in keeping the locomotives in proper condition, and also in bringing about real coöperation between the State and the railroads.

State Locomotive Inspectors.—"It will be noted that the law provides that screens or hoods on the smokestacks must give the 'most practicable protection' and that spark arresters must be constructed so as to give the 'greatest possible protection.' The question naturally arises as to who shall decide as to the most practicable device.

"The law provides that any locomotive inspector designated by the State Board of Forestry may reject immediately from service any locomotive, etc., and in case of disagreement appeal may be made to the State Railroad Commission.

"Particular attention is called to the fact that any defective engine can be ordered out of service and that it cannot be returned to service until the defects have been fully remedied. This provision of the law is extremely important and is far more effective than the usual fines, for any railroad company that was inclined to disregard the law would be quickly brought to its senses by having its locomotives ordered out of service.

Other Provisions.—"Minor though important provisions of the law are:

"*a.* Railroads must provide patrols for duty along their tracks in dangerously dry weather, and if any railroad company fails to provide such patrols after due notice, the State Board of Forestry may employ patrols and the cost shall be charged to the railroad company.

"*b.* Every railroad must at least once every year cut and burn, or remove from its right of way, all grass, weeds, brush, logs, and refuse material.

"*c.* No railroad company shall permit its employees to deposit fire, live coals or ashes upon their tracks outside of the yard limits, except they be immediately extinguished.

"*d.* Engineers, conductors, or trainmen who discover fires along the right of way, or on lands adjacent to the railroad, shall report the same to the agent at the nearest telegraph station.

COMMENT.

"The railroads of Wisconsin have come to realize within the last few years that they are more directly interested in preventing forest fires than any other great industry in the State, and as a result of this realization they are anxious to do their full share in putting a stop to forest fires that are caused by the railroads.

"The State Board of Forestry has a locomotive inspector who devotes his entire time from March 1st to December 1st to inspecting locomotives in the forest regions of the State, and he is constantly working with the railroad officials to perfect improved devices."

MICHIGAN.

The third of the Lake States, which has perhaps been more seriously denuded of timber and laid waste by forest fires than either Minnesota or Wisconsin, has at the present time the least effective fire protective system of the three. The weakness of its organization consists in part in its being combined with the game and fish warden system of the State.

Fire Wardens.—The State Game, Fish, and Forestry Warden, who is responsible to the Public Domain Commission, has charge of the prevention and suppression of forest fires. Supervisors are constituted fire wardens of their respective townships. In those townships in which the supervisor does not reside the State Warden appoints a fire warden. The forested part of the State over which this law is operative is divided into ten districts, each in charge of a deputy game, fish, and forestry warden, who is directly responsible to the State Warden. These deputy wardens receive a salary from the State of not to exceed $1,000 and their necessary expenses. In addition to this force, temporary fire wardens are appointed by the State Fire Warden in any locality which he thinks is inadequately protected. The State Warden is empowered to use such means under his command as he may deem necessary to prevent and suppress fires during dry and dangerous seasons, the expenses of which, to be paid by the State, must not exceed $10,000.

Fire wardens may summon all necessary assistance, and persons refusing to attend are liable to a fine or imprisonment. All fire wardens and employees engaged to fight fire are to receive for their services $2 per day for the time actually employed, two-thirds to be paid by the township and one-third by the State, with the proviso that no fire warden is to be paid for more than a total of fifteen days service in one year. The approximate cost of fire prevention during 1913 was $18,600, $10,000 of which was specially appropriated by the State Legislature for this purpose and the remainder was part of the receipts from hunting and fishing licenses.

Railroads.—All railroads operating within the State are required to use efficient spark arresters, and to keep their rights of way clear of combustible material. Employees are forbidden to deposit live coals within the vicinity of woodlands and trainmen are required to report fires at the nearest telegraph station. Railroad companies are also required to give particular instructions to their employees for the prevention and prompt extinguishment of fires, and to post warning placards furnished by the forest commissioner.

Efficient spark arresters must also be maintained upon all threshing or other portable steam engines.

Inspection.—Perhaps the two most effective features of the present administration of the fire laws are the careful and efficient inspection of railway locomotives and rights of way, and the inauguration and growth of the Boy Forest Scout movement. In the report of the State Game, Fish, and Forestry Warden for 1912 seventy pages are devoted to the subject of railway fires and the efforts being made, not only by the State but also by the railroads themselves, for their prevention and final elimination. It would seem from this report that the strongest and closest coöperation exists between the railroads and the Forestry Department, and that very gratifying results are being obtained.

Forest Scouts.—The Michigan Forest Scouts movement deserves special mention. In adapting the Boy Scout idea to the forest protective needs of the State of Michigan, Mr. William R. Oats, State Game, Fish, and Forestry Warden, has not only secured an invaluable auxiliary fire-fighting force for this State, but has started a movement which may spread with advantage over the larger part of the United States. Already New Jersey, Massachusetts, and Washington have taken it up, and the forestry officials of West Virginia are seriously considering the advisability of organizing such a force. There seems no reason why North Carolina could not take advantage of the enthusiasm and intelligence of her school boys and girls in the same way, as soon as there is some definite State organization under the supervision of which they may be enlisted.

"The Michigan Forest Scouts are school boys and girls between the ages of 7 and 19 years who have willingly enlisted as protectors of forests and property and become close students and exponents of reforestation. The movement has proven so popular that school boys and girls in all parts of the State have joined its ranks until now there are 3,000 members.

"Not only has the organization proved a great aid in the protection of forests and property, but it has resulted in a good moral effect on the members, bettering their health by giving them training out-of-doors, developing chivalry and increasing their appreciation of citizenship. In a general way knowledge of the importance of prevention of forest fires is assimilated not only by the boys and girls of the State, but through them their parents have a greater appreciation of the value of forest protection.

"A boy or girl to join the organization must pass a creditable examination on simple fire fighting and 'first aid' methods. A few of the things that candidates must know are how properly to use a knife, hatchet, ax, shovel, mattock; flails of brush, sacks or blankets; how to determine direction by a watch; height of a tree, and how to tie a death-grip, square, fisherman's halter, and lumber jacks' single and double timber hitch.

"Candidates must also be able to swim 20 yards, walk one mile in 12 minutes, row an ordinary boat, or paddle a canoe one mile in acceptable time, according to conditions. They must know the general State open season for the hunting of game or taking of fish, and their own county game law exceptions, if there are any.

"Candidates must also be able to distinguish and name three indigenous forest trees, three indigenous water plants, three indigenous ground plants, three domestic game birds, three migratory game birds that pass over Michigan, three game fishes and six fur-bearing animals. Other minor things about forestry, game, or fish conditions must also be answered satisfactorily by the lad who desires to join the movement.

"The general control of the Michigan Forest Scouts rests with the board of control, the Superintendent of Public Instruction and Secretary of the Public Domain Commission being at the head of the department of which they are auxiliaries. The field control rests with the field supervisor and immediate control of the scouts is with the State deputy fire or forestry warden of the accompanying district.

"In 1912 the scouts extinguished 509 fires in Michigan, besides reporting large fires to State Warden."*

"As a result of the educational campaign by the scouts," so the Forestry Warden reports, "it is doubtful if there is today any English-speaking adult in the forestry district who does not appreciate the disastrous effects of fires, or has not some knowledge of fighting them and of precautionary measures."

Summary.—Mr. Gifford Pinchot in a letter to the State Game, Fish, and Forestry Warden indorsing the forest scout movement, sums up the situation in Michigan in the following words:

"You must realize that the enlistment of boys of the State in this work cannot solve the fire problem. Michigan, I am sorry to say, is far behind most of the States in handling this question. The enlistment of the Michigan Forest Scouts must not be allowed to stand in the way of an effective body of fire fighters employed by the State.

"By far the best work in fire fighting now done in the United States is that of the National Forest Service. I recommend strongly the organization of work along the same lines for the State of Michigan. Such a service should stand on its own feet, and should not be merged in any organization with work other than that of forestry to look after. The forest question is far too important not to have an organization of its own."

*Michigan Forest Scouts, in American Lumberman, Jan. 31, 1914.

NORTHWESTERN STATES.

Of the five Northwestern States Wyoming is the only one which has not an effective State fire protective system. Out of the 10,000,000 acres of forest land contained in this State less than 1,000,000 acres is in the hands of the State or of private owners. All the rest is adequately protected by the Federal Government, either as National forests or part of the Yellowstone National Park.

Coöperative fire protection has reached its highest efficiency in these States where the Federal Government, the State, the counties, and associations of private owners all coöperate to prevent forest fires. (For a discussion of coöperative fire protection, see Economic Paper No. 33, Forest Fires in North Carolina During 1912 and National and Association Coöperative Fire Control.)

OREGON.

Perhaps the most effective fire protection in the United States is now practiced in Oregon. This is not only because there is a well organized State system, provided with an adequate appropriation, but because the law provides for and requires definite patrol on the part of woodland owners.

"Approximately 28,000,000 acres or 46 per cent of the area of the State is timberland or land upon which there is sufficient brush to make protection from fire necessary. About 16,000,000 acres are inside the boundaries of the National Forests and are patrolled by the United States Forest Service; while the remaining 12,000,000 acres are patrolled on a coöperative basis by the State and the private timberland owners."

State Board of Forestry.—In the act of 1911 a State Board of Forestry of seven members is provided for. The personnel shall consist of the Governor, the acting head of the Forest School of the Oregon Agricultural College, and five electors of the State of Oregon to be appointed by the Governor from and upon the authoritative recommendation of Oregon State Grange, the Oregon Forest Fire Association, the Oregon and Washington Lumber Manufacturers' Association, the United States Forest Service, and the Oregon Wool Growers' Association, each to select and name one of such electors. The members of the board shall receive no compensation, but shall be entitled to actual traveling expenses incurred in attending meetings.

State Forester.—The Board of Forestry must appoint the State Forester at a salary of not to exceed $3,000 and a Deputy State Forester at a salary of $1,800. Both officials are allowed necessary office and contingent expenses, and traveling and field expenses. Among other duties, the State Forester must appoint and instruct fire wardens; take action to prevent and extinguish forest, brush, and grass fires; enforce the forest laws, and coöperate with landowners, counties, or others in forest protection.

Appropriation.—The sum of $60,000 per annum is appropriated for carrying out the provisions of the fire protection law. In addition, county commissioners may appropriate money from the county funds for forest protection in their counties.

Fire Wardens.—Several different classes of wardens are provided for. The State may appoint proper citizens fire wardens, who shall serve voluntarily or under compensation by property owners or counties.

State and county officials whose duties make their *ex officio* services as fire wardens especially desirable shall accept appointments as such when requested by the State Board of Forestry.

Upon the recommendation of Federal forest supervisors, the State Forester shall appoint resident officers of the National forests *ex officio* fire wardens.

In times or localities of particular fire danger the State Forester may appoint and employ either independently or jointly with other agencies additional fire wardens. These last shall be paid from the State fire fund: *Provided,* each county in which such services are given shall be responsible for one-third the expense thus incurred.

A law passed in 1913 provides that all county judges shall be *ex officio* fire wardens, having all the powers of county fire wardens, with the special duty of issuing permits for burning.

In 1913 the following numbers of fire wardens of the different classes were employed in the State: Employed by individual timber owners 120, employed by associations 111, employed by counties 1, employed under the Weeks law 58, employed by United States Forest Service 122, serving without compensation 315, employed by State 32, making a total of 759.

The following sums were paid by the State, private, and county agencies in 1913 for patrol, improvement work, and supervision: Individual patrol $22,200, association patrol $47,400, county agencies $1,400, State agencies $16,500, Federal expenditures under Weeks law $8,700, making a total of $96,200.

Timberland Owners Must Provide Fire Patrol.—Under a recent law owners of timberland must furnish or provide a sufficient fire patrol during the season of the year when there is danger of forest fires. This patrol must meet with the approval of the State Forester. If the owner fails to provide such patrol the State Forester may patrol the land and levy the costs against the land not to exceed 5 cents per acre per year. The law recognizes the residence of the owner within one and one-half miles of the timberland as effective patrol.

This law, the State Forester says, has already proven a powerful help in advancing systematic forest fire protection. It was the chief factor in more than doubling the membership of the patrol associations and through its influence six new associations were formed in the spring of 1913.

Burning of Slashings.—Lumbermen are required to burn their slashings each year in such a way as to confine the fire to their own lands. Builders of trails, roads, or railroads must destroy or remove all inflammable material resulting from the constructing or clearing for such improvements.

Permits are required for the burning of such slashings, choppings, woodlands, or brush lands between June 1st and October 1st each year.

Spark Arresters.—All engines using fuel other than oil in or near forest or brush land must be provided with adequate spark arresters, kept in constant use and repair from June 1st to October 1st of each year. The escape of fire from any engine shall be *prima facie* evidence that such appliances have not been adequately maintained.

Railroads.—All rights of way of railroads must be mowed each year between June 1st and July 1st. If any railroad neglects or refuses to mow their right of way, the adjoining landowner may mow it and collect the costs from the county authorities.

Closed Season.—In addition to the requirement of permits for burning between June 1st and October 1st, which is designated the "closed season," the Governor may with the advice of the State Forester suspend all permits in times and localities of unusual fire danger. In addition, during the open season for hunting game he may by proclamation suspend the open season and make it a closed season for the shooting of wild birds or animals of any kind in order to prevent the use of firearms or fire by hunters.

WASHINGTON.

The State of Washington has 22,000,000 acres of timberland that requires protection. Of this area, 11,684,680 acres are within exterior boundaries of the National forests.

The State forestry organization and the State laws are quite similar to those of Oregon, its neighbor to the south. It has a State Board of Forest Commissioners with a State Forester, and a fire warden who has charge of the fire protective system.

"The law relating to forest fires passed in 1911 provides that where wood-waste material is destroyed in incinerators, they shall be equipped with effective spark arresters, and the same applies to smokestacks, chimneys, or any other outlet for sparks. Where forest products are being manufactured within one-quarter of a mile of forest material, the destruction of slabs and refuse must be provided for in a manner which will not endanger surrounding property. Locomotives, donkey engines, etc., must be provided not only with an effective spark arrester, but with devices which will successfully prevent the escape of live coals from fire boxes and ash-pans. The felling of trees so that tops lie in adjoining timber is prohibited, unless the permission of the owner of such timber is procured. Whenever rights of way are cleared, the slashings must be piled and the burning done at such time as the fire warden considers safe. Watchmen must be kept at donkey engines for two hours after operation ceases, and all snags over 25 feet in height within 50 feet of each donkey engine must be felled."*

Permits are required for the burning of slashings both for clearing land and as fire preventive measures. The holders of permits generally exercise great care to prevent fires from spreading beyond the limit of the slashings, and little loss is done by such burnings, so it is said.

There are three agencies for fire protection actively at work in the State: the United States Forest Service, the Washington Forest Fire Association, and the State organization. These three coöperate to the fullest extent in preventing and extinguishing fires.

Federal Protection.—"About one-half of the timbered area of Washington is protected by the Forest Service. In this work about 210 men are employed, and as an adjunct to protection 758 miles of telephone line and 1,270 miles of trails have been constructed and are maintained by the Forest Service. The cost of protection within the boundaries of the National forests, in the ordinary year, is about $80,000.

State Protection.—"The State has an appropriation of $37,500 yearly with which to maintain the office of State Forester and put wardens in the field. In addition to this fund, the State received the past year $10,000 from the Federal Government as its share of the Weeks law fund. The State has in the field one, and in some cases two, fire wardens in each county. These wardens receive $4 per day and necessary subsistence expenses when away from headquarters. Their duties are to enforce the law and, by doing so, prevent destruction by fire.

Washington Forest Fire Association.—"The Washington Forest Fire Association has a membership representing approximately two and three-quarter million acres. This association patrols all of the territory west of the Cascade Mountains outside of the National forest, or about 8,000,000. Its patrol and fire-fighting force consists of a chief fire warden, 12 inspectors, and from 75 to 100 patrolmen. For purposes of protection the State is districted, first into inspector districts and then into patrol districts. Each patrol district is in charge of a ranger, who, in addition to being responsible for the suppres-

*Forestry Quarterly, Vol. IX, p. 516.

sion of any fires that may start, is charged with the duty of law enforcement, issuing burning permits and seeing that the law requiring the burning of dangerous slashings is enforced.

"An inspection district is made up of several ranger districts and, as the name implies, is in charge of an inspector. These men are responsible for the work of the rangers in their districts and are selected for their wide knowledge and experience in fire suppression. All rangers and inspectors are responsible to the chief fire warden, who in turn is responsible to the trustees of the association. Inspectors receive from $90 to $125 per month and expenses and are employed for about five months of each year. Rangers receive from $75 to $100, no expenses being allowed.

Coöperation.—"To insure the greatest success, thorough coöperation between the three agencies engaged in fire prevention is necessary. Such coöperation exists. The Forest Service, the State and the Association coöperate under an informal agreement in looking after the areas along the National forest boundaries.

Needed Changes.—"The Washington law is good in most respects, and protection work in the State is of a high character. However, there is need of radical reform along lines which will free the State Board of Forestry, the State Forester, and the warden force from political influence. At the present time a portion of the State funds are held in readiness to meet emergency fire-fighting expenses. The result is that during the ordinary year a balance accumulates which is turned back to the State Treasury because of nonuse. Obviously the State appropriation being far too small, the maximum of benefit would be derived if all of the funds were expended in putting on a larger patrol force, leaving to some other agency the raising of funds with which to fight fire.

"It seems logical that besides its appropriation for fire protection in general, which is no more than is done by Oregon and other States without large grant areas of their own, Washington should also contribute additionally on an acreage basis for the specific care of its timber holdings, as does Idaho under the Fallon law."*

IDAHO.

Idaho contains approximately 20,000,000 acres of forest land, nearly half of which is owned and protected by the Federal Government as National forests. With the exception of about 250,000 acres owned by the State, the remainder is nearly all in the hands of lumber companies or other large owners.

The fire protective law, which is said to be one of the best in the country, is based on a system of coöperation between the landowners and the State.

Administration.—The fire law is administered by the State Board of Land Commissioners. They are required to divide up the State into districts, having due regard to the area of forests or timberlands therein.

*Report of Forestry Committee, Fifth National Conservation Congress, p. 308.

Upon application of the owners of the land, they are to appoint one fire warden to each district, who is to be paid by the property owners.

Fire Wardens.—The district warden is to appoint such fire wardens in his district as may be designated by the property owners. They likewise are to be paid by the property owners. They shall exercise all the powers and duties of State officers in enforcing the provisions of the fire law. They are to patrol, extinguish fires, and investigate fires, post notices, and compel assistance which will be paid for at a rate of not more than $2.50 per day.

Under this law the State, as a landowner, coöperates with and contributes to four timber protective associations, composed of timberland owners throughout the State. For the purpose of administering the law and paying its own pro rata share in the protective associations the State makes an appropriation of $15,000.

Disposal of Brush.—All persons engaged in cutting timber from "lands within the State of Idaho are required to pile and burn or otherwise dispose of the brush, limbs, tops, and other materials incident to such cutting which are 4 inches or under in diameter; and the times and methods of so doing shall be prescribed by the warden of the fire district in which said cutting shall be done."

Permit for Burning Brush.—Between June 1st and October 1st no person must set out fire for the purpose of clearing land without a written permit from the fire warden; and at no time can a fire be set out unless sufficient help is present to control it, and unless it is watched until it is out.

Railroads.—All railroads must keep the ground for 50 feet on each side of the track where it is a part of the right of way clear of all combustible materials. Railroad employees must not leave deposits of fire near woodlands, and trainmen on discovering fires adjacent to the track must report them at the next station.

Spark Arresters.—All users of spark-emitting locomotives, logging and portable engines, traction engines, or stationary engines between June 1st and October 1st must provide the same with good and efficient spark arresters.

Comment.—The president of the Northern Idaho Forestry Association says:

"In Idaho private timber owners, the State administration and the people at large believe in the protection of their forests from fire, and today there is probably no locality in the world, not even except Germany, where this branch of conservation is so efficiently handled as in the timber section of northern Idaho covered by our four local fire associations."*

---

*Report of the Forestry Committee, Fifth National Conservation Congress, 1913.

MONTANA.

Montana has a comparatively small amount of forest land, and the greater part of this is included in the National forests, which are thoroughly protected by the Government. However, Montana maintains a well organized fire protective system, which, except for the amount of the appropriation, which is $5,000 a year, is abreast of most of the western States.

Organization.—The State Forester, "who shall be skilled in the science of forestry and whose salary shall be $2,500 per annum and actual necessary expenses," and who is responsible to the State Board of Land Commissioners, has entire charge of the fire warden system. The fire wardens are of two kinds. The *volunteer fire wardens* are public-spirited citizens appointed by the State Forester in such numbers and localities as he may deem wise. On the other hand, the sheriffs, game wardens, and deputy game wardens are *ex officio fire wardens,* and are deemed paid fire wardens, though receiving no compensation except such as they receive in connection with their other duties. Fire wardens may summon assistance for putting out fires and perform such other duties as are required of them for the protection of the forests. No fire warden, however, may incur any expense in excess of $50 without expressed authority from the State Board of Land Commissioners.

Railroads.—Railroads are required to keep their rights of way clear of combustible material for a distance of 100 feet on each side of the track. All railroads are also required to plow fire lines 6 feet wide at a distance of 50 feet from the track wherever it passes through a range or grazing country. If any railroad fails to comply with this law, the county commissioners may plow such fire lines and recover the expense from the railroad.

Disposal of Brush.—Wherever timber is cut on State lands the operators are required to pile and burn the brush and slashings in such a manner as to prevent forest fires.

NEW ENGLAND STATES.

All six of the New England States have efficient fire protective organizations and fairly effective forest fire laws. Though these organizations are variously constituted, still the administration of the laws in each State is in the hands of a technically trained forester who is either responsible directly to a commission or to the chief official of such a commission.

MAINE.

Maine and New York are the only northeastern States which restrict their efforts at forest protection to what they call the forest region of the State. In the former State the lands which are protected are all in the hands of private owners; while in New York protection is exercised largely for the benefit of State lands, which constitute a considerable proportion of the area which is protected.

Forestry District.—The Maine forestry district comprises approximately nine and one-half million acres of land in the roughest portion of the State. The land in this district is specially taxed at the rate of 15 cents on the hundred dollars, or about 1⅔ cents per acre. This yields a revenue of something like $70,000, all of which is used for protecting this district from forest fires.

Forest Commissioner.—The administration of all the forest laws is in the hands of a forest commissioner, who is responsible directly to the Governor. His duties are defined as follows:

"The forest commissioner shall take measures for the prevention, control, and extinguishing of forest fires in said forestry district, and to this end he shall establish such sub-forestry districts as he may deem necessary for effective protection against loss or damage by fire. He shall have authority to establish lookout stations connected by telephone, and to equip and maintain depots for necessary tools for the extinguishment of forest fires."

Forest Fire Wardens.—The commissioner appoints one general forest fire warden for each district, and within the districts such numbers of deputy fire wardens as in his judgment are necessary. The general fire wardens receive compensation at the rate of $3 per day, with an allowance for expenses of not to exceed $2 per day, for every day they are on duty; while the deputy forest fire wardens receive $2 and subsistence for each and every day of actual service.

Lookouts and Patrols.—At the end of the fire season of 1913, 42 lookout stations were being operated in the forestry district, while 173 patrolmen were employed. While the lookout men were obliged to remain on duty at their posts throughout the season, the patrols were employed in the construction of telephone lines, trails, camps, etc., when the weather conditions would permit. During dry and dangerous seasons the patrols were used largely along the railroad lines and in regions where fishermen, hunters, and camping parties were using the woods, lakes, and streams. In addition to the patrols and lookouts, something like three hundred fire wardens are appointed in the forest counties and townships of the forest district. All wardens may, for the purpose of controlling and extinguishing fires, summon to their assistance citizens of any county, who shall be paid 15 cents per hour and subsistence during actual service.

Railroads.—Railroads are required to keep their rights of way clear of inflammable material, and to furnish all locomotives which run through forest land with spark arresters. Employees of railroads are forbidden to deposit live coals in the vicinity of woodlands, and are required to report fires found burning on or near the right of way. During the past year chief fire wardens have been appointed for the territory along the right of way of the railroads. These men were paid by the Forestry Department, and the State was reimbursed by the railroads. Under the direction of these chief wardens, patrols, fire trains, etc., were maintained and expenses paid by the railroads.

Comment.—The forest commissioner, who now is a technically trained forester, summarizes the work which he proposes to take hold of as follows:

"We plan to extend the system of lookout stations and to improve the stations already constructed as fast as possible. We believe that the lookout stations form the backbone of our protective system and that they should be supplemented by patrols when necessary. We expect to be able to build several lines of telephone, install additional boxes of fire tools, and in some instances furnish a camping outfit for a fire-fighting crew in central places."

NEW HAMPSHIRE.

Forestry Commission.—New Hampshire has a forestry commission of three members appointed by the Governor, who serve without compensation, but receive legitimate expenses incident to the carrying out of their duties.

State Forester.—The Forestry Commission appoints a State Forester at a salary of $2,500 a year and reasonable traveling, field and office expenses, who executes all matters pertaining to forestry within the jurisdiction of the State.

The State Forester is empowered to build, equip, and maintain mountain lookout stations connected by telephone lines, which stations are to be used for the discovery and control of forest fires. He may purchase or receive gifts of land and hold them in the name of the State for observatory sites, for rights of way, paths, and telephone lines; and if necessary sites cannot be obtained by either purchase or gift, the Forestry Commission may acquire the same under the power of eminent domain. The State Forester may call an annual conference of forest fire wardens and other employees for the purpose of improving the service. He may also establish supply stations for tools and apparatus used in fire fighting, etc.

Protective Force.—The State is divided up into four forest fire districts, each of which is in charge of a district chief. Under this chief three classes of men are employed:

(1) Patrol service performed by (*a*) Federal patrolmen paid by the United States. (*b*) Association patrolmen paid by the New Hampshire Timberland Owners' Association. (*c*) State patrolmen hired temporarily by the State during dry weather.

(2) The mountain lookout stations in charge of watchmen employed by the State.

There were operated in 1912 twenty permanent stations and five temporary ones. These stations reported that year 178 fires to the wardens and patrolmen, who proceeded without delay to extinguish them.

(3) Forest fire wardens:

One forest fire warden in each town* and one or more deputy wardens in each town. The list of forest fire wardens and deputies for 1912 includes some 650 names.

Fire Wardens.—Selectmen of all towns and mayors of all cities are required to recommend persons who are fit to fill the office of forest fire warden and deputy fire warden, and these men may be appointed to fill these positions by the State Forester. These wardens, under instructions from the State Forester, are required to patrol the woods of their respective districts, warn persons who are traversing the woods about lighting and extinguishing fires, post warning notices and arrest offenders against the forest law. The State Forester shall have power to remove the wardens from office at his discretion. The expense of fighting forest and brush fires and expenses locally incurred by forest fire wardens in preventing fires is borne equally by the town or city and by the State. Wardens have power to arrest without warrant any who are offending against the forest laws of the State.

Appropriation.—The appropriation for maintaining the Forest Fire Service amounts to $10,000 a year.

Brush Burning.—The law forbids the burning of brush in or near woodland between April 1st and November 1st without the permission of the forest fire warden.

Spark Arresters.—The owners and operators of portable steam sawmills are required to use spark arresters, which are approved by the State Forester.

*The New England "town" is an administrative division of the county, almost identical with our Southern "township," but with a larger share of self-government.

The section referring to this law reads as follows:

"No person, except when the ground is covered with snow, shall operate any portable steam mill unless the same is provided with a suitable spark arrester, approved by the State Forester. Such approval shall be in writing, signed by the forester, and said approval may be revoked by the State Forester in the same manner.

"It shall be the duty of the State Forester to examine all portable steam mills or cause them to be examined, whenever he deems it necessary, to determine whether the same are kept in constant use, as provided for in section 1 of this act. It shall be the duty of the town forest fire warden to examine portable steam mills, when requested to do so by the State Forester, and make reports on the same in such form as the State Forester may require."

Railroads.—New Hampshire seems to have no definite laws to control railroad fires. The Forestry Commission in their report for 1911-1912 recommends as follows:

"A few years ago the Main Central Railroad began a systematic work for fire prevention, viz., making it the duty of one man in each section crew to patrol the track, following trains. This work was especially effective during the dry season of 1911, patrolmen being provided with velocipedes so that they could keep their section well covered. They would carry on these velocipedes a shovel, or hoe, a bucket of water and a mop to put out small fires. On account of the heavy grades, this company has recently been using a number of oil burning engines, and these entirely eliminate the fire risk for the trains on which they are used."

VERMONT.

Vermont employs a technically trained State Forester, who is responsible to a State Board of Agriculture and Forestry. Mr. Robert M. Ross in an article on "Forest Fire Prevention in Vermont" in American Forestry, November, 1913, says that Vermont a few years ago had practically no system of fire prevention, but today stands well up in the list of States which are striving to reduce to a minimum the danger of forest fires. The State appropriation for forestry purposes amounts to something over $10,000 a year, though only $1,500 of this was used for fire prevention last year.

Fire Wardens.—A new law passed in 1913 provides that the selectman or chief township officer shall appoint a fire warden by January 1st of each year who shall meet the approval of the State Forester. If this appointment is not made by March 1st, the State Forester himself may make the appointment. This provision makes it possible to secure good wardens in forest towns and keep them in office as long as is desirable. These wardens are paid at the rate of $2 per day when actually engaged in fire work; all other men who are hired to do fire fighting work are paid by the town at the same rate as those engaged in work on the roads, which is usually $1.75 per day. Whenever the amount expended in fighting fire in a town exceeds 5 per cent of the grand list of the town, the State pays the sum over this per cent. Thus the poorer towns are helped by the richer ones, an arrangement which seems no more than right.

Lookouts.—The two main branches of protective work are a series of lookout stations and a system of patrolling. At the present time Vermont has four lookout stations in operation, with prospects of the erection of another one in the immediate future. Two of these stations have been erected by the owners of woodland in the vicinity of the stations, while the other two were constructed by the State itself on State forests. Men are kept at these stations during the dry periods of the year, that is, from May to October. These lookout men are connected by telephone with the town wardens, so that fires which have been discovered can quickly be extinguished.

A new law gives the State Forester authority to erect such buildings, lookout stations, etc., as may be desirable on State forests, the same to be paid for out of the general forestry appropriation.

Patrols.—"In several sections of the State patrols are of far more value than lookout stations. During this season we have had several patrolmen out, a few of whom we have kept along sections of railroad tracks where there is especial danger of fire starting. The others have confined their work to districts which are frequented by fishermen, hunters, and campers.

"In regard to establishing patrols in very dangerous sections, there is a law which empowers any warden of a town, with the approval of the State Forester, to appoint a patrolman during dangerous periods, said patrolman to be paid by the town in which his work is done.

"For the past two years the State Forest Service has kept its patrolmen busy during the months when the danger of fire is small, by having them work on trails in the mountainous sections of the State."

MASSACHUSETTS.

Massachusetts, with an estimated area of 2,000,000 acres of woodland and an additional 1,000,000 acres of so-called waste land capable of reforestation, has perhaps the strongest and most thoroughly organized forestry department of any of the New England States.

Supervision.—The State Forester, who is in charge of all of the forestry work, is appointed by the Governor with the consent of the council. He must be a trained forester who has had a technical education. He is to be an *ex officio* member of the State Board of Agriculture. The State Fire Warden is appointed by the State Forester to take entire charge of the fire protective work of the State. He is directly responsible to the State Forester. Under the State Fire Warden are one assistant State Fire Warden, one locomotive inspector, and four district forest wardens in charge of the four forest districts of the State.

Forest Wardens.—The forest wardens are appointed by the mayor and aldermen of cities and the selectmen in towns, subject to the approval of the State Forester. It is the duty of the forest warden to "take precautions to prevent the spread of forest fires and the improper kindling thereof, and he shall have sole charge of their extinguishment. He shall investigate the causes and extent of forest fires and the injury done thereby," etc. Forest wardens are compensated for making investigations for the State Forester at a rate not to exceed 35 cents per hour for the time actually employed by them. The payment to forest wardens, to their deputies and to the persons assisting them at a forest fire is at a rate prescribed by the town.

At the present time there are in the employ of the State 353 forest wardens with over 1,000 deputies.

Lookouts.—Massachusetts has an excellent system of lookout stations scattered over the forested part of the State. In the past year twenty-one of these stations were operated with very gratifying results. The observers form part of the State system of fire protection and are paid a salary by the State. The wardens, on the other hand, are considered township officers and are paid by the local authorities.

Forestry Conventions.—An excellent provision of the forestry law is that the State Forester may expend a sum not to exceed $2,000 in making necessary arrangements for conventions of forest wardens and in paying wholly or in part their traveling expenses to and from such conventions. By this means the fire protective force becomes a more coherent and intelligent body of men each year, so that steady improvement in effectiveness is insured.

Railroads.—Railroads are required to install and maintain spark arresters, and to clear off all inflammable material on each side of their track to a point 200 feet distant. In order to do this they are empowered to enter upon unimproved land adjoining their right of way, after giving due notice, and clear the land of dead leaves, dead grass, and dead wood to a distance of 100 feet from the track without thereby becoming liable for trespassing. Railroads are also forbidden to leave deposits of fire, hot ashes, or live coals upon their rights of way. They are required to post notices furnished by the State Forester. In addition, train hands are required to signal by blowing the whistle when fires are discovered, and to notify the section men. Section men or other employees are required when notified to proceed at once to the fire and extinguish it. Railroads are liable to the authorities for the cost of extinguishing any fire set by them.

RHODE ISLAND.

Rhode Island, which has an area of less than 683,000 acres, or little more than North Carolina's largest county, contains only 250,000 acres of woodland, practically all of which is in farm woodlots. Nevertheless, this small State has a Commissioner of Forestry and a State fire protective system.

Commissioner of Forestry.—The Governor is required to appoint a Commissioner of Forestry to hold office for three years. His duties are principally to collect and publish information relating to the forests of the State, their protection and perpetuation. The Commissioner is paid $1,000 a year and expenses. The expenses, however, together with the costs of printing, etc., must not exceed $500 annually.

Forest Wardens.—The town council of every town is required to appoint each year a forest warden and to notify the Forestry Commissioner of this appointment. In any town having 4,000 acres or more of woodland the town warden may divide up the town into two or more districts, and appoint district wardens for each. There were, in 1913, one hundred forest wardens in the State.

The compensation of wardens is fixed at 30 cents per hour and that of employees of the wardens at 18 cents per hour for actual services in extinguishing forest fires. They are paid for patrolling and serving as watchmen at a lookout station at 20 cents per hour. In addition to this, town forest wardens are paid $10 a year and district forest wardens $5 a year in lieu of all allowances for postage, etc.

Patrols and Lookouts.—"During a period of drought the town forest warden may require the district forest wardens to patrol their several districts, subject to the approval of the town council."

Fire wardens are required, when fires occur, to take measures to extinguish them. They are given "authority to summon any able-bodied male person in his town between the ages of 18 and 50 years to aid in the prevention or extinguishment of a forest fire, and may require the use of horses, wagons, and other property adapted to the purpose."

A minimum of five hours pay is allowed to persons who are officially summoned to assist in extinguishing forest fires, one-half to be paid by the town and one-half by the State.

Whenever two or more adjoining towns which contain an aggregate of 8,000 acres or more of woodland, or whenever any number of forest owners whose woodland in any two or more adjoining woodlands aggregate 4,000 acres, shall in any town establish, at their own expense and subject to the approval of the Commissioner of Forestry, a lookout station connected with the local telephone system for the purpose of protecting the forests from fire, the town forest warden of the town in which such lookout station is established shall appoint a watchman for the station during such period as the town forest warden may think advisable, not exceeding 300 hours in any one year: *Provided,* that not more than two such lookout stations in any one county shall be entitled to draw public money. One-half the expense for the service of watchmen and for telephone service shall be paid by the town and one-half by the State.

Appropriation.—The State of Rhode Island makes a total appropriation of $3,000 for forestry purposes, one-half of which is used for fire protection and the other half for the salary of the Forestry Commissioner and his expenses.

Permits for Burning Brush.—No fire may be set between March 1st and December 1st except by written permission of the town or district forest warden, except on plowed fields or on lands devoid of inflammable materials, when such a fire is at least 100 feet from any woodland.

Railroads.—Railroads are authorized to enter upon unimproved land adjoining their rights of way in order to clear at their own expense such lands of dead leaves, dead grass, and dead wood to a distance of 100 feet from the tracks, provided sufficient notice is given to the owner.

CONNECTICUT.

About one-half the State of Connecticut, which has an area approximately one-tenth that of North Carolina, is better adapted to the raising of trees than of any other crop, and the largest factor in handling the forest land is the fire problem. More than 4 per cent of the 1,500,000 acres of forest land was burnt over in 1911.

State Fire Warden.—The State Forester of Connecticut is an officer of the Connecticut Agricultural Experiment Station. He is appointed by the director of the station and is paid out of the general appropriation for the support of the Experiment Station. The State Forester is *ex officio* State Forest Fire Warden, and as such is given supervision of town fire wardens, and is required to issue notices and regulations to the wardens and cause violations of the laws in regard to forest fires to be prosecuted.

Fire Wardens.—Selectmen of the towns are required upon request of the State Forest Fire Warden to appoint town fire wardens, who shall act for a term of one year. Such town fire warden may establish two or more fire districts in the town and appoint district fire wardens for each. Town and district fire wardens are required to prevent and extinguish forest fires and enforce fire laws. Any fire warden may arrest without warrant any one violating the forest fire law. During a season of drought the town fire warden may establish a fire patrol in the town. He may summon necessary assistance for extinguishing fires and may also require the use of horses and other property needed for such purposes.

Compensation.—Town and district fire wardens shall receive 35 cents per hour for time actually employed at forest fires or otherwise discharging their duties; while the selectmen are to fix the prices per hour to be paid laborers employed by fire wardens and deputies, not exceeding 20 cents per hour. All expenses incurred by the town wardens, their deputies, and men employed by them, together with their own compensation, are paid for, one-half by the town, one-fourth by the county, and one-fourth by the State.

Lookouts.—In regard to lookout stations, the State Forester reports that two stations were maintained experimentally during 1912 with valuable results. If possible, other stations will be established during 1913, the State coöperating with towns and landowners when practicable. If the stations are equipped with telephones the observers will be able to locate fires definitely, and thus be able to inform the nearest wardens at once.

Railroads.—Only two laws relating to forest fire work by the railroads are at present in force. The first makes a railroad company responsible to the person injured when property is damaged by a fire from their engine.

The other law was a compromise measure. "The State Forester prepared a bill for the Legislature which would have made patrol compulsory on the part of the railroads, upon instruction from the State Forester. The railroads were opposed to any such measure, and they offered a substitute making themselves liable for the cost of fighting fires which they started. This seemed worth while accepting, and for the time being the idea of compulsory patrol was dropped. The measure was enacted into law in the summer of 1911."

Comment.—At the Weeks Law Conference in Washington, January, 1913, the State Forester said:

"I do not feel we need any law compelling patrol, for I think we can get the help of the railroads in this matter without compulsion. If we can get them to patrol voluntarily, it will produce a better coöperative spirit between the railroads and ourselves. It may be advisable for us in Connecticut to have a law compelling inspection of the locomotives, because it seems to me patrol work is not getting to the bottom of the trouble. We ought to go further back than that and eliminate the cause of fires."

NORTHEASTERN STATES.

More or less efficient fire protective systems exist in all of the six States here classed as northeastern. In three of them, however—Ohio, Indiana, and Delaware—where the forests occur chiefly in the form of farmers' woodlots, and extensive or destructive fires rarely occur, no effort has been made to develop effective working forces. In the three other States the systems are some of the most effective in the country.

NEW YORK.

New York does not maintain a fire protective system for the whole State, but only over what is known as the "forest preserve" area. This consists of approximately 10,000,000 acres in the Adirondacks and the Catskill mountains, about one-fifth of which belongs to the State, and is known as the State Forest Preserve.

Supervision.—Fire protection is under the general charge of the Superintendent of Forests and the immediate supervision of the Assistant Superintendent of Forests, who are in turn responsible to the State Conservation Commission. The Conservation Law provides for the division of the protected area into districts, each to be in charge of a district forest ranger, who shall receive an annual salary of not to exceed $1,500 and necessary expenses. The Adirondack region is divided into four fire districts and the Catskill territory into one.

Rangers and Lookouts.—These five districts are divided into definite territories, each in charge of a ranger. "The rangers' duties consist in patrolling the dangerous places, watching out for fire, meeting people, instructing them in regard to building camp fires, giving them literature and keeping in close touch with the entire territory. Also whenever a fire occurs he immediately summons help and endeavors to extinguish the same promptly. During the past four years fifty mountain observation stations have been established. Each of these observers, as well as the rangers, has connection with the Commercial Telephone System, and the observers are provided with a camp, field-glass, and map of their territory, together with a list of the rangers, fire wardens, landowners, etc., to be notified in case of fire." The fact that so many fires have burned over only small areas is due to their prompt discovery by lookouts who were able to get men to the fires quickly.

"Ninety-five per cent of the fires are detected by these observers while fires are in their incipient stages, and but very few fires occur which are not extinguished promptly."*

*American Forestry, Vol. XIX, p. 750.

Rangers receive a salary of $75 per month and necessary expenses. They may employ men and teams to fight forest fires and may summon necessary assistance.

Expenses.—All salaries, costs, and expenses incident to fire protection are paid by the State except wages and expenses incident to the actual work of fighting fires which are already burning, which shall be paid one-half by the State and one-half by the town in which the fire wardens and men so employed were actually engaged in fighting fires.

Camp Fires.—The law regarding camp fires reads in part as follows:

"Every person who starts a camp or other fire upon or in the vicinity of forest or wood land, for cooking, obtaining warmth, or any industrial purpose, shall, before lighting the same, clear the ground of all branches, brushwood, dry leaves, or other combustible material within a radius of 10 feet from the fire, and shall carefully extinguish the fire before quitting the place."

Emergencies.—The Governor may by proclamation forbid hunting, fishing, camping, etc., in the forest preserve counties on account of drought or other emergency. A very valuable provision has recently been added to this law (March, 1914). This allows the Governor to borrow from the State a sum not to exceed $100,000 for the purpose of fighting and controlling forest fires when in the judgment of the Conservation Commission "an emergency exists whereby through inefficiency of appropriations it is found impossible to protect the forests of the State from fire."

RAILROADS.

The forest fire laws regarding railroads seem to be very effective in New York. Though originally confined to the forest preserve counties, the law has recently been amended so that all railroad lines in the State are subject to inspection and are obliged to comply with certain laws and regulations. "The Conservation Law provides that every railroad company and every person operating a railroad in any part of the State shall properly clean its right of way, and shall provide each locomotive with practical and efficient spark-arresting devices, and furthermore said devices shall be approved by the Public Service Commission and shall be at all times maintained in good repair."*

Patrol.—All railroads are required to provide necessary patrol as the commission may direct between the first of April and the first of November; and if the railroads do not organize and maintain such fire patrols, or if they are inadequate, the commission is required to organize and

*Report of New York Conservation Commission, 1912.

maintain efficient patrols, the cost of which shall be paid to the commission by the railroads whose lines are thus patrolled.

Railroad Inspectors.—In addition to this, railroads are required to employ competent inspectors to examine all locomotives as they leave the division point or roundhouse between March 1st and December 1st, and to make reports on the condition of the fire preventive devices, which reports must be open for inspection by the Conservation Commission. All trainmen are required to report fires at the first station at which they arrive, and the station agent is required to notify the nearest State ranger or fire warden.

State Inspectors.—In addition to the inspectors employed by the railroads, the Conservation Commission maintains two chief inspectors for the northern and southern divisions of the State respectively. These inspectors receive an annual salary of $1,200 and expenses. Four additional inspectors are employed during the summer months to assist these chief inspectors. The Conservation Commission has power to require the withdrawal from service of any and all locomotive or logging engines which shall be reported as defective.

The railroads have been coöperating with the Conservation Commission in a very gratifying way, and the law seems to be working quite effectively. The Superintendent of State Forests reports that "the inspection of thousands of miles of right of way and many thousands of engines of various designs and types at numerous places has kept our force very busy. Conferences have been held between all general inspectors and superintendents of motive power and other officials of railroads. As a result a better understanding has been reached and the railroad officials have submitted drawings illustrating proposed changes in design for the approval of the Public Service Commission."

Oil Burning.—For the past few years all railroads operating in the Adirondacks during the summer season have used oil as fuel. The Superintendent of Forests says in regard to this:

"The use of oil as fuel for steam development eliminates sparks and cinders as a cause of fires. We know of no case where fires have been caused in New York State through its use. During the oil-burning season last year there were only two fires along the New York Central Railway from Utica to Malone, and both, I think, were caused by cigarettes or cigars thrown from smoking-car windows. However, while the use of oil is effective, a very large percentage of the fires can be prevented if the locomotives are equipped with proper devices to prevent the escape of sparks, coals, or cinders."

Portable Engines.—All donkey, traction, portable engines, portable steam sawmills or other engines, boilers, or locomotives which do not burn oil as fuel must be provided with a screen or wire netting to prevent the escape of sparks and cinders from the smokestacks, and with practical devices to prevent the escape of fire from ash-pans and fire boxes. Any violation of this law is subject to a penalty of $100, and in addition the offender shall be liable to treble damages.

Appropriation.—The appropriation for fire protective work is now $100,000 a year, and the commission says that at least $125,000 per year should be appropriated.

The chief weakness of the law seems to be that it does not apply to the whole State. The Superintendent of Forests says:

"New York is the only State in the northeast that does not exercise supervision or authority over forest fires in the entire State. The law should be amended to give this commission authority to organize, in any section of the State outside of the ninety-six fire towns in the forest preserve, where the forests are threatened and forest interests are sufficient, a suitable fire organization to be paid for by the territory protected and towns benefited."

Top Lopping Law.—This law, as at present amended, requires that every one felling evergreen trees for sale or other purposes shall cut off from the trees and the limbs thereof at the time of felling or at some time fixed by the commission, all limbs up to a point where the trunk or branch does not exceed 3 inches in diameter. The commission may decide that the limbs need not be lopped if in their judgment the danger from fire does not warrant it. The working of this law has been very carefully investigated by all interested parties, and the general conclusion arrived at is that when judiciously carried out the top lopping law does very materially increase the fire protection; that the thoroughness with which the lopping is done has much to do with the future results; that a limitation may be made beyond which it is not necessary to lop; that a reasonable extension of time should be allowed operators in order to accomplish their work at the minimum expense.

PENNSYLVANIA.

Pennsylvania was one of the first States to take up the question of forestry, and has been ever since a leader in this movement. However, largely on account of politics, she has of late years allowed many of the other States to get ahead of her in the efficiency of her forest fire administration. The forest commissioner claims that even now 5,000,000 acres of land are being kept nonproductive by forest fires. This area, he says, if properly protected, would yield at least one billion feet of timber per year.

Organization and Appropriation.—The Commissioner of Forestry, who is also President of the State Forestry Reservation Commission, and the Deputy Commissioner of Forestry are designated Chief Fire Warden and Deputy Chief Fire Warden respectively. These officials are given immediate supervision and control of the fire warden system. The Commissioner of Forestry is required to appoint in each borough and township, if necessary, one district fire warden, who is to be chosen for his physical fitness and good reputation for sobriety, honesty, and ability. It is the duty of the fire warden to extinguish fires. He is authorized to employ necessary assistants and has the power to compel the attendance of assistants if necessary. District fire wardens receive as compensation 25 cents per hour and actual expenses while engaged in the performance of their duties, and persons employed by them receive 15 cents per hour. No owner or lessee or person employed by them shall receive any compensation for extinguishing fire upon the lands of such owner or lessee. Assistant fire wardens may be appointed wherever needed, and their compensation is 20 cents per hour and necessary expenses.

Fire wardens may be required by the Commissioner of Forestry to keep daily patrol in regions which are especially hazardous, for which services they shall be paid a stated sum, not to exceed $25 per month.

For the carrying out of the provisions of this act, which was passed in 1909, the sum of $50,000 is provided biennially, or $25,000 a year.

Railroads.—There are no railroad laws to provide protection for forest lands as such. There is a law, however, which requires the use of spark arresters and the keeping of rights of way clear of inflammable material on lands in which oil wells and gas wells are situated. This law, of course, has a very restricted application.

Coöperation with Local Forest Fire Associations.—A law passed in 1913 greatly widens and strengthens the field of fire protective operations in Pennsylvania. By it the Department of Forestry is authorized to enter into coöperative agreement with local forest fire associations for the prevention and suppression of forest fires, and the department is authorized to spend a sum of money equal in amount to that expended by each of such associations for the employment of patrols during the forest fire season, provided that such expenditure does not exceed $30 a month for each patrolman. "When any group of landowners desire to organize themselves into a mutual forest fire protective association they shall promptly notify the Commissioner of Forestry of their intent, if it be the desire of such landowners to receive such coöperation from him."

It is presumed that the regular appropriation for forest protection must be drawn upon for carrying out the provisions of this act.

Pennsylvania owns nearly 1,000,000 acres of State forests and spends each year a large amount of money for their administration. Fire protection on these lands is fairly efficient. The State forest employees are empowered to assist in fighting fires on private lands in the same localities.

Summary.—The Commissioner of Forestry in his last report says in regard to the workings of the Pennsylvania law:

"At the present the part of the act which provides that during the spring and fall fire season each year wardens may be put on daily patrol, for which they are to receive a compensation of $25, is wholly inoperative, because no appropriation has been made by the Legislature to meet these provisions. The amount of the appropriation which the act was finally permitted to carry is inadequate. If fires are as bad in the next three fire seasons as they have been in the past, the $50,000 will scarcely last out the first year."

NEW JERSEY.

New Jersey, which is somewhat the shape and approximately one-sixth the size of North Carolina, and has in many respects quite similar forest conditions, contains an estimated forest area of 2,000,000 acres, 1,700,000 of which is now covered by the present system of fire protection.

Organization.—The fire protective organization is in charge of a State Fire Warden, who is responsible to the State Forester. Both of these officials are men of technical training and experience. The State Forester is appointed by and responsible to the State Forest Park Reservation Commission. This commission consists of the Governor, who is *ex officio* president, the State Geologist, who is termed the executive officer, and three citizens appointed by the Governor with the consent of the Senate.

Fire Wardens.—The State is divided into four divisions, each of which is in charge of a division fire warden. The township committee or governing body of every township, upon being notified by the commission, is required to appoint some suitable person to act as township fire warden for the entire township, or for such part of it as the commission shall determine, for a term of one year or until his successor shall have been appointed. Township fire wardens, when required to do so by the State Fire Warden, must divide their townships into two or more districts and appoint district fire wardens for each: *Provided,* that no district fire warden shall be appointed for the district in which the township fire warden lives.

Powers and Duties of Fire Wardens.—The section of the law dealing with the duties of fire wardens reads in part as follows:

"Township and district fire wardens shall enforce all statutes of this State now in force or that may hereafter be enacted for the protection of forest and timber land from fire, and shall carry out the directions of the State Fire Warden or division fire wardens regarding the prevention and extinguishing of forest fires. They shall have control and direction of all persons and apparatus engaged in extinguishing forest fires. They may plow land, or, in an emergency, set back-fires to check any fire. They may summon any male person between the ages of 18 years and 50 years who may live or be within the jurisdiction of such fire wardens to assist in extinguishing fires, and may also require the use of horses and other property needed for such purpose. Any person so summoned, who is physically able, who refuses or neglects to assist. or to allow the use of horses, wagons, or other material required, shall be liable to a penalty of $10. When a serious fire occurs the State Fire Warden or any division fire warden may summon to his aid fire wardens from surrounding townships with their assistants, and in such case the State shall bear the whole expense of paying the fire wardens and assistants who reside in townships which were not threatened. In every other case in which a fire is fought by men from two or more townships the cost shall be apportioned by the State Fire Warden among the townships in which the fire burned. or which were directly threatened."

If any township shall fail to appoint the fire wardens when directed by the forest commission to do so, or shall fail to make an appropriation sufficient to pay its share of the fire wardens' salary and bills incurred in fighting fires, assistance may be summoned by any fire warden, and persons so summoned shall be paid by the State.

Pay of Wardens.—The pay of fire wardens is regulated by law as follows:

"Each township fire warden shall be paid at the rate of $20 a year, and each district fire warden at the rate of $10 a year. Said sum shall be in lieu of all allowances for making reports, for postage. for posting fire-warning notices. and for issuing permits. For special services in investigating fires, and the causes thereof, and for all time in actual fire fighting, fire wardens and their helpers shall be paid at the following rates:

"Fire wardens. while engaged in fighting fires. $2 for five hours or less, and 30 cents per hour thereafter.

"Fire wardens, while otherwise employed, 25 cents per hour.

"Helpers, fighting fire, $1 for five hours or less, and 20 cents per hour for more than five hours.

"Helpers, on patrol or employed otherwise than fighting fire, 20 cents per hour."

Permits for Burning Brush.—Under the law permits are required to be obtained from the fire wardens before brush and other rubbish can be burnt by private citizens, unless the burning is to be in a "public road, garden, or plowed field at a distance of not less than 200 feet from any woodland, brushland, or field containing dry grass or other inflammable material."

Fires Must Be Watched.—The law which would be of the greatest assistance in North Carolina requires that "all persons who shall burn any pit of charcoal, or set fire to or burn any brush, grass, or other material whereby any property may be endangered or destroyed, shall keep and maintain a careful and competent watchman in charge of said pit, brush, or other material while burning."

Fire wardens, among other things, are required to post notices concerning forest fires, and a penalty is inflicted for tearing down such notices. Fire wardens may arrest without warrant any person found violating the forest laws.

Appropriation.—The State appropriation in 1912 for the support of the Forest Fire Service was $15,000, while the townships contributed for fire wardens' salaries and expenses something over $3,000. This sum enabled the State to maintain, in addition to the State Fire Warden, a force of four division fire wardens, 110 township fire wardens, 151 district fire wardens, and 3 fire watchers. In addition to this force, through coöperation with the United States Forest Service, a number of patrols are kept in the field throughout the dangerous season.

Lookouts.—At present New Jersey has done little in the establishment of lookouts, chiefly because telephonic communication is lacking in the remote forestry districts. With the increase in the number of telephones, however, the Forestry Commission plans to create a number of lookout stations, which, they are convinced, will insure much fuller protection.

Law Enforcement.—The commission lays great stress upon the value of strictly enforcing the laws. The State Forester reports that of the 545 fires reported in 1912, 252 are known to have been violations of the law. Of this large number, nearly half have been disposed of within the year, fines of various amounts having been inflicted in most cases.

"The only way we have found to cope with the problem is by endeavoring to penalize the people who start the fires. We put particular emphasis on getting the offender. If we can make a man pay a fine for starting a small fire, and the fact gets into the newspapers, it makes an impression on the people who frequent or use the forest. I believe we have done the greatest part of our educational work by making it expensive to start fires."*

Railroad Fire Lines.—In 1909 the Legislature of New Jersey passed a law requiring all railroads to build fire lines along their rights of way through woodlands. These fire lines were to be made by cleaning up

*Forest Fire Protection by the States, by J. G. Peters, U. S. Forest Service. 1914, p. 18.

and plowing a stretch 10 feet wide at a distance not less than 100 feet nor more than 200 feet from the track and keeping it clear of combustible material. The ground between the fire line and the track to be burned off or otherwise cleared of brush, grass, leaves, and dead wood.

A provision was inserted whereby objections of owners of property to the railroad constructing such fire lines would be considered by the Forest Park Reservation Commission, which commission would endeavor by peaceful means to overcome the difficulty and effect a satisfactory compromise. The weakness of this law, however, is in the fact that nothing can compel the owner to allow the construction of these fire lines, and, therefore, weak places occur at intervals along the lines. Railroads were not required to construct these fire lines all at once, but not exceeding one-fifth of their distance was to be completed each year, as determined by the Forestry Commission. Several of the principal railroads complied with the provision of this law and constructed many miles of fire line. Some of the railroads, however, fought the law, and it was finally declared unconstitutional. The fire lines, however, succeeded so well in preventing fires along the tracks that some of the roads still continue to construct and maintain them with good results.

The following comment by the State Forester on the local workings of the organization which appears in the publication of the United States Forest Service quoted above will be of interest:

"The State organization in north Jersey consists of a division fire warden as an assistant to the State Fire Warden and a township warden in each township where there is any appreciable amount of woodland, in addition to enough district wardens to adequately control the area. The aim is to assign a warden to each 5,000 acres of land. This force is composed of local men, who receive a small annual fee of $10 or $20 besides the money paid them for actually fighting fires. It is, therefore, a good deal of a voluntary service. These men, as soon as they hear of a fire, get together enough men to take care of it. They have authority to require assistance."

The Forester is confident that as soon as telephonic communication is extended to the forest area a lookout system can be installed in the northern part of the State which will cover the territory very satisfactorily, leaving the actual fire fighting and what little control is necessary to the local wardens.

DELAWARE.

Practically all the land in Delaware is adaptable to farming, and most of the forest is in the form of woodlots. For this reason fires are not common and may be easily prevented. Throughout the southern half of the State, however, more than one-third of the area is wooded, and it is estimated that 27 per cent of the whole State is still in woods.

In 1909, as a result of a forest survey of the State made the year before, a fairly good forestry law was enacted. It has, however, been practically inoperative, because no appropriation was made by the Legislature for its enforcement.

Organization.—The State Board of Forestry consists of five members: the Governor, Secretary of State, President of the State Board of Agriculture, Director of the Agricultural Experiment Station, and the Forester of the College. This latter official is *ex officio* State Forester, but as there is no Forester of the College, the Director of the Agricultural Experiment Station acts in the capacity of forester. It is said that only when the State employs a competent and technically trained forester whose sole duty it is to improve the forest conditions of the State will anything much along these lines be done.

Wardens.—The State Forester may, whenever he thinks it necessary, request the Governor to appoint certain men as forest wardens. These wardens are to receive no salary from the State, but only such compensation as the forester may allow them for special services actually rendered. The expenses incurred in fighting or extinguishing fire are to be borne by the county in which the fire occurs after the accounts have been approved by the State Forester.

Spark Arresters.—Logging and railroad locomotives, donkey or threshing engines, traction engines and other engines and boilers operated in, through, or near forests or brush, which do not burn oil or naphtha as fuel must be provided with appliances to prevent the escape of fire and sparks from smokestacks, ash-pans, and fire boxes.

Civil Liability.—An individual or corporation causing fires shall be liable to the State or to the county in which the fire occurs in an action for debt to the full amount of all expenses incurred by the State or county in fighting and extinguishing such fires.

OHIO.

Ohio has a Department of Forestry under the control of the Ohio Agricultural Experiment Station, and a forester appointed by that station. It has no fire protective system and very few fire laws.

"A section of the General Code of Ohio authorizes township trustees to call on the inhabitants of the township to assist in extinguishing forest or prairie fires; but this method is entirely inadequate, as a fire is likely to have caused great damage before the machinery for its control can be put in operation. Some provision should be made for a systematic patrol of the regions liable to forest fires during the small part of the year when there is danger from such fires. The necessary cost of such patrol would be far less than the present annual loss from fires."*

INDIANA.

Indiana is essentially an agricultural State, and only 17 per cent of its area, or 4,000,000 acres, are in woods, nearly all of this being in the form of farmers' woodlots.

Board of Forestry.—There is a State Board of Forestry composed of five members, including the secretary. The latter official is paid a salary of $1,800 a year and expenses. Practically the whole amount of the appropriation of $7,000 is spent for general and office expenses and for administering a small State forest reservation.

Fire Protection.—The only forest fire laws are (1) a law which forbids persons setting fire to the woods of another, (2) one which prescribes a heavy fine or imprisonment for setting fire to woods, marsh, or prairie maliciously or wantonly, and (3) one which makes it the duty of the township road supervisor to summon help and extinguish any fire which may occur in his district, the costs to be paid by the township.

PRAIRIE STATES.

The six prairie States, namely, Illinois, Kansas, Nebraska, Iowa, North and South Dakota, contain little or no forest land; and, with the exception of South Dakota, those States which have any forest policy have confined their efforts almost entirely to the encouragement of tree planting. Practically all of these States have at one time or another passed laws calculated to induce private individuals to plant woodlots, etc., usually with only indifferent results. Kansas now has a State Forester; most of his time, however, is devoted to teaching forestry in the State Agricultural College.

SOUTH DAKOTA.

Outside the National and State forests there is little woodland in South Dakota. At the present time the Federal Government controls about 1,200,000 acres and the State forests amount to about 60,000 acres more. Some 300,000 acres of farmers' woodlots are also reported. The forest administration deals almost entirely with State lands.

Administration.—The direction, management, and control of all State lands is in the hands of the Board of School and Public Lands. Among the duties of this board is the appointment when necessary of a forest

---

*Fourth Annual Report of Forest Conditions in Ohio.

supervisor, who shall have administrative powers, with authority to employ needed assistance in case of forest fire on or near any lands owned by the State. This official, who is called State Forester, was appointed in 1913, when a special appropriation of $3,000 a year for fire protection became available.

Fire Laws.—There are laws against willfully or negligently setting fires, and declaring a closed season in which no fires must be set in woods, marsh, prairie, grass or stubble lands. Any fire set must be kept in control and extinguished the same day on which it is set.

Railroads.—Railroads are permitted to enter upon private or State lands to construct fire guards along their lines.

Comment.—A comprehensive fire plan was inaugurated July 1, 1913. Several miles of telephone line were built and put into operation, and a lookout station established and equipped. This lookout has direct telephonic communication with the district ranger, with State forest headquarters, and with the nearest lookout on the National forest. Last year the State Forest Service was able, along with its other activities, to effect necessary fire patrol up to September 15th, when the money available was exhausted. The timely assistance of the Federal Government, however, under the provisions of the Weeks law, allowed for effective patrol till the end of the fire season.

SOUTHWESTERN STATES.

The Southwestern States have little forest land except in the mountains, and the greater part of this in most of these States is included in the National forests. Consequently it is adequately protected from fire by the Federal Government. Only two, California and Colorado, out of the six Southwestern States have any State fire protective system. Utah has a State Conservation Commission with a committee on State forest conservation, but no further State forestry organization. In Arizona, New Mexico, and Nevada there is little timberland in private ownership, but the States themselves own a considerable amount of forested school lands. As most of these are included within the outside boundaries of the National forests, no pressing need for their protection by the State has been felt.

CALIFORNIA.

California has an approximate area of 24,000,000 acres of forest land, or 24 per cent of its area. Of this amount, 14,000,000 acres is included in National forests and is thoroughly patrolled by the Federal Government. An additional 1,500,000 acres is included in National parks and other public lands; while nearly 1,000,000 belongs to the State. The remaining third of the forest area is owned one half by farmers and settlers and the other half by lumber companies. The forest fire laws at present are quite inadequate, largely because the appropriation is too small to carry them out effectively.

Organization.—There is a State Board of Forestry of four members, which supervises the State forestry work and convenes upon the call of the Governor or of its secretary. The State Forester, appointed by the Governor, is a civil executive officer who shall be a technically trained forester and shall receive a salary of $2,400 a year and necessary office and contingent expenses. There are two assistant foresters who each receive a salary of $1,200 a year and necessary expenses.

Fire Wardens.—The forester shall appoint public-spirited citizens to act as volunteer fire wardens, who may receive payment for their services from the counties or from private sources. The forester and fire wardens shall have the powers of arrest without warrant for violations of the State or Federal forest laws.

Fire Patrol.—In times and localities of particular fire danger the State Forester may maintain a fire patrol through the fire wardens, as the public interest may require, the expense of such patrol to be paid by the county. He may also, upon request of counties, corporations, or individuals, maintain a fire patrol on their forest lands, provided that the expenses be paid by those requesting the patrol.

Liability for Forest Fires.—Owners whose property is injured or destroyed by fire may recover in civil action the amount of the damage suffered if the fire occurs through willfulness, malice, or negligence. In addition, persons or corporations causing fires or violations of the law shall be liable for all expenses incurred by the State or county in fighting such fires.

Appropriation.—The sum of $7,000 a year is provided for the payment of all salaries and expenses and for carrying out the other provisions of the law.

County Coöperation.—Counties are allowed by law to appropriate from the general funds sums not to exceed from $10,000 to $20,000, according to the size of the county, for the purpose of aiding forestry work. This includes the preservation, reforestation, and protection from fire of forests upon public lands.

Spark Arresters.—Persons using logging locomotives, donkey or threshing engines, or other engines or boilers in or near forest, brush, or grass land must provide adequate devices to prevent the escape of fire or sparks from smokestacks, ash-pans, fire boxes, or other parts.

COMMENT.

"So far we have been without an appropriation for forest protection; consequently the State Board of Forestry has been prevented from organizing fire patrols and taking the first steps necessary to establish forestry principles.

"State fire wardens serve without compensation for their services and often incur considerable expense. For this they cannot be reimbursed by the State, since there is no appropriation for this purpose. It is imperative that the State make an appropriation for fire protection and for paying the necessary expenses incurred when fires do occur."

COLORADO.

Approximately 18 per cent of the area of Colorado, or about 12,000,000 acres, is forested. Of this amount, about 8,000,000 acres is under the control of the Federal Government, while approximately 4,000,000 is in private hands. The State itself owns some 600,000 acres of woodland.

The present forest law was passed in 1911, probably with the object of increasing the efficiency of the then existing fire prevention forces. When compared with the laws of some of the more progressive States, however, the Colorado law seems very inadequate, as it leaves the forestry work in so many different hands. This defect will be noticed in the following brief summary:

State Forester.—The State Board of Agriculture is authorized to appoint the State Forester, who shall be a professor of forestry in the State Agricultural College, and shall be under the control of the Board of Agriculture. His salary shall not exceed $2,500 a year. His duties, amongst others, are to advise, aid, and assist the Board of Land Commissioners in preventing and extinguishing fires on State lands; to advise or assist individuals, associations, corporations, etc., in the care of their forest lands; to aid and assist the associations of the various counties in extinguishing fires; to investigate fires and report derelictions of duty on the part of any officer of the State with relation to fires or forests, and to prepare notices concerning the prevention and extinguishing of forest fires, which the Commissioner of Game and Fish is required to post.

Fire Wardens.—Sheriffs of the various counties of the State are to report to the State Forester as soon as practicable the occurrence of any fire in any forests in the State, either on private or public lands, and shall then aid and assist in extinguishing the same.

Deputies appointed by the sheriff at present serve in the forty-two counties which contain forest lands. In all there are 392 such wardens.

In addition to these deputy sheriffs, 197 special forest fire wardens have been commissioned from the list of special deputy game wardens after several conferences with the State Fish and Game Commissioner.

Appropriation.—For carrying this act into effect the Legislature appropriates $10,000 for each successive biennial period, or $5,000 a year.

SOUTHERN STATES.

The South has allowed the western and northern States to outdistance it in the matter of forest protection. It is only within the last few years that any of the southern States have even talked of adopting State fire protection, and it is only the borderland States that have so far secured any fire protective systems. Maryland was the leader in this movement, and has continued to be foremost in the protection of her forests. Kentucky and West Virginia now also have State fire protection. North Carolina and Virginia have State foresters, while Tennessee and Alabama have forest laws; but all four are still without forest protection. Louisiana will no doubt have an excellent system as soon as its rather cumbrous machinery gets into working order.

The remaining southern States have done little or nothing in the way of forestry. Forestry laws have been introduced from time to time into the legislatures of South Carolina, Florida, Mississippi, and Missouri, but have failed to pass. Georgia has a forester connected with the State Agricultural College, while Arkansas and Oklahoma have apparently made no move towards any form of forestry. It is said that Texas is contemplating some action at the next session of the Legislature. With its 40,000,000 acres of forest land definite forest protection is certainly needed.

The southern States, like the lake States, have been greatly handicapped in their efforts to secure forest protection by the theory, fostered by many large landowners, that all of the cut-over lands are suitable for agriculture. The greater part of the pine lands of the South may eventually be adapted to farm use, but it seems certain that for many years to come there will be little demand for the greater part of it. This should, therefore, be adequately protected from the fire and allowed to produce a remunerative crop of timber.

MARYLAND.

Maryland, like North Carolina, has three forest regions, the Mountain, the Piedmont, and the Coastal Plain region. Altogether, Maryland has approximately 2,000,000 acres of woodland, most of which is greatly reduced in productiveness by repeated forest fires. The State Forester says that the forest fire question is the most important forestry problem in Maryland.

At the time of the passage of the forest law in 1905 the Maryland law was considered about the best in the United States. Since that time, however, several States have secured more effective laws.

State Board of Forestry.—"There shall be a State Board of Forestry, consisting of seven members, the Governor, Comptroller, president of Johns Hopkins University, president of the Maryland State Agricultural College, State Geologist, and one citizen of the State known to be interested in the advancement of forestry, and one practical lumberman engaged in the manufacture of lumber within this State, who shall be appointed by the Governor, to serve for a term of two years, which board shall act without compensation, save for actual necessary expenses incurred in the performance of their official duties."

State Forester.—The Board of Forestry shall appoint a State Forester who shall have a practical knowledge of forestry and shall be a trained forester. His compensation, fixed by the board, shall not exceed $2,000 per annum and reasonable traveling and field expenses. He shall have charge of all the forest interests of the State, shall have charge of and direct the forest wardens, take necessary action to prevent and extinguish forest fires, and enforce the forest fire laws. He has various other duties which are defined in the law.

Appropriation.—The law provides an annual appropriation of $10,000 for the work under the Board of Forestry and an additional appropriation of $6,000 for the publication of forest reports and maps.

Protective System.—"Our protective system consists of forest wardens, forest patrolmen, and lookout watchmen. The wardens are commissioned by the Governor, upon the recommendation of the State Forester, the law limiting us to the appointment of not more than one warden for each 15,000 acres of woodlands in the county. The wardens receive no salary, but are paid for services rendered, half by the State and half by the county. Since under our law there are no restrictions in the appointment of the wardens, except as to number, we have been able to select men who would make the best officers, most of them actuated by a high sense of public duty. The chief difficulty is that they are too far apart, and in order to overcome this we are appointing deputies for each warden, with the view of having the men within 2 or 3 miles of each other.

"The patrolmen, all of whom are Federal employees, are regularly commissioned forest wardens, assigned to patrol duty. They are usually farmers who know everybody in the community and who understand the local situation thoroughly. These men are assigned a territory covering from 85,000 to 100,000 acres each, and, as far as possible, they travel along the ridges, where a good view of the surrounding country can be obtained. They are mounted on horses, in which respect our system appears to be different from that of other States. The patrolman furnishes his horse and receives $3 per diem when actually employed, and his patrol is limited to days when it is dry enough for fires to run in the woods. This usually amounts to from 50 to 60 days during the year. By paying a dollar a day more for a mounted patrolman than for one on foot the efficiency, I believe, is at least doubled.

"The lookout watchmen aid very materially in the fire protection plan. We have a number of lookout stations in the mountains. Each one has a telephone connection with the forest wardens, so that a forest fire is quickly observed and reported to the nearest warden. We have found that under this system the fires have not only been reduced in number, but the average area burned over by each fire is very much less than before the system was inaugurated.

"In addition to the regular lookout stations there are a number of good observation points where we employ men living near-by to make three observations daily during the dangerous seasons, for which they are paid 50 cents a day. We find that this arrangement works very well and saves the expense of a regular station where we would not be justified in having an all-day lookout."*

Spark Arresters.—Railroad and logging locomotives, donkey or threshing engines, and other engines and boilers which do not burn oil as fuel must be provided with appliances to prevent the escape of fire and sparks from the smokestacks and to prevent the escape of fire from ash-pans and fire boxes.

Stock Law.—One mountain county in Maryland still allows live stock to run in the open woods. As a result of this practice fires have been set intentionally to burn off the young forest growth in order to improve the range for cattle and sheep. In one month twenty-nine fires occurred in this county, eleven of which were definitely known to have been set for this purpose. The fire warden system was unable to cope with the situation, and 55,000 acres were burned over in this county in May. The State Forester says:

"Any law which will encourage the burning of 30,000 acres of woodland, causing a loss of over $100,000, for a few hundred dollars worth of free grazing has certainly outlived its usefulness and should be repealed."

North Carolina confronts this same problem in a number of counties, both in the western and eastern parts of the State. It is to be hoped that she may soon do away with the menace of the open range.

WEST VIRGINIA.

West Virginia, which has an area of a little over 15,000,000 acres, or approximately one-half the area of North Carolina, contains about

*Forest Fire Protection by the States, by J. G. Peters, U. S. Department of Agriculture.

11,000,000 acres of forest land, the greater part of which has been cut over and much of it very badly burned.

A law passed in 1909 provided for a Forest, Game and Fish Warden, and subordinated fire protection to the protection of game. As only a very small appropriation was allowed for the carrying out of this law, little effective work could be accomplished.

Protective System.—Under this law the State Forest, Game and Fish Warden was made *ex officio* fire warden of the State, and all deputy game wardens were made deputy fire wardens for their respective counties. These wardens, in addition to their duties in protecting game, were required to extinguish any forest fires which were brought to their notice, and were empowered to hire volunteers or summon assistance to extinguish fires.

Deputy wardens receive $2 per day for the time actually employed at forest fires, and the various counties are empowered to fix the price paid to laborers at forest fires not to exceed $2 per day for services actually rendered. All services rendered at forest fires, both by deputy wardens and their assistants, are charged against the county, and the county court is required to pay such cost out of the county funds.

Recovery of Expenses.—The warden of any county in which has occurred a forest fire which has been extinguished by his efforts can recover from those causing the fire to the amount expended in extinguishing the fire, together with the costs of said recovery. This, however, shall not act as a bar to the recovery of damages by those injured by the fire.

This law has been greatly hampered in its execution by the county court refusing to allow claims for extinguishing fires or by fixing the per diem so low that it was very hard to get men to help fight fires.

Railroads.—Railroads passing through forest lands are required to move from their rights of way twice a year all grass, brush, and other inflammable materials. In seasons of drought they must employ sufficient trackmen to promptly extinguish fires on their rights of way. They must also provide locomotives with spark arresters and devices to prevent the escape of fire from ash-pans and furnaces. They are forbidden to deposit live coals on their track or rights of way near forest lands, are required to extinguish fires on or near their rights of way, and trainmen are required to report fires at the first station to which they come.

Appropriation.—Under the law of 1909 there was no appropriation which could be used for fire prevention. In 1913, however, the Legislature appropriated $25,000 for two years for the use of the forest, game, and fish warden in carrying out the provisions of the earlier law. Two-fifths of this is to be used for special fire preventive measures.

With the $5,000 a year for the next two years the Governor has decided to establish a State fire protective system. "Five lookout stations are to be erected at once (October, 1913) and properly equipped with field glasses and fire-fighting equipment. Telephone connections will be made with these stations from all the surrounding country and watchmen stationed there during all the dangerous season to give an alarm in case of the discovery of fire. This system will be extended throughout all of the forest area of the State as rapidly as proper coöperation with timber owners and organizations can be effected and Federal coöperation secured."*

Comment.—A more comprehensive law was introduced into the Legislature in 1913, providing for a special Forest Department, State Forester, a protective system, and a special appropriation. This bill was backed by the forest, game, and fish warden, but it failed of passage, owing to lack of time to consider it, due to a senatorial deadlock.

KENTUCKY.

Kentucky has approximately 10,000,000 acres of forest land or about 40 per cent of the total area of the State. Like North Carolina, there are three physiographic regions, the eastern or Mountain region, the central or Blue-grass region, and the western or Valley region. The permanent forests are in the mountains, which are perhaps rougher, though not so high as ours in North Carolina. As the larger part of the land in these mountains is better adapted for growing timber than for any other purpose, the necessity for protecting the forests from fires is obvious. Until recently, however, Kentucky has made no appropriation for fire protection.

In 1912, largely through the persistent efforts of the State Federation of Women's Clubs, a first-class forestry law was enacted and a State Forester appointed. Since that time a fire protective system has been formed and one or more local clubs organized to coöperate with the State in fire protection. Kentucky is now perhaps, with the exception of Maryland, the foremost amongst the southern States in the protection of her forests from fire.

State Board of Forestry.—The new law established a State Board of Forestry, consisting of six members, namely, the Governor, Director of the State Experiment Station, Commissioner of Agriculture, all of whom are *ex officio* members, and three persons to be appointed by the Gov-

*American Forestry, Vol. XIX, p. 748.

ernor with the advice and consent of the Senate. The members of the board shall receive no salary, but shall be paid necessary expenses incurred in attending meetings.

State Forester.—The State Forester shall be appointed by the board and he shall be a graduate of a school of forestry, a technically trained forester with both practical and theoretical knowledge of forestry. Among other duties, the State Forester is secretary of the Forestry Commission. He is given supervision and direction of all forest interests within the State and "he shall have charge over all forest wardens who may be appointed by the State Board. He shall take such action as is authorized by law to prevent and extinguish forest fires, enforce the laws pertaining to forests and woodland, prosecute any violation of such laws, etc." His salary is fixed by the Forestry Board and must not exceed $2,500 a year and reasonable expenses.

Fire Wardens.—"Whenever the State Board of Forestry considers it necessary, it may apply to the Governor to commission such persons as it may designate to act as forest wardens." These wardens shall receive not to exceed $2 per day for services actually rendered. Their duties are to protect the State forest reserves; to report violations of the law, and assist in apprehending and convicting offenders; to extinguish fires, and employ persons to assist as they may deem expedient. No provision is made for patrols or lookouts, which seriously reduces the effectiveness of the system.

Appropriation.—The sum of $15,000 per annum is appropriated for the use of the State Board of Forestry in carrying out the provisions of the forestry law. Only a small part of this, however, can be used for fire protection, as the law also provides for the purchase and administration of lands for State forests.

Spark Arresters.—"Logging and railroad locomotives, donkey or threshing engines, and other engines and boilers operated in, through, or near forest and brush, which do not burn oil as fuel," must be provided with spark arresters and devices to prevent the escape of fire from ash-pans and fire boxes.

Comment.—At the end of the 1913 fire season the State Forester reported that the county fire wardens in the eastern part of the State had been kept busy fighting fires. The efficiency of the work of the wardens has been thoroughly demonstrated.

VIRGINIA.

Virginia has a productive forest area of about 15,000,000 acres, or about 58 per cent of its total area, which is a somewhat less proportion of woodland than we have in North Carolina. The same three forest regions, the Mountain, Piedmont, and Coastal Plain, that we have here, occur there. A considerably larger proportion of the forest, however, is in the form of farmers' woodlots. Until recently little forestry work has been done by this State, and the laws have only been the usual ones against setting fire to the woods and the not so usual one requiring steam engines to use spark arresters.

In March, 1914, however, a comprehensive law was passed which when made effective by an appropriation will place Virginia in the front rank of the southern States which exercise forest protection.

State Forester.—The office of State Forester is created under the direction and control of the State Geological Commission, which is composed of the Governor, President of the University of Virginia, President of the Virginia Polytechnic Institute, Superintendent of the Virginia Military Institute, and one citizen from the State at large appointed by the Governor. The Forester is to be appointed by this commission. He must be a technically trained forester who has both a practical and theoretical knowledge of forestry. Besides the care and management of the State forest reservation and State nurseries, which are provided for in the bill, he shall have charge of all forest wardens and shall take necessary action to prevent and extinguish forest fires. His salary shall not exceed $2,000 per year, together with reasonable traveling and field expenses.

Wardens.—The State Geological Commission may apply to the Governor to commission certain persons to act as State forest wardens. These wardens receive no salary, but shall be paid by the State for services actually rendered, not exceeding $2 per day. It is the duty of the forest warden to extinguish forest fires and to summon necessary help for this purpose.

County Protection.—The boards of county supervisors are authorized by this bill to levy and appropriate money for purposes of forest protection, improvement, and management. "The State boards shall have recourse under an action at law for debt against any landowner, individual, or corporation on whose account they shall be obliged to pay out money for fighting fire for the amount which they shall have expended for such purpose."

Spark Arresters.—"Logging and railroad locomotives, donkey or threshing engines, and other engines and boilers operated in, through, or near forest or brush, which do not burn oil as fuel, shall be provided with appliances to prevent, as far as may be possible, the escape of fire and sparks from the smokestacks thereof, and with devices to prevent, as far as may be possible, the escape of fire from ash-pans and fire boxes.

Forest Reserve Fund.—"All money received as penalties for violations of the provisions of this act, less the cost of collection and not otherwise provided for, together with any amount obtained from the State forestry reserves, shall be paid into the State Treasury to the credit of the forest reserve fund, which fund is hereby created; and the moneys in said fund are hereby appropriated for purposes of forest protection, management, replacement, and extension, under the direction of the commission."

Appropriation.—This bill was passed so late in the session that no appropriation was carried through with it. A provision, however, was inserted by which the necessary funds for the work will be provided by the University of Virginia until the meeting of the next Assembly in 1916.

LOUISIANA.

Louisiana has an approximate forest area of 22,000,000 acres, two-thirds of which, it is estimated, is held by lumber companies and other large owners, and the remainder by farmers. As a result of repeated burning, some 4,000,000 acres of woodland are now barren.

The Department of Forestry was authorized in 1904, the Register of the Land Office being *ex officio* Commissioner of Forestry. A fire warden system was established by the parishes. In 1910 this law was repealed and a comprehensive law passed. The tax feature of this law was declared unconstitutional by the Supreme Court, so that an amendment to the Constitution was necessary. This was passed in 1912, and the law was again amended in the same year. Owing, however, to strenuous opposition to the collection of the tax imposed, the law has not yet been put fully into force.

Organization.—The State Conservation Commission consists of three persons appointed by the Governor with the consent of the Senate, who shall be men well informed on the three following branches: Conservation of wild life, game and the requirements for its conservation; oysters, salt- and fresh-water fish of the State; the forest and mineral resources of the State. The chairman of this commission receives a salary of $3,000 per annum, while the other two persons are paid $2,400 per annum each. Necessary traveling expenses are also allowed them.

State Forester.—Under the Conservation Commission and responsible to it, the Register of the State Land Office is appointed *ex officio* State Forester. A Deputy State Forester at a salary of $1,800 a year and an allowance of $600 a year for traveling and office expenses is appointed to take charge of the forestry work of the State. This official "shall be a person practically and theoretically educated in silviculture." (Owing to lack of funds, the technically trained forester has not yet been appointed.)

Among other things, it is the duty of the State Forester "to have direction of all forest interests and all matters pertaining to forestry within the jurisdiction of the State, to take such action as is authorized by the law to prevent and extinguish forest fires, enforce all laws pertaining to forests and woodland, and prosecute for any violation of these laws." With this authority it is presumed the Conservation Commission can organize and maintain an adequate fire-fighting force as soon as sufficient money is available.

Railroads.—All railroad companies operating through forest lands must keep their rights of way clear of all combustible materials and safely dispose of the same between November 15th and April 15th. No railroad company shall permit its employees to leave or deposit fire or live coals on its right of way, other than between the rails, in the vicinity of woodland. When trainmen discover fires along their right of way they shall report the same at the next telegraph station. In seasons of drought railroad companies must give particular instructions to the section foremen for the prevention and prompt extinguishment of fires originating on their right of way.

License Tax for Conservation.—In order to provide funds for the enforcement of the conservation law a special annual license tax is provided for in Act No. 209 of 1912, which is based upon the then recently passed amendment to the Constitution. This tax is levied each year "upon each person or association of persons, firm, or corporation pursuing the business of severing natural products, including all forms of timber, turpentine, and minerals . . . from the soil. The said person, firm, association, or corporation shall at the same time pay to the tax collector of the parish where said product is taken or severed from the soil a license tax equal to one-half of one per centum (½%) of the gross value of the total production thereof, less the royalty interest accruing to the owner thereof, the license on which shall be paid by said land or royalty owner. And the value of all products shall be computed at the place where the same are severed or taken from the soil; and the value of all forms of timber, for the purposes of this act, shall be computed in their manufactured state, after severance from the soil."

After several months of disagreement between lumbermen and the State Auditor as to on what basis returns for the license tax were to be made on the different species of timber trees cut, the following scale was agreed upon: Yellow pine, $2.50 per thousand feet; cypress, $3 per thousand; tupelo gum, $1 per thousand; cottonwood and red gum, $2 per thousand; hickory, oak, and ash, $3 per thousand. These figures represent the agreed value of the timber severed from the stump at place of cutting, so that the tax of ½ per cent is levied on these values.

Comment.—Louisiana is the only State which is trying to protect its forests with a direct tax upon the user of the forest. "He who severs, and profits by exhaustion of the natural resources of the State, in the creation of which he had no hand, should, in addition to the common burden of the expense of government, borne by all alike, bear an additional burden of taxation, the proceeds to go towards replacing either the resource which he has removed or, if that be impossible, toward renewing one which by its nature is renewable."*

The Conservation Commission speaks of this method of taxation as a new principle of government. It formulates this principle in the following words: "The exploiters of our natural resources should bear an extra burden of taxation, sufficient in a measure not only to regulate their own business, but to replace the resources which they exhaust."*

ALABAMA.

Alabama, with practically the same total area as North Carolina, has approximately the same amount of forest land or a little more than 60 per cent of the total area. Practically all of the woodland is in private hands, 44 per cent of it being owned and controlled by farmers. The remainder is in the hands of large lumber companies and similar owners. In 1907 a comprehensive forestry law was enacted; but as it carried no appropriation and none has been made since, the law has been inoperative—at any rate, as far as fire protection is concerned. The object of the law, according to the title of the act, was "to provide for the protection of the forests of Alabama; to establish and create a State Commission of Forestry, to consist of the Governor, a member of the State Tax Commission, the State Game and Fish Commissioner, the Commissioner of Agriculture and Industries, a member of the United States Forest Service, the Professor of Forestry in the Alabama Polytechnic Institute, and one practical lumberman; to declare the county game and fish wardens, forest wardens; to declare constables, justices of the peace, sheriffs and deputy sheriffs, *ex-officio* forest wardens, and to provide for the appointment of deputy forest wardens by the Governor; to exempt from taxation for a period of ten years land which shall be planted in trees; to appro-

*Report of the Louisiana Conservation Commission of 1910-12.

priate the sum of $500 annually for the purpose of carrying out the provisions of this act; to create a forest reserve fund, and to provide for the payment of all fines, forfeitures, and penalties arising under the provisions of this act into said fund."

Comment.—The law itself was copied more or less closely from the Maryland law, and as soon as a sufficient appropriation can be secured to put it into effect it will furnish Alabama with a fairly effective fire protective system.

TENNESSEE.

Tennessee with 15,000,000 acres of forest land has no fire protective system and appropriates no money for the purpose of forest protection. In 1907 a law was passed providing for a fire protective system in the Fish, Game, and Forestry Department. No appropriation, however, has been made and absolutely nothing has been done to carry out the provisions of the law.

The only work along forestry lines which has been done in Tennessee was carried out by the National Government in coöperation with the State Geological Survey. Three or more reports have been prepared by Government agents and published by the State Survey. In one of these occur the following passages:

"There is now a fire law on the statute-books which provides penalties for setting forest fires carelessly or willfully, but it lacks an appropriation to make it effective.

"The legislation in regard to forestry is of a very scattered nature. In addition to the fire law, it consists chiefly in giving investigative functions to three different departments—the State Geological Survey, the Department of Game, Fish, and Forestry, and the Commissioner of Agriculture. It is time to consider what legislation is needed in order to unify and round out a consistent and complete forest law."

During the past spring, namely, in February, 1914, the Geological Commission created a Division of Forestry in the Geological Survey. A State Forester has been appointed to take charge of this division, who is to assume his new duties the coming autumn.

Comment.—A complete forest law providing for a separate Forestry Department, a professional forester, etc., was introduced into the Legislature in 1913, chiefly through the efforts of the *Southern Lumberman*. It failed of passage for political reasons. Such a law, carrying a sufficient appropriation, is greatly needed.

NORTH CAROLINA.

North Carolina has no fire protective system and very inadequate fire preventive laws.* Nevertheless, for purposes of comparison the following facts are here given:

North Carolina has an approximate area of 31,000,000 acres. It is estimated that 63 per cent or 19,600,000 acres of this is forest land. The State is naturally divided into three regions, the Mountain or western, the Piedmont or central, and the Coastal Plain or eastern region. Approximately 75 per cent of the Mountain region is absolute forest land and should be kept permanently in woods. The greater part of the Coastal Plain region will eventually become agricultural land, but until the population is largely increased most of it should be growing a crop of timber. The Piedmont is largely a woodlot region, the forests constituting from 30 to 60 per cent of the average farm.

For the past five years the forests of this State have sustained an annual loss from fires of approximately $650,000 a year.† The worst fires occur in the Mountain and Coastal Plain regions.

North Carolina makes no appropriation whatever for forest protection, and no direct appropriation for forestry in any form. The Forester, however, is employed by the State Geological and Economic Survey to do educational and propaganda work throughout the State. Improved forestry laws have been introduced into each General Assembly for the past six or eight years, but there has not been sufficient public interest in the matter to secure their passage.

---

*For North Carolina fire laws, see page 17.

†See Table 2, page 9.

PUBLICATIONS

OF THE

NORTH CAROLINA GEOLOGICAL AND ECONOMIC SURVEY.

BULLETINS.

1. Iron Ores of North Carolina, by Henry B. C. Nitze, 1893. 8°, 239 pp., 20 pl., and map. *Out of print.*

2. Building and Ornamental Stones in North Carolina, by T. L. Watson and F. B. Laney in collaboration with George P. Merrill, 1906, 8°, 283 pp., 32 pl., 2 figs. *Postage 25 cents. Cloth-bound copy 30 cents extra.*

3. Gold Deposits in North Carolina, by Henry B. C. Nitze and George B. Hanna, 1896. 8°, 196 pp., 14 pl., and map. *Out of print.*

4. Road Material and Road Construction in North Carolina, by J. A. Holmes and William Cain, 1893. 8°, 88 pp. *Out of print.*

5. The Forests, Forest Lands and Forest Products of Eastern North Carolina, by W. W. Ashe, 1894. 8°, 128 pp., 5 pl. *Postage 5 cents.*

6. The Timber Trees of North Carolina, by Gifford Pinchot and W. W. Ashe, 1897. 8°, 227 pp., 22 pl. *Out of print.*

7. Forest Fires: Their Destructive Work, Causes and Prevention, by W. W. Ashe, 1895. 8°, 66 pp., 1 pl. *Postage 5 cents.*

8. Water-powers in North Carolina, by George F. Swain, Joseph A. Holmes and E. W. Myers, 1899. 8°, 362 pp., 16 pl. *Postage 16 cents.*

9. Monazite and Monazite Deposits in North Carolina, by Henry B. C. Nitze, 1895. 8°, 47 pp., 5 pl. *Out of print.*

10. Gold Mining in North Carolina and other Appalachian States, by Henry B. C. Nitze and A. J. Wilkins, 1897. 8°, 164 pp., 10 pl. *Out of print.*

11. Corundum and the Basic Magnesian Rocks of Western North Carolina, by J. Volney Lewis, 1895. 8°, 107 pp., 6 pl. *Out of print.*

12. History of the Gems Found in North Carolina, by George Frederick Kunz, 1907. 8°, 60 pp., 15 pl. *Postage 8 cents. Cloth-bound copy 30 cents extra.*

13. Clay Deposits and Clay Industries in North Carolina, by Heinrich Ries, 1897. 8°, 157 pp., 12 pl. *Postage 10 cents.*

14. The Cultivation of the Diamond-back Terrapin, by R. E. Coker, 1906. 8°, 67 pp., 23 pl., 2 figs. *Out of print.*

15. Experiments in Oyster Culture in Pamlico Sound, North Carolina, by Robert E. Coker, 1907. 8°, 74 pp., 17 pl., 11 figs. *Postage 6 cents.*

16. Shade Trees for North Carolina, by W. W. Ashe, 1908. 8°, 74 pp., 10 pl., 16 figs. *Postage 6 cents.*

17. Terracing of Farm Lands, by W. W. Ashe, 1908. 8°, 38 pp., 6 pl., 2 figs. *Postage 4 cents.*

18. Bibliography of North Carolina Geology, Mineralogy and Geography, with a list of Maps, by Francis Baker Laney and Katherine Hill Wood, 1909. 8°, 428 pp. *Postage 25 cents. Cloth-bound copy 30 cents extra.*

19. The Tin Deposits of the Carolinas, by Joseph Hyde Pratt and Douglas B. Sterrett, 1905. 8°, 64 pp., 8 figs. *Postage 4 cents.*

20. Water-powers of North Carolina: An Appendix to Bulletin 8, 1910. 8°, 383 pp. *Postage 25 cents.*

21. The Gold Hill Mining District of North Carolina, by Francis Baker Laney, 1910. 8°, 137 pp., 23 pl., 5 figs. *Postage 15 cents.*

22. A Report on the Cid Mining District, Davidson County, N. C., by J. E. Pogue, Jr., 1911. 8°, 144 pp., 22 pl., 5 figs. *Postage 15 cents.*

23. Forest Conditions in Western North Carolina, by J. S. Holmes, 1911. 8°, 115 pp., 8 pl. *Postage 15 cents.*

ECONOMIC PAPERS.

1. The Maple-sugar Industry in Western North Carolina, by W. W. Ashe, 1897. 8°, 34 pp. *Postage 2 cents.*

2. Recent Road Legislation in North Carolina, by J. A. Holmes. *Out of print.*

3. Talc and Pyrophyllite Deposits in North Carolina, by Joseph Hyde Pratt, 1900. 8°, 29 pp., 2 maps. *Postage 2 cents.*

4. The Mining Industry in North Carolina During 1900, by Joseph Hyde Pratt, 1901. 8°, 36 pp., and map. *Postage 2 cents.*

Takes up in some detail Occurrences of Gold, Silver, Lead and Zinc, Copper, Iron, Manganese, Corundum, Granite, Mica, Talc, Pyrophyllite, Graphite, Kaolin, Gem Minerals, Monazite, Tungsten, Building Stones, and Coal in North Carolina.

5. Road Laws of North Carolina, by J. A. Holmes. *Out of print.*

6. The Mining Industry in North Carolina During 1901, by Joseph Hyde Pratt, 1902. 8°, 102 pp. *Postage 4 cents.*

Gives a List of Minerals found in North Carolina; describes the Treatment of Sulphuret Gold Ores, giving Localities; takes up the Occurrence of Copper in the Virgilina, Gold Hill, and Ore Knob districts; gives Occurrence and Uses of Corundum; a List of Garnets, describing Localities; the Occurrence, Associated Minerals, Uses and Localities of Mica; the Occurrence of North Carolina Feldspar, with Analyses; an extended description of North Carolina Gems and Gem Minerals; Occurrences of Monazite, Barytes, Ocher; describes and gives Occurrences of Graphite and Coal; describes and gives Occurrences of Building Stones, including Limestone; describes and gives Uses for the various forms of Clay; and under the head of "Other Economic Minerals" describes and gives Occurrences of Chromite, Asbestos and Zircon.

7. Mining Industry in North Carolina During 1902, by Joseph Hyde Pratt, 1903. 8°, 27 pp. *Out of print.*

8. The Mining Industry in North Carolina During 1903, by Joseph Hyde Pratt, 1904. 8°, 74 pp. *Postage 4 cents.*

Gives descriptions of Mines worked for Gold in 1903; descriptions of Properties worked for Copper during 1903, together with assay of ore from Twin-Edwards Mine; Analyses of Limonite ore from Wilson Mine; the Occurrence of Tin; in some detail the Occurrences of Abrasives; Occurrences of Monazite and Zircon; Occurrences and Varieties of Graphite, giving Methods of Cleaning; Occurrences of Marble and other forms of Limestone; Analyses of Kaolin from Barber Creek, Jackson County, North Carolina.

9. The Mining Industry in North Carolina During 1904, by Joseph Hyde Pratt, 1905. 8°, 95 pp. *Postage 4 cents.*

Gives Mines Producing Gold and Silver during 1903 and 1904 and Sources of the Gold Produced during 1904; describes the mineral Chromite, giving Analyses of Selected Samples of Chromite from Mines in Yancey County; describes Commercial Varieties of Mica, giving the manner in which it occurs in North Carolina, Percentage of Mica in the Dikes, Methods of Mining, Associated Minerals, Localities, Uses; describes the mineral Barytes, giving Method of Cleaning and Preparing Barytes for Market; describes the use of Monazite as used in connection with the Preparation of the Bunsen Burner, and goes into the use of Zircon in connection with the Nernst Lamp, giving a List of the Principal Yttrium Minerals; describes the minerals containing Corundum Gems, Hiddenite and Other Gem Minerals, and gives New Occurrences of these Gems; describes the mineral Graphite and gives new Uses for same.

10. Oyster Culture in North Carolina, by Robert E. Coker, 1905. 8°, 39 pp. *Out of print.*

11. The Mining Industry in North Carolina During 1905, by Joseph Hyde Pratt, 1906. 8°, 95 pp. *Postage 4 cents.*

Describes the mineral Cobalt and the principal minerals that contain Cobalt; Corundum Localities; Monazite and Zircon in considerable detail, giving Analyses of Thorianite; describes Tantalum Minerals and gives description of the Tantalum Lamp; gives brief description of Peat Deposits; the manufacture of Sand-lime Brick; Operations of Concentrating Plant in Black Sand Investigations; gives Laws Relating to Mines, Coal Mines, Mining, Mineral Interest in Land, Phosphate Rock, Marl Beds.

12. Investigations Relative to the Shad Fisheries of North Carolina, by John N. Cobb, 1906. 8°, 74 pp., 8 maps. *Postage 6 cents.*

13. Report of Committee on Fisheries in North Carolina. Compiled by Joseph Hyde Pratt, 1906. 8°, 78 pp. *Out of print.*

14. The Mining Industry in North Carolina During 1906, by Joseph Hyde Pratt, 1907. 8°, 144 pp., 20 pl., and 5 figs. *Postage 10 cents.*

Under the head of "Recent Changes in Gold Mining in North Carolina," gives methods of mining, describing Log Washers, Square Sets, Cyanide Plants, etc., and detailed descriptions of Gold Deposits and Mines are given; Copper Deposits of Swain County are described; Mica Deposits of Western North Carolina are described. giving Distribution and General Character, General Geology, Occurrence, Associated Minerals, Mining and Treatment of Mica, Origin, together with a description of many of the mines; Monazite is taken up in considerable detail as to Location and Occurrence, Geology, including classes of Rocks, Age, Associations, Weathering, method of Mining and Cleaning, description of Monazite in Original Matrix.

15. The Mining Industry in North Carolina During 1907, by Joseph Hyde Pratt, 1908. 8°, 176 pp., 13 pl., and 4 figs. *Postage 15 cents.*

Takes up in detail the Copper of the Gold Hill Copper District; a description of the Uses of Monazite and its Associated Minerals; descriptions of Ruby, Emerald, Beryl, Hiddenite, and Amethyst Localities; a detailed description with Analyses of the Principal Mineral Springs of North Carolina; a description of the Peat Formations in North Carolina, together with a detailed account of the Uses of Peat and the Results of an Experiment Conducted by the United States Geological Survey on Peat from Elizabeth City, North Carolina.

16. Report of Convention called by Governor R. B. Glenn to Investigate the Fishing Industries in North Carolina, compiled by Joseph Hyde Pratt, State Geologist, 1908. 8°, 45 pp. *Out of print.*

17. Proceedings of Drainage Convention held at New Bern, North Carolina, September 9, 1908. Compiled by Joseph Hyde Pratt, 1908. 8°, 94 pp. *Out of print.*

18. Proceedings of Second Annual Drainage Convention held at New Bern, North Carolina, November 11 and 12, 1909, compiled by Joseph Hyde Pratt, and containing North Carolina Drainage Law, 1909. 8°, 50 pp. *Out of print.*

19. Forest Fires in North Carolina During 1909, by J. S. Holmes, Forester, 1910. 8°, 52 pp., 9 pl. *Out of print.*

20. Wood-using Industries of North Carolina, by Roger E. Simmons, under the direction of J. S. Holmes and H. S. Sackett, 1910. 8°, 74 pp., 6 pl. *Postage 7 cents.*

21. Proceedings of the Third Annual Drainage Convention, held under Auspices of the North Carolina Drainage Association; and the North Carolina Drainage Law (codified). Compiled by Joseph Hyde Pratt, 1911. 8°, 67 pp., 3 pl. *Out of print.*

22. Forest Fires in North Carolina During 1910, by J. S. Holmes, Forester, 1911. 8°, 48 pp. *Out of print.*

23. Mining Industry in North Carolina During 1908, '09, and '10, by Joseph Hyde Pratt and Miss H. M. Berry, 1911. 8°, 134 pp., 1 pl., 27 figs. *Postage 10 cents.*

Gives report on Virgilina Copper District of North Carolina and Virginia, by F. B. Laney; Detailed report on Mica Deposits of North Carolina, by Douglas B. Sterrett; Detailed report on Monazite, by Douglas B. Sterrett; Reports on various Gem Minerals, by Douglas B. Sterrett; Information and Analyses concerning certain Mineral Springs; Extract from Chance Report of the Dan River and Deep River Coal Fields; Some notes on the Peat Industry, by Prof. Charles A. Davis; Extract from report of Arthur Keith on the Nantahala Marble; Description of the manufacture of Sand-lime Brick.

24. Fishing Industry of North Carolina, by Joseph Hyde Pratt, 1911. 8°, 44 pp. *Out of print.*

25. Proceedings of Second Annual Convention of the North Carolina Forestry Association, held at Raleigh, North Carolina, February 21, 1912. Forest Fires in North Carolina During 1911. Suggested Forestry Legislation. Compiled by J. S. Holmes, Forester, 1912. 8°, 71 pp. *Postage 5 cents.*

26. Proceedings of Fourth Annual Drainage Convention, held at Elizabeth City, North Carolina, November 15 and 16, 1911, compiled by Joseph Hyde Pratt, State Geologist, 1912. 8°, 45 pp. *Postage 3 cents.*

27. Highway Work in North Carolina, containing a Statistical Report of Road Work during 1911, by Joseph Hyde Pratt, State Geologist, and Miss H. M. Berry, Secretary, 1912. 8°, 145 pp., 11 figs. *Postage 10 cents.*

28. Culverts and Small Bridges for Country Roads in North Carolina, by C. R. Thomas and T. F. Hickerson, 1912. 8°, 56 pp., 14 figs., 20 pl. *Postage 10 cents.*

29. Report of the Fisheries Convention Held at New Bern, N. C., December 13, 1911, compiled by Joseph Hyde Pratt, State Geologist, together with a Compendium of the Stenographic Notes of the Meetings Held on the Two Trips taken by the Legislative Fish Committee Appointed by the General Assembly of 1909, and the Legislation Recommended by this Committee, 1912. 8°, 302 pp. *Postage 15 cents.*

30. Proceedings of the Annual Convention of the North Carolina Good Roads Association held at Charlotte, N. C., August 1 and 2, 1912, in Coöperation with the North Carolina Geological and Economic Survey. Compiled by Joseph Hyde Pratt, State Geologist, and Miss H. M. Berry, Secretary, 1912. 8°, 109 pp. *Postage 10 cents.*

31. Proceedings of Fifth Annual Drainage Convention held at Raleigh, N. C., November 26 and 27, 1912. Compiled by Joseph Hyde Pratt, State Geologist. 8°, 56 pp., 6 pl. *Postage 5 cents.*

32. Public Roads are Public Necessities, by Joseph Hyde Pratt, State Geologist, 1913. 8°, 62 pp. *Postage 5 cents.*

33. Forest Fires in North Carolina during 1912 and National and Association Coöperative Fire Control, by J. S. Holmes, Forester, 1913. 8°, 63 pp. *Postage 5 cents.*

34. Mining Industry in North Carolina During 1911-12, by Joseph Hyde Pratt, State Geologist, 1914. 8°, 314 pp., 23 pl., 12 figs. *Postage 15 cents.*

35. Good Roads Days, November 5 and 6, 1913. Compiled by Joseph Hyde Pratt, State Geologist, and Miss H. M. Berry, Secretary. 8°, 102 pp., 11 pl. *Postage 10 cents.*

36. Proceedings of the North Carolina Good Roads Association, held at Morehead City, N. C., July 31 and August 1, 1913, in coöperation with the North Carolina Geological and Economic Survey. Statistical Report of Highway Work in North Carolina During 1912. Compiled by Joseph Hyde Pratt, State Geologist, and Miss H. M. Berry, Secretary. 8°, 127 pp., 7 figs. *Postage 10 cents.*

37. Forest Fires in North Carolina During 1913 and a Summary of State Forest Fire Prevention in the United States, by J. S. Holmes, Forester, 1914. 8°, 82 pp. *Postage 8 cents.*

VOLUMES.

Vol. I. Corundum and the Basic Magnesian Rocks in Western North Carolina, by Joseph Hyde Pratt and J. Volney Lewis, 1905. 8°, 464 pp., 44 pl., 35 figs. *Postage 32 cents. Cloth-bound copy 30 cents extra.*

Vol. II. Fishes of North Carolina, by H. M. Smith, 1907. 8°, 453 pp., 21 pl., 188 figs. *Postage 30 cents.*

Vol. III. The Coastal Plain Deposits of North Carolina, by William Bullock Clark, Benjamin L. Miller, L. W. Stephenson, B. L. Johnson, and Horatio N. Parker, 1912. 8°, 509 pp., 62 pl., 21 figs. *Postage 35 cents.*

Pt. I.—The Physiography and Geology of the Coastal Plain of North Carolina, by Wm. Bullock Clark, Benjamin L. Miller, and L. W. Stephenson.

Pt. II.—The Water Resources of the Coastal Plain of North Carolina, by L. W. Stephenson and B. L. Johnson.

Vol. IV. Birds of North Carolina. *In press.*

BIENNIAL REPORTS.

First Biennial Report, 1891-1892, J. A. Holmes, State Geologist, 1893. 8°, 111 pp., 12 pl., 2 figs. *Postage 6 cents.*

Administrative report, giving Object and Organization of the Survey; Investigations of Iron Ores, Building Stone, Geological Work in Coastal Plain Region, including supplies of drinking-waters in eastern counties, Report on Forests and Forest Products, Coal and Marble, Investigations of Diamond Drill.

Biennial Report, 1893-1894, J. A. Holmes, State Geologist, 1894. 8°, 15 pp. *Postage 1 cent.*

Administrative report.

Biennial Report, 1895-1896, J. A. Holmes, State Geologist, 1896. 8°, 17 pp. *Postage 1 cent.*

Administrative report.

Biennial Report, 1897-1898, J. A. Holmes, State Geologist, 1898. 8°, 28 pp. *Postage 2 cents.*

Administrative report.

Biennial Report, 1899-1900, J. A. Holmes, State Geologist, 1900. 8°, 20 pp. *Postage 2 cents.*

Administrative report.

Biennial Report, 1901-1902, J. A. Holmes, State Geologist, 1902. 8°, 15 pp. *Postage 1 cent.*

Administrative report.

Biennial Report, 1903-1904, J. A. Holmes, State Geologist, 1905. 8°, 32 pp. *Postage 2 cents.*

Administrative report.

Biennial Report, 1905-1906, Joseph Hyde Pratt, State Geologist, 1907. 8°, 60 pp. *Postage 3 cents.*

Administrative report; report on certain swamp lands belonging to the State, by W. W. Ashe; it also gives certain magnetic observations at North Carolina stations.

Biennial Report, 1907-1908, Joseph Hyde Pratt, State Geologist, 1908. 8°, 60 pp., 2 pl. *Postage 5 cents.*

Administrative report. Contains Special Report on an examination of the Sand Banks along the North Carolina Coast, by Jay F. Bond, Forest Assistant, United States Forest Service; certain magnetic observations at North Carolina stations; Results of an Investigation Relating to Clam Cultivation, by Howard E. Enders of Purdue University.

Biennial Report, 1909-1910, Joseph Hyde Pratt, State Geologist, 1911. 8°, 152 pp. *Postage 10 cents.*

Administrative report and contains Agreements for Coöperation in Statistical Work, and Topographical and Traverse Mapping Work with the United States Geological Survey; Forest Work with the United States Department of Agriculture (Forest Service); List of Topographic maps of North Carolina and counties partly or wholly topographically mapped; description of special Highways in North Carolina; suggested Road Legislation; list of Drainage Districts and Results of Third Annual Drainage Convention; Forestry reports relating to Connolly Tract, Buncombe County and Transylvania County State Farms; certain Watersheds; Reforestation of Cut-over and Abandoned Farm Lands on the Woodlands of the Salem Academy and College; Recommendations for the Artificial Regeneration of Longleaf Pine at Pinehurst; Act regulating the use of and for the Protection of Meridian Monuments and Standards of Measure at the several county-seats in North Carolina; list of Magnetic Declination at the county-seats, January 1, 1910; letter of Fish Commissioner of the United States Bureau of Fisheries relating to the conditions of the North Carolina fish industries; report of the Survey for the North Carolina Fish Commission referring to dutch or pound-net fishing in Albemarle and Croatan sounds and Chowan River, by Gilbert T. Rude, of the United States Coast and Geodetic Survey; Historical Sketch of the several North Carolina Geological Surveys, with list of publications of each.

Biennial Report, 1911-1912, Joseph Hyde Pratt, State Geologist, 1913. 8°, 118 pp. *Postage 7 cents.*

Administrative report, and contains reports on method of construction and estimate of cost of road improvement in Stantonsburg Township, Wilson County; report on road conditions in Lee County; report on preliminary location of section of Spar-

ND - #0015 - 140926 - C0 - 229/152/19 [21] - CB - 9780331341188 - Gloss Lamination